TEACHING AND LEARNING

To π

TEACHING AND LEARNING

Lessons from Psychology

Richard Fox

BLACKWELL PUBLISHING
350 Main Street, Malden, MA 02148-5020, USA
108 Cowley Road, Oxford OX4 1JF, UK
550 Swanston Street, Carlton, Victoria 3053, Australia

First published 2005 by Blackwell Publishing Ltd

Library of Congress Cataloging-in-Publication Data

Fox, Richard, 1945–
    Teaching and learning: lessons from psychology / Richard Fox.
        p. cm.
    Includes bibliographical references and index.
    ISBN 1-4051-1486-X (hardback: alk. paper) − ISBN 1-4051-1487-8 (pbk.: alk. paper)
    1. Teaching.   2. Learning.   3. Educational psychology.   I. Title.
    LB1025.3.F694   2005
    371.102–dc22

                                                                    2004009016

A catalogue record for this title is available from the British Library.

Set in 10/12.5 Rotis Serif
by Graphicraft Limited, Hong Kong
Printed and bound in the United Kingdom
by TJ International Ltd, Padstow, Cornwall

The publisher's policy is to use permanent paper from mills that operate a sustainable forestry policy, and which has been manufactured from pulp processed using acid-free and elementary chlorine-free practices. Furthermore, the publisher ensures that the text paper and cover board used have met acceptable environmental accreditation standards.

For further information on
Blackwell Publishing, visit our website:
www.blackwellpublishing.com

Contents

Contents

Foreword

Ted Wragg

Many books have been published on the psychology of teaching and learning. Some are strong on teaching but not so hot on learning, whereas others are the opposite way round. Several have been put together by psychologists with tenuous links to the classroom, while a number have been written by people well tooled up to teach children but rather rustier on the central precepts of educational psychology.

The strength of Richard Fox's book is that it is well grounded in all these areas. As an experienced educational psychologist, Richard has a formidable grasp of both the theory and applications of psychology. Moreover, as a teacher and teacher trainer, he understands the intricacies of daily life in the classroom. Few people can match that sort of range, which is why this book has such all-round credibility.

Another strong point is that the book takes a very broad view of psychology, spilling readily over into philosophical or sociological issues when the need arises. The school curriculum, classroom processes, individual issues like 'motivation', 'assessment' or 'bullying' cannot be seen in isolation. The context in which they occur, and the principles and values on which they are built, are also part of the wider teaching and learning story.

The climate of the classroom is effectively captured by the frequent use of transcript and illustration from real lessons. Teachers often find books on teaching and learning remote from their everyday experiences and aspirations, so these classroom examples help to bridge what can sometimes appear to be an almighty gulf between theory and practice.

I have no doubt that this book will be of immense value, not only to student teachers and their mentors but also to experienced teachers who think deeply about their craft. Teaching is both an art and a science. It can perhaps best be seen as an art form with a scientific and philosophical foundation.

Medical practitioners are highly esteemed as a profession for the substantial background knowledge on which they are able to ground their craft. Teaching is also a professional activity which can and should be evidence based. Even those who like to busk it will be fascinated by the many insights in this thoughtful and well-researched book.

Acknowledgements

A book such as this has a long intellectual history, strewn with debts all along the way. I would like to thank especially my friends and colleagues at the School of Education, University of Exeter, who, for a period of some ten years, involved me in the friendliest way in their 'long conversation' about education. I am also more indebted than I can really say to all the teachers, particularly in Devon, who have allowed me to watch them at work and to learn from them.

Professor Charles Desforges deserves my special thanks because it was he who initially involved me in this project and who has continued to help me make sense of it. I owe thanks, also, to Maureen and David Lewis for reading and commenting on sections of the book, when they were already too busy, and to Liz and Tony Clayden for their support and encouragement with my writing. To my three anonymous reviewers I send sincere thanks for pointing out many errors and for making a number of helpful criticisms. One of them, a newly qualified teacher, actually gave up part of her precious half-term break to do this work, which is dedication of a high order. Her criticisms and insights were much appreciated and I hope have made this a better book. I also wish to extend my thanks to Will Maddox and Sarah Bird at Blackwell Publishing, who backed me to carry out the project and have helped me throughout with great tact and professionalism.

Finally, I thank my wife, for her love, patience and support over many, many years as well as for helpful criticisms of this text as it emerged.

The author and publishers gratefully acknowledge the following for permission to reproduce copyright material:

Alexander, R. (2000) *Culture and Pedagogy*, pp. 458–60. Oxford: Blackwell Publishing.
Donaldson, M. (1992) A table of the modes. In: *Human Minds*, p. 269. London: Penguin Books.
Open University (1991) INSET pack *Talking and Learning 5–16*. Audio cassette, band 2.
Rowland, S. (1984) *The Enquiring Classroom*, pp. 80–1. London: Taylor & Francis (incorporating Falmer Press).

Introduction

This book is for anyone who is interested in teaching. It started as an attempt to map out and summarize reliable knowledge about teaching and how it functions to aid learning. It was written, in the first place, mainly for students training to become teachers and for newly qualified teachers. In the course of writing the book, it has turned into something of a personal exploration of the territory, a selection and interpretation of the research that I now feel to be most significant for all teachers. It takes, as its context, the school system in England and Wales, with its National Curriculum, its four Key Stages and its national assessment regime. (Brief notes on this system for those not familiar with it are provided in the section on pp. 4–6.)

When I started teaching, some 30 years ago, I was a graduate in psychology, but I was soon made aware both of how little that qualification helped me in the classroom and of how meagre the literature was in those days, which could have given me a useful foundation of knowledge for teaching. Since then, I feel that the situation has gradually and steadily changed for the better. For those who possess some intellectual curiosity and a readiness to learn, it is now possible to set out a great deal of useful general knowledge about teaching and learning. It may be difficult to apply, but it can still provide a valuable context to essential practical experience. This is the claim that, more than any other, underpins the present book.

Teaching is frequently an emotionally draining occupation. It is often physically wearing and psychologically stressful. People commonly become teachers because of their love of children and because of deep-rooted wishes to help other people. Teachers often make strong relationships with those they teach and yet have to retain an even-handed professional stance of interest and fairness towards all their students and, indeed, their parents. So absorbing is teaching as an occupation that it is hard not to take its issues home and worry over them, even during the night. Teaching is thus a job that demands much from the self, from the resilience and integrity of the person within. Although I know all this to be true, I have not referred to these strong feelings or to this sense of personal commitment very often in what follows. I do, in Chapter 16, look at the strong emotions and the investment of self that are involved in becoming a teacher. For the most part, however, I have stuck to the cognitive side of the story, assuming that all teachers will discover the affective side of teaching for themselves soon enough, and that it is probably best discussed with those one likes and trusts.

The book attempts to cover issues of common interest to all teachers, or at least to those who teach students between the ages of 5 and 16. To this end I have tried throughout to give varied examples right across this age range and across different school subjects. (Apologies, in advance, for some subjects which get scarcely a mention: this does not reflect their relative importance but rather the availability of suitable examples.) This is a very ambitious undertaking and, in Chapter 16, I accept that teachers also need specialist knowledge, of one or more subjects, to become qualified professionals. Nevertheless I have been surprised to discover how much of the material seems as germane to Key Stage (KS)1 as to KS4, and how many issues impact on each and every school subject across the curriculum. Teachers perhaps have more in common than they realize. I also believe that all teachers will profit from understanding something about how things work in subjects and age groups that may be remote from their own particular 'patch'. Much of what I say is also relevant to the pre-school years and to post-16 teaching, but I have had to draw the line somewhere. Nor have I attempted to write about the broader social and political context of education. It is not that I think this context is unimportant, merely that there is not enough space to cover it here, even if I were competent to do so, which I am not.

It is an irony of educational research that we do not possess a really good model of how teachers develop from being novices to becoming experts at what they do. I am adopting a simple, and I hope robust, view here that this process involves building up knowledge and experience of three main kinds:

- practical knowledge, based on experiences of teaching;
- knowledge of how to teach particular curriculum subjects, to students of a given age range; and
- general pedagogical knowledge of teaching, learning, learners and schools.

This book makes its contribution to the third and last category. If you imagine each type of knowledge as residing in one of three overlapping circles, the region in which all three overlap is potentially of the greatest importance. It is here (I imagine) that teachers try to articulate to themselves how their teaching is actually done. Their specific practical experience has here to be interpreted in the light of what they know about how to teach this subject to this age group, and what they know about learners and about teaching in general. The specific knowledge should gradually illuminate the general and the general knowledge should inform the specific.

Some teachers probably rely almost entirely on practical knowledge and are not much interested in reading about teaching or learning, unless it be to discover some new 'recipes' for lessons. However, I confess I am not impressed by this stance. Who, aspiring to be a professional teacher, would not want to know as much as possible about this fascinating job? Surely we owe it to the students we teach, and indeed to ourselves, to find out as much from other people and from research as we possibly can. If professionals are people who make professionally informed decisions and engage in professionally relevant actions, then these decisions and actions should be based on the best available knowledge, used in the best interests of their students. Moreover I maintain that part of the continuing interest of teaching, as an occupation, lies precisely in finding out more about how it works. Good teachers are also good learners.

Research is often written by researchers for other researchers and consequently is dense with technical language and difficult for the general reader to evaluate. Hence the need for books such as this, written as an introduction for a more general audience. I should come clean and admit that, in spite of the book's title, much of the research I review is educational rather than strictly psychological, though it often has its roots in psychology. I also confess that in writing it I have not been able to rely on objective and well-established research findings alone. In effect I have used my own experience, as a parent, a teacher, an educational psychologist and a teacher trainer, to provide some of the practical advice and underlying convictions that glue the various ideas of the book together. Thus I have drawn on 'craft knowledge' and on my own experience where I felt I needed to.

Inevitably I have been selective in the research that I have considered interesting and relevant and I have tried to concentrate on certain powerful themes and ideas. I have also drawn on my own values and beliefs where necessary in order to try to produce a reasonably coherent account. Where these intuitions, values and opinions have led me to steer things in a particular direction I have tried to make this plain. But without this kind of personal 'voice' breathing some life into the text, I believe that the book would be a duller and a less useful one. Yet I also have to concede that the reader will need to keep his or her critical faculties alive and alert, so as not to be lured unreasonably by my opinions into territory that lies beyond the path actually illuminated by solid research evidence.

The general plan of the book is a simple one. Part I consists of a course for beginning teachers in understanding what goes on in classrooms. It considers the repertoire of teaching in Chapter 1 and the main phases of learning in Chapter 2, together with how they match up with different sorts of teaching and tasks. Chapter 3 provides an overview of the social context of the classroom, as a very particular kind of environment for learning. Chapters 4 and 5 provide introductions to two of the immediate problems facing beginners, namely keeping order and planning lessons. Craft knowledge is prominent in Part I and there are regular examples of episodes from real lessons to illustrate the argument.

In Part II, I take a look at the main areas of research that have contributed to our understanding of learning, teaching and motivation. In this section, psychological and educational research findings predominate and we stray from the day-to-day demands of the classroom, while always keeping an eye on why the research matters to teachers. Thus, Chapters 6, 7 and 8 all consider learning, moving from the easiest and most natural varieties to the more difficult kind of deliberate learning that I believe is central to the work of schools. Chapters 9 and 10 look at motivation, first in general and then more specifically in classrooms. Chapter 10 also includes material on teaching learners to manage their learning more effectively. Chapter 11 provides a sketch of the developing mind and its intellectual journey. Chapter 12 is about individual differences in intelligence and personality, and about the relative influence of parents and peers on learners.

In Part III, we return more directly to the classroom, to extend the coverage of teaching to a range of more advanced topics. Chapter 13 tackles special educational needs, together with bullying and child abuse. Chapter 14 looks at the impact of gender and ethnicity on schooling, whereas Chapter 15 focuses on the vital topic of assessment. In the last chapter, Chapter 16, I consider the development of subject expertise, what we know about teachers' knowledge and its growth, and the demands made on teachers as professionals.

I had better admit, as we set out on this tour of an enormous landscape, that in spite of much helpful advice from friends and colleagues, I am bound to have left some important places unvisited and to have got lost now and again. I hope these shortcomings do not disfigure the book too much. The remaining mistakes are all my responsibility.

I have used the term 'student' rather than 'pupil' throughout the book, although with some misgivings. I think this is because 'pupil' is beginning to sound a touch old-fashioned and patronizing, whereas 'student' is more neutral, even if its range does not usually include 5 year olds. Throughout the book there are examples, questions and exercises for the reader to try out, as a means of engaging with the text and trying to learn from it. There are lots of cross-references between chapters, to help the reader make links between related sections. Thus numbers in parentheses, such as (10.2), refer to a chapter (10) and a section (2) where other material on the same topic can be found. The book can be read in any order, but there is no penalty for starting at the beginning and working your way through to the end.

Notes on the school system of England and Wales

Most of what follows is true throughout the UK, although Scotland and Northern Ireland retain control over their own educational systems. Children are currently required by law to attend school between the ages of 5 and 16. Many children start school at the age of 4+ years and continue beyond the age of 16. Teaching is organized via a National Curriculum in five age groupings as follows:

Foundation stage (age 3–5 years): pre-school and Reception (R). This has its own curriculum, with early learning goals in six 'areas of learning'. An obligatory assessment in the form of a foundation stage profile is made on entry to KS1.
KS1 (age 5–7 years): Year (Y)1, Y2.
KS2 (age 7–11 years): Y3, Y4, Y5, Y6.
KS3 (age 11–14 years): Y7, Y8, Y9.
KS4 (age 14–16 years): Y10, Y11.

Many, but not all, schools are arranged as either primary schools (KS1 and KS2) or secondary schools (KS3 and KS4). At KS1, class sizes are restricted to 30 or fewer pupils. About 94% of children attend maintained (or state) schools, with some 6% being educated in private (or independent) schools.

The National Curriculum was established by the Education Reform Act of 1988 and was revised in 2000. It applies to all pupils from age 5 to 16 in maintained (state) schools. It is made up of core subjects, i.e. English, mathematics and science, and foundation subjects, i.e. art, design technology, history, geography, information and communication technology, modern languages (at present from KS3 but in the future from KS2), music and physical education. Religious education, personal, social and health education, and citizenship are also compulsory subjects but are outside the full National Curriculum framework, having only 'non-statutory guidelines'. At KS4 fewer subjects may be studied.

Each core and foundation subject in the curriculum is organized around programmes of study (the content of the curriculum) and attainment targets (learning objectives arranged in a hierarchy of levels, from level 1 to level 8 plus one for exceptional performance). There are obligatory National Curriculum tests (formerly called Standard Assessment Tasks, or SATs) at the end of KS1, KS2 and KS3 in the three core subjects only. At the end of KS4, students sit a varying number of subjects for the General Certificate of Secondary Education (GCSE) at age 16+. Results for this examination are graded from A* (the highest) to G (the lowest).

In 1999, national frameworks were established for the teaching of literacy and numeracy, which were given protected curriculum time, known colloquially as the 'literacy hour' and the 'numeracy hour'. These had a significant impact on teaching across KS1–3 and were subsequently replaced by a broader 'primary strategy' and 'national strategy'.

The Department for Education and Skills (DfES) is the ministry overseeing the school system. It is assisted by the Office for Standards in Education (Ofsted), which is responsible in particular for the inspection of schools, and by the Qualifications and Curriculum Authority (QCA), which oversees developments in the curriculum, assessments and examinations. The Teacher Training Agency (TTA) currently has overall responsibility for teacher training. All these agencies maintain websites, as does the General Teaching Council for England (GTC).

There are some 423,600 teachers working full time in schools in England and Wales, with an additional 122,400 teaching assistants (figures from 2003); 48.8% of the teachers are in secondary schools, 46.6% in primary schools and 4.5% in special schools and units. There is considerable turnover in the teaching force. Currently some 31,000 individuals start on a course of teacher training each year, of whom about 88% complete their course and some 60% actually enter teaching. Although figures vary from year to year, around 20% of these newly qualified teachers leave the profession, at present, within 3 years of starting. However, some two-thirds of entrants stay on for 10 years or more.[1] Most students qualify as teachers via either a 4-year (undergraduate) Bachelor of Education degree or a 1-year Postgraduate Certificate of Education (PGCE). There are also some school-based and 'flexible' part-time training courses. Student teachers work towards attaining **Qualified Teacher Status (QTS)**, after which they can seek to be employed in a maintained school and enter into an induction year as newly qualified teachers. Following further observations and assessments of their progress they may pass their probationary period and become fully qualified teachers.

The reader is warned that facts change rapidly in this field and an introduction such as this will probably date rather quickly. Useful basic websites include the following:

www.dfes.gov.uk
www.ofsted.gov.uk/
www.qca.org.uk/
www.standards.dfes.gov.uk/
www.nc.uk.net/
www.gtce.org.uk/
www.bbc.co.uk/learning
www.ngfl.gov.uk/
www.teachernet.gov.uk/
www.canteach.gov.uk/

NOTE

1. The figure of two-thirds comes from a speech by David Miliband, Minister of State for School Standards, given on 24 June 2003. Most of the other statistics quoted in this introduction come from the DfES Research and Statistics Gateway website (www.dfes.gov.uk/rsgateway).

PART I

Beginning to Teach

This part of the book introduces the main tasks of the teacher.

- Chapter 1 considers the repertoire of teaching, ranging from direct instruction, through interactive teaching to the setting and supervision of independent work.
- Chapter 2 relates teaching to a series of different phases of the learning process, from first encounters with a topic through to routine practice and revision.
- Chapter 3 considers the social world of the classroom as a special context in which to learn and work.
- Chapter 4 provides an account, with advice, on how to manage order in the classroom.
- Chapter 5 concerns planning and the design of lessons.

CHAPTER ONE

The Repertoire of Teaching

1.1 Introduction

In this chapter teaching as a professional activity in schools is introduced. The question of the kinds of knowledge that teachers draw on, in learning to teach, is raised, partly in order to clarify the function of this book. Teaching is analysed into three main categories:

- direct teaching and demonstration;
- interactive teaching; and
- independent practice and problem-solving.

These three different kinds of teaching are illustrated using transcripts of classroom lessons. The involvement of values and judgements in the business of schooling is emphasized and the way in which values enter into the life of classrooms is introduced via the idea of 'ethos'.

1.2 Teaching and Learning

Humans are specialists in adapting to their circumstances by learning. We carry our knowledge and skills about with us in our heads, in the form of memory, and this, to some degree, enables us to understand, predict and control our lives. Teachers work to aid learning. Schools have grown up as institutions whose special purpose is to ensure that a culture's most valuable knowledge is learned by its children. However, it is as well to realize from the start that much of this learning goes on out of school. Moreover, learning is always invisible and intangible and the learner does not necessarily even know that it has taken place. Schools concentrate resources for learning and attempt to generate the conditions in which many learners can benefit from them as efficiently as possible. However, any classroom is a compromise, with a

history, a budget and a timetable, where there are often conflicting views and traditions about what is worth doing and worth learning. Values, choices and judgements
thus enter into schooling from the very start.

It is the teacher's job to organize and manage the learning environment in school
and also to be sufficiently knowledgeable and competent to guide learners effectively
through the approved curriculum. But the children, the students in schools, already
have knowledge, values and habits that they bring with them. In the encounter
between a teacher and his or her class, the mental world of the teacher meets the
mental worlds of the students. Both students and teacher will probably learn from
these encounters but it is far from easy to ensure that the students' learning is what
the teacher intended it to be, or indeed that anything new is learned at all. For,
in spite of a great deal of hard work and many excellent intentions, much of the
activity that goes on in schools, although busy and conscientious, is more or less
useless in terms of new learning taking place (see sections 3.6, 3.8).

How difficult is it to teach? Just as almost anyone can cook, in that they can boil
an egg, almost anyone can do some simple teaching; it does not require special
talents or training. We all act as informal teachers of one another, from time to time.
Indeed we are generally adept at showing, telling, describing and explaining in our
everyday lives, especially when we are confident and familiar with the topic we are
dealing with, whether it be how to bake a cake or how to send text messages on a
mobile phone. But teaching a class in a school, across the full range of the curriculum, is extremely difficult, just as cooking an ambitious menu for many clients in the
pressurized atmosphere of a restaurant kitchen is very difficult. Although it may be
easy to teach simply or badly, it is very difficult to teach 20–30 students consistently
well. To become an expert in this field, as in so many others, it is essential to have
practical experience over a prolonged period of time. In fact one of the greatest
satisfactions of teaching is that good teachers continue to learn, for as long as they
teach. To turn an old insult on its head, we may say that those who can, teach, and
those who teach continue to learn.

1.3 How Teachers Learn

As well as the **deliberate practice** needed to become a good teacher, it is helpful
to have some knowledge about what is likely to work. Some of this will come
from watching other teachers at work and from talking with one's fellow teachers.
But the claim of this book is that useful knowledge, and some valuable principles,
can also be learned from the systematic research that has been done on teaching
and learning. Much of this research is psychological in nature, although not all of
it started off, or ended up, in psychology as a discipline. Increasingly, when it is
carried on in classrooms, either with or by teachers, it is simply called **educational research**.

To some extent teaching is an art, for the teacher has to 'perform' his or her
teaching in real time, making hundreds of spontaneous decisions about what to do

and say on the spur of the moment, guided only by some general principles and values and by a search for quality. There is also a good case for considering teaching as a craft, a set of repeated activities that have been shaped gradually into expert routines and habits through a long period of apprenticeship, and that are constantly adapted skilfully to the materials at hand. Much of the expertise of teachers is of this pragmatic kind, which I shall call **craft knowledge**. Craft knowledge can be summed up as a feeling for what works, learned from one's own experience and from that of others. However, there is also a body of knowledge, built up from research, which can inform what teachers do. Thus we can say that whereas the actual activity of teaching has elements that make it both an art and a craft, in its conception and planning teaching can draw on the findings of disciplined scientific enquiry. The most difficult trick is to use this knowledge fluently to inform the activity of teaching itself.

What is it, then, that skilled teachers do? It is time to take a look at some teachers at work.

1.4 Teachers at Work

I use excerpts from transcripts of teaching throughout this book. Describing lessons by way of transcripts of what people say is helpful, but necessarily limited. The bare words on the page are incomplete and all the expressive qualities of the speech, together with the non-verbal communication, are lost. Nonetheless, we can recapture some of what went on in these classrooms. Oblique slashes (/) mark a pause. An ellipsis (. . .) indicates a section missed out.

Example 1.1 Painting the sky: young children and art[1]
A man, with a rich bass voice, is telling some 6-year-old Russian children a story about an old woman, a babushka, who goes for a walk to the woods in autumn. As he talks, he acts out the story.

Teacher: Oh, she walked along all crooked [*hobbles round the room with stooped back, eyes on the ground*], her back was old and bent, old and bent [*clutching painful hip*] and oh, the stiffness! And she came at last to the wood. She came to the wood and [*looks up*] raised her head, and what do you think she saw? [*Nominates a child, A, by bending towards her, still in babushka posture*]
Child A: [*Rapidly*] The leaves falling, the leaves falling.
Teacher: Yes! But that's not all she saw. / What else did she see?
Child B: [*Calls out*] The sky!
Teacher: [*Stands up straight and sweeps his arm in a celestial arc*] Yes! The sky. And [*bending towards B*] what was the sky like?
Child C: [*Calls out*] Light blue.
Teacher: Light blue, yes. Now, what we have to do is this. [*Clasps hands, speaks more earnestly*] We have to show this scene, with the leaves falling. [*Mimes falling leaves*]

That's what we have to make today. So, what do we have to start with? / What do we have to do first? Anyone?

Child D: The sky!

Teacher: Yes, we start with the sky. Right, let's open up the paints. Have you all got yellow, red, dark blue and white?

Students: Yes.

Teacher: Good. Now don't use any others, just keep to the yellow, red, blue and white.

...

Teacher: And now I need a *huge* brush, a really big brush to help me. [*Students hold up their paint brushes*] Oh yes, let me have that for a minute, can you? [*Takes brush offered by A and holds it up*] Now look, this brush is really large, so we'll be able to do everything we need to really quickly using this one, won't we? We can't afford to do it slowly, you know, otherwise we'll never be able to help Grandma, will we? Now look this way, please. The first thing you do is to dip the brush into the water, [*does so*] then get just a very little paint onto the end of the brush. [*Dips brush into paint. To two students who are standing up to look*] Sit down please, sit down.

Child E: [*Calls out*] Should we start from the bottom and work up?

Teacher: Of course! Now watch the way I do it. First of all, the bottom line [*paints a line across a piece of paper fixed to the portable blackboard, then recharges his brush*] and then some very little blocks, just tiny little ones, like this: one, two, three. [*Dabs small blocks of colour above the line and then rinses his brush*] And now what colour paint do we need? Which colour do we need just a little of?

Child F: Dark blue?

Teacher: Not dark blue. [*Charges his brush*]

Child F: Yellow?

Teacher: Yes. Just a little yellow, like this: one, two, three, four. [*Paints four more blocks of colour*] And now a few more strokes with the brush, what colour this time?

Child A: Dark blue!

Teacher: Dark blue, yes.

Child F: Lots and lots of it!

Teacher: [*Paints*] One, two, three, four.

Child G: And now we want some white.

Teacher: We want some white, yes. And in what direction do we put the white on?

Child G: In little blocks?

Teacher: I said in what direction? From the top or from the bottom?

Students together: From the top! From the bottom!

Teacher: From the bottom, yes. And this is the way I do it, do you see, [*painting as he speaks*] over everything else that hasn't been painted yet. Here we go! Here and here, and all over, and out comes a really beautiful sky. Now, [*gestures towards the class, returns A's brush*] you try it please.

In this first example, the teacher is the dominant figure. He takes charge and the students' job, in the first part of the lesson, is mostly to listen and watch. This is an example of our first kind of teaching: **direct instruction** and **demonstration**. It is perhaps the most obvious kind of teaching, occurring when a teacher tells students something they did not know before, or demonstrates a new skill to them, as here.

But telling students things, or even showing them skills, are not in themselves sufficient for learning to occur. **Assimilation** of new information, for example that you can use several colours to paint a sky, requires that the learner also does two things: (i) manages to fit the new information into his or her existing knowledge, so that it makes sense; and (ii) remembers it. If it does not make sense, the learner will not be able to use the knowledge sensibly. If it is forgotten, the learner will not be able to use it at all.

Exercise

Try, now, to make a brief list of the sorts of things that this teacher said or did, which you think would have helped these students to understand and remember how he painted the sky. Then read the analysis that follows.

Analysis of Example 1.1: direct instruction and demonstration

This teacher was actually not a professional at all, but a local painter who gave his time to this Russian kindergarten in Kursk, unpaid. He nevertheless teaches with confidence and skill. The general moves that he makes as a teacher, which are typical of this kind of teaching, are indicated in italic in what follows.

The teacher first shows a talent for *dramatic story-telling* and for *skilful demonstration*. Acting out the story of the babushka was a way of *engaging the full attention* of these young children. He also invited them to participate, by *asking them questions*. Their answers helped him to *gauge their understanding* and *drew them into the discourse*. Having *elicited contributions* from the children he often *confirms* and *repeats* them ('Yes, we start with the sky ...'). But he is also prepared, on occasion, to give them *direct instructions* ('Now don't use any others ...') or to *correct* them ('Not dark blue ...'). He *informs* them, about the colours, the size of the brush and so on, in a clear and unfussy manner. He then *demonstrates* how to paint the sky, step by step, which probably both aids their learning and maintains their interest. No doubt his skill as a painter, as well as his *skills as a communicator*, were strong means of *giving the activity value* in the eyes of the children. Finally, he *initiates activity*, getting them to start painting, in imitation of his lesson, without delay.

We might note in passing that these young children have not yet been fully socialized into the strict Russian traditions of the classroom, whereby students have to raise their hands in an approved manner in order to make a contribution. They still shout out their answers, volunteer information and ask questions, from time to time. Yet the teacher is already beginning to shape their behaviour by his pattern of responses, without ever being harsh or deviating from the content of his lesson. In the Russian tradition, there is an approved way to begin the painting of skies, bound by rules and conventions, and the lesson has a strong element of direct instruction, which may make it a little unusual to Western eyes and ears. The lesson continued with the children doing their paintings. The teacher continued to instruct while **monitoring** their work and, finally, there was a **plenary** discussion in which the children viewed and commented on each other's paintings.

Example 1.2 Decimal fractions: KS2 maths[2]
The teacher of a Y4 class (8–9 year olds) writes '0.1' on his whiteboard.

Teacher: Here's 0.1. What different ways could I use to describe this?
Student: 10%.
Teacher: Well done. What else?
Student: One-tenth.
Teacher: OK, what else?
Student: 1 over 10.
Teacher: Right. Now, if this [*writes 1.0*] is a centimetre on your ruler, what would this
   be [*writes 0.1 centimetre*]?
Student: Half a centimetre?
Teacher: Umm, might there be a problem there?
Student: 1 millimetre.
Teacher: Who agrees with 1 millimetre?
Students: [*Lots of hands go up*]
Teacher: Tell me why that's true. [*Indicates child*]
Student: Because one-tenth of a centimetre is 1 millimetre.
Teacher: OK, so how many millimetres in 1 centimetre?
Students: [*Several voices*] 10!
Teacher: What fraction of a centimetre is 1 millimetre?
Students: [*Several voices*] A tenth!
Teacher: Right, so 0.1 centimetres is the same as 1 millimetre. So, how could we write
   3 millimetres? [*Indicates child with hand up*]
Student: 0.3 centimetres.
Teacher: And 9 millimetres? [*Indicates child*]
Student: 0.9 centimetres.
Teacher: Really good! Now, what if I write 12 millimetres? Be careful! [*Indicates child*]
Student: 1.2 centimetres.
Teacher: 1.2 centimetres, who agrees with that? [*Most hands go up*] Well, I'm really
   pleased. At the beginning of the year you wouldn't have said that! What about
   26 millimetres? [*Indicates child*]
Student: 2.6 centimetres!
Teacher: Right. Nice to see all the hands going up.
Student: [*A boy*] You just have to move it one place to the left!
Teacher: Let's see who . . . here's one for those who are feeling clever, 123 millimetres?
   [*Indicates child*]
Student: 12.3 centimetres!
Teacher: OK, you've got enough information for the next part of my task . . .

Analysis of Example 1.2: interactive teaching

Interactive teaching is appropriate in a wide variety of situations. We use it when
we want to awaken or rehearse existing knowledge, to practise routine skills or
problem-solving and also when we want to extend knowledge. The students have
to have some relevant knowledge in order to take part, but this knowledge may

be relatively poorly remembered, vague or fragile. Here, the teacher leads the whole class through a series of examples about representing decimal fractions and the relationship between centimetres and millimetres, using question and answer. Although not new to the class, these ideas have not been addressed recently. He is careful to proceed quite slowly until he gets the sense that the class understands. Then he tries some harder challenges. Interactive teaching frequently involves this mixture of:

- using questions to gain attention, initially;
- rehearsing what is known and applying it to exemplary problems;
- informally assessing the students' existing level of understanding and fluency, as a preparation for further work;
- arousing as many students as possible to participate actively in the exchanges;
- using easier and also harder questions to challenge differing levels of understanding across the same class.

There is an emphasis in this example on being able to represent the same mathematical concept in several different ways that are equivalent, so as to promote conceptual fluency in moving between **representations** (0.1, $^1/_{10}$, 10%). This is both a test of understanding and a powerful way of encouraging students to make links themselves. This teacher uses the strategy of 'Who agrees with that?' to try to get children to think for themselves and to commit themselves to an answer even if they have not raised a hand. He asks 'Why is that true?' to press them to justify an answer. He gives a prompt ('Be careful!') to warn them of a commonly encountered problem. He uses praise freely, praising not only their correct answers but also their willingness to participate. Several of his strategies can be seen as converging on the aim of building up the students' confidence in doing arithmetic. He is gentle with an early error ('Umm, might there be a problem there?'), makes a positive 'metacognitive' comment on the progress they have made during the year and challenges them with sensitivity ('Here's one for those who are feeling clever'). At one point, a boy attempts to generalize about the examples, but was not heard by the teacher.

This kind of interactive whole-class teaching has become very common in the context of the UK's literacy and numeracy strategies. It allows a single teacher to work with all the students in a class at once and to try to involve as many of them as possible actively in the lesson. Its organization is admirably simple and at its best it provides students with plenty of opportunities to learn, via listening or speaking. A tight rein can be kept by the teacher on the relevance of the talk and challenging problems can be set. In the example given here there is a high degree of concentration on the planned content of the curriculum (in this case maths) and a high apparent degree of attention by students to the task. The **pace**, in terms of both the rapidity of questions and the introduction of ideas, is brisk and this, too, seems to help with student attention. Teachers and students probably get a sense of satisfaction from successful examples like this as everyone can see and hear that appropriate work is being done, and celebrated. Besides, there is no time to be distracted or bored. The whole class is thus helping to orchestrate a performance that can bring pride to one and all.

However, there is a risk in whole-class interactive teaching, namely that one or more children fail to understand and thus fall behind or, conversely, never find the work sufficiently challenging. Differential questioning can be used to try to avoid this pitfall of the 'one size fits all' approach. The teacher also needs to be fluent and skilled in rapidly producing questions, or examples, at varying levels of difficulty, in checking the accuracy of students' answers and in making assessments of their understanding and **engagement**. It is particularly easy to fall into the fallacy of assuming that a string of correct answers from two or three students means that the whole class understands the work at hand, which may not be the case. Another potential drawback of this kind of teaching is that students have little chance to ask their own questions or offer their own contributions. Poorly motivated students may refuse to answer or try to avoid the teacher's attention. (Note that interactive teaching may also be carried out with an individual or a small group, rather than with the whole class.)

In Example 1.2, although both teacher and students are actively involved in the dialogue, the teacher is still very much in control of what is said. As we will see later, there are other kinds of interactive teaching in which the students gradually take on rather more initiative in the dialogue. But first we need to look at a third general kind of teaching in which the student is given much more initiative.

Example 1.3 Dice throwing: KS2 maths/science investigation[3]
Stephen Rowland, a primary teacher and researcher, worked in another teacher's class for a year and here describes his dialogue with a student and his observations of her work.

Sarah had been doing some fairly routine work from a textbook introducing probability. It involved throwing dice and making estimates and tallies of the results. When I came to her she explained the work to me and appeared to have some, albeit imprecise, notion of ratio or proportion. For example, she guessed that out of 100 tosses of a coin she would expect 'heads' to come up 50 times; and that from 600 throws of a dice she would expect 'about 100' sixes.

Field notes: 8 January
I asked Sarah if there were any other questions which she could raise concerning the work so far... After only a moment's thought, she said, 'I wonder if it makes any difference to the number that turns up on the dice which number shows when I roll it?' She explained how she had been rolling the dice off the palm of her hand. She wondered if it would make any difference to the result if, say, the number 1 was initially uppermost when the dice was on her hand. With virtually no assistance from me she went on to describe how this could be investigated experimentally. First, with 1 uppermost in her hand, she would roll the dice and record the 'score'. This would be repeated 25 times. (She initially said that 60 times would be better but that it would take too long.) She would then make a bar chart of the results. The experiment would then be repeated with 2, 3, 4, 5 and 6 initially uppermost. By comparing the charts with what

might be expected had she tossed the dice 'just anyhow' she would be able to see if the initial position affected the outcome. Sarah followed this procedure and soon produced the first bar chart. (For the sake of economy, I reproduce her results here in the form of a table rather than bar charts.) Her first results, starting with 1 uppermost, were:

Face	Frequency
1	0
2	3
3	3
4	7
5	6
6	7

Having completed this,[4] she examined the dice, noting that 1 and 6 appeared on opposite faces. With no prompting from me she suggested the following tentative hypotheses to explain her results.

1 Since the frequency of 1 was zero, then perhaps the initial face will not become uppermost in the final position of the dice.
2 The face opposite the starting face (here 6) will always score high.

I asked her if she could offer any explanations for the initial face not turning up at all. She said, 'Because the dice would have to rotate completely round to end up in this position.' I replied, 'But don't you think there is enough space for it to make one complete turn?' (It appeared to me that the dice, in rolling off her hand, had made at least one complete revolution.) She said, 'Yes, perhaps it does rotate once, but there's not enough space for it to go round twice.' Her explanation seemed most plausible and not only accounted for the low frequency of the initial face, but also for the high frequency of the opposite face (face 6 scoring 7). Sarah now went on to the second part of her experiment, repeating 25 rolls with face 2 initially uppermost.

Analysis of Example 1.3: independent problem-solving

In the original account, Sarah takes her investigations further, but eventually runs up against some difficulties with inconsistent results, which she finds hard to explain. Although the example starts off from some routine problem-solving in a maths book, it develops into an informal science investigation into dice throwing. For our purposes, however, the important points to notice about the example have to do with the altered balance of power between teacher and taught, compared with Examples 1.1 and 1.2. Here the teacher, or observer, starts by asking the student a general **open question**, to which she does not know the answer. The student comes up with an answer that is a genuine question of her own: does the initial position of the dice on her palm affect the results of her throws? The student is then allowed considerable freedom to carry out her *investigation* and only *consults* the teacher/observer from time to time when she wants help. In her investigation, she *applies her knowledge* of probability and also of bar charts and demonstrates her intuitive ideas about *testing hypotheses*.

The teacher's role is no longer to inform or demonstrate. And although he is involved from time to time in dialogue with Sarah, it is not so much in order to teach her as to try to help her to apply her own knowledge and to extend it. He thus helps to set up an opportunity for *independent problem-solving* and he *monitors progress*. He uses his interactions with Sarah to *hypothesize* about her thinking and to *assess* her level of understanding of both maths and science. Finally he *evaluates* the outcomes of her work, partly as feedback to her and partly for his own purposes of recording her learning.

Does this count as teaching? In one way, it is quite difficult to see any teaching going on. But if we define teaching as **facilitating learning**, then clearly this is teaching, albeit quite an indirect form of it. It is important to note that if we never give students such opportunities to use their knowledge independently, we will never be able to judge what they can, in fact, do for themselves. And if they never practise investigations, they will not find it easy to extend their knowledge for themselves, away from the teacher and the classroom. Such independent work may vary from the most routine kind of working through examples in a textbook to more open-ended and ambitious investigations and projects.

1.5 The Repertoire of Teaching

So far we have distinguished between three main kinds of teaching, summarized briefly in Table 1.1. In addition to these three main varieties of teaching, teachers of course do other things. For example, they plan, organize, assess, record, display work, answer questions, think aloud, encourage, sympathize, supervise out-of-class activities, drink coffee and tea, make jokes and intervene to keep order. It should be

Table 1.1 The teaching repertoire

Type of teaching	Teacher's main role	Student's main role
Direct instruction and/or demonstration	To inform, explain or show how	To listen, watch and sometimes imitate
Interactive teaching	To engage, question, rehearse, prompt, challenge, extend, correct, confirm, praise, assess	To contribute to the dialogue as appropriate
Independent practice and problem-solving	To set up opportunities, monitor, assess, evaluate	To apply knowledge, practise and solve problems

clear, however, that the central business of aiding learning can be done in several main ways, all of them involving communication and management, but each of them differing in the extent to which the teacher is either controlling the talk, activity and lesson content, or transferring to the students a greater degree of control over these things. Together, the three varieties make up a basic **repertoire of teaching**, which any competent teacher should be able to use across different sorts of lesson.

Let us now bring the three varieties together in another way. Teachers generally should try to make their teaching match the existing level of the students' skill or understanding. This adapting of teaching to learning is sometimes called **contingent instruction** (or **scaffolding**). If this is so, we can state a principle of contingent instruction very simply: when a learner gets into difficulty with a task, immediately offer more help; when a learner succeeds at a task, with a given level of help, reduce the level of help next time around. Eventually the aim is for the student, or group of students, to be able to operate independently. This is an easy principle to articulate but a very difficult one to put into practice consistently. The 'offering more help' can, of course, come in many shapes or forms, across all the different types of teaching we have considered.

We have already seen that if the students know little or nothing about a topic, then it is appropriate for the teacher to use direct instruction. The teacher is the active communicator and the student's role is to listen and learn. Similarly, if a student has no idea how to, say, join a clay handle onto a clay pot, it is appropriate for the teacher to demonstrate how to do it. When the students have some knowledge or skill, but cannot manage entirely on their own, then the teacher should move to interactive teaching. I will break down interactive teaching into three subclasses.

- **Prompting**: here the teacher actively supports the learner's early efforts by giving some kind of support, clue or prompt. She might start a sentence, for example, hoping that the learner will complete it, or say something about the general nature of the required answer, or even guide a young child's early handwriting physically with her own hand.
- **Coaching**: here the teacher does not provide physical help, or deliberate clues that form part of the required answer, but instead looks at, or listens to, the child's efforts and then gives verbal feedback on their quality. This could include such things as evaluating writing, pointing out where a line of thinking has gone wrong or suggesting a further line of work.
- **Dialogue** or discussion: here the teacher allows the student, or students, to make more decisions about what should be said or done. As in a true conversation, the participants, teacher and students, are on equal terms and anyone can attempt to make a relevant contribution, whether it be to provide information, ask a question or make an evaluation.

As we move from prompting to coaching and then to dialogue, the control of the talk and action gradually passes from the teacher, as solely in charge, to students and teacher having an equal part to play. Since teachers have overall responsibility for both their students' general welfare and their learning, and since teachers often (though not always) know more about a topic than their students do, it is actually rather difficult for teachers to start a genuine conversation between equals in a classroom. However, this does not mean we should never try.

Moving on from interactive teaching, the final stage of handing over control of the problem to the student is **independent practice and problem-solving**. This, too, can be divided into different sorts of practice. Relatively low-level practice involves merely the routine application of existing knowledge and skill to already familiar contexts and problems. In more challenging kinds of practice, such as in genuine investigations, the student meets situations and contexts which are unfamiliar. These demand that, as well as applying knowledge, he or she has to decide in the first place what knowledge is applicable and then how a solution should be tested, checked or evaluated. They may also involve extension or elaboration of the student's existing knowledge.

So far, little has been said about the process of learning. Nor have any distinctions been made about teaching different age groups or types of student, or indeed about teaching different school subjects or disciplines. The claim so far is that there are some **generic processes of teaching**, which apply to all subjects, to all age groups and to all sorts of learner. Three further ideas need to be mentioned at this stage. Until now, no questions have been raised about the **motivation** of students, although some examples (dramatic story-telling, orchestrated question and answer, the student's own curiosity) have been mentioned in passing. Motivation is seen by most teachers as central to the success of lessons. Teachers also have to pay attention not only to the particular topics being taught but also the general thinking, reasoning and feeling of their students. A useful general term for 'thinking about thinking' is **metacognition**. Let us say, then, that teachers need to pay attention to the metacognition of their students, i.e. to the way in which they manage, think and feel about their own learning.

1.6 Ethos

Because all education involves judgements about what should be taught, and how, we have already seen that values enter into the choices that teachers make. Also, teachers live with children in classrooms and have to organize a way to get along together. The classroom is a miniature society, with its own rules and traditions. We will use the general term **ethos** to describe all the attitudes and values that are expressed, or lived out, in the classroom, whether they are explicitly mentioned or remain implicit in the ways in which the different participants communicate with, and relate to, one another. When the teacher in Example 1.1 says 'Look this way please' he asserts his right to give orders, but remains polite to his young charges. When the teacher in Example 1.2 says 'Nice to see all the hands going up' he is both commenting on a 'meta' aspect of the lesson (student readiness to answer) and showing that he values this positively. When the teacher in Example 1.3 asks

'But don't you think there's enough space there for it to make a complete turn?' he is implicitly entering into a real discussion with Sarah, in which he shows that he values her ideas. All these examples show one or other aspect of ethos at work.

In some ways, the general ethos of any classroom is quite quickly and easily noticed by any observer. It is apparent in language, for example the way in which the teacher addresses students and they address the teacher. It shows in the displays on the walls and in the layout of the room. It is indicated by the way in which work is discussed and by the questions that are asked. It may be revealed in examples of conflict or disorder or in the humour displayed in defusing them. As teachers, we are all probably aware of some of the values we are trying to embody in our teaching. We might, for example, want our students to feel comfortable with taking risks, or want them to grow in confidence and independence. We might desire that they treat one another with respect and kindness. It is less easy to notice the ways in which we may compromise our values, for example to keep order or perhaps from anxiety over making some mistake or from a general wish to fit in with the values and traditions of the school. The moral atmosphere of a class is perhaps its most important and overriding feature, but it is diffused among hundreds of encounters and a thousand details. It can also be difficult to influence, especially as a newcomer. As you evaluate lessons, it is worth pondering on the ethos that is developing in your class, how you are made aware of it and how you intend to try to develop it.

1.7 Questions and Extension Tasks

At the end of each chapter you will find some questions. The first ones are designed partly to help you check your understanding of the chapter. In answering them, however, you will also provide yourself with a summary of the main ideas in the chapter. A more open-ended question for discussion follows.

1 How does teaching as a professional activity differ from informal episodes of teaching something to a friend?
2 How do values enter into teaching?
3 In what main ways were teachers said to learn about their work?
4 What three main kinds of teaching have been distinguished?
5 What are the main advantages and disadvantages of whole-class interactive teaching?
6 Why is it important to include opportunities for independent problem-solving in the repertoire of teaching?
7 What three subclasses of interactive teaching were defined?
8 What is meant by the 'ethos' of a class or school?
9 **Discussion question**: what kinds of 'ethos' have characterized the classrooms where you have so far worked or observed? What kinds of tell-tale signs, or language, helped you to understand the unwritten rules and values that were at work?

To conclude this opening chapter, you may wish to read Example 1.4 in Appendix A, which provides a longer account of a whole lesson. It aims to illustrate, once again, particular examples of the various generic processes of teaching and offers you the chance to see if you can recognize them.

NOTES

1. Example 1.1 comes from Alexander (2000), pp. 458–60.
2. Example 1.2 comes from a set of unpublished observations of teachers by Richard Fox.
3. Example 1.3 is taken from Rowland (1984), pp. 80–1.
4. Sarah appears to have included 26 rather than 25 throws in her table.

CHAPTER TWO

Learning and Task Demands

2.1 Introduction

In introducing teaching, I made use of a threefold classification of the main kinds of teaching. Now I intend to do the same with learning, in order to provide a useful entry point to the subject. This chapter introduces a simplified model of learning that classifies it into three broad phases, from the first encounter with a topic to its final revision. Two further intermediate phases are then added to make it more complete. This analysis is useful because it enables us to try to match the right kind of task, and the appropriate kind of teaching, to each phase of learning. Five kinds of task are introduced to match the five phases of learning. The scheme is used here to analyse five different extracts from lessons, which illustrate in different ways the various **task demands** involved and some of the difficulties that arise in practice. The same set of ideas is then used to show how the connection of teaching with learning can sometimes break down for quite predictable reasons.

2.2 Three Phases of Learning

The classification of learning that I will use in the present chapter comes from an account of complex human learning by two American psychologists, Rumelhart and Norman.[1] These psychologists considered all learning to be a matter of organizing experience in what they called **schemas** (or schemata). These are units of organized information, represented in our minds. We might, for example, have a number of existing schemas available to help us know how to paint a sky in a painting (schemas to do with relevant materials, knowledge of what the sky looks like, ways of making marks on the paper, etc.). In learning, new experiences and new information have somehow to be integrated into our old existing schemas, so that they are to some degree transformed. The Russian art lesson (Example 1.1) will provide us with examples of how this transformation may occur. There are three main processes involved: accretion, restructuring and tuning.

Accretion refers to learning a new fact, idea or skill. Here, new knowledge is being added to the system. When the art teacher in Example 1.1 chose to use a large brush to paint his sky, one of the children might have received this suggestion (about choosing an appropriately sized brush) as a completely novel idea, which he or she then started to put into practice. Another child might have learned, for the first time, that the background of a picture might be painted before the foreground.

The second process, **restructuring**, is a matter of gaining new insight, or understanding. No absolutely new knowledge is added but rather one's existing schemas of knowledge are shifted around, elaborated or reorganized. Sticking to Example 1.1, we could imagine that a child may have watched the painting demonstration and thought for the first time about how the sky might be painted using more than one colour. The sky is not a new idea, and the colours are already familiar, but a multi-coloured sky might be a new **concept**, requiring a restructuring of schemas. A different example of restructuring might be that a child, impressed by the performance of this large, bearded artist, comes to think for the first time that it might be *worth* painting a picture of leaves falling against an autumn sky. His or her attitudes to what are suitable subjects to paint may thus have changed.

The third process, **tuning**, refers to the gradual process whereby skills and understanding become smooth and automatic patterns of response. New knowledge gradually becomes organized into accustomed routines. Thinking of Example 1.1 again, we might imagine that over a series of art lessons, the loading of the brush with paint gradually becomes an automatic and easy skill, at least for some of these children. That is, with repeated practice, their initial errors are gradually eliminated and they become adept at loading the brush with just enough paint, but not too much, without having to think consciously about how to do it.

These three **basic processes of learning** (accretion, restructuring and tuning) may all occur together in the course of learning. Accretion and restructuring, for example, seem to blend into one another. However, if we looked at a learner at a single moment in time, say in the Russian art lesson, we would probably find one of the processes predominating. When a topic is quite new, we would expect that accretion dominates: the learner is preoccupied with accumulating and assimilating new ideas and/or skills. If this was the first art lesson these children had ever experienced, then probably all sorts of new ideas were bombarding them, to the general effect: so this is how it's done!

After this initial learning of new facts, concepts or skills, there is likely to be a period in which restructuring dominates. Patterns and links between new and existing knowledge are being noticed, organized and integrated. Thus, after a series of art lessons, perhaps the children would begin to notice how certain techniques of the teacher clash with the way they have formerly (intuitively) made their pictures. Then, they might start to make choices that involve taking on some of the teacher's skills and strategies as their own. They might repeatedly try to use small blocks of paint, shall we say, instead of painting in large zig-zag strokes. They might habitually start to think about how colours might be combined. They might consciously think of compositions in terms of background and foreground.

There may then be new lessons in which accretion again dominates. Perhaps the artist shows them how to use a broad wash or a dark outline. The repertoire of types of painting marks and strokes starts to expand. Then in a further period of learning, the children may start to learn how to apply this repertoire strategically, across a range of different pictorial problems (**strategic application**). Finally, at least some aspects of the repertoire are practised until they become relatively automatic processes of choosing and painting different subjects, parts or details of a picture skilfully. This would be the period in which tuning predominates.

2.3 Task Demands

One of the main points of Rumelhart and Norman's scheme is that it enables us to think about which kinds of learning are most likely to be demanded by different tasks, set by teachers.[2] In particular, we can distinguish between the following.

- **Incremental tasks** involve the process of accretion, in the acquisition of new facts, skills, rules or procedures. If this was the first time the Russian children had seen a sky being painted using more than one colour, this may have been the main thing they remembered from the lesson and tried to imitate in their own paintings. Direct instruction and demonstration is obviously particularly appropriate to this kind of new learning.
- **Restructuring tasks** involve the student in inventing, realizing or constructing a new way of dealing with familiar material. Thus the Russian children may have been prompted by the artist to try to start at the bottom of the sky and work upwards. Although they may have painted pictures, even of skies, before, let us imagine that this is first time they have thought of starting from the bottom and working upwards. Or perhaps, for some children, the notion that one could use the colour yellow, or dark blue, or both of them, for the sky was something of a revelation. They know these colours but they have never thought of using them like this. Interactive teaching may be needed to prompt or challenge them to actually notice such things and put them into practice for themselves.
- **Problem-solving tasks** demand the use of familiar knowledge but in new contexts. They extend the range of application of a concept, fact or skill. We can imagine the Russian children painting first the sky and then leaves, flowers or trees in successive lessons, each time learning how to use small blocks of paint as one means of building up a complex image. Problem-solving exercises with arithmetic and familiar writing tasks, such as narratives or reports, would typically involve this kind of strategic application of existing knowledge to new contexts. They fit the kind of teaching associated with independent problem-solving (see Chapter 1) but are also often supported by interactive teaching.
- **Practice tasks** demand the process of tuning existing knowledge. Here, the student is familiar with both the problems and the contexts and simply has to work on

building up fast, accurate, routine responses. A handwriting lesson or an arithmetic quiz might typically involve this kind of routine practice.

* **Revision tasks** are introduced in order to prevent forgetting, rather than to add to or change existing knowledge. Material is evoked which was once familiar. At first the student is rusty in bringing to mind and using the appropriate facts, concepts and skills, but soon fluency and accuracy are re-established.

It is important to realize that these different types of task demand are not to be thought of as better or worse than one another: they are simply appropriate to different phases of the cycle of learning. All of them are appropriate at different times and all of them can contribute to learning of different sorts. We cannot always be sure which processes are in action, across the different students in a class. What demands restructuring from one child may only demand routine practice from another. One student may be learning about, say, colour mixing for the first time, whereas another may have already experienced it often at home. Note that two extra concepts have now been added to Rumelhart and Norman's threefold scheme: strategic application and revision. Strategic application requires the learner to select and apply knowledge appropriately to new problems. Revision requires the learner to revisit knowledge and recall it. It acknowledges that fact that we often forget what we have learned. Table 2.1 sums up the links between types of task and learning process.

We have reached an important point: many new ideas have already been introduced and you need to take stock and check that you understand all the terms used in Table 2.1. Being able to work out what demands different tasks are likely to make on learners is a crucial part of effective teaching. We are shortly going to make use of the concepts in Table 2.1 in order to analyse a whole sequence of examples.

Just to emphasize the links: incremental tasks clearly match up with the initial learning process we have called accretion. Equally, practice (and revision) tasks are clearly linked to tuning. However, the distinction between restructuring and problem-solving is a harder one to keep clear. In a restructuring task, the learner has to come

Table 2.1 The links between types of task and learning process

Kind of task	Dominant learning process	What's new?
Incremental	Accretion	Facts, concepts or skills
Restructuring	Restructuring	Acquiring new means for solving familiar problems
Problem-solving	Strategic application	Applying existing knowledge to new problems
Practice	Tuning	Fluency in problem-solving
Revision	Recall and tuning	Recovering fluency

up with a new way of thinking about a familiar problem. For example a child might always have dealt with sums like 'What are three lots of four?' by repeatedly adding, as in $4 + 4 + 4 = 12$. Learning that the same problem can be thought of in terms of multiplication, as in $3 \times 4 = 12$, involves conceptual change and thus restructuring.

In a problem-solving task, the learner is faced with a new problem and has to use appropriate, but existing, knowledge to solve it. For example, a child who has learned the three times multiplication table and is used to sums that take the form $3 \times 4 = 12$, is now given the problem 'I find three piles of chairs, each with four stacked chairs in them. How many chairs have I found?' The initial question for the child is: which knowledge is applicable? In reality, many sorts of tasks that are given to children involve a mixture of restructuring and problem-solving. That is, to some extent the task demands the reshaping of relatively new and unfamiliar ideas (or skills) and to some extent the strategic application of these ideas to new contexts, or problems. Restructuring is thus often combined with strategic application.

2.4 Analysing Examples of Task Demands

Let us now look at some further examples of lessons, and think about the demands they may have made on the students concerned. The point of this is, firstly, to begin to see how the analysis can be useful in thinking about how teaching should fit in with the main phases of learning. Secondly it can suggest how learning may go wrong.

Example 2.1 Artesian wells: KS3 geography[3]
A Y7 class of 29 students (aged 11–12 years) were given two successive geography lessons on the Great Artesian Basin in Australia. (An artesian well is a well dug down to underground water, trapped under great pressure between two layers of impermeable rock. When the well is drilled, the pressure forces the water up through the hole. Such wells can be highly valuable, for example in areas of low rainfall.) In the second lesson the teacher started by re-explaining orally the principle of artesian wells, using a diagram drawn on the blackboard. He described the diagram as being like a slice, or cross-section, through a cake. He explained that there were two kinds of rock: one with 'large spaces between the grains . . . like a sponge' called 'porous' rock, whereas in the other kind the grains were close together and water did not 'get into it'. He wrote the word 'porous' on the board. He went on to describe the subterranean movement of water, falling on higher ground, soaking into the ground and through rock and collecting above a layer of non-porous rock at the bottom of the 'basin'. All this was linked to work done in the previous lesson, and the observer's notes refer to the teacher's 'very clear explanation' and the 'very clear worksheet'.

The teacher next moved on to describe how clouds lose their moisture before they reach the artesian basin, comparing their drying out with clothes on a line in the wind. He asked, 'Will there be a lot of moisture or a little?' His tone was colloquial: 'What he [a farmer] does is drill a hole . . . What's going to happen if there's a dry summer?' There was mention of a water shortage, of 'artesian' and 'sub-artesian' water, and of the 'Eastern and Western Highlands'. The students were then required to complete a worksheet, answering questions about how artesian wells work, using a passage in a textbook for reference, a passage which repeated the cross-sectional diagram of an artesian well and used terms such as 'the rainfall is light', 'poor quality pastures' and 'porous rock'. The passage ended 'Water enters the porous rock and seeps through to the lower part of the basin, where it is trapped between layers of non-porous rock, turning the porous rock into a reservoir'.

We need to make some assumptions in interpreting the task demands of this lesson. We know that it was the second time that these students had encountered the concept and vocabulary of artesian wells. However, the detailed explanations and diagrams provided suggest that the teacher expected much of the material to be new. It can therefore be classed as an incremental task, requiring accretion, in terms of our scheme. This is especially so in the first part of the lesson, where the teacher uses direct instruction to introduce a number of key new ideas. In completing the worksheet, however, it seems that this teacher hoped that the students would be able to use their new knowledge to solve some pencil and paper problems, which both applied and tested their understanding. To this extent, the worksheet was a problem-solving task. However there is doubt about whether the students had managed to assimilate the new knowledge sufficiently. Perhaps they had not yet restructured their ideas so that they could apply their knowledge effectively. Perhaps the worksheet demanded some restructuring of their everyday concepts. Robert Hull, the observer, had this very suspicion and later gave a series of written questions to a sample of 75 students, from three parallel classes, who had all experienced versions of these two geography lessons taught by the same teacher. Four of the questions were the following.

1 Which of these four sentences, A, B, C, or D, has the same meaning as 'the rainfall is light'?
   A Not much rain falls there.
   B Rain falls there gently.
   C The rain glitters in the sun when it falls.
   D There is a lot of rain there.
2 What are 'pastures'? Why are the pastures 'poor'?
3 What does 'porous' mean?
4 Has finding water in dry places anything to do with artesian wells?

Another of the questions asked the students to draw a simple sketch of an artesian well.

The responses to question 1 were as follows: A, 42; B, 26; C, 3; D, 4. Adding B, C and D, we can see that 33 of 75 students (44%) were confused over the phrase 'the rainfall is light'. They were no doubt familiar with the words 'rainfall' and 'light' but they seem to have failed to realize that they needed to restructure their understanding of 'light' in this new context. Hull does not give raw scores for questions 2 and 3 but implies that many students were not very sure what 'pastures' were and misunderstood the concept of 'porous' to a lesser or greater extent. One, for example, wrote 'POROUS – stored (doesn't soak through)' and then 'NON-POROUS – soaks through'. Many others thought that 'porous' meant 'holds in'. Nine students (12%) seem to have answered 'no' to question 4, suggesting that more or less the entire lesson had gone over their heads. Hull also found a wealth of varied misunderstandings in the children's sketches of artesian wells. Very few students had understood that a continued process of water seeping down from higher ground at the edges of a basin could eventually lead to pressure on the water trapped at the bottom between layers of non-porous rock.

Hull also had a discussion with a group of four of the same students, one of whom made the following comment, contrasting English homework, which she saw as open-ended, creative and 'fun', with geography homework.

> But with geography or history or maths you haven't got to sort of think about it, you've just got straightforward sums. You know, you just do 'em. An' geography, you know, you just . . . you haven't really got to think how you know about artesian water. You've just got to look it up in the dictionary or the library, or som'ink, just copy it up. You don't have to think 'em, you can't think of lots of different ways to write about artesian water because only one way's right.

It seems clear that these students simply did not appreciate that, along with accretion, considerable restructuring of their everyday knowledge was required in order to effectively assimilate all the new words and ideas from their geography lessons, so that they could be put to good use sensibly and accurately. The teacher, in fact, had made several attempts to **bridge** the gap between the students' everyday experience and the new set of concepts, by using appropriate **analogies** to do with cakes, sponges and clothes drying on a line. Nevertheless, it is tempting to conclude that the restructuring that was in fact required had failed to occur for many of these students. A task that seemed to demand problem-solving was actually one that demanded restructuring as well. Even worse, the particular student quoted above, and perhaps many of her friends, did not realize that restructuring needed to occur. They assumed that they could move straight from accretion to strategic application. Metacognitively speaking, they were in the dark. This kind of tragic misunderstanding may well be played out again and again in classrooms, each and every day.

Example 2.2 Maths quiz: KS2 maths[4]
A Y4 class of 24 children (aged 8–9 years) started their numeracy hour with a routine mental arithmetic quiz, the children writing down their answers to the following questions posed by the teacher.
  If 15 times 6 is 90, what is 15 times 3?
  Find the product of 7, 6 and 2.
  How many quarters in 7 wholes?
  The area of a square is 36 square centimetres; what is the length of one edge?
  I think of a number, add 5 and double it. The answer is 18. What number did I think of?

After 10 questions, they swapped books and marked one another's work. As they went through the problems, the teacher persistently asked them to explain their solutions.

Teacher: How did you get that, Ollie?
Student: I timesed 7 times 6 to make 42, and then 2 times 42, which is 84.
Teacher: Good. How many quarters in one whole, Ellie?
Student: Umm, 4.
Teacher: Right, so how many in 7 wholes?
Student: 7 times 4, 28.
Teacher: Right, 28 of what, Tim?
Student: Quarters.
Teacher: Right. If the area of the square is 36 square centimetres, what is the length of one edge, umm, hands up! Tommy?
Student: 36 centimetres.
Teacher: Uhh, what do you make it, Sharon?
Student: 9.
Teacher: Who agrees? Erm, Ollie?
Student: No, because it's 6 times 6, 'cause a square has all equal sides.
Teacher: Who agrees with that? Right, just about everyone. Good. I'll have to talk to you later, Tommy, about how you got 36. Right, we'll do the marks later. Swap your books back.

He next launched into the main topic for the lesson.

This maths quiz appears to be a straightforward example of a practice task. The teacher certainly intended this, as he told the observer that all the problems were familiar ones to the class. It would also be reasonable to claim that there was an element of revision intended, as the lesson occurred near the end of the school year and reached back across topics that had been learned and practised in previous terms. The results also bear this out, as the great majority of the class got eight or more of the ten problems correct.

There is also the possibility, however, that some of the contexts for the calculations were (unintentionally) new ones, at least to some students, so that an element of problem-solving, and thus strategic application, came into it. The teacher tried to use the marking session to assess the children's underlying grasp of the various concepts, checking whether they had really been understood. It seems that Sharon and Tommy both needed further help with relating the edges of a square to its area but, without further probing, we cannot tell whether they had missed the teaching (lack of accretion), had failed to understand the concepts (lack of restructuring), had applied the wrong knowledge (failure of application) or had just made a careless error in calculating (lack of tuning).

Example 2.3 Safety in the home: literacy, health and safety[5]
In this example from an occupational training programme, the tutor was following up aspects of literacy that related to health and safety regulations in the workplace. There were five trainees, aged between 16 and 18, in the group.

Tutor: [*Looking round the group*] Before we start, can anyone give me any ideas of the kinds of accidents that might happen in the home?

Kay: Leaving toys on the stairs.

Tutor: That's good. Anyone else?

Steve: Trailing wires such as on an iron . . .

Tutor: Fine.

Steve: . . . where a little child could pull it down.

Tutor: Pull it down. Yes, fine. Can you think of anything, Amanda?

Amanda: Just leaving things hanging around and everywhere, putting pots away . . .

Tutor: Mmm. [*Nods*]

Amanda: . . . and things like that.

Tutor: So being tidy is one of the main areas. I agree with you.

This example of interactive teaching is taken from near the beginning of the first occasion on which this group had met. The demands of the tutor's questions are deliberately low-key. She uses the typical moves of eliciting ideas, confirming them, repeating some of them and finally reformulating one answer as a generalization, which also acts as a summary, or **recap**. Up to this point the task is merely a revision one, if it can be said to involve any learning at all. Interestingly, by moving to a generalization ('So being tidy is one of the main areas') the tutor may have 'upped' the challenge of the task very slightly by implying that she would prefer answers in the form of further, and different, generalizations. If so, a tiny demand for restructuring has crept into the session, although its main aim was to make the trainees feel at ease in the new situation.

So far as we can see, there was no attempt here to produce accretion and there is scarcely a problem, as yet, to which knowledge has to be strategically applied. Of course, if lessons make only these sorts of light demands on learners, it is unlikely that any new learning will take place. This leads us to a key warning to teachers, which I will call the **fallacy of experience**. This states that while having experience is necessary for learning, not all experiences lead to learning, because not all *require* any learning. So far, these trainees could get by with their existing knowledge. Simply to have some 'experience' does not guarantee that one will learn anything new from it. Indeed, two different teachers may each have, say, 10 years of teaching experience, but whereas one of them might have learned continuously from each and every year, the other one might have had the equivalent of ten lots of one year's experience, learning little or nothing new after year one. Experience does not amount to the same thing as learning.

Example 2.4 Tartarin of Tarascon: equivalent of KS2 French (mother tongue)[6]
This extract has been translated from French. Twenty French students, aged 9–10, have been working for about 12 minutes in silence, writing their individual answers to a series of written comprehension questions, related to a passage from a class reading book, Tartarin de Tarascon. *(In the passage, Tartarin is involved in a deception, pretending that he is a great traveller.) Now the teacher moves to the front of the class, the textbook in her hand.*

Teacher: Question 4e.

Student A: [*Reads*] 'But is it true? Where did Tartarin get the weapons and plants? What are his books for?'

Teacher: Can we give a definite answer to this question?

Students: No.

Teacher: No, we can't be sure, we don't know. If it says 'Where did Tartarin get his weapons and plants?' How do we know?

Students: We don't know.

Teacher: We don't know. We can only guess. First guess?

Students: [*Raise hands and call out*] He might have bought them.

Teacher: He might have bought them. Second guess?

Students: [*Call out*] He might have been on a journey.

Teacher: He might have really been on a journey, and brought them back with him from where they grow. What are the books for then?

Student B: To know if there are lots of exotic plants growing there . . . / exotic things.

Teacher: [*Other students begin calling out as B's answer tails off. Some students raise their hands*] Shh. C?

Student C: To impress his / er, visitors.

Teacher: To impress visitors.

Student D: To impress people.

Teacher: To impress people. What are the books for if he hasn't been on a journey? / If he didn't bring the plants back with him, if he bought them . . .

Student D: To make people think that he goes hunting?

Teacher: Yes, but with regard to the plants and trees?

Student D: That he . . .

Student E: [*Calls out*] If he can't travel, the books tell him what it's like.

Teacher: Yes.

Student C: If he bought them, he wouldn't know where he had found them, so he reads about it in books. If he had a visitor who asked him where he bought something, he wouldn't know what to say. If a visitor asked him where he bought, for example, [*glances at her textbook*] the boa . . . bo . . .

Teacher: Baobab.

Student E: He er, he er bought it in, in Africa. If er, Tartarin doesn't know the answer and he says he bought it in America, the visitor would know he wasn't a great traveller.

Teacher: *Yes*. He mustn't make any mistakes in his answers. He mustn't say . . .

Students: Just anything.

Teacher: . . . just anything.

This interactive teaching example reveals several possible levels of task demand. Initially it seems to be pitched mainly at the level of problem-solving (strategic application of familiar knowledge to new contexts). Yet reading can make demands on the learner at every one of the levels of our scheme. Considered simply as a matter of routine word recognition, reading may often require only the practice and fine-tuning of highly familiar perceptual and cognitive skills. But reading the passage in the book and understanding its meanings at different levels may also require problem-solving (and hence strategic application of knowledge), since knowledge of language and general knowledge have to be brought together to find answers that can be justified by reference to this previously unknown text. Notice that reading may also demand restructuring of concepts (restructuring), and indeed accretion, where novel words, ideas and contexts are encountered for the first time (as perhaps you are finding with this book).

In the passage above, the teacher's attention has shifted to the answers to a series of problems (comprehension questions) that the students have initially been solving on their own. The teacher uses interactive teaching to **elicit** contributions, which she mostly accepts, via repetition. Perhaps this is still at the level of a fairly low-level problem-solving task. Then, however, she seems to push for a deeper understanding of the implied meaning of the passage. Tartarin, it appears, is faking his knowledge of exotic animals and plants but this must be inferred from the text, as it is not explicitly mentioned. Now the students have to put their reasoning together with their knowledge of the text, in order to get at both what the text states and what it implies. If this is a relatively new way of thinking about the meaning of a text we might argue that this amounts to a demand for the restructuring of knowledge, which is needed to reach a new level of understanding.

Robin Alexander, from whose work this comes, certainly argues that this French primary teacher is inducting her students into reading as the interrogation of a text, via evidence: 'The children learn to draw the line between what the text implies and what it states, what they may read into it and what they can read *in* it.'[7] Thus the teacher's question 'Can we give a definite answer to this question?' is at a different level to a question such as 'Where did Tartarin get the weapons and plants?' Alexander also points out that by asking a question at this higher (or deeper) level, the teacher is matching her discourse to one of the basic processes of the discipline of studying literature (interrogating a text). The lesson is in this sense a genuine example of literary study. The same is true of our next example.

Example 2.5 The cause of the black coating: KS3 science[8]
Small groups of students, in the school laboratory, have been heating various materials. One student noticed some black coating on a tube and asked 'Where did the black coating come from?' The teacher suggested that ideas should be collected about possible causes, or sources.

Teacher: Let's think of *all* the items involved. What were they?
Student A: Flame . . . foil.
Teacher: Yes . . . what else was there? What else could it have been?
Student B: The tongs.
Teacher: The tongs . . . All right . . . let's put that down . . . maybe . . . the tongs . . . let's put that down as a possibility. It may be *unlikely*, but it's still a possibility until we've proved that something else was responsible. Right, are there any other possibilities?
Student C: The air.
Teacher: Yes, the air. What else is in the vicinity? Have we got all the various agencies involved?

Student C: Gas?

Teacher: It may have come from the natural gas ... let's put that down. It may have. It's a possibility. Now, who would like to summarize what these possibilities are for causing the black coating on the tube?

Student A: The copper coating, flame, tongs, gas, air ...

Teacher: Right, now how do we find out which was responsible?

Student D: By an experiment?

Teacher: Right, we need to design another experiment after half term. What should we do?

Student E: We could scrape off the coating ... and work out why ...

Teacher: We could ... we could analyse it ... Good, right now ... who found it weighed more after it had been heated?

This discussion, or interactive teaching example, was not directly relevant to the main curriculum content of the lesson. It arose out of a question asked by a student, which the teacher could not foresee. However, he decides to make use of the question, at least for a short time, to illustrate a series of points about science as a process of enquiry. The level of task demand implied by his series of questions is again at the level of problem-solving, though we cannot rule out the possibility that it demanded restructuring for some students. He expects the students to be able, with the help of the cues supplied by his questions, to articulate the fundamental scientific processes of considering relevant variables as causes, and testing to see which of them caused the effect of the black coating. What does not seem to occur is any checking that the students really understand these processes. Restructuring, perhaps the most elusive of the processes of learning, is again missing from our analysis. We might argue that if the teacher had actually asked the students to plan an experiment to find the cause of the black coating, and then to justify their designs to one another, they might have been pushed to extend and elaborate their knowledge, rather than simply to apply it, with considerable support from the teacher.

This example also illustrates a very common strategy of teachers, which is to reinterpret, or **reframe**, some experience shared by the class, describing it in terms of the 'official' vocabulary and concepts of the relevant subject or discipline. Thus the students use an everyday vocabulary ('tongs', 'air', 'gas'), whereas the teacher uses many scientific words and phrases ('all the items', 'possibility', 'responsible', 'proved', 'agencies', 'causing', 'design an experiment', 'analyse'). Teachers may thus attempt to induct students into the ways of thinking, speaking and acting which typify, or even constitute, the different academic disciplines (16.4). But it is easier, as the teacher, to use these terms in context, hoping that some accretion and restructuring will, as it were, rub off on the students, than it is to press the students to start to use them appropriately for themselves. (For some reason, several examples chosen in Chapters 1 and 2 show a marked reluctance on the part of teachers in England to have their students use the correct term 'multiply' rather than 'times', but that is by the by.)

2.5 Patterns of Teaching

One purpose of the examples in this chapter is to illustrate some typical patterns of teaching. Over and over again, it is possible to see a common pattern to these examples of (largely) interactive teaching. First, the teacher asks a question (**initiation**); then one or more of the students answer (**response**); then the teacher accepts, rejects or evaluates the response (**evaluation**). This **IRE pattern** has been found to typify the discourse of many teachers, of all age ranges, across classrooms in all parts of the world. It has both strengths and weaknesses, as we shall see, but it is remarkably common. What is less often noticed is the kind of demand made by the initiating question. Is it a question that challenges the students to revise, practise, strategically apply or restructure their knowledge? Questions can be pitched at all these levels of demand. The *intellectual challenge* of the teaching can thus vary greatly within apparently similar IRE patterns of interaction, from virtually nil to a demand for some radical restructuring of thinking.

A second theme that emerges from this chapter is that certain kinds of failure in the processes of learning are actually completely predictable from teaching that does not make certain demands on the learner. These **predictable breakdowns** in the chain of teaching and learning are summarized in Table 2.2. All these failures are failures of teaching, which lead in different ways to failures in learning. (Of course it is always a possibility that learners will somehow make the demands upon themselves, and thus succeed in learning despite the teacher, but we would be unwise to rely on this taking place). However, important though they are, these predictable breakdowns are not the only ways in which a failure to learn can occur.

It is important to emphasize that the responsibility for learning is always shared between teacher and taught. Learners, too, can contribute to their own downfall, for

Table 2.2 Predictable breakdowns in the chain of teaching and learning

Teaching lack	Associated learning failure
No incremental demand	The lesson never introduces students to new facts, concepts or skills and therefore no accretion of new knowledge occurs
No restructuring demand	The lesson never challenges students to restructure their existing body of knowledge, so they do not
No problem-solving demand	The lessons never require students to select and apply their knowledge to new problems in an insightful way so they do not learn how to do this
No demand for practice	Students are not required to practise routine problem-solving to 'tune' their competence, so they remain lacking in fluency and/or accuracy
No demand for revision	Students are not required to return to past topics and therefore fail to recall and further tune their knowledge

example by failing to attend to teachers or tasks, not attempting to understand new ideas, not applying themselves diligently to problem-solving, not asking questions when they are confused, or not practising and revising. Understanding why these things happen will be a theme of later chapters. Meanwhile, we might suggest a tentative hypothesis about the processes of classroom learning, based simply on the examples studied so far: of all the processes of learning, it is restructuring and strategic application that are the two hardest ones both for learners to achieve and for teachers to reach and affect. To put the same thing another way, tasks that demand accretion or tuning (incremental tasks and routine practice or revision) are easier to plan and carry out than tasks that genuinely demand, and get, restructuring and strategic application of knowledge (restructuring and problem-solving tasks).

2.6 Summary of Key Ideas

I have introduced a great many new ideas about teaching and learning in this chapter. For this reason I am adding a brief summary of the key ideas.

- Learning was initially divided into three main phases: accretion, restructuring and tuning. Then the two further phases of strategic application of knowledge and recall were added, to make five in all. The assumption being made is that effective long-term learning will depend on students moving through all these five phases.
- Five corresponding kinds of task were delineated: incremental, restructuring, problem-solving, routine practice and revision. If you are able to establish where your students have reached with their learning, you should be able to begin to design suitable tasks for them, choosing a task with suitable learning demands and matching it with appropriate teaching.
- The various examples of lessons illustrated how we might try to use the idea of task demands to analyse what is happening in lessons.
- The examples are also intended to show how there can be predictable breakdowns in the connection between teaching and learning. In spite of much hard work in classrooms, new learning does not always come about, or last very long.
- Restructuring ideas and applying knowledge to new problems seem to be the most difficult kinds of learning to bring about in the classroom.

In order to assimilate this new knowledge, my own analysis suggests that you will have to see how far your existing understanding has been transformed, or restructured, whether you can apply the ideas to new examples of lessons and whether, eventually, you can make their application a routine part of your fluent practice as a teacher. In other words, learners have to make journeys in thought for themselves. As one piece of help with this demanding process, I supply a final example of teaching for you to analyse and also a further exercise.

But first, take a look at the glossary of key terms on p. 283. This provides you with a way of checking your understanding of the main educational concepts used in this book. Many will still look unfamiliar. However, a number of the key concepts from the first two chapters are listed there and should already be familiar. See if you can find some of these. When you have checked out the glossary, return to the following revision and extension tasks.

2.7 Questions and Extension Tasks

Read Example 2.6 below and see which of the key concepts from the first two chapters seem, without forcing the issue, to apply to the example. In particular:

- What sorts of teaching, if any, take place? (Remember Table 1.1.)
- What task demands are made on the learners? (Remember Table 2.1.)
- What kinds of learning may have taken place? (Remember Table 2.1 again.)

Make your own written notes, analysing what you understand the example to be illustrating. Then compare your efforts with my analysis, provided in Appendix B.

Example 2.6 Maximum box: KS3 maths[9]
A group of girls in a London school worked together on a maths problem. The problem was this: 'You have a square sheet of card measuring 15 centimetres by 15 centimetres and you want to use it to make an open cuboid container by cutting out the corners. What is the maximum capacity the container could have?' One of the students, Emily, was considered by her teacher to be quite confident and able in mathematics. The other students in the group are referred to by the letters A, B and C. At the point the transcript begins the girls have successfully made their container out of card, which is marked out in centimetre squares, but Emily is unhappy that the box seems to have got 'bigger' despite having lost its corners. This is because she has a fundamental misunderstanding about what they are doing. As you read, try to work out what her difficulty is.

> Emily: this box is bigger than what it should be 'cos if you get 15 by 15 you get 225, but if you times um 9 by 9 times 3 you still get 243 and I haven't got that much space in my box.
> A: You have.
> Emily: But the 15 by . . .
> B: It can be, it can work, I think.
> Emily: . . . but surely . . .
> B: You cut off corners.
> Emily: Yeah but that should make it *smaller*.
> B: I think that is right.
> Emily: [*Counting squares marked on the paper*] Hang on, one, two, three, four, five.
> C: You're not going to get to 243.
> Emily: I shouldn't get 243 'cos if the piece of paper only had 225 then, um . . .
> C: Hang on, look . . . 9 times 9 times how many was it up?
> A: But don't you remember Emily it's got all this space in the middle.
> Emily: Yeah, but . . .

A: It's got all that space in the middle.

C: It is right, Emily, it is, it should be that number.

Emily: But if I have a piece of paper with 225 squares, why should I get more?

A: Because you have all that space in the middle.

Emily: [*Sounding exasperated*] No, it hasn't got anything to do with it. If my piece of paper had only 225 squares on it, I can't get more out of the same piece of paper.

A: You can because you're forgetting, things go *up* as well, not just the flat piece of paper like that.

Emily: Oh yeah.

A: It's going up.

C: It's going up ... it's because, look, down here you've got 3 and it's going up.

A: You're going 3 up, it's getting more on it. Do you see it will be 243?

Emily: Yeah.

C: It's right, it should be.

As a second task, read through your notes (or start writing some) on the first two chapters. Add to these notes until they form a summary, for yourself, on everything that has struck you as new, interesting or controversial in these two opening chapters.

The following questions are designed to help you check your understanding of the chapter.

1 What are the three phases of learning distinguished in Rumelhart and Norman's model?

2 What two other phases of learning were added to them?

3 What is meant by the 'fallacy of experience'?

4 How can intellectual challenge be varied within the IRE pattern of teaching?

5 What were said to be the two hardest kinds of learning to include in lessons?

6 **Discussion question**: even if you can find out the phase of learning appropriate to each student in a class for a particular topic, it is unlikely that they will all be in the same phase at the same time. Does this make the idea of task demands useless? How would you try to deal with this problem?

NOTES

1. Rumelhart and Norman (1981).

2. The analysis of task demands originates from the work of Charles Desforges.

3. Example 2.1 is taken from material in chapter 2 of Hull (1985). It has been edited for present purposes.

4. Example 2.2 is from an unpublished set of observations of teachers by Richard Fox.

5. Example 2.3 comes from Mercer (1995), pp. 34–5.

6. Example 2.4 comes from Alexander (2000), pp. 462–3.

7. Alexander (2000), p. 464.

8. Example 2.5 comes from Hull (1985), pp. 141–2.

9. Example 2.6 is taken from Mercer (1995), pp. 12–13. It originated with an audiotape (band 2) from the Open University (1991) INSET pack *Talking and Learning 5–16*.

CHAPTER THREE

The Social World of the Classroom

3.1 Introduction

The two most urgent priorities facing student teachers are probably (i) how to plan effective lessons and (ii) how to keep order in the classroom. However, a direct confrontation of these two key issues will be delayed just a little further, in order first to clarify the kind of social world the teacher has to plan for and in which she or he needs to keep order. Without some understanding of this context, teaching can easily go wrong. Teachers need to learn something of the beliefs, rules and traditions that lie beneath the surface of classroom behaviour. In this chapter the perspectives of teachers and students are compared. The interests and concerns of both are seen to result in a working consensus, which often includes a good deal of low-level routine work and a resistance to intellectual challenge. Examples are given of how students sometimes fail to understand what the teacher intends that they should learn and strategies are suggested for introducing change gradually to a class. The influence of assessment and problems of transferring school learning to other settings are introduced. The chapter finishes with a survey of students' views on what makes a good teacher.

3.2 Classrooms as Environments for Learning

The social world of a classroom is a very particular one, in which particular conditions apply. New classrooms may be compared to foreign countries, or at least subcultures, in which certain languages are spoken and certain traditions followed. If, as a newcomer, one ignores the basic rules of the subculture, one is likely to come seriously unstuck! You should enter a new school, or a new classroom, much as an anthropologist enters a new culture: be on the lookout for how they do things. What are the rules, written and unwritten, that people are using to cope with the demands and opportunities of life? What does the look of the place and the language being used tell you about the ethos and priorities of the local inhabitants? How are you going to fit in?

Initially it seems obvious that classrooms bring students together with a teacher, along with some material resources, with the intention that some new learning shall take place. But there are two (often unspoken) prior aims: that the participants remain unscathed and that the institution itself survives. Only when these two conditions are satisfied is learning likely to be considered. Students and teachers have more important things to worry about than learning if they feel that their safety or self-respect is under threat. In addition, all institutions, schools included, seem to give a high priority to the survival of the institution itself. Pay attention, particularly in school assemblies or staff meetings, and see if you can judge whether more time is spent on institutional matters or on the business of learning. It is surprising how often the mundane business of timetables, car parking, dinner money, social occasions and school photographs absorb valuable time in the school day. Moreover, classrooms are not always easy places in which to learn.

It may seem odd to say that classrooms are difficult places in which to learn, but in spite of everyone's good intentions it can often be the case. Sometimes there are straightforward problems to do with space, resources or noise. Overcrowding and temperatures that are too high, or too low, are commonplace problems. (I retain vivid memories of teaching in one particular mobile hut that was so cold in winter that we all had to get up, roughly once per half hour, and bounce up and down on the spot for a minute just to get our circulations going again.) Pneumatic drills or noisy neighbouring classes can also be a serious distraction. Although these physical difficulties are real enough, they are not the focus of this book.

3.3 What Are We Here To Do?

A more relevant, though invisible, problem is that the teacher and the students are likely to come into the classroom with quite different views of what is going on. Here is one teacher's view of exactly this invisible gap in aspirations.

Example 3.1 Helping students on a journey
John Holt, writing as a teacher, felt that he had finally seen through a common fallacy among teachers.

> Thus teachers feel, as I once did, that their interest and their students' are fundamentally the same. I used to feel that I was guiding and helping my students on a journey that they wanted to take but could not take without my help. I knew the way looked hard, but I assumed they could see the goal almost as clearly as I and that they were almost as eager to reach it. It seemed very important to give students this feeling of being on a journey to a worthwhile destination. I see now that most of my talk to this end was wasted breath. Maybe *I* thought the students were in my class because they were eager to learn what I was trying to teach, but they knew better. They were in school because they had to be or because otherwise they would have had to be in another class, which might be even worse.[1]

This wry acceptance of the compulsory institutional basis of most schooling may come as a shock to you, or it may confirm what you have already thought for yourself. The logic of the classroom situation is one in which typically one teacher confronts many children, who are not free to come or go. The teacher, in this respect, represents society's decision that all children should go to school.

Secondly, children generally perceive school in a simple and practical way: as a place to meet their friends (or even enemies) and as a place where one does 'work'. Work is very prominent and important in our society. But work is not the same as learning. School as a social context, for interacting with one's peers, can easily seem more important to children than the school's adult-determined curriculum. From the teacher's point of view the classroom is also an intensely busy world of work. Jackson[2] estimated that on average teachers engage in some 1000 personal exchanges per day, with groups or individuals. However, although the teacher's perception is likely to be one of constant interaction with individuals, groups and the whole class, the perspective from the student's point of view is radically different. Most interactions with the teacher take place as a member of a larger group or class. Individual encounters and conversations with the teacher are relatively rare. A large-scale study of British primary classes[3] found that 56% of teachers' time was spent in interactions with individuals, whereas each student could expect only a few individual encounters with a teacher per day. Thus the teacher's impression of what is going on is radically different from that of a single student.

The same researchers found that teachers, in their talk, generally focused on managing behaviour and on how tasks should be completed, rather than asking searching questions designed to encourage their students to think deeply. At first glance this state of affairs may seem odd, but there are reasons for it, as we will see. Nor does the teacher see everything. John Holt likens the teacher's own attention to that of a person in the woods at night with a powerful flashlight in his or her hand.

> Wherever he turns his light, the creatures on whom it shines are aware of it, and do not behave as they do in the dark. Thus the mere fact of his watching their behaviour changes it into something very different. Shine it where he will, he can never know very much about the night life of the woods.[4]

3.4 Task Demands and the Working Consensus

In classrooms, teachers are linked to learners by the tasks they set up. For the learner, one of the main adaptive tasks, therefore, is to discern what the teacher wants from a task. This is likely to be interpreted by students as what kind of 'work' the teacher will reward. Thus, for example, teachers may say that they want originality and imagination, but only assess neatness and spelling. The students are likely to draw their own conclusions. Walter Doyle[5] points out that the academic tasks set in schools are regularly evaluated and thus can be characterized as involving different degrees of uncertainty and risk for the students. An uncertain task, in this context, is one that cannot be completed by a precise and predictable formula, or a routine response. A risky task is one that involves tough standards of teacher evaluation, which may not be met. Students are likely to react uncooperatively to both uncertain and risky tasks.

Doyle describes a study of three classes in the USA, all taught English by the same, very experienced, teacher. One of the main findings was that if a task required 'higher-level' independent thinking, the students immediately sought to reduce the task to something more familiar, using strategies like asking repeated public or private questions and slowing down the pace of classroom events until the teacher compromised on her more open-ended and challenging goals in order to maintain order. (You may like to look out for similar strategies at work in your own classes at university.) Such strategies may be learned very early on in a school career, as the following example suggests.

Example 3.2
Mary, aged 5 years 5 months, is a Y1 student being interviewed by a researcher.[6]

> Interviewer: What do you do if you are doing some maths, if you are not sure what to do? Or if you come to something really hard?
> Mary: Some people cry.
> Interviewer: Do they?
> Mary: Sometimes I cry.
> Interviewer: Do you? What happens when you cry?
> Mary: Miss S. helps you a bit and things like that.
> Interviewer: Is it best to cry, or ... I mean, why don't you just go and ask her what to do before you cry?
> Mary: Sometimes ... she doesn't get cross. But sometimes you cry because you are a bit worried, and you think she'll tell you off. Do you know, when other people cry, you feel like you could cry, don't you? That's what I think.
> Interviewer: Have you been told off at all?
> Mary: Not much.
> Interviewer: How do you manage to be good?
> Mary: I just ask her things and I say, 'Can I do my writing?' and things like that.
> ...
> Interviewer: What do you think about your work in school?
> Mary: Maths is easy for me and sometimes writing is a bit hard, 'cos there's lots of things you could do and you can think what to choose. Word cards help us a bit and the word books help us.
> Interviewer: Do you like learning new things?
> Mary: I like it. If it's difficult, we just ask the teacher. If the teacher is busy, we just wait.

Mary has only been at school for a term or two but she has already found some powerful strategies for reducing the uncertainties and risks of the tasks the teacher sets her. She can avoid risk by simply waiting and doing nothing, until the teacher actively helps her. She can ask the teacher for reassuring confirmation of what it is she should do, rather than thinking it out for herself. She can seek the teacher's help to make the task easier. And when things get really tough, she can burst into tears!

3.5 The Working Consensus

Andrew Pollard[7] argues that students and teachers cope with the fundamental social context of school life by negotiating a series of understandings and rules about behaviour in classrooms that become taken for granted. The product of these negotiations is what he terms a *working consensus*, which then governs relationships. By making some common-sense assumptions about people's motives, he is able to suggest various ways in which new learning may be threatened by the nature of the consensus that commonly evolves. All parties in the classroom face a social situation in which learning, and its evaluation, are often on display. Both know that some form of appropriate 'work' should go on. In this context, Pollard argues, both the teacher and the students are likely to have what he calls various 'interests at hand' that they will attempt to satisfy. These are summarized in Table 3.1.

The interests listed in Table 3.1 by no means exhaust the various aims and intentions that people may have in classrooms: they simply pick out some of the most common. Teachers have more power than students, in that they are expected and authorized to initiate work and direct students. But students, especially if acting collectively, are by no means powerless. Each 'side' may use a variety of strategies to cope with the demands made on them, in the light of their interests at hand. The major strategies include conforming to the working consensus, rejecting it or trying to re-negotiate it.

This analysis suggests that the opportunities for a student to learn, within a class, will be affected not only by the quality of teaching and the demands it makes on

Table 3.1 Common concerns of students and teachers

Students' interests at hand
Maintaining their own dignity and self-respect
Maintaining the approval of the teacher by doing appropriate 'work'
Maintaining the approval of the peer group by following their norms of behaviour
Searching for interest and amusement, rather than boredom or anxiety
Keeping the burden of work to a manageable level

Teachers' interests at hand
Maintaining his or her dignity and self-respect
Carrying out the approved functions of a teacher: to keep order and to teach
Maintaining the approval and respect of the students
Keeping the burden of work to a manageable level

Source: After Pollard.[7]

the learner (see Chapter 2), but also by the social strategies that both teacher and students use to reach their working consensus. Many strategies are possible, of course, but some are more likely to occur than others. If students feel vulnerable, for example, to humiliation or failure then they are likely to adopt defensive strategies. An unusually demanding teacher may either threaten the self-esteem of a student, so that he or she feels likely to fail, or demand that the student acts in a way which would be disapproved of by the peer group. In such a case the student is very likely to try to avoid the demand. He or she may try to minimize exposure to questions, play safe when answering or try to re-negotiate the nature of a task so as to make it easier. One should never underestimate the strength of our determination not to make fools of ourselves in front of others. To give another example, if students find they are either bored or confused it is likely that they will try to re-negotiate the unspoken 'rules of the game' so as to get more interest and amusement from the situation. When a student says 'it's boring' remember that this may be an indirect way of saying that she or he does not understand or is feeling confused. A more general prediction is that students will be restless and uncooperative whenever they perceive the demands made on them to be either too great or too small.

3.6 The Problem of Low-level Routine Work

Teachers, for their part, may also act so as to minimize the risk of an activity not 'working', in the sense of not producing appropriate 'work' by the students or threatening good order. They may also act so as to avoid the threat of professional failure, or the threat of unmanageable amounts of work, by keeping their demands on the students within the limits that students find acceptable. The implication is again that there are pressures on both teacher and taught to keep life within manageable bounds, to within the unspoken levels of difficulty and effort of the prevailing working consensus. The disastrous result of this commonplace state of affairs is likely to be a great deal of undemanding routine activity that results in little or no new learning.

Turning to relevant empirical studies, Neville Bennett and colleagues[8] found that almost 60% of language and number tasks given to 7 year olds, across 16 classrooms, demanded only routine practice of familiar problems. Some 25% introduced new material (i.e. were incremental) and only 7% required restructuring or strategic application. An earlier study of KS3 secondary school classes, by Ted Wragg and others, concluded that 'few tasks make adequate demands on the able, in many cases not even on the average students; and that much time is spent on tasks which are simply trivial'.[9]

In a more recent study, Robin Alexander surveyed language and mathematics lessons in primary schools across no fewer that five different cultures (England, France, India, Russia and USA). He found that:

everywhere primary students spent a great deal of time practising skills already acquired, but the critical difference came in the way this emphasis was balanced (or not) by the introduction of new knowledge and opportunities for students to embed such knowledge through tasks which invited application and restructuring.[10]

This takes us back to the concerns of Chapter 2, of the need to mix tasks that demand incremental learning with tasks that require conceptual restructuring, problem-solving and routine practice. You will recall that restructuring and problem-solving seem to be the most demanding kinds of learning. But now we can see that they may also be the rarest to be found in classrooms. Alexander found that in India, Michigan (USA) and England routine practice tasks were dominant, whereas in France there was a greater emphasis on application (problem-solving) as well as lots of practice. Only in Russia was there an insistent emphasis on restructuring tasks, alongside incremental tasks, problem-solving and practice. The distinctive pattern in these Russian schools, by the way, was of a great deal of student–teacher dialogue, in a whole-class setting, with individual students being asked to give quite lengthy explanations and justifications of their problem-solving, under direct questioning from the teacher.

3.7 Routines

We can begin to see that routine low-level work is likely to feature prominently in classrooms because it fits the working consensus and is less stressful for one and all. But it should also be clear by now that this is not good for the students' learning. Walter Doyle[5] considered the classroom as an ecological system, in which the inhabitants typically adapt to their environment. This environment is one that is rich in information resources, such as books, diagrams, displays, talk of various kinds and non-verbal behaviour. Many people are taking part, all at once, and all are simultaneously trying to make sure that their various interests and purposes are served. The result is a complex, information-rich environment. But the teachers and students, who inhabit this world, can only attend to a limited amount of information at any one time. Their information-processing capacity is limited. One way in which they will adapt to the complexity of the situation is to try to make many actions into predictable routines.

The salient fact about routines is that they do not require constant decisions or mental effort. The less risk and uncertainty there is in the situation, the more likely the students will be able to maintain their approved quota of 'work' (and thus the approval of the teacher) and also interact with their friends. For the teacher, too, routines are not only calming but also essential to good order. Low-level work, which keeps everyone busy, is thus good for appearances and for the teacher's own sense of risk and uncertainty. Unfortunately, the common question 'Are you getting on with your work?' has very little to do with the matter of learning something new.

In the classroom, students will try to work out how to adapt to the strategies of a particular teacher and this will involve forming expectations about which sorts of work will 'pay off' in terms of teacher approval. Doyle summarizes the situation as one in which the dominant activity of the participants in a classroom will be 'an exchange of work for grades'. Four clear implications can be drawn from this analysis.

1 The assessment regime operating in a classroom will tend to dominate the kind of work that students choose to do.
2 Once students have adapted to one kind of work pattern, they will resist any abrupt change that threatens their adaptive habits.
3 If students are confused because they cannot understand what it is that is demanded by a task, they will be unsettled.
4 'Work', i.e. any activity that seems to lead to favourable assessment, is likely to be more salient to students than the elusive matter of learning something new.

3.8 Getting the Point: Work versus Learning

If 'work' is more salient than learning, it is not surprising that students may pay very little attention to the learning goals that lie behind an activity. This is one of the most important messages of this book.

Example 3.3 Why do we need numbers? KS1 maths[11]
The children in a reception class ($4^1/_2$–$5^1/_2$ years old) were industrious workers and cheerfully completed the tasks their teacher, Mrs W, gave them. Over several weeks the focus in mathematics had been the development of counting skills. When Mrs W asked the class 'Why do you think we need numbers?', the following conversation took place.

> Michelle: We need to count the numbers.
> Simon: We need to draw the numbers.
> Mrs W: Why do we need to draw the numbers?
> Lisa: So we can copy them.
> Mrs W: But why do we need numbers at all?
> Lisa: So we can colour them in.

The children had indeed been counting, drawing, copying and colouring in numbers, but they had apparently failed to understand what longer-term aims might lie behind the work. As Charles Desforges[12] put it:

> Children work hard in classrooms. Unfortunately, hard work is not necessarily associated with mindful learning . . . the overarching characteristic of learning is the deliberate and committed pursuit of new competencies . . . quality learning is mindful of the goal of learning; the goal is not incidental.

In the following example, the goals of a lesson are again drastically misconstrued because the students make their own sense of a lesson for which their teacher has not given them clear aims.

Example 3.4 Castaways: KS2 social studies and drama[13]

A Y3 class took part in a drama lesson in which they pretended to be stranded on a desert island and had to organize themselves as castaways would. The teacher intended the lesson as a social studies exercise, in which the children would learn how communities of people have to come to mutual decisions about the rules and laws governing their lives. After the exercise the teacher conducted a discussion.

Teacher: Can we now leave the island for a moment and come back home. In this country there is a law that says that all children when they reach the age of 5 must attend school. How could you change that law? What could you do? Angela?

Angela: You could say your child was a younger age.

. . .

Jimmy: Miss, if we're on the island anyway Miss / you wouldn't get into trouble. There's no police or anything there.

Teacher: Yes, but Jimmy you will remember that I have said that we have now left the island and are back home. And there is this law that says you must attend school once you're 5 years old.

Jimmy: Miss we can just skive out of school Miss.

After the lesson, the researchers interviewed the children about what they thought it had all been about, what they had learnt and what they thought their teacher hoped they would get from what they had done. Two of the children responded as follows.

Angelina: [*After a few moments' hesitation*] I would think that I would learn that I would never go on a boat trip again.

Joanne: It teaches you about what would really happen if you were on a desert island, what it's like on a desert island.

In this instance, young children have clearly missed the whole point of the lesson, in so far as the teacher intended them to ponder the basic conditions of human societies and their rules. To the children it was all to do with boating accidents or life on a desert island.

It seems that a 'production line' metaphor, centring on 'work', is all too easily internalized by both students and teachers in classrooms, so that new learning is pushed unintentionally to one side. (Remember, also, our hypothesis in Chapter 2 that tasks involving restructuring and strategic application are harder to carry through, both for teachers and learners, than tasks that ask only for accretion or tuning.)

Both Pollard and Doyle, in their accounts of classroom life, emphasize the way in which a working consensus is likely to be built up over time. Routines and habits that have proved adaptive will not be easily or willingly given up. It is not surprising, in the light of all this, that Ted Wragg[14] found that when experienced secondary school teachers met their classes at the start of the school year, their main preoccupation and concern was to impress their students with the practices and routines that they liked students to follow. For the students, the task was to learn all the different routines and priorities that characterized the lessons of each different teacher. Students are adept at doing this.

3.9 Introducing Changes

If then, as a teacher, one wishes to change the ethos of a class or to introduce new routines or raise the level of intellectual challenge of lessons, what is one to do? The moral of the story so far is not that it is impossible to bring about change, but rather that one should fully expect certain difficulties to arise and take them into account. Some of the most important implications include the following.

- Teachers should make it as clear to students as they can what the aims of any task are. You must make the goals of learning plain.
- It is important for teachers genuinely to reward the sorts of work and learning that they wish for. You must use assessment to steer learning in the right direction. (This topic will be taken up in Chapter 15.)
- As a novice teacher, first learn to manage a class using the existing rules and routines, before introducing any radical changes. Otherwise you are likely to be met by strong and unmanageable resistance.
- As a newcomer to a class, observe and learn the local rules, signals and routines, even the unspoken ones, as quickly and thoroughly as possible. Only then will you be in a position to keep order effectively and to plan good lessons. You have to start from where the students are even if you want to end up somewhere different.
- If change is required, expect to have to explain it clearly and bring it about by introducing new routines, which are first negotiated and then practised, in manageable steps.
- Do not expect that students will meet a sudden rise in the level of intellectual challenge of tasks willingly or easily.

These 'ground rules' of teaching are by no means meant to encourage a passive acceptance by new teachers of old habits or low standards. Rather, they are intended to make the process of realistic change feasible. One has to build foundations for any lasting change. We all want to raise the level of intellectual functioning of our students, but such a desirable aim is likely to misfire if one ignores the social realities of the classroom as a context for learning. Establishing order is a necessary first step towards making effective learning possible, but if you stop at that, the result is likely to be only a good deal of low-level routine work. Pushing beyond this will require further steps, as subsequent chapters try to make plain.

3.10 Authenticity

A friend of mine once related a sad story to me about teaching in a KS1 classroom. A small boy asked her, in an art and craft session, if he could make a washing machine. Delighted by this sign of initiative, the teacher set him up with cardboard, scissors and glue. The boy duly made his model but did not seem very happy with the result. My friend tried to find out what was wrong. After much coaxing, the child said, 'But I wanted it to work.' The realization dawned on the teacher that this boy had hoped to make a real washing machine. It was not a cardboard model that he was after.

Classrooms can often simulate the real world, but it is difficult to make them authentic sites for learning. This is a large issue and will only be touched on here. Firstly, it seems to me, that teachers are right to seek at least some degree of authenticity in their lessons. Science lessons should really involve thinking that is scientific, history lessons should look at the nature of historical evidence and French lessons should use the French language extensively for communication. Teachers should thus try to 'enact' the deep structures of each subject in the way that they teach. But the other side of the coin is that only so much can be done along these lines, and students know this perfectly well. In science, a prominent aim is for students to learn some of the colossal amount of scientific knowledge that we already have, not to reinvent it all. Historians generally need a vast amount of knowledge of an historical period before they can usefully begin to interpret or evaluate new evidence. Beginners at French cannot say very much in French.

A compromise seems to me to be essential. If we teach poetry writing to children, for example, we do want them to function as much as possible as real poets. We want them to have an authentic experience of poetry writing. But we also have to accept that real poets do not usually compose their work because it is English on Wednesday mornings and because Miss says we are doing poetry today. Students know that they are writing poems because it is an English lesson and that part of the point of the activity is to get better at writing, regardless of whether they are ever going to be poets now or in later life. But if we accept this compromise, in a spirit of realism, we also need to note that it produces problems of its own. It means that much of what is learned in schools is learned in a special social context, away from the real contexts of its application.

We build models of washing machines but not real ones. We write poems in English lessons when told to. We draw maps in geography without making any journeys. And as a result we should not be surprised to find that school learning may not transfer very easily to settings outside the classroom. All too often, in other words, school knowledge cannot be easily used away from school. It is too fragile, too dependent on the context in which it was learned. Away from the classroom, the student forgets the knowledge or forgets how to apply it. The relevance of classroom 'work' is tragically often perceived by children to be confined to the classroom (but see Chapters 7 and 8 for more on this). A final brief point, in a more optimistic vein: some authenticity is made possible by bringing the real world, in the shape of people or artefacts or natural objects, into the classroom; and some authenticity can be reached by taking students out of the classroom and into the community, on visits, for their learning.

3.11 Students' Perceptions of Teachers and Classrooms

Researchers have regularly asked students of different ages what they think about their teachers and classrooms. Naturally, the ability of students to conceptualize and talk about teaching and learning develops considerably with age and experience. Nevertheless a strikingly consistent picture emerges, at all ages, of what children think makes a good teacher.[15] The essential attributes are clustered around the twin poles of 'caring' and 'competence'. In terms of competence, students value teachers who are knowledgeable, enthusiastic about their subject, skilful at explaining things and able to adjust flexibly to changing situations. They like teachers to set clear, achievable targets and tasks. They like lessons which are 'fun and interesting', which include a variety of activities and which offer chances for the students to participate. On the caring side, students appreciate teachers who are fair, considerate and who value individuals. Thus, they praise teachers who go out of their way to support and help those with difficulties, who spend time getting to know them as individuals and who care about them enough to chat to them outside the classroom as well as within it. A third common theme is that children think that good teachers can keep order, without being unfair. They appreciate a teacher who is 'strict but kind', who is firm but 'able to have a laugh'. They also like, or think they like, consistent treatment in terms of discipline.

These descriptions of the 'good teacher' seem eminently reasonable, but there are also some snags. There is some evidence that students feel that it is the teacher's responsibility to motivate them to work. Thus they will work hard for a teacher who can make lessons 'fun and interesting' but may think it perfectly fair to make little or no effort if a lesson seems boring or irrelevant. They may thus perceive the success or failure of a lesson as being the teacher's responsibility rather than a joint responsibility of teacher and students working together. It is as if they see the lesson as being somehow for the teacher's benefit rather than for theirs. In a similar way, although they like teachers to keep order, they may see a weak disciplinarian as fair game, as not deserving their respect. They may then see nothing wrong with 'messing about' in such lessons.

Thus students quite unintentionally make life harder for teachers, for they do not have either the same long-term perspectives or a feeling of overall responsibility for what happens. It is comforting to rely on the teacher. There are some gender differences in these attitudes, with boys in general being rather less prepared than girls to take responsibility for their own behaviour and learning. Girls may show a tendency to blame poor results on themselves and to attribute successes to the effects of good teaching. Boys, in contrast, may more often attribute success to their own efforts and blame teachers for any failures. Thus girls may in general need to learn to feel less helpless in the face of difficulties, whereas boys may need to learn to take more responsibility for their own poor attention and work[16] (10.2).

Another series of difficulties stem from the institutional nature of schooling and the gap that may open between a school's aspirations and what it can actually provide for the individual student. Thus secondary students have been critical of the impersonal atmosphere of large schools, of the inability of teachers to really get to know them as individuals or to have the time to listen to their problems and do something effective about them[17]. They understand that teachers often have heavy workloads but may feel that in consequence teachers' attempts at pastoral care, or at preventing bullying, are ineffective. Some report that their learning is disrupted by other students, with distractions and noise resulting from poor class control by some teachers.

Unfortunately, problems such as large classes, impersonal surroundings (e.g. corridors and playgrounds), a curriculum perceived as irrelevant or too difficult and teachers unable to control their classes may have a particularly strong impact on the most vulnerable students, those who already suffer from emotional and behavioural difficulties and/or learning difficulties. On a brighter note, students are also ready to lavish praise on the teachers who they say respect them, have time for them and who teach them well. Classrooms are crowded places and it is important for the teacher to look out for individuals, the quiet and undemonstrative ones as well as the loud and most noticeable ones.

3.12 Questions

The following questions are designed to help you check your understanding of the chapter.

1 Why approach a new class as if you were an anthropologist?
2 What other priorities sometimes get in the way of learning in classrooms?
3 How is the average student's view of school likely to differ from that of a teacher?
4 What is the significance of the production line metaphor?
5 What common 'interests at hand' were described for teachers and students?
6 How was it claimed that students might often miss the point of lessons?
7 What view of the problem of 'authenticity' of learning was advanced here?
8 How may students unintentionally make life difficult for the teacher?
9 **Discussion question**: the strategies outlined in section 3.9 might be criticized for being contradictory. On the one hand they seem to privilege order (and perhaps a quiet life). On the other hand they suggest that intellectual challenge is a priority. Can these two aims be reconciled?

NOTES

1. Holt (1984), pp. 37–8.
2. Jackson (1968).
3. Galton, Simon and Croll (1980).
4. Holt (1984), pp. 33–4.
5. Doyle, W. (1986).

6. Example 3.2 comes from Pollard and Filer (1996), pp. 56–7.
7. Pollard (1985); see also Pollard and Filer (1996).
8. Bennett et al. (1984).
9. Kerry and Sands (1984).
10. Alexander (2000), p. 249.
11. Cockburn (1995).
12. Desforges (1993).
13. Example 3.3 comes from Edwards and Mercer (1987), pp. 50–4.
14. Wragg (1984).
15. Ruddock, Chaplain and Wallace (1995).
16. Younger and Warrington (1999).
17. Wise and Upton (1998).

CHAPTER FOUR

The Management of Order

4.1 Introduction

Keeping order in a classroom is mostly a matter of good relationships, effective communication and carefully planned work. In this chapter these factors are analysed and advice is supplied, along with a series of classroom vignettes, to illustrate how good order can be affected by apparently small differences in teaching behaviour and style. A sequence of possible strategies for intervention by the teacher is described, from the least to the most serious, with examples. This is followed by discussion of a framework of rules to protect the rights of teacher and taught and consideration of the likely pattern of early relationships with a class.

4.2 Order and Disorder

Schools are mostly (at least in the UK today) very orderly places.[1] However most teachers can remember being in charge of disorderly, even chaotic, lessons where things have gone wrong. It is well worth keeping in mind, as you struggle to contain rebellion and chaos in 3B on a Thursday afternoon, that research has consistently shown that the overwhelming majority of children want classrooms to be peaceful, orderly places. Even though it may seem otherwise at times, you almost certainly have the silent majority on your side. You should also be prepared at all times to seek out help and support from other teachers and staff. Staff in good schools go out of their way to help one another. Following on from what has been said in the previous chapter about the working consensus that normally exists in classrooms, there are three common causes for students becoming restive and trying to reject, or subvert, that consensus.

1 Poor relationships between teachers and students. These include teachers who fail to be sufficiently assertive communicators and those who are over-assertive, to the point of using bullying tactics.

2 Inadequate setting of tasks, which leads to uncertainty, confusion or boredom.
3 Teachers who are not sufficiently aware and alert to what is going on around the classroom or other teaching spaces and who let small incidents grow into major ones.

On the basis of my own and my colleagues' experience of teaching and of supervising student teachers in schools, I would argue that by far the most common reasons why beginners fail to keep order are linked to these same three causes. Thus most failures stem from:

- a lack of sufficient assertiveness in communicating with students;
- inadequate planning, leading to lessons in which students are not provided with tasks that engage them fully, at an appropriate level of difficulty;
- failure to deal quickly with small problems before they escalate.

To these common problems it is fair to add one more, which applies only to some classes:

- disorder may repeatedly break out in difficult classes, with recalcitrant students, who are alienated to some degree from their schooling and who are difficult even for experienced teachers to manage.

4.3 'Withitness'

Developing awareness for behaviour throughout a classroom seems to be a skill that takes some time to develop, probably because initially student teachers have all their attention taken up by what is going on immediately around them. They tend to get absorbed with one student, or group, and fail to notice what is happening on the other side of the room. With experience, teachers develop what Kounin[2] called 'withitness', an ability to split attention between the student they are talking to and the rest of the class, so as to 'have eyes in the back of their heads'. They sweep the classroom rapidly with their eyes from time to time and are adept at noticing any signs of trouble early. You should be aware from the start of the need to do this kind of routine monitoring of order, even if you find it difficult to put into practice. You can try to practise it from the start.

4.4 Assertive Communication

By 'assertive' communication I mean verbal and non-verbal communication that is firm, confident and positive, but not aggressive. Assertive teachers maintain their own basic rights without trampling on those of their students. A detailed analysis of how teachers can do this is provided in Robertson.[3] There are several ways in which this style of communication can fail to develop successfully.

1 A teacher may be too *unassertive*, effectively allowing dominant students to control the working consensus for their own ends.

2 A teacher may be *over-assertive*. She or he is aggressively determined to keep order, brow-beating the class into a passive and sulky state of obedience, often using sarcasm or threats, which succeed in 'keeping the lid' on trouble but which fail to win the trust or respect of the students.

3 A teacher may be *indecisive*, failing to take the initiative in interacting with a class. In this situation a dangerous kind of communication vacuum arises, which will quickly be filled by the students. The teacher then finds it hard to re-take control of the pattern of interaction.

Consider the following examples.

Example 4.1[4]
Miss White enters her KS3 classroom ready to teach a maths lesson to a class of 12 year olds for the first time. A boy drops a book as she walks by and, without thinking about it, she stoops down and picks it up, giving him a smile as she puts it on his table.

> **Student A:** Are you our new teacher, Miss?
> **Teacher:** Yes, I am. [*She smiles again*]
> **Student B:** I hope you're better than the last one we had! [*Laughter from the class*]
> **Teacher:** Yes, well . . .
> **Student A:** She was a right old bag! [*More laughter*]
> **Teacher:** Now, really, that's enough.
> **Student B:** It was enough for us!
> **Teacher:** Now, let's have your attention, please . . .

This tiny episode, which lasted only a few seconds, could set a pattern for communication during the whole lesson, unless Miss White changes her style very rapidly. She is understandably nervous as she enters, and smiles at her new students out of a wish to seem friendly and also because she is feeling tense. She picks up the book because she is habitually helpful to other people. A student asks a friendly enough question and she smiles again and answers. In doing this she is both giving out non-verbal signals that she wants to placate the class and also allowing the students to start to control the communication. She responds indecisively to the first impolite remark from student B and is then interrupted by student A. She responds to the cheeky remarks and laughter with a weak reprimand and student B immediately follows up with another joke, at her expense. She responds by asking for their attention. She thus finds herself reacting to events, while the students set the tone and dominate the interaction. Small details, like the smiles, the picking up of the book and the 'please' requesting attention, all give out a message of slightly submissive behaviour. She might have done better to ignore student A, take up a central position in front of the class and instruct them to pay attention. Then she might have introduced herself briefly and started almost immediately to focus on work. As it is, Miss White is in danger of coming across as both unassertive and indecisive. The students in this class have established that, for the moment at least, their peer group solidarity and values are unchallenged and in control.

Example 4.2

Mrs Green is teaching history to a KS3 class of 13 year olds. She stands outside her classroom door before the lesson and contemplates the students, who are still arriving.

> **Mrs Green:** Samantha Jenkins, why are you chewing? Come here. Here, I said! You're not deaf as well as dumb, are you?
> **Samantha:** No, Miss.
> **Mrs Green:** No, Mrs Green.
> **Samantha:** No . . . Mrs Green.
> **Mrs Green:** Put it in the bin. [*She gestures inside the classroom. Samantha disappears to get rid of the offending sweet*] Now. Straight line. No talking. James Wilson, if you want a detention you're going about it the right way. There's always one sad case, isn't there? [*A few students laugh. A girl puts up her hand.*]
> **Girl:** Please, Miss . . .
> **Mrs Green:** No, Emma, not now. Right! [*She raises her voice*] Class 5 . . . I am waiting! [*There is now silence*] Thank you. I see you're gracing us with your presence today, Carl; wonders never cease. When you enter the room you will be so good as to sit exactly where I placed you last week. Is that clear? And I hope you've all remembered your books this time. Right. Are we ready? Enter!

Mrs Green is certainly assertive in this opening exchange. The trouble is that she is in danger of establishing her rule by a kind of bullying domination. She is prepared to use sarcasm and to humiliate individuals in minor ways, all in the cause of good order. The result may be that she does indeed have an orderly class but she will not be either liked or trusted. If, for example, a student such as Emma came to her class with a serious problem, she would be unlikely to trust Mrs Green sufficiently to confide in her. And if Mrs Green had difficulty, say in operating a tape recorder, the class would probably prefer the pleasure of watching her struggle to that of helping her.

Example 4.3

Mr Brown is beginning a science class with his KS2 class. He has set up a demonstration concerned with electric circuits and switches on his table at the front of the class. His 10- and 11-year-old students straggle into the room from their lunch break. Several boys are still arguing about their recent football game.

> **Mr Brown:** Now settle down everyone! Settle down . . . we're going to do some science this afternoon, so you'll need your science jotters. John, don't put your bag there. We don't want the gangways cluttered up.
> **Student A:** Sir! Sir! Can we open the windows? It's really hot in here.
> **Mr Brown:** We'll see about that in a minute. Now I want you all sitting down . . . hurry up. Is Leonie here? Leonie, now your mother has phoned in. She can't meet you after school today; you're to go home with Natasha's mum, OK?
> **Student B:** Are we going to do experiments Mr Brown?

Mr Brown: All in good time. John, would you open the windows, please? That's right. Open both of them. Yes, both of them. Now, are we all ready?

Student C: Mr Brown, can we work in pairs today?

Mr Brown: We'll see.

Student C: You said we could last time.

Mr Brown: Yes, yes. We may have time for some work in pairs. We'll have to see how things go. John, what's the problem? The window's jammed? I think it's probably that blind getting in the way . . . no, not that one, the one on the left . . . isn't it that? Go and help him, would you, Suzanne. Now, have we all got our science jotters? [*Several students now get up from their seats and go to get their jotters from trays at the side of the room*] Now, this afternoon, we're going to go on with our work on electricity. You remember that last week we looked at simple circuits and switches.

Student D: Sir! Sir! My Dad showed me a special kind of switch from his work.

Mr Brown: Did he, now? Perhaps you can tell us about that later, Nicholas. Your Dad knows a lot about electricity, doesn't he?

Student D: Yeah. He's got a new van and all. It's bigger than his old one . . . [*At this point a child wanders into the room*]

Mr Brown: William, what are you doing coming in late like this? Where have you been?

Student E: I've been seeing Mrs Harvey about the photographs.

Mr Brown: Photographs? I thought all that had been seen to long ago.

Student E: Ours had to go back and be re-done. They gave us the wrong lot at first.

Mr Brown: Well, anyway, you'd better get your science jotter out and come and join us.

Student E: My science jotter?

Student D: He's got a new drill and all . . .

Mr Brown: Yes, your science jotter. I'm afraid we haven't got time for that now, Nicholas. Hurry up, Will. No just sit there for now. Now, last time I wasn't able to show you how a real switch would work, because we didn't have the right sort. We had a few problems with that, didn't we? But we won't worry about that for now. Today we're going to look at a different kind of circuit. Now, can you all see? [*Cries of 'No!' 'Colin! You're in the way!'*]

Mr Brown: Sit down, Colin, or the ones behind you won't be able to see, will they? Now this is what is known as a parallel circuit. No, no, John, I didn't tell you to stand up. I tell you what: I think you'd better all gather round the table here, right at the front, so you can see properly . . . [*There follows a minor stampede, as 28 children push their chairs noisily back and rush together towards the front of the room, to get a good place. Natasha drops her science jotter and falls to her knees with a wail to save it. Colin tries to prevent a boy from sitting in the seat next to him, reserving it for a friend; an argument breaks out. James trips over a chair and falls to the floor, much to the merriment of his peers. Sally and Sharon start to wrestle with each other over possession of a chair. James drops his pencil case and the contents spill out all over the floor. It takes Mr Brown some considerable time to restore order*]

. . .

Mr Brown: Now, let's see where we were. Leave Sally alone, James. Now when I show you how this works I want you all to think about why it does what it does. You see science is all about explaining things. You might want to jot down some notes in your books. [*Five students stand up noisily and start to make their way back through the crowd to their tables where they have left their books*] Oh dear, oh dear! I said you'd need your jotters! [*Fifteen minutes of the lesson have already gone by*]

Mr Brown is an example of an indecisive teacher, who does not prioritize suffici-ently, and a teacher who is not well organized. Movements of a class, from one place to another and also transitions between one activity and another, are both prime occa-sions for disorder to emerge, unless they are carefully planned and executed. If this teacher needed the class to be sitting around his table, with their science jotters, then he should have moved them, one group at a time, with their books and pens, to seat-ing that he had prepared at the front of the room. The problem with the window leads to a long pause, or flat spot, in which any initial momentum in the lesson is lost. The windows should have been opened before the children arrived. The message for Leonie could have waited until a quieter moment, later. This was not the time to encourage Nicholas to talk about his father's work; nor is the lack of a switch in last week's lesson relevant to this one. Late arrivals should be dealt with briskly, post-poning any lengthy explanations until later. Notice that none of the students has yet been either really difficult or uncooperative, yet the lesson has got off to a truly disastrous start.

4.5 A Checklist for Successful Management of Order

Teachers do not have extensive powers to coerce students into obedience. Effective teachers keep order partly through the quality of the work they initiate and partly through good relationships, built up over time by effective communication. When they have to respond, or intervene, to deal with behaviour problems they seem to follow a number of unwritten rules, some of which include the following.

- Stay calm and do not shout. Remain polite and cool. Escalating noise and aggres-sion are unhelpful. Speak clearly and firmly.
- Learn to stop the class. Avoid the 'steam-train' effect of constantly saying 'Shh!' as a way of reducing noise levels. It is rarely effective. Instead, give a clear signal to get everyone's attention (e.g. 'Stop what you're doing . . . pens down and face this way . . . everyone listening.') Insist on absolute quiet at such moments, then be ready to talk briefly to the whole class about a work-related problem or issue.
- Be aware of non-verbal communication. Your position in the room, your body language and your pattern of eye contact with students are all sending signals about your confidence and competence. Move about the class; take up a promin-ent position from which you can see and be seen when you want to talk to everyone; use eye contact with individuals to communicate your determination; look confident, even if you do not feel it.
- Communicate with enthusiasm and energy. Try to use your voice expressively, varying the pitch and volume. Occasionally, try speaking deliberately *quietly* as a way of getting attention. If the class is dispersed, for example in a gymnasium or hall, bring them back together, near to you, in order to make major teaching points without shouting. Make sure you interact with the students, make eye

contact and listen carefully to the feedback they give you. Make sure you are heard without shouting.

- Keep up lesson momentum. Be aware of the dangers of breaks in continuity, lengthy introductions and talk that sidetracks you away from the main theme. Do not allow queues of students to form at your desk; negotiate useful ways of dealing with 'wait time' and move yourself, to see children in their places. Plan how to manage all major transitions and movements from place to place.
- Do not make a series of threats that you cannot follow through. Threats are almost always counter-productive so try never to use them.
- Avoid procrastination. Do not get involved in long arguments with students over incidents of misbehaviour. In particular, avoid getting sucked into disputes over secondary aspects of the situation. Speak briefly, addressing the primary behaviour in question and then try to re-focus on work-related issues.
- Avoid confrontations with individuals in front of the whole class. Give the student a clear choice to return to work and say you will deal with him or her afterwards. Then remember to do so.
- Use humour, if you are able, to defuse tense situations.
- Avoid, so far as possible, all talk about 'bad behaviour'. Whenever you can, avoid a 'negative spiral' of nagging and reminders about what has gone wrong. Try instead to build 'positive spirals' of talk which either comment on positive aspects of working relationships or redirect students to matters to do with the lesson. Keep students' attention on the work at hand.
- Be prepared to insist on periods of silent work, when students need to concentrate on individual problem-solving.
- Make notes of any serious incidents or sanctions given and follow them up with determination.

4.6 Strategies for Intervention, from the Least to the Most Serious[5]

When a student misbehaves there are a number of strategies you can use, from the least to the most serious, which you should keep firmly in mind. You will appear more effective and confident if you can react to problems decisively, choosing appropriately from the steps on the following 'ladder' of responses.

Tactical ignoring and the meaningful look

Minor distractions and misbehaviours are best dealt with by either overriding them altogether, paying attention instead to what students should be doing, or with a silent look fixing the miscreant firmly in the eye and frowning or perhaps shaking your head. Some teachers use a gesture of the hand or an expressive sound ('Uh?') to the same effect. (Major issues, however, cannot be ignored.)

Example 4.4
Mrs Grey is reading from a textbook to her class. A girl is playing with her pen; Mrs Grey passes by her desk, removes the pen from her hand and puts it down, without pausing in her reading. A boy taps the shoulder of a friend in front of him, to distract him; Mrs Grey pauses slightly; the class orient to her, following the unexpected silence; she shakes her head at the boy, who desists; Mrs Grey resumes her reading.

Naming an individual and giving a simple reprimand

The teacher calls out the name of an offending student. She issues a mild reprimand.

Example 4.5
Mrs Grey looks up from her monitoring of one child's writing. She sees two girls fussing with a pencil sharpener. She says, 'Samantha! Jodie! Leave it alone; get on with your work.' She then turns immediately back to her work, in the expectation that she will be obeyed. Some 10 seconds later she looks across the room to check that the girls are now working.

Eliciting a rule and redirecting

The teacher asks the offending child to recognize what he or she is doing wrong and redirects them to work.

Example 4.6
Mrs Grey sees a boy lifting a chair dangerously over the heads of some neighbours.

   Mrs Grey: Keith! Stop! Why shouldn't you be doing that?
   Keith: Urm. I'm not holding the chair right?
   Mrs Grey: That's right. I've shown you how to move a chair safely. Now do it properly.
      [*He does so*] Good boy.

Rule restatement and choice

Where a basic rule has been broken, the teacher asks the student to restate an agreed class rule and then offers him or her a choice to conform or face more serious consequences. The consequence would usually be to work in isolation, to apologize, to see the teacher at the end of the lesson or to make up work later in free time.

Example 4.7
A boy in Mrs Grey's class swears, audibly, at another boy. Mrs Grey reacts quickly but calmly.

   Mrs Grey: Roy! I heard that. What is our rule about language in the classroom? [*Roy says nothing*] What is our rule about swearing? Come on, Roy!

Roy: [*Eventually mutters*] We shouldn't use, like, bad words.

Mrs Grey: That's right. We don't show aggression or disrespect to others in our language. That was out of order, Roy, and you know it. Now, you can either apologize for using bad language, or I'll have to see you afterwards.

Roy: [*Considers this for a moment and then mutters*] Sorry.

Mrs Grey: [*Accepts this*] Now, we've got just ten more minutes to finish this piece of writing. Let's see everyone doing their best!

Offering a choice together with a minor sanction

In more serious incidents, students may break a rule more than once or threaten to defy the teacher's authority. The teacher responds by putting the responsibility back on the student's shoulders and offering a way out of the situation, without backing down or escalating the conflict.

Example 4.8

Jodie is upset about her history work. She reacts to Mrs Grey's request to do the work again by throwing her book on the floor and bursting out.

Jodie: No! Stop picking on me! You cow!

Mrs Grey: Pull yourself together, Jodie.

Jodie: It's not fair. You always pick on me!

Mrs Grey: I'm coming back to see you in just one minute. I want you to calm down and think about how you should speak to a teacher. [*She moves swiftly away to another desk and talks to another student. Without further attention, Jodie puts her head down on her arms and sobs. After about 30 seconds, Mrs Grey returns to Jodie, takes a spare chair, and sits beside her. She talks to Jodie very quietly. The rest of the class look at them for a few moments and then, seeing no drama, reorient to their work*]

Mrs Grey: Now, Jodie, what have you got to say for yourself?

Jodie: [*Tearfully*] I wasn't the only one who didn't do it right. You always pick on me.

Mrs Grey: It may feel like that, Jodie, but it's not true. I simply want you to do the work properly. Now, why don't you take your things over to that spare table [*indicates an empty table at the back of the room*] and get down to some proper work. If you're stuck, just ask me for help.

Jodie: S'not fair. It's always me!

Mrs Grey: Jodie, the choice is yours. Either you move your things to that table and get on with your work now, as you know you should, or I'll have to arrange for you to do it later, in your own free time. It's up to you. [*Jodie thinks about this for a moment and then picks up her things, still in a huff, and moves to the spare table. Mrs Grey ignores her and attends to the whole class, making a point about the next stage of the lesson. A few minutes later she returns to Jodie, praises her work, and encourages her to continue. Jodie is still sulky but has calmed down considerably*]

Note that Mrs Grey played down Jodie's defiant language and ignored the book on the floor. She refused to get involved in a secondary issue about what was, or was not, fair. She stuck to the primary point at issue: that Jodie should do the work again. She did not raise the temperature of the confrontation or try to settle it with a shouting match overheard (with delight) by the rest of the class. She also gave Jodie a way out of the situation, without either of them losing face.

Use of time out

When all else fails, the teacher states the situation and what needs to be done, and if the child refuses to comply orders him or her to leave the room and cool off in a specified, supervised space. (**Time out** requires an agreed school-wide policy.)

Example 4.9

John has been in a fight with another boy. He then repeatedly refuses to join in a lesson and finally shouts at his teacher. Mrs Grey has already been through the steps outlined in Examples 4.4 and 4.5.

Mrs Grey: OK, John, it's time to calm down and do some work. You know we've been through this already.

John: Get lost.

Mrs Grey: [*Still calmly*] Right. You know very well you shouldn't talk to a teacher like that, John. I think it would be best if you went to Mrs Temple's office right now, and stayed there for 10 minutes. Then we'll have a discussion at the end of the lesson. Off you go. [*On this occasion, John complies, slouching out of the room and slamming the door behind him. Mrs Grey ignores this drama and gets on with her lesson. She knows that Mrs Temple is briefed to receive students under these circumstances. Ten minutes later, Mrs Temple escorts John back to the class. At the conclusion of the lesson, Mrs Grey asks John to stay behind. She asks him for an account of his behaviour and is sympathetic to the fact that he had reasons for feeling upset. She persuades him to apologize. She writes a brief note, outlining the incident, which she passes on to the head teacher*]

Further notes on time out

'Time out from reinforcement', to give it its full title, is a non-violent but effective sanction if used correctly. Isolating a child from the classroom in this way for a period of 5 or 10 minutes is probably the most disruptive and serious short-term sanction a school will use. It does, however, depend on an agreed policy across a whole school, with proper procedures in place. In particular, the room or place to which the student goes must be safe, supervised, but devoid of all social contact and amusement. It is meant to be boring. School secretaries or classroom assistants will sometimes supervise, at a distance. One minute of time out for each year of the student's age is a good rule of thumb. Periods of time out beyond about 15 minutes are most unlikely to improve the effects of this sanction. It is only a short-term strategy and must not be used too often. Children may also be asked to make some appropriate restitution for their wrong-doing at a later point in time.

Some schools and teachers organize systems of 'swapping' students across classes, for brief cooling-off periods. The offender is sent with some set work to the alternate class and works alone. Some classrooms have convenient quiet areas, partitioned off or just outside the door, which can be used for time out. Some schools have evolved a warning 'yellow card' followed by a 'red' (sending off) card, in the manner of soccer referees. However, asking a child to stand outside a classroom door is *not* a good idea if they then spend their time making faces at their peers through a window in the door. Nor is it sensible to send a child outside if there is any risk that he or she will run out of school. If a child refuses to leave the room when ordered, there should be a system in place for a senior member of staff to be called to escort them. If they still refuse, the most likely strategy is to remove the rest of the class for the remainder of the lesson, leaving the offender on his or her own, but under supervision.

Many schools still use a system of work during free time, or detentions, as a sanction for older students although, as with time out, it needs to be a formal, organized procedure and should not be overused. Rogers[6] recommends the use of a '4W' form as a constructive minor punishment. The form demands that the student, after a period of cooling off, write answers to four questions.

1 What I did against our class (school) rules.
2 What rules (or rights) I broke or infringed.
3 What is my explanation?
4 What I think I should do to fix things up or work things out.

One advantage of the 4W form is to focus the student's thought on what has happened and why. It can lead into discussions about how to improve behaviour and also prompt thoughts about appropriate restitution.

Incidents of misbehaviour that go beyond those outlined above probably need longer-term programmes of response, involving senior members of staff and, on occasion, parents. These are likely to involve some form of restitution for damage done or negotiation of a behaviour contract, which is then carefully monitored. Where such programmes fail, schools are likely to consider suspension or, eventually, exclusion. The issue of bullying is dealt with separately in 13.6.

4.7 A Framework of Rules

A classroom is a social microculture, with its own history and traditions. If, as a student teacher, you arrive to teach in the middle of the school year, some kind of working consensus, and an underlying ethos, will already be in place. As we have seen (3.6), this working consensus often leads to an emphasis on work, but rather rarely to one on learning. A more basic problem for new teachers, however, is to ensure that a viable working consensus is accepted rather than rejected by the students. Without a stable basis of order, all learning is at risk. This need for order,

Table 4.1 The rights of students and teachers

Students' rights	Teachers' rights
To feel physically and emotionally safe	To feel physically and emotionally safe
To be treated with dignity and respect	To be treated with dignity and respect
To be allowed to learn without harassment	To be allowed to teach without harassment

so that learning may flourish, is the main justification for teachers to manage behaviour. But teachers also have a more fundamental responsibility for the general safety and welfare of their students. Over the years, British courts of law have maintained that responsible teachers are *in loco parentis*. This Latin phrase simply means that teachers are expected to act so as to protect the welfare of their students, just as reasonable parents would in a similar situation.

If the keeping of order is to be rational and reasonable, it should be founded on the same values that inform the general ethos of the class and the school. We can express a minimal list of such values in terms of the rights of those taking part. Such rights, which should be protected, might look as shown in Table 4.1.

If they are to become more than empty claims, rights must be linked to responsibilities and these can be expressed as a simple set of class (or school) rules. The rules, in their turn, must be linked to clear consequences for rule breaking and to systems of support to bring this about. Class rules must fit within school rules and teachers should, of course, seek for consistency. Depending on the age of the students, it is sensible not only to explain the basic rules but also to negotiate them in a language that the students understand and accept. If they feel some genuine ownership of the classroom rules, through having helped to make them, they are more likely to accept them as a reasonable basis for discipline.

The key areas in which teachers generally find that formal or informal rules are needed include the following:

- basic respect and concern for other people, in terms of language and actions;
- issues of safety;
- proper concern for property and possessions;
- movement during lessons, to protect learning;
- rules of communication, to protect mutual respect and learning;
- rules for settling conflicts.

In practice, most schools find that other issues, such as clothing and jewellery, food and drink, and time keeping also have to be governed by rules.

Humour is a key 'lubricant' of classroom life, making it possible to defuse tensions and potential conflicts. However, it should not be used to damage children's self-respect. As children grow older their own wit may become a weapon that they use against one another and against teachers, with greater or lesser discrimination. In the following example, both teacher and student trade mock insults, in a friendly way, and the teacher comes off second best.

Example 4.10 KS4 English lesson[7]
A teacher, perhaps priding himself on his good rapport with his students and his sense of humour, was discussing a piece of work they had done.

Teacher: Mmm, well, do you know Tracey, it hurts me to say it, but for you it's not a bad piece of work.
Tracey: Gee, thanks.
Teacher: No, I mean, just think, if you really got stuck in, you know, really tried, you could be almost average.
Tracey: Who'd want to be like you anyway?
Student: Come off it, sir, she'd never make average.
Tracey: Hey, if I was average, bird-brains, I'd be top of the class.
Teacher: [*Laughing*] Nice one, Porky, nice one.
Tracey: You must be a not-average teacher, having us.
Teacher: Dead right, I'm not average.
Tracey: That's what I said.
Teacher: [*Laughing*] Right, one to you.
Tracey: You can't count either.

4.8 Getting to Know You

Establishing good working relationships with a new class takes time and energy. Research by Wragg[8] and others has found that new teachers tend to have a brief 'honeymoon' period with their classes, in which their very novelty and unknown personality have a restraining influence on students' conduct. In the second week or so of such encounters, however, this novelty effect wears off and is succeeded by a process of testing the limits of what the teacher will allow. As a new or student teacher, it makes sense to be prepared for this 'delayed misbehaviour' effect and to be prepared to work on establishing ground rules for a good working consensus right from day one. Planning for the management of order thus needs to take its place alongside planning for learning. Experienced teachers spend considerable time early on with their classes establishing routines and procedures, for such things as seating, beginnings and endings of lessons, managing resources and asking questions. In this chapter the management of order has been dealt with rather in isolation, in order to give it a clearer focus, but in reality experienced teachers manage students' behaviour to a considerable extent via the routine ways in which they manage tasks and activities. This links classroom order to other aspects of planning and teaching in a more integrated fashion (see Chapter 5).

If you find it difficult to keep order, talk about it to a mentor, another student or an experienced teacher and, if possible, have them observe you, with a checklist (such as that shown in section 4.5) at hand, to analyse what is going wrong.[9] However, good order is not only a matter for individual teachers. The policies and practices of the whole school are very important and staff should communicate about these and support one another in implementing them.

4.9 Questions

The following questions are designed to help you check your understanding of the chapter.

1 What three causes of failure to keep order were said to be most commonly found among beginning teachers?
2 What are the main strategies through which effective teachers were said to keep order (quite apart from 'strategies for intervention')?
3 What kinds of strategies do you need to practise as a beginner teacher in order to help maintain good order?
4 What kinds of non-verbal communication should you be aware of in your own teaching?
5 If naming a student and giving a reprimand are not effective, what strategy would you try next?
6 How long is it reasonable to keep a student in 'time out'?
7 What change in student behaviour might you expect in about the second week of a teaching practice?
8 **Discussion question**: consider the following quotation.

> Traditionally the image of the teacher is one of a forbidding figure ... like a prison warder or an army sergeant. The inefficacy and indignity of this way of preserving the order appropriate to learning were rightly challenged. Unfortunately, however, it has been replaced in some quarters by that of the benign child-minder who keeps in the background and manipulates children by appealing to their interests. The teacher, in other words, has identified himself with the attitudes of a consumer-oriented society. The techniques of the supermarket have succeeded those of the prison.[10]

Do you feel there is now any truth in this argument? How would you answer the writer?

NOTES

1. The annual report of the Chief Inspector of Schools for 2000/2001 states that behaviour was found to be 'unsatisfactory' in only about 1% of primary schools and 8.3% of secondary schools (Ofsted 2001).
2. Kounin (1970).
3. Robertson (1981).

4. Examples 4.1–4.9 are all fictional vignettes, based on many of the author's observations and classroom experiences.
5. This section draws on ideas from Rogers (1991).
6. Rogers (2000).
7. Example 4.10 comes originally from O'Connor (1983), as quoted in Mercer (1995), p. 52.
8. Wragg (1993).
9. Further helpful and more detailed reading on this subject can be found in Rogers (1991, 2000) and Wragg (2001a,b).
10. Peters (1966), p. 263.

CHAPTER FIVE

Lesson Design

5.1 Introduction

Planning for teaching involves imagining the future. It is difficult to do this if, as a student teacher, you know relatively little about the present. You lack detailed knowledge about the individual students you are going to teach, about the curriculum you are taking on and about the resources available to help you. Firstly, you need to acquire just enough information about each of these elements in the situation to get started. Then you need to continue to learn as much as you can about all of them, as you continue working in a particular class and school. In this chapter the process of planning is described and is illustrated with examples of simple lesson plans through to more complex planning issues and links to schemes of work.

5.2 Simple Plans

These days, much of the curriculum, in the form of schemes of work, is outlined for each class in the school's planning documents. As a student teacher you are most likely to be given some part of this agreed outline and asked to take on responsibility for teaching it. Aside from these officially agreed school plans, experienced teachers carry much of their day-to-day planning in their heads. For student teachers, however, the compiling of lesson plans serves more than one function. In the first place a good lesson plan is for you: it should be a practical tool, to think out what you intend to do. But its second function is to provide others with evidence of your thinking about teaching and learning. As such, your written plans will almost certainly form a part of the evidence that is used by those responsible to judge whether you are becoming competent to teach. It is thus a public document, which others need to understand.

Good plans contain information, or estimates, about a minimum of five things:

- what you intend the students to learn;
- how you mean to help them to learn;
- what materials and conditions are needed for this learning to occur (resources and organization);
- what the sequence and timing of activities will be;
- how you intend to find out what has been learned, by the students and by you (monitoring, assessment and evaluation).

Here is a very simple example, a maths lesson for 5–7 year-olds, that tries to do these five things.

Example 5.1 KS1 maths: balancing sums

Aims for students' learning

- To think about the 'equals' sign (=) as showing that two sides of a number sentence are in balance; to understand 'equals' as 'balanced' or 'same'.
- To think about addition and subtraction as inverse operations.

Aims for teaching

- Asking questions at different levels of difficulty to particular students.
- Efficient distribution of materials.
- Checking understanding by questioning during plenary.

Resources

A set of scales, some Multilink (or similar) cubes, a whiteboard and pen. More cubes (or other regular weights) and paper or plastic cups for the students to use as 'scales' and one die per pair of students. A worksheet with six to ten problems, showing stick figures of people balancing on a see-saw, representing balancing sums (e.g. $6 + 5 = 2 + ?$, $8 + 4 = 15 - ?$).

Sequence of activities

1 Demonstrate how the pans on a simple set of scales only balance when you put an equal number of Multilink cubes in each pan. Add some cubes to one side and ask how many there are on that side now. Ask how many we have to add to the other side to make it balance. Record each operation as a number sentence on a whiteboard, e.g. $5 + 4 = 5 + 4$. Repeat a couple of times. Next remove some cubes from one side and ask how many are left. Ask how many must be removed from the other pan to balance it. Record the number sentence. Continue adding and taking away cubes until the children all seem secure with the idea of balance, through adding and subtracting.
2 Indicate a big 'equals' sign on the board and ask what it means ('is equal to'). Point out that each side of a number sentence with an 'equals' sign in it has to 'balance' the other side. Model some examples that do and do not balance. Ask for help to identify the ones that balance. Cross out the ones that do not balance.

3 Arrange the class in pairs, with their maths jotters and a pencil. Ask two children to give out two paper cups and a die to each pair. Ask another two children to give out about 20 cubes to each pair. Explain how the two cups represent their 'scales'. They are to throw the die and put that many cubes in one 'scale pan' (i.e. paper cup) and record the number. They then throw the die again and put that many cubes in the second cup. Next they have to add or subtract a number from one 'scale pan' to make the pans balance. Then they record the whole number sentence, using an equals sign. Rehearse this with one pair of children while the others watch. Then set the class to work.

4 When they are confident at the operations, give out a prepared worksheet to each child with six to ten see-saw problems to complete. (You can adjust the problems to suit the varying needs of your class. They should be easy to start with and challenging to finish with.)

5 Plenary: stop the class. Ask about how they completed the see-saw worksheet. Ask the following questions. Does this sum balance? Shall we add or subtract? Is there another way to find a balance? What do we need to do to make it balance? Who can make up a new balancing sum? See if they can remember the definition of the 'equals' sign by mixing up correct and wrong definitions. Praise good answers. Finish by rehearsing the meaning of the 'equals' sign.

6 Students to put all materials away. Dismiss class. *Assessment*: after the lesson check the accuracy of solutions on the worksheets. Evaluate how well the students answered your questions and whether you achieved your own teaching goals.

You need to teach many simple lessons, or shorter episodes, using simple plans like this (though the format is up to you). In each case, after the lesson think about what you would now like to have put in your plan. What would have been useful to add to it? Make sure you include some aims for your own teaching as well as for the students' learning.

Most teachers probably start their lesson designs with some curriculum content that they intend to teach. Then they mostly think about one or more key activities that their students will find interesting and challenging. Around this core they then build their lesson. At first, if you are a KS1 or KS2 teacher, you will need to raid all kinds of sources for good ideas about tasks and activities. Ask teachers for ideas, look in education magazines, consult the Internet, ask your friends and look at printed collections (such as those for the literacy and numeracy strategies). Teachers of KS3 and KS4 are more likely to use their own specialist subject courses as a source. One very rich source of lesson plans is the Internet, but be warned: although there are literally thousands of lesson plans on offer, many of them are not so much plans as brief descriptions of activities for learning, or simply worksheets that you can download. The following is a typical example.

Example 5.2 KS2 English: words borrowed from other languages[1]
Learning objective: to identify words from other languages.

Here are some words which originated in Italy: confetti, graffiti, ghetto, opera, spaghetti, studio.

Task 1: write dictionary definitions for each word. (Use your own words. Give careful explanations and try not to use the original word in its definition.)

Task 2: look carefully at the words. What do they have in common, in terms of their spelling? Explain this carefully in a complete sentence.

Task 3: make a list of other words which you think may have come from Italy. (Clue: some of them are very tasty indeed!)

It would be easy to criticize this as a 'plan' but really it is just an idea for an activity, for anyone to borrow and, as such, it may even be useful. What it lacks as a proper plan are at least the following ingredients, which you would need to add if you borrowed it.

- Clearer objectives for the students' learning, related to the National Curriculum English programme of study and to what they know already. (As written it is not even clear that the stated objective will be met by the activity described.)
- Some practical information about how the lesson is to be taught. Include ideas about timing. Where will the dictionaries come from? Where will answers be written? What will students do if they finish this series of tasks? What is the teacher's role?
- Attention to the students, in terms of what they might know already, whether they are all to complete exactly the same tasks in exactly the same way and how you intend to assess what they have learned. (Not so easy with this task, apart from seeing if they have completed the tasks set. Assessment is dealt with in more detail in Chapter 15.)

In the early stages of your teaching experience, you will probably find that you are mostly focusing on quite simple practical aspects of lessons. Did you manage to keep the class on task? Did you get the room cleared up and the lesson finished on time? Did the students complete the tasks you gave them? Was there too much or too little to do in the time available? Did the students seem engaged by the tasks you set them? Such matters of practical organization, communication and management of order are the most common preoccupations of beginners, which is perfectly understandable. But having dealt with lessons at this level, you will need to move on. (It is quite likely, therefore, that you will need to return to this chapter more than once, at various points in your progress.)

5.3 More Detailed Plans

Much of the development of planning consists of extending the basic ingredients we have already encountered to provide more detail and more thought. It also seems fair to say that not all your lesson plans will be as detailed or thorough. The occasional one can be nothing more than an aide-memoire which shows that you have given a minimal degree of thought to a teaching session. I have in mind 'plans' of the following sort: 'Class 5b, 2 December, 13.30 to 14.15. Mental maths quiz, followed by finishing off the graphs they started yesterday'. However, you also need to write proper detailed plans that show you are really thinking about your developing work and about the students' learning. Let us look at a further example.

Example 5.3 Y5 history lesson: Aztec agriculture
This lesson was taught by A.U., a student teacher on KS2 teaching practice in a medium-sized school in a coastal town. The class of Y5 students was one she had taught before, but she did not yet know them well. The school had instructed her that she was to teach a sequence of lessons on Aztec history and culture, then one of the prescribed units of the KS2 national history curriculum. In this lesson, the second of the series, she wanted to achieve two main things. The first was to explain to the class how the Aztecs, living in their city of Tenochtitlán, had little access to good land and built floating gardens, called chinampas, on a lake in order to provide food. The other aim was to introduce the class to the kinds of foods that the Aztecs ate. For her own teaching, she was mainly concerned with two quite specific points: she wanted to teach the lesson in such a way that it would appeal to boys as much as to girls, and she wanted to try to involve all the students in discussions, no matter what their existing knowledge or cultural background was. She was particularly aware that some boys might be scornful of work on 'cooking' and that there were two ethnic Japanese students in the class, both fluent speakers of English. Here is her plan for the 1-hour history lesson for year group 5C on 14 May.

Learning objectives

- To describe the significant features of Aztec agriculture.
- To recognize the foods and eating habits of Aztec society (NC: 13: 2a, 5c).

Teaching objectives

- To take account of the varying interests and previous knowledge of the class, including boys and girls and students from different cultural backgrounds.
- To involve as many students as possible in the discussion on food.

Resources

- Prepared OHT on Aztec foods.
- Worksheets on *chinampa* gardens.
- Selection of books with material on Aztecs.

Introduction
Two main topics written on board. Ask for prior knowledge about what the Aztecs ate and where their food came from. Why did living near a lake present problems? Describe chinampa *garden system with diagram. Show OHT of Aztec foods and discuss.*

Main activities

- Use textbooks and information on board to complete worksheet on food and farming. (Model use of textbook to locate information.)

- T.H. to support L/A groups with completing sheet. Urge H/A groups to complete concept chart on Aztec farming and to add other information they have found.

Plenary

Discuss ideas for Aztec meals; draw together their accumulated knowledge. Key assessment question: can they come up with explanations for why the Aztecs used chinampas? Can they list some of the problems they faced?

Before reading on, think about the strengths and weaknesses of this plan. Where is it providing helpful detail? What, if any, important issues seem to be missing? The strong features of the plan include the following.

- The lesson has a simple but clear structure.
- It has some general aims for learning, linked to National Curriculum objectives.
- There is a good focus on particular aims for teaching in this lesson, to do with cultural diversity and participation.
- There is some consideration of slower and faster learners (L/A, low attainment; H/A, high attainment), in terms of what they might accomplish, and how a teaching assistant (T.H.) might help.
- A key assessment question has been included in the plenary session.

The main weaknesses seem to be as follows.

- Clearer, more specific targets for learning are needed. Which concepts and facts about the Aztecs are central? How might the targets differ for different students? What specifically historical skills and ideas are being taught? Rather ominously, for a history lesson, there is no mention of when the Aztecs lived.
- Rather little thought is given to the management of resources or to timing. If gathering information from texts is central, then we need to know more about which texts are available, how they will be distributed and whether students will work individually or in groups. What skills will be modelled? The use of information and computer technology (ICT) does not get a mention, though it might have been very helpful as a source of information. It is not clear what ideas about the lesson have actually been shared with T.H., the teaching assistant, or what her responsibilities are.
- Is the focus of the lesson on farming or on food? Should it be on one or the other?
- Does the worksheet enable the students to learn new facts and restructure their concepts about the way of life of the Aztecs? It may degenerate into a matter of low-level work, of 'filling in the blanks'.
- Assessment has at least been considered, but not in much depth or detail; if targets for learning were clearer, then assessment of the written work and of the oral answers might be more pointed and useful (15.3).

In her evaluation of this work, A.U. commented particularly on a number of lessons she felt she had learned. She was critical of the speed of her introduction;

she felt she did not spend enough time drawing out the students' initial knowledge and ideas. She wrote about this in terms of engaging their attention, but it would have been equally important as a means of informing herself about the level of their initial understanding of this remote people. She now felt that the discussion of food, and of Aztec meals, had diverted attention from the main focus on farming and food production. It had been a distraction that could have waited until the next lesson. She was pleased that many of the students had indeed participated in the discussion and that she had managed to draw out the Japanese students' rather different experience of foods with sensitivity and tact. Her references to popular male TV chefs had seemed successful in engaging the boys in the discussion.

A.U. also went on to comment on the students' use of the textbooks. They had been easily distracted by exciting illustrations of topics irrelevant to her aims for the lesson; they had floundered when it came to using the index to look up other words than 'agriculture'; some had copied text straight from the book onto the worksheet. She was not sure that the more able students had been sufficiently challenged and she felt the whole class needed more teaching on finding and using information in nonfiction texts. What perhaps she missed in her (very good) evaluation was whether or not this was a successful *history* lesson. She did not really consider what she wanted the students to remember, or understand, that they did not already know. She did not think of her teaching in terms of the learning demands of the tasks set. Accretion was central to this new topic of Aztec agriculture.[2] Restructuring would be needed in terms of concepts relating to farming, food production and technology. Which concepts would she focus on? How would the students know what they should be learning? The work drew on existing skills involving reading for information and this aspect of the task could be seen more as 'independent problem-solving', although many students turned out to need additional teaching in this area. Nevertheless, it was by no means a bad lesson; it is always easy to comment with hindsight.

5.4 Getting Clearer about Learning Objectives

One of the commonest problems of lesson planning is to stop short at describing tasks or activities, without thinking through what you want students to learn from completing them. There is also an important distinction to be made between 'aims' for learning and 'learning objectives'. An aim is more general and vague, an objective more concrete and specific. In her history lesson A.U. had an aim to teach significant 'features' of Aztec agriculture. To translate this into some specific objectives she would need to specify key facts and concepts that she wanted all, most or some of her students to understand and remember. These might have been to do with 'floating gardens', 'maize', 'soil fertility' and 'rainfall' for example. She might profitably have concentrated on the contrasts between a technology based on wood/leather/stone and manual labour versus one using metals and machines. Turning to reading for information, this is an important cross-curricular skill and there are a number of specifics that could have provided A.U. with a sharper focus for her teaching, including making brief written summaries and the more flexible use of an index.

The outcomes of learning objectives are observable; one can apply the 'Hey Mum' test to them. To carry out this test imagine a student demonstrating his or her new learning at home by saying 'Hey, Mum, look at me (or listen to me) doing so and so.' For example, one of A.U.'s students might have said 'Hey, Mum, look at me locating information by using an index, making use of several different words related to farming.' This (however implausible it might sound) counts as passing the test, because you *could* show Mum this. If, however, the student said 'Hey, Mum, look at me improving my understanding of Aztec history' it would count as a fail. Mum might respond 'So how exactly has your understanding improved? Show me!' The 'Hey Mum' test has its failings, but it may help you to focus your mind on specific observable outcomes of learning. These will usually be focused on facts, concepts or skills.

Not all learning outcomes are observable, or easy to observe. Increased understanding of concepts of agriculture, changed attitudes towards remote cultures, growing degrees of understanding of the nature of historical enquiry: these are all longer-term aims. Yet, although not easily observable they are important. (In fact teachers will still be on the look out for evidence of them.) When we teach students to write stories, or history essays, we cannot predict all that they will invent. We can check their spelling but it is much harder to assess their imagination and understanding. It is reasonable, therefore, to include longer-term and broader aims for teaching in your planning, particularly for the medium and long term. These aims may mostly be specified in medium-term schemes of work, rather than in individual lesson plans. Yet pinning down specific learning objectives, lesson by lesson, has real advantages. Firstly, it will focus your attention on the priorities of a lesson and what will count for you as relevant or irrelevant contributions and questions. Secondly, it will make it much easier for your students to get a clear grasp of what it is they are supposed to learn. Thirdly, it will make assessment easier. (More is written about targets and target-setting in connection with assessment in 15.3.)

5.5 More Complex Planning Issues

Lessons can be designed in many formats, the most common being that formalized in the 'literacy hour' and having the so-called 'diamond' shape.

Whole class introduction

/ | \

Group and individual activities

\ | /

Plenary summation/evaluation

You may well wish to vary this basic 'shape' but whatever clear structure you come up with, you will need to check that your lessons meet some general criteria for success. The following checklist may help.

1 Usually you will need to begin by attracting the students' attention and interest and engaging them in thinking about a topic. How will you try to do this? Can they all see and hear you properly? Are they actually paying attention? Have they the materials they need?

2 What do they already know that is relevant to your lesson, and where is their learning going in future lessons? Think about how you will make your intended objectives for their learning explicit to them. Can you include an **advance organizer,** a brief written description of the main content and activities with which they will be engaged? This can help students understand where you intend going with your teaching.

3 Consider the key ideas you are going to talk about and how they might be represented and linked to students' existing knowledge and interests. What kinds of learning demands will your lesson make on your students? To what extent are you making demands for accretion, restructuring or problem-solving (see Chapter 2)? Are there some well-known misconceptions that you need especially to guard against? What key new terms need clear definition and what key questions will help you to assess their current level of understanding? Are there some skills or cross-curricular themes you need to think about, in addition to your principal subject focus?

4 Think also about managing behaviour. Have you anticipated the major transitions in your lesson, especially those which will involve distributing resources to the class or moving them from one location or seating arrangement to another? These are 'accident black spots' where you need to be clear about what should happen and clear in communicating to students what they are to do. Are there times in the lesson where you need to insist on quiet or silent work? Think about how you might allow some talk before and after such periods of individual concentration. Do you need to give signals warning them of how much time they have left to finish a task? What other aspects of managing behaviour might you bear in mind? (See Chapter 4.)

5 Remember that in the final stages of the lesson you are likely to want to see how far knowledge, understanding or skills have progressed. How will you assess this? Are you clear about the main priorities for your teaching and their learning? How are you going to involve them in evaluating their own progress? What homework is to be set, if any?

6 Most classes contain a wide range of individual differences in terms of existing knowledge, attitudes, maturity, interest, background culture, gender and ethnicity. Most classes contain some students with special educational needs (see also Chapter 13 for a more detailed treatment). The teaching that you plan and the learning outcomes of the various groups and individuals in the class need to take proper account of this diversity. This will lead to giving somewhat different

treatment to different individuals, a process generally referred to as the 'differentiation' of teaching.

Differentiation is one of the most important ways in which you will begin to extend your lesson designs, as you get to know more about your students. The main forms of differentiation include the following:

- Differentiation by task: different students undertake different tasks, which are appropriate to their needs as learners.
- Differentiation by outcome: students work on the same tasks, but you expect different levels and quantities of work to emerge for different students. Outstanding students are set greater challenges; slower learners are expected to achieve only the more fundamental outcomes or understanding.
- Differentiation by teaching or support: students work at the same tasks but some are given more independence, whereas others are supported with special materials or aids or with extra teaching. Some may simply require close monitoring by a teacher or teaching assistant, whereas sometimes a different teaching style or approach may be suitable for some students and not others.
- Differentiation by questioning or challenge: as students are working you will be engaging them in discussions, asking them questions and setting them challenges. In this interactive teaching you can vary the level to suit the needs of different students, including those of high ability.

Besides differentiation, there are a number of other key issues that good detailed planning should address, and these are discussed below. They are not all equally applicable to every single plan or scheme of work you make, but they should appear in your planning.

Expectations, pace and intellectual challenge

Once, as a teacher, you attune yourself to the various levels of attainment specified for the different subjects and key stages of the National Curriculum, you will be increasingly aware that every lesson on a given topic can be more or less challenging. Student interest, too, is crucially dependent on whether the lesson challenges them in ways that they can see are relevant to their lives. Management of order, also, is greatly aided by giving students plenty to do, at a level that is neither too hard nor too easy, and by keeping lessons moving at a brisk pace. It is all too easy to fail to challenge the most knowledgeable and to fail to realize the extent of the confusion of the least knowledgeable students.

Variety in activities and resources

Lessons need to be designed to include a variety of tasks and types of activity. Periods of direct instruction need to be mixed with interactive teaching, independent problem-solving and practice or revision. You will need to draw as appropriate on verbal and visual stimuli, on texts, slides, posters, films, tapes, videos and computer images. Practical and group activities provide a welcome break from written work and teacher talk. Think about the amount of time during which your students can usefully concentrate on one kind of task: sometimes shorter, brisk activities are the most productive; sometimes you may deliberately give sufficient time for extended investigations, role-play or art making.

Selecting and managing resources

Often you will need to consider health and safety issues, the proper use of equipment or its accessibility. Often, also, you will need to think about the level of skills that you are assuming, even in such apparently simple matters as reading a work card, using a ruler or designing a table of data. Lessons can all too easily get bogged down in difficulties over such practical matters. In the case of texts, you will need to build up a wide repertoire of knowledge about key texts for the curriculum you teach. Your use of human resources, too, in the shape of other adults in the class, presents a huge challenge: they need to know what your main intentions are, and how they can best contribute to making materials, teaching or assessment. They may also be very helpful contributors to your plans, if given a chance.

Use of ICT

The effective use of ICT goes well beyond the remit of this book. It is relevant to both your own professional preparation for teaching, your assessment and record keeping and to the teaching of different subjects. However, one key question to ask when thinking about its potential contribution to a lesson is: will ICT genuinely improve the lesson's quality? If so, in what ways? It will often require careful rehearsal and organization to be effective. Fluency with equipment is also important to the business of keeping order. Its use may relate to the kind of representations you can use in a lesson or to the special educational needs of some students, or even to what homework you set. It has a somewhat different contribution to make in each different subject area, which you will need to research. Not all commercial software is of good quality, however, and you need to build up a repertoire of programs and websites that you value and can use effectively. Finally, in your planning you need to consider how your students need to progress in terms of their own understanding and use of ICT.[3]

English as an additional language

Once again, this is an important issue but one that goes well beyond what can be included in this book. As a student you will not be expected to be an instant expert on teaching English as a second or additional language. Yet you need to realize that teaching and learning are crucially affected by language competence. With the help of more experienced staff, you can expect to begin to learn both how to assess your students' abilities to learn in English (and perhaps other languages of the community) and also the different kinds of language demands made by the different tasks and activities that you are planning to use.[4]

Work in out-of-school contexts

Schools make regular use of the local environment and of visits out of school. Even work in the school's own grounds may be very profitable, but needs careful planning. You will need to think, once again, about health and safety issues and about whether you need extra help in the basic supervision of your students as they move about outside the classroom. Often it will be necessary to punctuate a lesson with a clear signal to come back together as a group, to check on progress, to give further instructions or re-engage attention on the work in hand. For visits out of school, the school will have policies in place and you will need to consult with other more experienced staff over such matters as getting parental permissions, acceptable levels of adult supervision, reconnaissance of the place to be visited and preparations for making the visit a success. Once again, think about what exactly the visit is likely to promote, in terms of learning, and how the students are going to be informed about this. What knowledge will they need to have in advance in order to get full value out of the trip and how will you follow the visit up in the classroom?

5.6 Beyond Single Lesson Plans

As you progress with your teaching, you will need to share your planning with other members of staff in subject or year-group teams. Teaching assistants (or learning support staff) and parents also need to be in the picture, if they are to contribute. You will quite quickly be expected to plan a sequence of lessons, running for perhaps half a term or a term, and such medium- and long-term planning will make different demands on your thinking. The way in which your students are to find continuity and progression in such sequences of lessons becomes crucial. You will also probably need to think more about independent problem-solving, practice and revision as phases of learning. The importance of analysing the learning demands of any task have been much emphasized in Chapter 2, but this may not be stressed by other teachers and tutors you come across and, unless you habitually pay attention to it, it may get lost to view.

If you are now rather perplexed and worried about the sheer number of different issues which all seem to need to be taken into account in planning, be reassured that over a period of time, say a year, they will start to fit more naturally into your thinking. Planning will develop, from the simplest outlines to more and more detailed and knowledgeable plans and sequences of lessons, as you learn more about students, the curriculum and your own teaching. We will now examine one last example of a plan, which is then put in a broader context in order to appraise its strengths and weaknesses.

Example 5.4 Y9 art: working on printing for book illustrations

The following lesson plan was used by a student teacher, M.D., in teaching an art lesson to a Y9 class in an independent school. It plunges us into the specialized world of secondary art teaching. (The demands of subject specialisms will be further discussed in Chapter 16.) The lesson involved making linocuts and prints and was the second in a series related to a project on book illustration. Previous lessons in the scheme had introduced students to fifteenth-century northern European book illustration, with a particular focus on the work of the Limbourg brothers. Students were also learning how to use drawing as a preparatory stage of printmaking. The headings under 'Programmes of study' come directly from the National Curriculum for art (KS3); for each lesson the teacher would tick the entries relevant to the learning objectives being covered.

Lesson plan 2

Class W3, 14/01/03, 10.25 to 11.40
Concept/theme/process: printed book illustration
Culture/period/style: fifteenth-century European art

Programmes of study

Exploring/developing ideas

- Record/analyse/select   ☐
- Question/discuss critically   ☐
- Organize/present information in different ways   ☑

Investigating/making

- Investigate/combine/manipulate   ☑
- Apply/extend knowledge of materials; control tools/technique   ☑
- Experiment/select methods/approaches appropriately   ☑

Evaluating/developing work

- Analyse/evaluate/express judgements   ☐
- Evaluate/adapt/refine/develop work   ☐

Knowledge/understanding

- Matching visual codes/ideas/purposes   ☑
- Understanding visual codes/conventions for representing ideas/values/beliefs   ☐
- Understand continuity/change in contexts, different roles, functions Western/non-Western art   ☐

Learning objectives

- All students must: complete a first print; show some understanding of gauge types and line quality; show understanding of how simplicity of design will impact on lino cut.

- Most students should: draw out the visual code of 'dots and lines' of lino cutting and convert into a representation of a landscape. Print second (light green) print. Show improved design by testing line quality in drawing.
- Some students could: complete grid in sketchbook. Trace/transfer de Worde woodcut.

Homework
Locate and print Limbourg brothers' illumination from specified web page.

Health and safety reminders
Always to cut away from body and not towards anyone else. Use of bench-hooks; do not put free hand in front of cutting blade (demonstrate). Wash hands thoroughly.

Materials/equipment
Lino plates, iron, lino handles ×24, lino cutters ×24 (No. 2 blade), bench-hooks ×24, old towel rags/oven gloves for protection of non-cutting hand, sugar paper/newsprint, tissue/ brushes/matt medium for extension, worksheet 4, coloured pencils, tracing paper, Pritt sticks, scissors, dark and light green printing ink, rollers, press, sheets of newsprint, homework handouts, sketch books, de Worde woodcut photocopies, display materials, examples of printed marks in students' previous work.

Lesson sequence

10.25 *Introduction*: settle round front table and register students. 'Aprons on'.
10.30 Gather students. Explain aims, printing lists and order of printing for lesson, both dark and light green prints. Stress: health and safety 'golden rules'; gauge types and lines/marks (use plane landing metaphor). Highlight lesson's aims on whiteboard. Check to see who has started or has completed dots and lines worksheet already. Explain that all will need to finish this. Check identity of monitors. Monitors to distribute blocks, boards and tools, paper and pencils for rubbings.
10.36 Explain to all, especially light greens that they will be cutting out dots/lines/marks in landscape. With biro, draw these onto surface of lino. Model, using dark pen and light paper. Also biro onto model lino plate. Must not cut lino until I have seen design. Stress: how will we know if our blocks will make a good print? (Demonstrate block rubbing to check quality of line.) Explain tasks while not cutting/making print, i.e. collages, grid, de Worde tracing. Check for anyone not sure what to do.

Transition: students to move to their various tasks.

10.45 *Main episode*: dark greens begin printing. Cutting, printing, extension work.
11.00 When first light green is ready, demonstrate to whole class how light green is to be printed. Are you happy with block 1? Did you make a rubbing to check it?
11.05 Light green printers should have begun printing.
11.25 Have class begin to clear up. Pack away and clean equipment and tables.

Transition: packing away and sitting to receive homework. Stress: only monitors need to move around, as last week. Everyone to help tidy tables. Gather lino blocks and rubbings on front table.

11.30 Set homework: go through requirements and check understanding of task. Ask students to pick examples of lino blocks/rubbings and comment on success criteria. What was difficult/easy about today's lesson? What have you learned about drawing for printmaking? What are the main limitations/advantages of linocuts for illustrations? Praise effort and good work.

Conclusion: dismiss class when all assembled and ready.

11.40 Lesson ends.

Exercise
Before reading on, consider what seem to you to be the main strengths and any weaknesses of this plan and note them down.

This was a lesson that involved complex resources, tight timing and attention to health and safety issues. The practical demands alone of organizing the lesson are considerable but not unusual for secondary art lessons. The strengths of the plan seem to lie in its evidence of detailed thinking about a number of issues.

- Rich and interesting activities, linked to good examples.
- Some attention to pace and intellectual/artistic demands.
- Good attempts to refer to key learning aims and objectives.
- Some attention to differentiation, by outcome.
- Careful attention to resources needed and to their management.
- Careful attention to timing, so that all activities are fitted in.
- Inclusion of appropriate ICT for homework.

At first sight, the weaknesses seem mainly to be the scant attention paid to the students, their past knowledge, their cultural background, their level of skill or their interests. The learning demands of the lesson are not made very explicit, in terms of accretion, restructuring, etc., and we hear rather little about assessment. Nor are aims for the teacher's own developing teaching made explicit. However, to be fair, all these matters were dealt with in the student teacher's background scheme of work.

In the **scheme of work** the student teacher had considered her students, the curriculum and assessment at greater length. In particular she had considered how to bridge the gap between the art being taught and the students' own interests and world. Cultural diversity and special needs were not in fact major factors with this class. Many kinds of book illustration were to be examined, including genres more immediately appealing to this age group. A focus of the scheme of work was to build students' understanding of the ways in which drawing systems can be used to shape and inform printing processes such as linocutting. Much of the work was new, involving (in this lesson) an appreciation of fifteenth-century art and practising the key skills of drawing and making blocks for printing in new ways.

In the scheme of work the student teacher drew on her specialist curriculum course to differentiate between:

- **declarative knowledge,** i.e. knowledge *that* certain things are the case (e.g. that wood blocks were used in the fifteenth century for printing or that different blades produce different marks); and
- **procedural knowledge,** i.e. knowledge of *how* to do something (e.g. how to use drawing to indicate marks for linocutting or how to make a two- or three-colour print).

This distinction had been used to think productively not only about student learning but about the assessment of that learning over the period of a term. This involved two formative assessments in which students were required to reflect on their learning in relation to targets, with a view to improving it as the scheme progressed. The teacher intended to provide critical feedback to individuals during each lesson and also to make a summative assessment of the entire project with a view to setting new targets for the next term. (For the significance of the terms 'formative' and 'summative' see 15.2.)

Student teachers are normally expected to evaluate their lessons on a regular basis. In the case of the art teacher we have been considering, she had an ongoing dialogue with a mentor and a visiting tutor, which involved a written record examining her progress in teaching. (Hence the lack of aims for teaching in the lesson plan: they appeared elsewhere.) If you have difficulty knowing how to set about evaluations, ask yourself what aims you had in your planning for your own teaching and for the students' learning. If these were present in your planning, you have the starting points for your evaluation. Then ask yourself what events in the lesson surprised you or were unplanned. Consider how these affected the process of learning and the outcomes. Try to write not only about practical points of classroom management, but also about your own developing teaching and your assessment of the students with whom you were working: what have you learned about them? And what have you learned about the curriculum you were teaching? Think about whether you can recognize issues that have been raised by your reading of this book, or by your course, and see if you can recognize connections with what happened in your lesson. Lastly, consider how your evaluation will feed forward into your future plans.

With so much emphasis on planning it is easy to lose sight of the fact that some events and outcomes in lessons may not have been planned at all. This, however, is not necessarily a bad thing. However the unexpected and spontaneous will face you with the need to make judgements about whether the new idea or line of thought is relevant to the curriculum you intend to teach. Some tasks will also be fairly predictable and constrained in how they turn out, whereas others will be much more open and allow a greater degree of student choice. Even if you are constrained as to the content of the curriculum you teach, you should be able to find plenty of opportunities for students to make choices, to become involved in their own learning and even to contribute to its planning. The more you let them in on the secret of what school is all about, the better opportunity they will have to understand how to manage their own learning effectively (10.6). The quality of planning should follow through into the quality of lesson evaluation. This should then inform future planning, in a regular cycle. If they are working properly, you should be able to gather clear evidence both of effective teaching and also of your own development as a teacher.

5.7 Questions

The following questions are designed to help you check your understanding of the chapter.

1 What particular difficulties with planning do you face as a newcomer to a school?
2 What five elements should be present in a simple lesson plan?
3 There are many lesson plans available on the Internet. What is one of the problems of using them?
4 Do all learning aims need to connect with observable outcomes?
5 What advantages and disadvantages are there to observable learning outcomes?
6 Name several of the 'more complex issues' that planning should address, when appropriate.
7 What might you write about in a lesson evaluation, apart from practical issues?
8 **Discussion question**: 'The key to effective lessons is the careful design of the task.' How far do you agree?

NOTES

1. With thanks to www.primaryresources.co.uk
2. Strictly speaking the Aztecs were practising horticulture not agriculture, but this is a dimension of subject matter knowledge that was understandably absent in this KS2 lesson.
3. For further reading on the use of ICT in teaching see, for example, Sharp et al. (2002), Kennewell et al. (2002) and Drage (2002–3).
4. For further reading on English as an additional language see National Literacy Strategy (2000).

PART II

The Psychology of Human Learning and Motivation

This second part of the book is concerned with the psychological knowledge base for teaching. It will set out what I believe to be the most important things we know about how people learn and how teachers support them. It will start with a series of three chapters about human learning, which aim to show that learning in school has a relationship with other more general kinds of learning but also that it has some distinctive features of its own.

- Chapter 6 is about relatively simple intuitive forms of learning.
- Chapter 7 is about our innate mental capacities and about cultural forms of learning.
- Chapter 8 concerns the challenge of deliberate learning, which is the main preoccupation of schools.

Thinking and learning are much influenced by our emotions, feelings and motives.

- Chapter 9 provides a broad survey of human motivation.
- Chapter 10 concerns influences on student motivation in the classroom, including their beliefs and theories about the self.
- Chapter 11 considers the general development of the mind, including material concerned with thinking, emotion and interests.
- Chapter 12 explores some individual differences among learners, focusing on intelligence, temperament and parental influence.

CHAPTER SIX

Intuitive Learning

6.1 Introduction

We have already encountered learning in Chapter 2, where it was introduced by way of Rumelhart and Norman's model, which emphasized the main phases of the learning process over time: accretion, restructuring and tuning. In this chapter we step back from the classroom to take a broader view of the nature and variety of human learning. Various kinds of informal learning are surveyed, including:

- learning through imitation;
- habituation and perceptual learning;
- learning associations between events;
- informal problem-solving;
- implicit learning.

All these forms of learning have in common the fact that they are relatively spontaneous and natural ways of adapting to the world. They occur across all human cultures, whether or not schools or teachers exist.

6.2 Effortless Learning

Schools are a relatively modern invention, dating from a few schools for the elite in ancient civilizations, such as Greece and Rome, and medieval schools, which mostly sought to train priests, doctors and lawyers. Only in the nineteenth century did the phenomenon of mass schooling first appear, in Britain and other newly industrialized nations. Long before that, however, humans were learning in more informal ways how to adapt to the way of life into which they were born.

Example 6.1 Imitative play

Colin Turnbull spent some time living with the BaMbuti pygmies, a hunter-gatherer people who lived in the heart of the Ituri forest in Zaire, Africa. He describes typical play among the children.

> Like children everywhere, [BaMbuti] children love to imitate their adult idols, and this is the beginning of their schooling, for the adults will always encourage and help them. What else do they have to be taught except to grow into good adults? So a fond father will make a tiny bow for his son, and arrows of soft wood and with blunt points. He may also give him a strip of a hunting net. The mother will delight herself and her daughter by weaving a miniature carrying basket, and soon boys and girls are 'playing house'. They solemnly collect the sticks and leaves, and while the girl is building a miniature house the boy prowls around with his bow and arrow. He will eventually find a stray plantain or an ear of corn, which he will shoot at and proudly carry back. With equal solemnity it is cooked and eaten and the two may even sleep the sleep of innocence in the hut they have made.[1]

This account describes a timeless scene, which has been played out in every human culture, across space and time. Imitation is a fascinating ability, which deserves more space than it will receive here. Considerable brainpower is needed to imitate human actions successfully. Babies only a few days old have been shown to watch the movements of people's mouths and to imitate simple mouth opening and tongue protrusion. To do this, they have somehow to coordinate their visual perception with their face muscles so as to produce a 'match', for after all they cannot see their own faces. At 18 months of age, children will sometimes imitate an adult's action, completing the action even when the adult model did not complete it.[2]

In contrast to this ability to 'read' the intention behind, or likely shape of, an action, Stephen Pinker[3] cites the example of a chimpanzee raised by the researcher Laura Petitto in a human house. Her project involved teaching the chimp sign language, at which he proved adept. This intelligent animal (affectionately named Nim Chimpsky) used to imitate some of the actions of washing up plates, but never cared whether or not the plates got clean. Only the rough circular washing movements of the human model were being imitated, not the activity of cleaning dishes. Human children, in contrast, do become aware of the goals of actions. The children observed by Turnbull in their typical imitative play in the forest were no doubt perfectly aware of what they were doing, at one level, but may not have realized that they were learning vital skills. Spontaneous play is a rich context for learning of many kinds, but children play not to learn but because they like playing.

For most of the time that humans have lived on the earth they have not felt any need for schools. Our 'environment of evolutionary adaptation', i.e. the way of life for which we evolved and to which our biological heritage is best fitted, is generally thought to be that of hunting and gathering.[4] Hunter-gatherers, of whom only a few groups still survive, live in small nomadic bands. Generally the men hunt animals and the women gather nuts, roots and other edible plants. In such cultures, children generally become adults at around the age of 12–16 years. They learn a complete way of life, often involving extensive knowledge of the landscape, plants, animals and other natural materials, together with many skills necessary for survival. Typically, hunter-gatherer children observe adults carrying out all the many activities that make up their way of life and imitate them. They practise many skills through play and participate along with adults in social activities, often fulfilling minor tasks such as fetching and carrying materials. Occasionally they will ask older respected adults for advice or instruction but this is relatively rare. Observation, imitation, practice and informal social participation suffice for most learning.[5]

In case the example above sounds somewhat idyllic it may be as well to state that life for hunter-gatherers is, in many respects, very tough indeed. They literally depend on their wits and their accumulated knowledge to survive. Hunting and gathering was the only way of getting by for some 95% or more of our time on earth. About 10,000 years ago, humans learned how to domesticate certain crops and animals. Agricultural societies were born and, on the basis of the surplus food they produced, a settled way of life developed, which led to extensive trade, specialized crafts and the building of cities. In traditional agricultural societies, which still exist in many parts of the world, the way to expertise in the various skilled crafts lies through a long apprenticeship, full of mundane low-level practice. This generally takes place under the guidance of a 'master', but it is usually notably short on formal instruction. Once again, observation, imitation and long practice suffice, although the practice might often be conducted under the beady eye of the master, who supplies verbal feedback. Typically, only small numbers of children have been educated to become literate professionals, such as priests and scribes.

Informal, intuitive kinds of learning are thus typical of the early history of humans and predominated right up until the Industrial Revolution. This chapter concentrates on such intuitive learning, which is often an effortless side-effect of experience and which certainly still goes on in schools. It is not centrally dependent on language or teaching and it is often unconscious, in the sense that the learner 'picks up' certain habits and skills without deliberately setting up learning as a goal. I am not arguing that no teaching ever took place, anywhere, before schools were common, but rather that formal teaching was relatively rare whereas intuitive learning was common.

6.3 Perceptual Learning and Habituation

The easiest example of such learning is the way our perceptual systems tune in to familiar faces and voices. Without ever deliberately setting out to learn them, we all recognize the voices of friends and family over the phone and the faces of most people with whom we regularly interact. We do not have to try; it just happens as a side-effect of living. Similarly, we learn our way about familiar places and we learn everyday skills, of dressing, eating, cooking and managing household appliances. This latter kind of skilled behaviour also depends on a good deal of trial and error practice, although imitation and perceptual learning may contribute. Such simple examples of learning are quite similar to the even simpler processes of light adaptation and habituation. If we move from a bright to a dark place, our eyes take a little time to become adjusted to the new level of illumination but the adjustment happens automatically.

If we experience almost any sensations or perceptions repeatedly, we gradually pay them less and less attention until they may become an unnoticed part of our surroundings. This process is called **habituation**. For example, you are so habituated to the feel of your clothes against your body that you are probably unaware of any such sensation as you read this. But when reminded, you can easily 'dishabituate' and pay attention to the tactile cues of your clothes against your body. When we learn to ride a bicycle (a learned sequence of skilled movements), at first we have to attend with great care to what we are doing. But with practice we eventually reach a point at which the brain once again 'takes over', regulating our balance and steering, while we are free to attend to other things, such as the passing countryside or a friend's conversation. (Even the absence of a normal stimulus may result in the opposite of habituation, i.e. dishabituation. People who live near a railway line sometimes wake up in the night because a regular train has not passed by!)

In all these simple examples, learning is taking place, in the form of adaptation, recognition of a voice, habituation or management of skilled movements, without our being aware of how it occurs. Indeed we do not even have to pay conscious attention to what is going on. Habit and habituation tune us in to the routines of everyday life. They relieve us from the constant necessity to think about what to do next and they account for a very wide range of everyday behaviour.

6.4 Learning Associations and Beyond

The mechanisms for learning, including those responsible for habituation and habits, are embodied in our nervous system, the brain together with its specialized perceptual and memory systems. We were born to learn. Learning has also been shown to start from very early on in life.

Example 6.2 Babies control sucking for visual or auditory rewards
Bruner[6] summarizes the brilliant work of a number of psychologists who studied the innate reflex behaviour of sucking in babies, and showed how they could start to use it voluntarily from an extraordinarily early age. Luckily for us, babies know how to breathe, swallow and suck instinctively, without any teaching or learning (though sometimes they try to do two of these things at once and run into problems). Their instincts take time to perfect, however, and they need some days to learn to become expert suckers for milk. Early efforts to 'connect' with the supply are often clumsy and frustrating for one and all. But babies also suck non-nutritively, probably as a sort of comfort procedure, at a regular rate, regardless of whether they are hungry. Moreover, while sucking starts off as embedded within the instinctive system for feeding and digesting food, the mouth eventually becomes one of the baby's main methods of exploring the world. Give a baby almost any manageable object, from a strawberry to a set of car keys, and it will put it to its mouth to explore orally.

Babies normally suck with their eyes closed. By about 9 weeks they will suck, pause and look, and then suck again. By 3–4 months, roughly, they can suck and look at the same time. Bruner describes experiments with 3-month-old infants who were shown projected coloured pictures on a screen. The babies were able to learn to vary their sucking actions, sucking either more or less when this activity resulted, via some ingenious machinery, in making the picture become brighter or keeping it in focus. The babies would increase (or if necessary decrease) their rate of sucking in order to obtain the visual reward of a clear picture. Later, DeCaspar and Fifer[7] were able to show that even babies in the first 2 days of life were able to control the rate of their sucking, on a specially designed rubber nipple, so as to switch on a tape recording of their mother's voice as opposed to a stranger's voice. They preferred to listen to their mother's voice and could use the process of trial and error learning, using feedback, to gain access to it. Thus babies are able and active learners from the very start of life and will often vary their behaviour to gain pleasure and avoid pain or discomfort.

All learning must result in some change to our memory, for if we remember nothing we simply have not learned anything. But although learning and memory are two sides of the same coin, we are by no means always conscious of what we have learned. A smell, say a certain kind of furniture polish, or the taste of a biscuit dipped in a cup of tea can sometimes catch our attention and reawaken a memory of a similar smell from a far-off place, years ago, which we never attended to with our conscious minds. An old friend gives us a call and in seconds we recognize the voice as familiar (although putting a name to it is sometimes rather harder!). This kind of memory, which some psychologists call **episodic memory**, is like sediment from our experiences, laid down without effort, unconsciously and automatically. Much of it is forgotten within a few weeks or months, unless we repeat the experience often or the experience was important enough to be frequently called to mind again. You can probably remember exactly what you did this morning when you woke up, but what about yesterday? What about a week ago? What about this same day a year ago? In fact episodic memories may still be stored somehow, but we generally lack the power to access them by recall. Everyday forgetting may be a simple economy for the brain.

Many species of animals learn and their learning is very much like this kind of intuitive human learning. Early theories of learning assumed that both humans and animals learned basically by associating one thing with another. If a dog heard a bell often enough just before food was presented, it would start to salivate when it heard the bell. If a pigeon were rewarded with water for pecking at a disc, then it would learn to peck the disc when thirsty. Perhaps the babies described above simply associated sucking with a picture that came into focus or with their mother's voice? However, although we, along with these other animals, do learn to make associations, especially when they seem to predict the future pattern of events, it is not enough to say that learning consists of making associations, together with a bit of observation and imitation.

When a child learns to talk, for example, she learns not merely sequences of repeated sounds, paired with objects in the world, but the rules which link word endings and word order to sense. She learns that 'the cat licked my brother' is different in meaning from 'my brother licked the cat' or from 'my brother liked the cat'. She learns that 'the village green' means something other than 'the green village'. Moreover a child who learns to say something like 'car go vroom!' could not have learned to do so simply as a result of imitating adult speakers, who never say such things (unless they are imitating a child), or from having simple chains of sounds repeatedly rewarded. It seems altogether more probable that the child is operating creatively with its own version of a set of rules for producing grammatical sentences in English.

6.5 Informal Problem-solving

Still sticking with simple intuitive forms of learning, the way our minds work by using reasoning and strategy in our actions can also be illustrated from work on children's trial and error problem-solving. When children encounter a new situation or problem for which they have no well-tuned solution, they have to start to think strategically, and to experiment in an informal way. Anne Brown and her colleagues have shown how such trial and error problem-solving grows in power during childhood and yet retains some common features of its overall shape.

Example 6.3 Strategies for problem-solving

DeLoache and colleagues[8] watched pre-school toddlers (2–4 years old) trying to work out how to fit together a set of 'nested' plastic cups they were given to play with. They were originally shown the full set put together and then the cups were taken apart and given to the child. The youngest and least experienced children tended to try to fit any pair of different-sized cups together, at random. If a pair did not fit, the child tried brute force, pushing harder in an attempt to make them fit. If this failed they abandoned the two cups and tried a new pair. A more successful strategy, tried by some, was to keep hold of one of the cups and search for a better partner for it but if this failed, again the child was likely to drop the cups and start again. Slightly older and more experienced toddlers had learned two more strategies: sometimes they tried reversing two cups, trying to fit 'a' into 'b' instead of 'b' into 'a'. Sometimes they had learned to take a cup and insert in between two other cups in the correct order in the sequence.

One noticeable feature of this study is that the younger and less successful children seemed to experiment at random with the cups, whereas the older and more successful ones seemed to be able to think, to some extent, about each cup as one member of a complete series. Their overall understanding of the problem was thus a more powerful one. Another interesting feature is that all the children persevered with the problem for a considerable time without help or encouragement. They worked away at the problem and they corrected some of their mistakes. They kept going in spite of frustration. Their curiosity and desire to 'master' the task seemed powerful motive forces.

Brown and Reeve[9] then carried out a very similar study with older children aged from 4 to 7 years. These children were shown a simple model train track, made out of eight pieces of inter-linking plastic track, some straight and some curved. The track was dismantled and they were asked to reconstruct it. Once again, younger children tended to start with any two pieces, trying to fit them together, whereas older children considered each piece in relation to the whole set. Less successful children again tried to use brute force when dealing with a hopeless arrangement of the pieces. They tried the odd local correction and if this did not work they would disassemble the track and start again. The more mature and successful children incorporated the strategies of reversing a piece and/ or inserting a piece between two others in order to help their solutions. A few children even moved on to innovate, finding two different ways of assembling the complete track.

Other psychologists have shown a similar pattern of developing strategies over longer periods of time in more complex learning, for example in studies of children's progress in drawing maps of a model landscape[10] and in revising drafts of their writing.[11] Over longish periods of time and repeated attempts at the problem, there is a ragged forward progression towards competence, with minor advances and retreats along the way, and the gradual acquisition of new strategies, implying a better understanding of the problem situation (see also Example 7.8). Older children generally (but not always) perform more competently across a very wide range of tasks and this is a result both of the gradual natural **maturation** of the nervous system and of their experience with the world. It is, of course, notoriously difficult to separate these two contributors, maturation and learning. The brain becomes more efficient as it grows, but its growth is also influenced by experience.

Putting the last few examples together, there seem to be some very general stages in the progress of everyday problem-solving, which relate both to a learner's age and to his or her initial degree of knowledge. We can describe the broad stages as follows:

- initial curiosity and trial and error investigation;
- partial understanding;
- consolidation of an effective strategy for solution (or failure and rejection of the problem);
- elaboration of the solution;
- renewed innovation;
- ability to describe both the problem and its solution.

With little or no knowledge of a problem, both children and adults make relatively blind trial and error attempts at solution, which typically involve looking for familiar patterns, engaging with isolated elements and often encountering frustration and failure. Partial understanding leads to partial solutions, which may work only with much time and effort or which ignore troublesome parts or cases that do not fit. A complete or satisfactory solution often leads to a new understanding of the nature of the problem, and how it relates to other problems. Further practice may then lead to a smooth and practised routine solution or to the discovery of alternative solutions.

6.6 Becoming Aware of Knowledge

Turning a solution into a routine may involve a number of moves, such as *describing* the problem and its solution in words and concepts, *memorizing* key facts, *honing* skills or learning to *apply rules* (thus moving on from the simple kinds of intuitive learning described so far in this chapter). Annette Karmiloff-Smith[12] argues that children start off with simple implicit knowledge of a concept or skill, which is closely encapsulated within the original context of learning. But once it is learned, at an intuitive level, the child then spontaneously initiates a process of **representational redescription**. This involves producing a new and simplified version of the knowledge in conscious, often verbal, thought. It loses many of its original perceptual details but becomes more abstract, manageable and can be used across different situations, or domains of knowledge.

A zebra, for instance, becomes a 'stripy animal'. The connection of the animal with a 'zebra crossing' is then a relatively easy move for the child to make. To take another example, knowing how to play a game starts as intuitive knowledge about simply joining in, but eventually can be described, to the self or to others, in terms of the goals, the rules and the moves of the game.[13] In this way we humans seem to make repeated cycles through the stages of problem-solving, developing slowly from no understanding at all to a routine solution process that can be applied with relatively little thought. We may finally evolve an abstract representation of the solution, which can be generalized and communicated to others. These later stages of the cycle, however, involve exactly the elements of language and social interaction that we shall look at in the next chapter.

Meanwhile let us summarize the forms of learning so far considered as examples of intuitive learning. These are listed below and can be seen to share a number of features:

- perceptual learning;
- habituation;
- observation and imitation;
- informal practice at skills;
- informal trial and error problem-solving.

All these can be found in other animals as well as humans. They are rooted in perception linked to memory and action. Sometimes they may include some deliberate thought, as when a person focuses their attention on imitating an action or deliberately trying to solve some problem, but often they are unselfconscious. The learning frequently occurs as an unconscious by-product of experience. Even in the case of problem-solving, the person may focus on the problem and its solution but give little or no thought to the learning that the solution involves.

6.7 Implicit Learning

Intuitive forms of learning are not merely relics from the past or confined to the years of childhood; indeed they probably saturate our everyday experience. This applies not only to habituation and perceptual learning, which are going on more or less all the time, but more generally to **implicit learning**. We often seem to have an intuition about how to do something (make friends, dance, beat an opponent at tennis, act a part, imitate an accent) without pausing to articulate our proposed solution, to see if it makes sense. This may be because we do not have the time, in the flow of events, or because we simply do not know how to put our skill or knowledge into words. We can do it but we do not know how we do it. We know more than we can say.

Example 6.4 Implicit learning
Berry and Broadbent[14] investigated a computer task, or game, which simulated the job of running a factory. The subjects of the experiment had to juggle with many factors, such as the size of the workforce, hours worked, pay and the cost of materials, so as to stabilize the factory's output at a certain level. The subjects were allowed to play the game for quite a long period and they generally succeeded in getting the factory to produce the output required. However, when questioned about what moves they were making or why they had chosen them, they were mostly unable to give clear answers. They tended to say things such as that they were 'following a hunch' or that a move 'felt right'. Over several days, with a complex version of the problem, their practical ability to run the factory ran far ahead of their explicit knowledge, articulated in answers to questions. Explicit knowledge did eventually emerge, but well after practical solutions had been found. They groped their way forward.

This experiment describes what is probably a familiar enough situation to most of us. Musicians, teachers and athletes are other groups who are often better able to operate skilfully in a complex situation than to articulate exactly how they do what they do. They are operating intuitively but skilfully. Guy Claxton[15] contrasts such implicit learning, or 'learning by osmosis', with (i) instantaneous instinctive reactions and (ii) what he calls 'd-mode thinking', where the 'd' stands for deliberation. In instantaneous reactions, say to suddenly losing one's grip on a glass and then catching it again or slamming on the brakes when a dog walks out in front of your car, the action is far too fast for conscious thought. The perception–action parts of the brain simply do what they can, executing their best guess as to what might work. At best, such fast reactions are a matter of 'having one's wits about one' as we say.

In d-mode thinking, in contrast, we consciously try to use our knowledge to solve problems that we first define for ourselves *as* problems. We wrinkle our brows and try to think. Deliberate thinking is purposeful and effortful. It seeks for explicit, clear, satisfying answers. But in 'osmotic' learning, Claxton's third kind of thinking, the brain discovers patterns, and tunes our habitual responses to well-known situations, quite unconsciously and non-deliberately. This kind of 'slow thinking' also operates in a playful, leisurely, contemplative way when we are relaxed and off-guard, not focusing our thinking deliberately on anything in particular. Ideas sometimes 'pop' suddenly into our minds or just 'occur' to us at such times. Claxton's main point is to argue that these three different modes, or speeds, of thought are all useful but for somewhat different kinds of problem-solving. Intuitive 'slow' thinking may be best at producing creative ideas for example, and conscious d-mode thinking at analysing and evaluating them critically. Clearly, d-mode thinking (and learning) is non-intuitive thinking and yet it is central to the kind of thought (and learning) we consistently try to promote in classrooms.

6.8 Learning as Adapting to New Situations

We have begun, then, by thinking about learning as the means by which humans adapt intuitively to situations, making use of their innate intelligence and their experience. Each person brings a personal history of learning to any new situation encountered. With repeated experience the person learns how to be competent in that situation by making use of what we might call the 'know-how' they bring with them. The 'situation' to which the person is adapting is itself made up of many elements, including the physical and material surroundings, people, objects and tools, and social and institutional rules and language, to name some of the most important. What any one learner notices in a situation will depend on that person's prior history and current purposes. She or he will then typically begin to act, using whatever competence seems appropriate to the situation.

If there is no match between the person's 'know-how' and what the situation seems to afford them, they are likely to try to leave it, seek help or become passive. If the match between 'know-how' and situation is very high, the person will simply act, using their existing knowledge, and nothing new, or almost nothing, will be learned. But very often a new situation is only partly familiar and then the learner will try to adapt, or 'tune in', to the situation so as to cope or succeed.[16] Once the learner is satisfied with a certain level of competence in that situation, he or she is likely to stop learning. His or her 'know-how' or 'understanding' may fit that particular situation, but it will not be a perfect fit to any other. But how are we to describe what has been learned? The outcomes of learning, or changes to what I have called 'understanding', can exist in a bewildering variety of forms. Some of the most important are listed below:

- physical adaptations and habituation;
- perceptual learning;
- imitated sequences of actions;
- learned sequences of skilled movements;
- change in attitudes or values;
- discovery of a new strategy;
- understanding of concepts;
- remembering facts;
- learning of a rule;
- increased conscious awareness of our own thinking, learning, etc.

This list is not intended to be the last word on what one might learn, but rather an attempt to indicate how varied the outcomes of learning may be. Anything that can be part of memory can be an outcome of learning. In this chapter, we have considered only the first six of these outcomes, deliberately postponing the last four, which all commonly make use of language and culture, to the next chapter.

6.9 Questions

The following questions are designed to help you check your understanding of the chapter.

1 What kinds of learning were common among hunter-gatherers?
2 What is habituation?
3 What is episodic memory?
4 What are the main stages of everyday trial and error problem-solving?
5 What does Guy Claxton mean by 'osmotic learning'?
6 Name some of the varied outcomes of informal learning.
7 What links together the different kinds of learning considered in this chapter?
8 **Discussion question**: comparing the treatment of learning in this chapter with that in Chapter 2, what similarities and differences can you find?

NOTES

1. Turnbull (1984), p. 119.
2. Meltzoff (2000).
3. Pinker (2002).
4. Barrett, Dunbar and Lycett (2002).
5. Lee and De Vore (1976).
6. Bruner (1969).
7. DeCaspar and Fifer (1980).
8. DeLoache, Sugarman and Brown (1985).
9. Brown and Reeve (1987).
10. Feldman (1980).
11. Graves (1983).
12. Karmiloff-Smith (1992).
13. Piaget, J. (1932, 1965).
14. Berry and Broadbent (1984).
15. Claxton (1997).
16. Resnick (1994).

CHAPTER SEVEN

Innate Capacities and Cultural Learning

7.1 Introduction

In Chapter 6 we looked at the simple and almost automatic ways in which we adapt to the world and pick up memories of our experiences along the way. So far learning seems both natural and easy. In this chapter we shall move on from such simple intuitive forms of learning to slightly more complex forms, which are strongly influenced by the operations of our language and culture. But first we need to take a brief look at cognitive psychology, the dominant psychological approach to studying the mind. This research has made much use of the analogy between minds and computers, both of which represent and transform information. Cognitive psychology has also led to speculations about the extent to which we are born with some innate mental capacities that are a consequence of the long process of human evolution. These may be important in making some kinds of learning more 'natural' than others. After this, however, the chapter will turn to the vital contributions of culture to human learning. These include playful interactions with the world, conversations with adults and more serious encounters with work. The chapter ends with a section on the ways in which children develop new ideas and strategies.

7.2 The Computational Theory of Mind

In the past 20–30 years, psychologists have been trying to work out how humans do all the apparently simple but actually fearsomely complicated things that we do with our senses and our thinking and language.[1] For us nothing could be easier or more natural than to walk down the street, recognize a friend coming towards us, start a conversation, exchange some news and walk on, remembering the last time we met. But trying to figure out how a machine, or a mechanism such as the brain, could achieve these taken-for-granted accomplishments is extremely difficult. Cognitive psychologists, working with other disciplines such as linguistics and neuroscience, have also been trying to explain how much of the structure of our minds is inborn, or innate, and how much is developed from our experiences of life.

Now, for teachers this fundamental research has had rather little interest or pay-off. Teachers are all too aware that Ashley can talk, recognize friends and remember what happened last night; they want to know why he always forgets his PE kit. They know that Lucy can switch her attention between her maths book and her neighbour's new shoes and crack jokes as she does so; they want to know how to get her to concentrate better on her work. Teachers, in other words, do not care all that much about *how* such things are done. They are more concerned with how learning so often goes wrong, and how to improve it. But to the cognitive psychologist these abilities are the basic functions of the mind's artful web: attention, perception, memory and language, not to mention emotions and passions. Thus most of cognitive psychology has become quite technical and most teachers do not read it.

Cognitive psychologists argue that the brain is somewhat like the hardware of a very flexible and powerful computer, whereas our knowledge and our memories are like the software and data that make the computer work. We will take a glimpse at this computational theory of mind, in order to make clearer the kinds of cognitive abilities that humans routinely use yet which we tend to take for granted. It is not that psychologists these days believe that the mind *is* a computer or even that it shares many features with the lumps of plastic and silicon that sit on our desks. Rather, the computer operates as an analogy for the mind, because of a key similarity between them. Both minds and computers process information about the world. They both deal in representations of the world and they both carry out operations on those representations in order to make sense of the incoming data and to predict future outcomes. Computers are also useful for testing explicit and very detailed theories of how parts of our minds might work. Essentially you run a version of your theory on a computer and see if its output shows similarities to the achievements and errors typically made by humans faced with the same task. If so, the logic underlying the computer program is inferred to be the same as that used by the mind.

The earliest computer models of the mind made use of programmed series of instructions, as in a digital computer program, to simulate processes such as perceiving, remembering and thinking. Although they had their successes, they proved limited in various ways. One key problem was that they were quite poor at pattern recognition. This is the extraordinary human ability to recognize any number of different versions of a symbol, such as the letter 'a', whether it is hand written or typed, printed in different fonts, or scrawled in paint on a wall. It is exactly the sort of perceptual ability we take completely for granted. We can do it automatically yet we cannot explain how we do it. The exact form of a written or printed 'a' changes in myriad ways and yet amazingly we can still rather quickly and easily recognize each version as the first letter of our alphabet. Building a machine that can do this trick has proved very difficult. A second generation of models of the mind, which use general purpose 'neural networks', has proved to be rather better at pattern recognition.

These so-called 'connectionist' models imagine the mind as a series of networks. Each network consists of elementary units, containing representations of the world (at some level), which are linked together and communicate with one another. Units affect other units by exciting or inhibiting them. A single unit is influenced by the overall input it receives from all the other units linked to it, 'firing' if the sum exceeds some threshold value. This threshold at which a single unit fires can alter with feedback, thus changing the way the network as a whole functions. As the network goes through cycles of repeated stimulation, it changes the thresholds of its units so that gradually the overall output alters to fit some desired pattern (the goal of the system). Since our brain cells are also known to form such networks, the analogy between the computer and the brain seemed a promising one. However the simpler kinds of connectionist models still lack both the flexibility and structure that seem to typify human cognition. They are quite good at pattern recognition, but not so good at language or reasoning with categories.

Steven Pinker[1] gives a number of examples illustrating ways in which humans do more than just alter the weightings of simple neural connections during thinking. For example, when we recognize that the phrase 'a Venetian blind' is very different in its meaning from the phrase 'a blind Venetian', we are showing that the elements 'blind' and 'Venetian' can each operate either as an adjective or as a noun, as a describer or as a thing described. Somehow the cognitive system has to represent this difference, which is just one of simply thousands of such distinctions used in language alone. Connectionist models struggle to do this economically. Another problem concerns individuals. When we hear that 'our cat got stuck up a tree today', we know that a particular individual cat is being described. Like all cats, it will probably have whiskers, a tail and paws but we cannot even be sure of this; it might be a tail-less cat or have one leg fewer than the normal ration. In any case, not all the features that define or characterize cats will belong to 'our cat' and vice versa. Bob Dylan is not to be confused with other Bobs, or other Dylans for that matter. Even if we replace one table with another identical one, we know that we are dealing with two separate tables, even though they may share every feature we can think of. Again, accounting for this in a connectionist model, which simply defines any table as the sum of all the properties of a table, leads to complications, involving layer upon layer of elements with more and more specialized functions, until the model seems unrealistic and cumbersome.

A third problem concerns our ability to think either 'fuzzily' or precisely about concepts. We often think of a concept via a stereotype, such as a typical bird or a typical mother, or whatever. In the case of 'bird' we seem to focus on a rather small bird with wings and a beak, like a sparrow or blackbird. Birds, we think to ourselves, are feathered creatures that fly, eat worms and build nests. But of course not all of them do: there are flightless birds, birds that eat fish and birds which breed in burrows. However, in experiments, people do recognize the stereotyped visual image of a bird more quickly than they recognize images of less conventional birds, such as penguins, eagles or owls. They say that a blackbird is a 'better' example of a bird than a seagull, which is strange in one way but matches our intuitive way of thinking about such things. This fits connectionism well, because it suggests that our concept of bird is strengthened the more bird-like properties (connections?) an example projects to us. But we can also be fussier when we choose to be. We can think like biologists do about the exact criteria that define the class 'bird', or indeed 'mother' or 'table'.

Kinship terms illustrate this nicely. All human cultures recognize kinship relations, such as mother, aunt, cousin, sister and so forth, and they have precise rules for each one (e.g. first cousin means an offspring of the sibling of a parent). The rules vary a bit from one culture to another, but in each they are used in precise ways, for instance to decide on questions of inheritance. We can reason with these concepts and rules and make inferences. We know, for example, that if we have a first cousin then we certainly also have, or had, an uncle or aunt. We know that our own grandmother also had a grandmother, who in turn had a grandmother, and so on. Somehow we carry both the fuzzy stereotype (a little old grey-haired lady of a grandmother) and the sharper rule-generated classification (which might include, say, Joan Collins) around in our heads at once. Connectionist models are not good at modelling such systems of concepts and rules that we can thus use so flexibly and productively.

7.3 Innate Structures of Mind

Psychologists who are critical of connectionist models are not necessarily giving up the computational theory of mind. Many of them simply think we need theories that equip the mind with more built-in innate structures. These structures would be the products of natural selection, evolved over many generations to solve specialized kinds of problems that faced humans in the environment to which we are biologically adapted. One likely candidate for such a specialist structure is our visual system. This perceptual system has variable focus, stereoscopic vision, an ability to judge how far away an object is, a facility for recognizing faces and an ability to track the movements of objects in space. Mostly it works without any conscious attention on our part at all; indeed we cannot 'see' its workings with our conscious mind. Like many parts of the mind it remains 'non-conscious'.

Example 7.1 Infants notice odd visual events
Infants have been shown to have surprisingly advanced abilities to make sense of objects moving about in space, with little or no opportunity to learn about them. Many such studies measure the infant's habituation to a repeated display. This simply means that an infant will get bored and pay less and less attention to a display as it is shown over and over again. The experimenter then tests to see if the infant shows signs of renewed interest (dishabituation) when a difference in the display is introduced. If he or she does, then we infer that the infant has noticed something new. Thus Elizabeth Spelke[2] and others have demonstrated that infants aged 3–4 months old react with renewed interest to a variety of 'anomalous' visual events. In a typical example, the infants were repeatedly shown an object disappearing behind the left-hand end of a screen and reappearing at the right-hand end, until they paid it little attention. Then the same object again disappeared behind the screen but reappeared not at the right-hand end of the same screen but from

behind a different screen, some way off to the right, without traversing the space in between. Normally this would be impossible and sure enough the infants showed renewed interest in this strange happening, suggesting that they had at least noticed that something different had occurred.

In another example the infants were shown a ball falling behind a screen. The screen was then removed to show the ball, stopped by a hidden shelf. After habituation to this original display had occurred, a second shelf was placed below the first one. When the ball fell behind the screen it was revealed as having ended up on the lower shelf. The infants, amazingly, reacted to this with renewed interest. There was something anomalous about the situation, as the ball seemed to have passed 'through' the upper shelf onto the lower one and these very young infants somehow appeared to perceive the oddity of what had happened. Such experiments suggest that a considerable amount of potential knowledge about objects moving through space is 'hard-wired' into our neural circuits in the course of evolution. Infants seem to expect objects to be cohesive solid bodies that move and interact in consistent predictable ways. When these assumptions are upset, the infants show a special interest.

Such examples illustrate that we bring certain capacities and understandings with us into the world at birth. Or we might say that a baby implicitly *anticipates* that the world will be a certain kind of place. A human intelligence is very different from that of, say, a seagull, a spider or a chimpanzee. Each species has evolved specialized forms of adaptive perception and behaviour; each is adapted to a particular way of life. Recent research has been building up a strong case for the existence of a number of specialized 'modules' in the human brain.[3] But if many of our mental structures have evolved and are ready and waiting in the structure of our brains at birth, does this mean that learning and culture are unimportant? People tend to get worried about this, but the answer is a resounding 'No!' One of the special evolved features of the human brain is precisely its amazing ability to learn. Learning only exists and works because our brains and perceptual systems are designed by evolution to learn. More copies of our ancestors' DNA were produced because learning turned out to be a powerful strategy, which helped them survive and reproduce. Culture is also a human speciality, involving such things as language, social organization, tool use, soap operas and scratch cards. These are everyday things we can deal with but they are totally dependent on the integrity of our nervous systems. For better or worse, both soap operas and scratch cards are restricted to use by humans.

Language, to take a single example, exists because we have evolved brains that can understand and produce grammatical sentences. Even though it is a thoroughly cultural affair, for after all there are thousands of different languages, each with an arbitrary set of sounds that combine to form words, language is also a part of the natural physical world. Words are sounds, vibrating in the air, or they are ink marks on paper, or some other form of matter and energy. Our explanations of, say, hearing will depend on references to physical matters such as sound frequencies, eardrums and auditory nerves. Our explanations of understanding sentences, to give a contrasting example, will depend on cultural concepts such as word sounds (phonemes), word meanings and syntax. Neither kind of explanation (the physical or the cultural) will displace the other, for each is needed at its own level. Rather than thinking of nature and culture as opposed forces, with opposing systems of explanation, we should recognize that culture emerged out of nature, and that nature has been transformed, in its turn, by culture. Culture and nature have to get along with one another.

There are those who oppose the computational theory of mind, arguing that it cannot do justice to our sense of meaning, of significance and subjectivity.[4] Otherwise, cognitive psychologists are currently mainly concerned with the dispute over how much of our mental life is accounted for by special evolved structures in the brain, such as a module for sentence comprehension, and how much it depends on more general, content-free neural capacity. These psychologists passionately believe that such research will one day have pay-offs for practical fields like education. So far, however, teachers are probably not convinced. For teachers, the overwhelmingly important fact is simply that we accept that children do recognize patterns, understand sentences, reason about family relationships and so forth. But it matters that we are appreciative of what children can do, quite early on, in the way of learning.

7.4 Early Competence

It is not easy to do justice to the innate capacities we are born with, the influence of the social context (or *situation*) on our performance and the influence of the transferable knowledge that we carry around with us from one situation to another, as memory. At the end of the last chapter, we left human learning at the point at which language and social interaction were about to enter the picture, to make a significant difference to more solitary intuitive methods. First, however, let's have a reminder of how young children use perception and action in an intelligent and playful exploration of the world.

Example 7.2 Making the coffee pot lid rattle[5]
Standing by the side of a low table, a 12-month-old girl bangs on a pegboard with a block she has been holding; at the far end of the table the lid on an improperly closed coffee pot produces a loud rattle. The little girl freezes; her eyes explore the tabletop. She hits the pegboard again, and the small movements of the lid attract her attention. She moves over, picks up the lid and rattles it against the pot; then back to her pegboard and block. She bangs: the lid rattles. The little girl gurgles, a wide smile appears on her face. A glance at her mother – still with that enormous smile – and on with her banging and the pot's rattling, to an accompaniment of gurgles, babblings, and small bounces of delight.

This little girl has found through her play a connection in the world and discovered that she can use her own actions to control it. Children love this kind of mastery of their surroundings and search it out in their everyday play and problem-solving. In a way, the situation itself evoked the problem. But children live surrounded by other people, who talk to them and interact with them. From about the age of 1 year or 18 months, they start to respond by talking back, first in one-word utterances and then, amazingly swiftly, with two- and three-word combinations. By the age of about 5 years, they can understand and use most of the main grammatical structures of their mother tongue. This undoubtedly depends on complex innate capacities that happen to underpin even the use of sign language by hearing-impaired children.[6] The acquisition of language, in turn, makes a huge difference to children's learning, as the following example illustrates.

Example 7.3 Anthony learns about paint[7]
Anthony (3¹/₂ years old) is watching his mother, who is painting the bathroom.

Anthony: You're painting.
Mother: Oh yes. Dreadful stuff, paint. It gets everywhere.
Anthony: What it do?
Mother: Gets on everything . . .
Anthony: [*Acknowledging*] Mm.
Mother: . . . and everywhere, when it's wet.
Anthony: Oh God! Does it get over me and er, my Daddy?
Mother: No. Mind out the way, sweetheart.
Anthony: My Daddy get it on him?
Mother: When he does painting, he does, yes.
Anthony: He does, doesn't he? He gets it on his hair.
Mother: Does he?
Anthony: Mm, and he gets it on his jacket.
Mother: I don't think Daddy would paint with his jacket on, darling.
Anthony: With his coat on, he do.

In such situations, the child's curiosity leads the talk, with his interest controlling what is talked about. This moves away from the present observable situation to things about the 'paint problem' that cannot be seen and are quite abstract and general. The mother does a good job helping Anthony, giving him information and offering corrective feedback. Anthony even takes the initiative towards the end, insisting on what he knows about his Daddy, when it comes to paint. This kind of dialogue, rooted in the child's own interests, is surely a rich context for learning about words, about paint and about parents. Anthony simultaneously learns about language and about the world. By the age of 4¹/₂ years, when many British children start school, they are already knowledgeable members of their culture. They may be tongue-tied in the Reception class, but not only can they understand and use the major types of spoken sentence, but they can also recognize and use concepts, remember facts, understand simple analogies and metaphors, search for the causes of events and interpret the intentions and beliefs that lie behind typical human actions and the characters in stories. As an example, consider the ideas involved in the following conversation between a parent and an American child of 4 years 2 months, who had seen several Judy Garland films on video.

Example 7.4 Reasoning about events[8]

Child: Did Judy die because she was old?
Parent: No, she wasn't very old when she died.
Child: Then why'd she die?
Parent: She got sick.
Child: Why'd she get so sick if she wasn't old?
Parent: I think because she didn't take care of herself. I remember reading that she ate and drank all the wrong things, things which weren't healthy.
Child: Why? Didn't she know what was good to eat?
Parent: I think she did but I read that she was sad and I guess she didn't think about taking care of herself.
Child: She was sad? What made her so sad like that?
Parent: I don't know, but it makes me sad for her.
Child: Me too. Why was she so sad? Why wasn't she happy and proud that she had made all those beautiful movies?

This child shows that she knows that there are causes of death, that old age may be accompanied by ill-health, that health depends partly on knowing what one should eat, that sadness (depression) has causes and that success and achievement normally produce feelings of happiness and pride. Her general knowledge, her linguistic competence and the way she pursues a line of questioning are all impressive. Focusing on her language for a moment, we can note her use of such words as 'because', 'why', beautiful' and 'proud'. Studies of children's vocabularies have concluded that they must somehow acquire an astonishing average of some seven to ten new words every day. This sounds impossible but typical 6 year olds have a receptive vocabulary (i.e. can understand the use) of around 14,000 words.[9] This early vocabulary growth mostly occurs via comparatively effortless, or implicit, learning, and before the child learns to read. Much of it happens in everyday dialogues with a parent and others. From here onwards, however, the rate of vocabulary growth depends a great deal on schooling, and especially on reading and writing. One study[10] estimated that 11 year olds in the USA were learning an average of 4875 words per year, but that this varied staggeringly from a low of 1500 words to a high of 8250 words per year, depending largely on how avid a reader the child was.

7.5 Theory of Mind

One of the most important abilities of young children is to understand other people's behaviour. Without this ability to go behind the observation of actions, to infer what people are trying to do, what they want and what they know, most of the social world would remain baffling. Infants like to look at faces, particularly at eyes. By 6 months of age, infants can tell if they are being looked at and by 1 year they can follow their parent's direction of gaze, attending to whatever the adult is attending to.[11] This 'joint management of attention' is crucial to learning with and from other people. At around 18 months to 2 years, children typically start to 'pretend' in their play, making a distinction between pretence and reality, one that they often share with their caregivers. They know, for instance, that a mother who pretends that a banana is a telephone, putting it to her ear and talking, is just playing, rather than having gone completely crazy.

Probably as a result of another specialized innate 'module' in the brain, they also quickly start to make guesses about the beliefs and desires that lie behind other people's behaviour, formulating an intuitive psychology. By about 4–4$^{1}/_{2}$ years of age, this 'theory of mind' as it has been called, is quite sophisticated, as has been shown in tests of 'false belief'.[12] In a classic experiment, a child is shown a tube of Smarties (for Americans, M&Ms) and asked what they think is inside. Not surprisingly they say sweets. But then they are shown that this particular tube actually contains pencils (a typical psychologist's trick!). Next they are told that a second child will be coming into the room and seeing the tube. What do they think this second child will think is in the tube? To succeed at this (by saying 'sweets'), the child has to distinguish between his or her own knowledge (that the tube contains pencils) and the beliefs of the new child (who has not yet seen inside the special tube). At around 3–4 years of age children often fail this test, saying that the new child will think there are pencils in the tube, but from 4–4$^{1}/_{2}$ years they start to succeed.

Knowing that someone else has different beliefs and different desires to yours is fundamental to understanding their actions. Children with autistic spectrum disorders are often incapable of this kind of intuitive psychology, i.e. reading the minds of others.[13] They seem to be stuck in a world in which if an adult puts a banana to her ear, she is just one (large familiar) object moving another (small yellow) object next to a sticking out bit near the hair on top. This 'mindblindness', as Simon Baron-Cohen has named it, turns out to be a constitutional fault in the system, a limitation of the innate mechanisms of mind, which although varying considerably in its intensity and effects, may limit the autistic person's participation in the world in many ways. It is a striking, if tragic, example of how we depend for our normal human intelligence on an intact and normal human brain.

7.6 Learning as Apprenticeship

Many psychological studies of learning take place in university laboratories and they often treat learners as individuals operating on their own. But as we know, humans typically live in cultures and are intensely social animals. In their home setting children usually have all kinds of social support for their everyday problem-solving. They can often watch more competent adults; they can ask for help; they can take part in social tasks by taking on the less skilled parts of the task. Some psychologists have seen these socially interactive ways of building up competence as central to how humans can and normally do learn. They treat learning as a kind of **apprenticeship** for living in a culture.

This kind of learning features lots of opportunities to watch how adults do things, and active support from more competent others when the child makes an attempt. Common routines and real purposeful tasks typify such learning, which thus contrasts quite dramatically with much classroom learning. Competence in this apprenticeship tradition is seen as a by-product of **guided participation** and as inextricably mixed up with the tools, routines and language used in each everyday context.

Example 7.5 How street sellers learn maths

In many developing countries children live on the streets and have to earn a precarious living without the benefits or security of schooling. In Brazil, one way that children earn a living is by selling small packets of candy (sweets). Aged between 5 and 15, the children buy the different sorts of candy from wholesale shops and then have to decide at what price to sell them. At the time when Saxe[14] studied them, they were dealing with a Brazilian currency, the cruzeiro (Cr$), that was suffering from an appalling inflation rate of 250% per year. Currency notes ranged in value from about Cr$100 to Cr$10,000, and the children had to not only receive money and give change, when selling different combinations of items, but also make sure that they had priced the items so as to make a profit yet remain competitive with the local competition. In spite of their woeful lack of a formal knowledge of arithmetic, the children coped amazingly well. For example, they would commonly use more than one pricing ratio, selling say one bar for Cr$200 and three for Cr$500 rather than $600, but they generally knew which ratio would make them a larger profit. If they sold two bars for Cr$500 and five bars for Cr$1000, giving a discount for the larger quantity, they realized that this eroded their profit margin.

They mostly recognized the value of the bills they were handling from the colours and pictures on them, rather than by reading the standard notation of figures. When Saxe asked them to put lists of large numbers, written in the standard form, in order (e.g. 1000 > 500 > 200, etc.) their performance was poor, with only about 40–50% of the problems correctly solved. When comparing actual currency notes, however, with the standard figures taped over or cut out, their ability to compare and order the same sums shot up to over 90% correct. They could add a pile of 17 different bills to a sum of Cr$17,300 and correctly give change for a purchase of Cr$7600 from a bill of Cr$10,000.

Saxe found that the youngest children, aged around 6 and 7, were much less competent in their calculations and in fact relied on the wholesale shopkeepers and older peers to help them price their goods. They started off with only a few items for sale and with simple prices. However, with experience and supported by the social network of the family, other street sellers and sometimes sympathetic customers, they quickly learned more sophisticated strategies and calculations. No doubt the knowledge that they might be cheated, or fail to turn in a profit, contributed strongly to their motivation to learn. The older more experienced sellers could solve problems such as the following: 'Suppose that you bought this bag of Pirulitos, and you must decide the price you sell the units for in the street. Let's say that you have to choose between two ways of selling: selling one Pirulito for Cr$200 or selling three for Cr$500. Which way do you think that you would make the most profit?'

Some of the older children did have experience of learning arithmetic in school but this group did not perform significantly better than their peers who had no school experience with these sums, except on the one task which involved using the standard form for writing numbers.

These street sellers had built up an effective, but very narrow, type of arithmetical competence, closely embedded in the social practices of their lives as sellers. However, they could not transfer their methods easily to formally presented school arithmetic problems, any more than their schooled peers could transfer their classroom arithmetical knowledge to the currency problems of the candy sellers in the street. If one approaches learning in this way, 'learning as participation' tends to be a dominant idea. It is then natural to think of learning as 'tuned', or closely attached, to the situation: the people, the materials and the format of the activity itself. The commonly observed failure of people to **transfer** their learning from one context to another is then not surprising. A concept such as addition or subtraction will continually evolve with each new social occasion of use. Learning, in this version of events, is always under construction and always rooted in context. Sometimes knowledge is said to be 'distributed' between people, tools and materials in the situation.

However, it is possible to think of transfer in another way. One might instead think of classroom learning as a rather special attempt to reach a deeper, more thorough and context-free kind of knowledge. By the end of schooling, we might argue, the core of a student's knowledge should be so robust that it will survive transfer across most situations. Solving the problem of transfer would then be a matter of recognizing that only a deep and thorough understanding, together with an accurate memory of, say, arithmetical problem-solving, will result in learning that successfully survives changes in context. A highly numerate person can quickly solve problems to do with buying and selling, in any currency and in any social situation. A literate person can make some sense of almost any text. True independence as a learner, in other words, depends on very sound learning that can be generalized. If this is so, however, we must also immediately confess that school learning has often failed in this aim. This is a matter to which we shall have to return in the next chapter.

7.7 Acquiring New Strategies and Ideas

In Chapter 6 the emphasis was on intuitive ways of learning, which are often subconscious, easy and non-deliberate. In this chapter we have still kept clear of classrooms and teaching, but have moved on to consider innate capacities, social interaction and oral language as the greatest resources available to the young human learner. A child, or indeed adult, can hit upon a new idea or strategy in a number of ways: he might be told it by someone else, such as a teacher in direct instruction; he might infer it from what someone else says; he might himself mentally draw an analogy between this problem and one he can already solve; he might spontaneously notice something new while problem-solving; he might deliberately think the problem through and reason his way forward to a new synthesis. Observation, listening, dialogue, reasoning and imagination are all possible ways forward. Sometimes the new idea will first appear unconsciously, implicit in action; sometimes it will begin as a consciously understood, verbalized idea. Implicit and explicit learning can both work. One common form of learning involves reasoning by analogy.

Example 7.6 Finding analogies

Reasoning by analogy involves comparing one problem, say how to share out a pizza, with another problem already experienced, say sharing out slices of a cake. The two problems correspond, in that cutting into slices will solve each one. Analogies thus depend on spotting the relevant correspondence. (An example of a more imaginative analogical solution involved how to scrape frost off a car windscreen, when no proper scraper was available. My wife seized an outdated plastic credit card and used it, very effectively, to clear the windscreen. She had spotted the correspondence between an ordinary plastic scraper and a plastic credit card.)

It has been claimed that children as young as 11–13 months are able to reason by analogy in the context of getting hold of a toy.[15] In this study, to reach the toy each infant had first to push aside a barrier (a box), then draw a cloth towards them, on which lay a string, attached to the toy. Pulling on the string brought the toy within reach. Following the first trial, the problem was repeated with a new toy, with the added difficulty that two cloths and two strings were presented, only one of which was attached to the toy. The toys, boxes, cloths and strings were also changed in appearance for each trial. Amazingly, some of the older infants solved the very first trial without help, although most needed their parent to model the solution for them first. Once the first problem was solved, however, most of the 13-month-old infants readily applied the same strategy to the analogous problems. The 10-month-old infants needed more help, for example by keeping the toy the same for each trial, but then were often successful. Did the infants really reason by analogy or were they learning simply by observation and imitation? It is hard to say.

A more convincing demonstration is provided by studies of a more difficult kind of analogical reasoning, known as 'relational reasoning'. This takes the form 'A is to B, as C is to −?' Thus a child might be asked to find a picture to complete the series 'bird is to nest, as dog is to −?' The possible picture solutions offered are of a bone, a cat and a kennel. Usha Goswami[16] showed that, provided they were dealing with familiar pictured materials, even 3 year olds could solve such problems as 'chocolate is to melted chocolate, as snowman is to −?' Of course to solve any of these problems, one has to notice the similarity involved. Anne Brown has shown, in a whole series of studies,[17] that children only tend to notice the crucial similarity, or correspondence, if they have actually represented it to themselves as part of the remembered structure of a previous example. Brown also showed that cueing the children to notice the relevant feature, or repeating a series of similar problems, or directly teaching the children about the correspondence all greatly enhanced their performance. This has obvious relevance to teaching children about relationships, analogies and similarities of all kinds. Whether children notice the vital correspondences in analogies is a rather hit or miss affair, but we can point them out; we can teach them! Goswami herself has shown that children commonly read new words (e.g. 'knight') by analogy with familiar ones (e.g. 'light', 'fight').

Strictly speaking, it is clear from some of these examples that analogies can and do suggest themselves to learners quite spontaneously, without either social guidance or even language being involved. However, teaching and cueing are so helpful in this process that analogical reasoning has been included in the present chapter, rather than in Chapter 6. As well as acquiring new ideas (accretion), learning can consist of making new links between ideas, working out a more effective understanding (restructuring) or executing existing solutions more effectively (tuning). The need for spontaneous concepts to be restructured by more systematic teaching in school is highlighted by the following example.

Example 7.7 The shape of the earth
Stella Vosniadou[18] has studied children's understanding of the shape of the earth by asking them a series of questions, such as 'If you were to walk for many days in a straight line, where would you end up?' Although most children have learned somehow from their culture that the earth is 'round', it turns out that they have conceptualized this 'roundness' in many ways. In a study in Urbana, Illinois (USA), 60 middle-class children at an elementary school, evenly divided between ages 6, 9 and 11 years, were asked individually to answer this and many other similar questions. Examples from the resulting dialogues are as follows.

> Jamie (third grade, 9 years old)
> E: What is the shape of the earth?
> J: Round.
> E: Can you draw a picture of the earth? [*Child draws a circle to depict the earth*]
> E: If you walked for many days in a straight line, where would you end up?
> J: Probably in another planet.
> E: Could you ever reach the end or the edge of the earth?
> J: Yes, if you walked long enough.
> E: Could you fall off that end?
> J: Yes, probably.

> Terina (fifth grade, 11 years old)
> T: The earth is round but when you look at it, it is flat.
> E: Why is that?
> T: Because if you were looking around it would be round.
> E: What then is the real shape of the earth?
> T: Round, like a thick pancake.

Vosniadou eventually categorized all the results in six groups, depending on models of the earth as a sphere, a flattened sphere (so you can walk on it), a hollow sphere (with people living on a flat surface inside), a dual earth (a sphere, and also a disc which people live on), a disc (or pancake shape) and a rectangular earth (flat but square). A true sphere was the choice of just three 6 year olds, eight 9 year olds and twelve 11 year olds (38% of the total sample). Vosniadou went on to carry out similar studies in some other cultures and found the same overall picture, with interesting cultural variations. Thus Indian children commonly said the earth was a disc, or dish, supported on water; this corresponds with a traditional Indian cosmology.

Vosniadou argues that in all cultures children begin by assuming that (i) the earth is flat and (ii) unsupported objects fall downwards. They are then told that the earth is 'round' or spherical and try to work out a model that preserves their two primitive assumptions together with the new information. Thus we can see that in science, our conscious deliberate learning requires us to abandon many of our most natural ideas in favour of strange scientific notions. We have to learn to put our misconceptions, our notions of 'common sense', on hold in order to grapple with difficult new ideas.

Such results remind us once again that simply giving children information does not ensure that they will learn adult concepts directly from it. Restructuring remains a crucial process, which can be greatly helped by mediation provided by a teacher. Secondly, the results, and others like them, suggest that common-sense views of the physical world are naturally and consistently different from current scientific accounts and that science teachers have somehow to take these naive misconceptions into account in their teaching.

Newton's laws of motion have repeatedly been shown to be counter-intuitive even to university students. Common sense suggests that objects stay still until acted on by a force; also that moving objects will gradually slow down and stop from some kind of inertia, unless kept moving by some effort, or energy. Contrary to these two assumptions, Newtonian physics states that linear motion is a state; only changes in motion (such as acceleration) require an explanation in terms of a force. In an ideal vacuum, objects will continue to move unless acted on by a force. Again, when asked to draw the path of an object, either dropped from a moving plane or from the basket of a person walking along the street, many people draw the object falling at right angles to the original path of the plane or person, failing to take into account the initial forward momentum of the object itself.

Lauren Resnick[19] argues that the original design of the brain, in terms of domain-specific modules, means that some curriculum knowledge will be easier to learn because it simply extends, or builds on, naive preconceptions, whereas other items, such as Newton's laws of motion, appear contrary to our spontaneous reasoning. As argued in section 7.3, the mind is not a blank slate at birth, but carries in its specialist structures certain evolved expectations about the world. Research on early conceptions of number and counting is an example of knowledge that partly fits and partly fails to fit well with later schooled arithmetic. Although children as young as 3 and 4 years can add simple sums such as 'two apples add one apple makes three apples', they cannot do the (apparently identical) problem 'add two and one'. They say things like 'two and one what?'[20] Although the explanation for this is not agreed on, it seems likely that it has to do with the connection that primitive counting has with the world of everyday countable things. Two apples can be seen and handled; 'two' cannot.

The splitting away of sets and numbers from everyday actions and perceptible quantities was a tremendous cultural leap (as was the association of letters with sounds, rather than words, in the invention of the alphabet). For children to make the leap they require help. However, the properties of commutativity and associativity of numbers seem to be assimilated quite easily by children as a single rule that numbers can be combined additively in any order. Thus 7 and 8 year olds were shown by Resnick sometimes to deal with problems such as 23 + 8 by first decomposing 23 to give (20 + 3) + 8, then reconfiguring the problem as (20 + 8) + 3, then counting on 3 from 28 to give the correct answer.

We have already looked at accretion, restructuring and tuning. Siegler[21] draws attention to yet another way forward: making increasingly adaptive choices between alternative available solutions.

Example 7.8 The overlapping strategies theory and early arithmetic
Robert Siegler has found that children often have alternative strategies in their repertoire, which are used on different occasions to solve the same kind of problem. These strategies may coexist over long periods but, with experience, faster more accurate strategies gradually replace slower or less accurate ones. At any given moment, more than one strategy may be used by the child, though each one will have a different probability of use. Siegler has found that most young children use at least three different coexisting strategies in his studies of time-telling, remembering lists of memorized items, arithmetic and spelling. For example, in learning to add simple single-digit numbers such as 3 + 5, young children use some or all of the following strategies.

1 Sum strategy: count one number (perhaps using your fingers), then count the other number (sticking up extra fingers), then count the total of both numbers (count all the fingers used). Thus 3 + 5 is dealt with by counting '1, 2, 3 (pause) 1, 2, 3, 4, 5 (pause) 1, 2, 3, 4, 5, 6, 7, 8'.
2 Shortcut sum strategy: counting on from the first number '1, 2, 3 (pause) 4, 5, 6, 7, 8'.
3 The 'min' strategy: counting on from the larger number '5 (pause) 6, 7, 8'.
4 Memory strategy: simply recalling the number bond from memory '8!'

By studying children intensively over a period of weeks, while several of these strategies were in play, Siegler was able to show that the shortcut sum strategy was a transitional one, often preceding the child's spontaneous discovery of the 'min' strategy. In the shortcut sum strategy the child still starts off from 1 (as in the sum strategy) but only counts each number once (as in the 'min' strategy). The 'min' strategy may then appear as a realization of redundancy in the count up to the first number, and the added realization that if one starts from the larger number, one saves time.

In any case, children often hang onto an older strategy after learning a new one. This may be because they are more confident in the efficacy of the old method (the sum strategy may be tedious, but after all it does work) and because they make more errors when first using a new strategy. When you are almost sure that 3 + 5 = 8, you may still not trust your memory if there is a lot at stake (e.g. if the teacher calls on you to answer in front of the whole class). This trade-off between confidence, accuracy and speed means that change in strategy use is a gradual process.

Secondly, children sometimes discovered a new strategy after successfully solving several problems with an older strategy. Sometimes it was failure that led to experimentation with a new strategy, but sometimes it was success. The children are probably not aware that all this is going on, but it may still be an example of growing conscious insight into a problem, as they work on it. To them it may just be a matter of trying to work out a sum, but slowly they build up more conscious awareness of how they do it (6.6).

Siegler found a tendency for children to learn faster if they initially used a variety of strategies rather than sticking always to one. It seems that flexibility is good and too much inflexibility (linked to anxiety?) is bad. Siegler suggests that flexible approaches may reveal more about the problem domain. Interestingly, the new strategies that children used generally made some sense even when they did not always yield correct solutions; they showed a developing understanding of the problem. Siegler points out that his research has parallels in studies of changes in the brains of animals learning a task. In such studies a new task has been shown to lead at first to a proliferation of new neural synapses (connections between brain cells) followed, after further experience, by a process of 'pruning' to a smaller set of, presumably efficient, connections. Lastly, Siegler claims that asking children to explain both why correct answers are correct and why incorrect answers are incorrect produces better learning than questioning only about correct answers. It seems to lead children to generalize more effectively about the whole set of problems, uncovering new strategies and new understandings.

7.8 Summing Up: Cultural Forms of Learning

We have, at last, arrived at an example of learning in the classroom. The main aim of the present chapter, however, has been to continue to argue that humans can learn in many different ways, and to suggest that language and culture, together, provide powerful resources for going beyond the simpler forms of intuitive learning considered in Chapter 6. Building on our innate mental capacities, we use language and social interaction to construct an elaborate model of the world. The main additions to our list of types of learning are summarized below:

* learning through dialogue;
* learning through guided participation;
* learning by reasoning, as in the use of analogy;
* learning from being told.

These are all still 'natural' kinds of learning, in that they often happen quite spontaneously and informally. In the next chapter we will look at more formal teaching, in relation to learning, and also at the roles of practice and transfer.

7.9 Questions

The following questions are designed to help you check your understanding of the chapter.

1 If our brains are the 'hardware' what is the 'software'?
2 What key similarities have been noticed between minds and computers?
3 Name one of the difficulties faced by connectionist models of the mind.
4 What features of mother–child dialogue seem to aid learning at home?
5 Describe the 'false belief' test. At about what age is it first passed?
6 Give two examples of possible innate (human) mental structures.
7 What is meant by 'guided participation'?
8 What is the 'problem of transfer'?
9 How is teaching often helpful to learning by analogy?
10 What implications might we draw, as teachers, from Vosniadou's findings about children's conceptions of the earth's shape?

11 **Discussion question:** to what extent are you learning to teach by using the kinds of learning described in Chapters 6 and 7? Are these sufficient? Do you need anything else?

NOTES

1. Eysenck and Keane (1995); see also Pinker (1997, 2002).
2. Carey and Spelke (1994).
3. Pinker (2002).
4. For example, Searle (1992).
5. Bronson, quoted in Flavell (1985).
6. Petitto and Marentette (1999).
7. Wells (1986).
8. Schulman (1991), p.16.
9. Smith (1992).
10. Nagy, Herman and Anderson (1985).
11. Lee and Homer (1999).
12. Gopnik and Welman (1994).
13. Baron-Cohen (1995).
14. Saxe (2002).
15. Chen, Sanchez and Campbell (1997).
16. Goswami (1998).
17. For example Brown, Kane and Echols (1986).
18. Vosniadou (1994).
19. Resnick (1994).
20. Hughes (1986).
21. Siegler (2002).

CHAPTER EIGHT

The Challenge of Deliberate Learning

8.1 Introduction

The message of Chapters 6 and 7 was largely to do with how humans can learn without formal instruction, or teaching. But schools aim to extend learning far beyond everyday knowledge. Good teaching can speed up learning and, at its best, inspire and encourage as it does so. One could argue that learning in school with professional teachers is, in one sense, 'unnatural' in that children are grouped together, away from the struggles of other adults making a living, with the deliberate intention that they should learn the content of a carefully prepared curriculum. Although learning in the classroom presents some special problems (see Chapter 3), its potential power to transform people's lives is considerable. There is a case for seeing learning in school as a specialized form of *deliberate learning*, with much higher goals than those of the craft apprentices, street sellers or children learning intuitively we encountered in the previous two chapters.

The chapter starts by explaining the work of Vygotsky, a Russian psychologist who has had a strong influence on the way we think about teaching. It continues with an example of a kind of teaching (reciprocal teaching) that was deliberately modelled on Vygotsky's ideas. Next, the main features of a contrasting tradition, teaching by direct instruction, are considered. Then the main difficulties of deliberate learning are set out, in terms of remembering, understanding and applying knowledge. This is a kind of learning that is seen here as central to the work of schools. A project that tries to meet at least some of these problems (Cognitive Acceleration of Science Education, CASE) is then briefly summarized. The chapter goes on to look at how practice affects learning and focuses specifically on a provocative research programme that suggests that deliberate practice can be extremely powerful in its effects. It concludes with some personal reflections on the implications for schools of the view of learning set out in Chapters 6, 7 and 8.

8.2 Vygotsky on Teaching and Learning

School learning sets out to develop the mind in ways that have the potential to free people from the limitations of their everyday culture, by inducting them into the most powerful disciplines of knowledge that humans have so far discovered. However, this rather lofty aim has to be reconciled with the gritty reality of life with children in a classroom, who do not always understand what is at stake. It also has to be reconciled with the more mundane but perfectly reasonable aim that schools should prepare children for working life, in a rapidly changing democracy. We all desperately want school learning to succeed, but how do we go about achieving it? We cannot examine how best to teach without considering what view we take of learning, especially learning which is deliberate and conscious rather than casual and intuitive. This turns out to have some quite unexpected and unpalatable consequences that I shall try to explain at the end of this chapter.

One of the most persuasive accounts of how teaching works is that provided in the sparse but brilliant published works of the Russian psychologist Lev Vygotsky, who died in 1934. His writing was rediscovered in the West and translated into English in the 1960s and 1970s.[1] Vygotsky started from the observation that children born into any culture acquire the language, social skills and knowledge required by that way of life, mainly by participating in activities with experienced others. His thinking thus fits neatly into the view of learning already introduced in Chapter 7.

Vygotsky also thought that culture, with all its resources of people, knowledge and technology, was the key to the education of the mind. He argued that not only knowledge itself but also the main psychological functions of the mind – such as memory, reflective thinking, planning and problem-solving – first developed in children through the process of social interaction with other more knowledgeable members of a culture. He thought that each new major mental accomplishment comes about in two steps. Firstly, it is experienced at a social level, in interaction with others. Then the child takes this new way of thinking into his or her own mind and operates with it independently. Thus, to give a simple example, young children at first usually encounter instructions from their parents and learn to follow them. Later, however, they begin to instruct themselves, using similar words and phrases, planning and monitoring their own activities with the help of language. Verbal thought comes about in this way, Vygotsky believed, starting with the outer exchanges of social conversation and then being put to work in a silent inner dialogue with the self. With young children, some of the dialogue with the self is still spoken aloud, and thus can be overheard.

Example 8.1 From dialogue to reflective thought[2]
Simon, aged 4 years 9 months, has just eaten an apple and is examining the pips. He explains to his mother what he might do with them:

A pip is a seed. So he can grow. And we might be able to grow some now. Got some apple seeds – apple pip seeds – and if I put even more, Daddy and me might go out one day, which isn't a rainy day, and we might be able to plant the seeds. Or I could plant them tomorrow.

Here Simon is using words and phrases that he has undoubtedly heard his parents use. Now, however, he appropriates them for himself, beginning to use language as a tool for his own thinking and planning.

Vygotsky stressed that with development children gradually learn self-regulation, by such means as planning, monitoring and self-criticism. Children are first drawn into these self-regulating activities by way of guided participation in socially valued activities. More experienced others take over those aspects of the task that the child cannot yet manage alone, supporting or 'scaffolding' the child's efforts. Adults or teachers thus act as mediators between the child and the culture. Through such support, or scaffolding, the child is enabled to reach a new level of competence, which she or he could not have attained alone. Thus parents, elder siblings and other teachers stretch the child's efforts towards new learning and higher standards, only relinquishing their aid when the child can take over the performance on his or her own. This process of teaching has been called **assisted performance**.[3] Children's readiness to profit from instruction, or from practice, depends of course on where they have reached in their learning. Vygotsky[4] described the need for teachers to assess what he called the **zone of proximal development** for a particular child. This is the level of competence with any given problem that goes just beyond what the child can manage alone.

A child can continue to make progress in learning within the zone of proximal development, but only with some skilled assistance. Teaching thus operates by attempting to move the learner forward via assisted performance. This is identical to what we described as interactive teaching in Chapter 1. The teacher may support the learner's partial solutions, suggest new strategies or provide helpful feedback about the current state of understanding. Later in the cycle, teaching moves on to the setting of problems for independent practice and encouragement of a clear understanding of how a solution was reached.

The transfer of activity from the outer social context to the inner private world of the mind results in the development of what Vygotsky called the 'higher mental functions'. These higher functions or advanced forms of thinking, such as planning, reflecting, reasoning and evaluating, are typically conscious and deliberate. They often make use of the symbolic resources of the culture, its language and symbol systems, its ways of thinking and concepts. The richer the culture is in symbolic languages and representations, the richer the potential for the child's learning. One of the results of such conscious deliberation is to free the child, bit by bit, from the domination of his attention by immediate events happening around him. He (or she) can begin to regulate thinking and attention, resisting the 'capture' of attention by every passing sight and sound. Children who go to school have such extended thinking supported by the resources of literacy and numeracy, together with all the concepts and ways of thinking encountered in other school subjects.

A further idea of Vygotsky's is that children's own early intuitive experiences lead them at first to form informal or 'spontaneous' concepts from particular instances, which lead only to hazy generalizations. 'Triangle', for example, might initially be understood by a child to refer to just one particular plastic shape found in a box of construction toys, or several such shapes. However, when triangles turn up as a concept in a school maths lesson, they include each and every three-sided plane shape that could ever exist. These 'schooled' concepts (Vygotsky called them 'scientific concepts') are more explicit and systematic. They gradually lead the child's thinking in the directions of abstraction and generalization. Thus, for Vygotsky, school should move the child gradually away from the restrictions of everyday experience and towards the shared languages of a literate, educated society.

Vygotsky was largely a speculative thinker and he died before his work was complete. Other scholars have since attempted to develop and test his ideas in more detail, but perhaps Vygotsky's great popularity in recent years has been mostly a consequence of his relatively simple and clear conceptual account of teaching. Teaching aids learning by bridging the gap between the student and the knowledge within a culture. It does this job of **mediation** via the process of assisted performance. Assisted performance operates effectively within a zone of proximal development for a given problem and student. This way of seeing things gives teachers a strong role in the process of schooling, without denying the natural ways in which humans are capable of learning on their own.

Example 8.2 Reciprocal teaching
Examples of educational research that actually develop and test effective new methods of teaching are regrettably rare. However, one successful example, developed by Ann Brown and colleagues,[5] examined reciprocal teaching. It owes an acknowledged debt to Vygotsky's ideas. Reciprocal teaching was developed to help a specific group of readers, aged around 7 to 13 years, who are able to recognize words fairly well but are poor at comprehension. A teacher, specially trained to use the method, works with a group of about six students at a time, each having a copy of the same text. They all read a short paragraph silently. The teacher then models four processes of comprehension:

- asking a question about the meaning of the passage;
- summarizing the main meaning of the passage;
- predicting what the next passage is likely to be about;
- raising any questions or matters for clarification, if appropriate.

Having modelled these procedures, the teacher asks the students in turn to take the role of teacher, proceeding through the sequence of asking a question about its content, summarizing the main message, predicting what the next passage will be about and, if appropriate, raising matters for clarification. The teacher continues to monitor how well the students succeed at these tasks, scaffolding their efforts and using the normal tactics of interactive teaching. Here is a short excerpt from a reciprocal teaching session, with the extract first and the dialogue following.

The second oldest form of salt production is mining. Unlike early methods that made the work extremely dangerous and difficult, today's methods use special machinery, and salt mining is easier and safer. The old expression 'back to the salt mine' no longer applies.

L: Name two words that often describe mining salt in the old days.

K: Back to the salt mines?

L: No. Angela?

A: Dangerous and difficult.

L: Correct. This paragraph is all about comparing the old mining of salt and today's mining of salt.

Teacher: Beautiful!

L: I have a prediction to make.

Teacher: Good.

L: I think it might tell when salt was first discovered, well, it might tell what salt is made of and how it's made.

Teacher: OK. Can we have another teacher?

With daily sessions of this kind, of about 30 minutes, comprehension of the text has been shown to increase dramatically over about 6 weeks, with gains transferring to reading comprehension outside the specific training sessions and lasting over a period well beyond the training.

More recently, reciprocal teaching has been combined with playing a taped reading of the text to students.[6] This taped reading supported children with poor word recognition skills (poor decoders), thus broadening the reach of the technique, as well as supplying a model of fluent expressive reading. With age-appropriate texts of suitable interest level, this particular study showed both good and poor decoders making significant gains in comprehension, with transfer to an independent test of reading.

8.3 Direct Instruction

Viewing teaching as 'assisted performance' is arguably more relevant to interactive teaching than to direct instruction, or to independent practice (see Table 1.1). Direct instruction has its own, rather different, tradition of research[7] which has shown that various features of direct teaching are associated with effectiveness, in terms of student learning. These features can be summarized as follows.

- The teacher has clear and appropriate goals for the students' learning.
- Clear explanations are given at an appropriate level for students to understand, with new terms and ideas being highlighted.
- Lessons are clearly structured: major ideas are broken down into meaningful segments and put together in a coherent sequence.
- Expositions by the teacher are relatively brief (no more than about 10 minutes at KS1/KS2 and 20 minutes at KS3/KS4).
- Good use is made of analogies, metaphors and examples that relate directly to the students' experience and interests.

- The teacher pays good attention to verbal and non-verbal signals that the students are following what is said, and regularly checks their understanding with questions.
- Both exposition and questions are designed to vary, so as to match the needs of different students across the class.
- Direct instruction is followed up by appropriate practice and problem-solving by the students.
- The teacher assesses students' work to ensure that the learning goals have been achieved and provides them with feedback.

You may feel that such lists are not far from the promptings of common sense. (Did anyone suppose that learning would thrive if teachers had no clear goals, talked incoherently at enormous length and never asked questions? Surely not.) Also, such lists are a good deal easier to prescribe than actually to follow. Nevertheless there are a great many important ideas summarized here. They provide a basic checklist for good teaching and they are supported by research evidence suggesting that they work. All teachers use direct instruction some of the time and it is important that it is both done well and used appropriately. The way it fits into the overall repertoire of teaching has already been set out in Chapter 1. How much we should depend upon direct instruction, however, and how much on interactive teaching and independent work remains controversial.

8.4 Three Challenges for Successful Teaching and Learning

In this section we will try to go beyond the basic skills of good teaching to consider the longer-term challenges of deliberate classroom learning. We learn in school only because we hope that the knowledge will somehow enrich our lives, but this is made possible only if we understand, remember and can apply what we have learned. These three challenges are so important that I shall expand on each of them. Students must meet them all if learning in school is to succeed and therefore effective teaching, too, must address each of them.

Setting clear goals for learning and assessing what has been learned are probably the two items most frequently prescribed for effective teaching. Unfortunately, however, learning is invisible. If only we could see or feel the changes in our bodies and brains as it takes place! As it is, we cannot even examine or inspect our own learning directly, let alone that of another person. It is a fallacy to imagine that learners necessarily know more about what they have learned than do teachers. If we want to know whether we have learned something new, we have to test ourselves, in some way, to find out. Thus if I want to know whether I now understand some of the general outlines of Einstein's theory of relativity, which I have just been reading about in a popular science book, I either have to ask myself questions and see if I can answer them or try to tell someone else about it or write something down. What is c in $E = mc^2$? What happens to light when it approaches a large body such as a planet? I have to conduct some kind of internal dialogue of this kind to have any idea of whether my reading has resulted in any learning. And I should check back with the book, too, to see if my answers are right. So when we judge that we, or anyone else, have actually learned something, we are always making a doubtful inference, a fallible judgement that may easily be wrong.

Deliberate learning is actually difficult, compared with the informal learning surveyed in Chapters 6 and 7. It is effortful and also slow. There is a Japanese proverb that says 'Don't learn it, get used to it!' We need patience and perseverance to learn new material thoroughly and it takes time. We can sometimes intensify our efforts, but after a certain point real learning cannot be hurried. Moreover the main satisfaction we get from such learning comes exactly from knowing that we have overcome its very real difficulties. But is it really the case that the kinds of easy 'informal' learning described in Chapters 6 and 7 are completely distinct and different from the hard 'deliberate' learning described in this chapter? No, it is not. They are more like two ends of a continuum that merge into one another. However, I have deliberately made a strong contrast between them so as to clarify why it is that school learning is often so slow and effortful.

You may remember that in Chapter 6, reference was made to 'episodic memory', the kind of automatic record of experience that is laid down in our heads with no conscious effort. Now we need to contrast episodic memory with **semantic memory**, the memory we construct consciously out of our mental representations in an effort to remember. Generally speaking we are more likely to remember new items of this kind, to the extent that we rehearse them, operate with them and recall them many times over. Sheer mental activity and good organization seem to be the keys to successful semantic memory.

Deliberate learning is made much harder by the simple fact that we forget very easily. Our learning (both in episodic and semantic memory) comes and goes. One important contributor to its stability is the context in which it was learned. Learning may be a covert intellectual process but it is also a social practice. I might get my sums right in a maths lesson but be thoroughly confused and muddled when an arithmetic problem crops up in the hectic atmosphere of, say, shopping in a hurry. (What is a quarter of a quarter? How many euros are there to the pound sterling?) Another important factor is how frequently we put our knowledge to use. We need to revisit knowledge and skills often, revising them until they are second nature to us, to prevent forgetting. But memory is also helped along by greater understanding.

Sometimes, in the history of schooling, either understanding or remembering has tended to be neglected as an aim. My classmates and I were required, long ago, to learn the prayer called 'The Collect for the Day' every Sunday from the prayer book. This was quite a demanding piece of rote learning, yet no one ever checked, or indeed showed any interest, in whether we had understood what we had learned so wearily in order to recite aloud. This seems a clear case of emphasizing memory to a ridiculous degree at the expense of understanding. The superficial knowledge we acquired slipped away and, so far as I know, never had any impact on our conduct, though perhaps some unconscious learning about language may have occurred. The first problem to be avoided is thus the *failure to understand*. Teaching someone else is, funnily enough, itself a great aid to understanding. Teachers often work on explaining ideas clearly and explicitly to themselves in a kind of mental rehearsal, before venturing to teach them to others. The result is sometimes that one faces up to areas of difficulty or poor understanding for the first time. The consequence of this can be a wonderful feeling of having understood something thoroughly for the first time.

However, understanding by itself will not really do either. If you understand all about the importance for teaching of the learning demands of different tasks (2.3), then well and good. But if you have forgotten all about these new ideas by next week then you will not be able either to use them in planning a lesson or communicate them to anyone else. If they turn out to be really important, you might just have to learn them all over again! (At least it will be easier the second time around.) The question of what is really worth learning by heart, or even **overlearning** as psychologists say, so that the subject matter sticks in memory and is resistant to forgetting, is both controversial and different for each school subject.

It is often argued that mere rote learning, or memorization, is useless outside the narrow world of the examination. One can always look facts up, people say, rather than slogging away at remembering them. There is indeed some truth in this. But remembered facts, skills, strategies and concepts are vital to all forms of expert performance. Skilled historians pounce on a particular fact and recognize its importance only because they interpret the fact against a huge backdrop of factual knowledge they possess about the period. Mathematicians work on complex problems only because they have a phenomenal fluency with simple operations on numbers. Novelists spend their time thinking productively about such things as character development and plot tension because they do not have to spend their time thinking about spelling and punctuation. Professional musicians think about the expressive qualities of their playing only because they do not have to think at all, at a conscious level, about where their fingers are. In short, all expert performance is built on a rich foundation of overlearned knowledge about some range of subject matter and skill.

Thus it does matter that children learn such things as spellings, number bonds, dates and scientific or mathematical formulae, because by committing them to memory they enable themselves to use their limited span of conscious attention to think about more important and interesting things. If you watch a 5- or 6-year-old child trying to write, this becomes painfully clear. He or she has to wrestle with the formation of every letter and with the spelling sequence of every letter within each word. Each is a problem that has to be solved consciously. Even the business of leaving a space between words is a decision that has to be thought about, endangering the flow of intended meaning. Remembering things is crucial to us because we only have a limited mental space to use for our thinking and we want to use this tiny allowance to move up the ladder to more complex sorts of problems, to escape from the tyranny of the elementary. The second problem that has to be evaded is thus *failure to remember.*

Remembering things is also important because without it we often cannot apply our knowledge in new situations, away from the original learning. Understanding and remembering therefore have to go together. But much of our remembering happens automatically, simply as a result of the frequent use of knowledge. 'Use it or lose it' is the mantra for remembering everyday facts. Journalists and others, who work via telephones a great deal, often keep dozens, even hundreds, of telephone numbers in their heads (or used to, before mobile phones remembered them automatically). In the same way, darts players can add any three numbers together and subtract them from 301 with lightening rapidity and ease. Bookmakers and gamblers play with the complex arithmetic of probabilities and odds effortlessly.

In the case of school learning, of such things as dates, facts, formulae and definitions, whether to commit the information to memory is a strategic decision. It is only worth spending time actually learning something by heart, learning it so thoroughly that it will always come to mind when wanted, if you are going to make use of the information often, but at irregular intervals, or if remembering it is going to enable you to move to a higher level of thinking, to tackle more complex problems. Essentially the memory for such things enables us to use our thinking in more powerful ways; it speeds up problem-solving and opens up new areas for thought. It is worth adding that a well-stocked memory, for poems as well as for science or history, is tremendously useful in allowing us to make use of such knowledge when far away from the classroom, library or computer search engine. It makes us more independent.

To test memory we try to recognize something (a relatively easy task) or to recall it (which is harder). To test understanding we have to ask questions and supply answers. Understanding is a relative matter. We have a deeper understanding of an idea, or event or principle, to the extent that we can answer more and more questions about it, moving ever further from the original focus and linking the knowledge with other pieces of knowledge. Just as remembering is important when we try to apply our knowledge, so depth and breadth of understanding are also important to knowledge application.

Of the three problems of deliberate learning that effective teaching has to overcome, the one most neglected by schools has probably been knowledge application. And yet without it, much school learning is, to put it bluntly, a waste of time. Not long ago, British children were tested on their knowledge of arithmetic by being asked, among other things, to work out the sum $225 \div 15 = ?$ Of the 12 year olds who were tested, 80% got this correct. Then, a little later, the same children were asked to solve the following problem: 'Suppose a gardener had 225 bulbs to place equally in 15 flower beds, how many would he put in each bed?' This time only 40% got the answer right.[8] As we have already noted, applying one's knowledge to a new context or a new problem is fraught with difficulties. These children may have learned to multiply and divide but perhaps their ability to apply the knowledge appropriately to new problems had not been a focus of their schooling. To apply knowledge, we need to be able to see what knowledge is relevant to the problem at hand, bring it to mind accurately and see how to use it strategically. To do all this we also have to have appropriate attitudes; we have to be prepared to have a go, to persevere, keep an open mind and avoid careless errors. The third problem is thus the *failure to apply knowledge successfully*.

If these three problems, of understanding, remembering and applying, are so crucial to successful learning, how are teachers to address them? One part of the answer is to attempt to build all three processes into the regular structure of lessons, so that they are frequently practised. One programme that has developed a systematic approach to teaching, which goes some way towards addressing these aims, is the Cognitive Acceleration of Science Education (CASE) project.[9]

Example 8.3 Teaching to speed cognitive development
Cognitive development is concerned with the general development of thinking and knowing from earliest childhood to adult maturity. Michael Shayer and Philip Adey wanted to intervene in schools not only to teach science more effectively but also to accelerate the general development of the minds of students in ways that could also be applied to other subjects and other problems. It has long been a dream of psychologists to do this. Cognitive acceleration has the promise of making students more effective thinkers and learners generally, a goal that would obviously result in more effective schooling and better performance outside of school, too.

Many attempts to carry through such a programme have been made, with some showing distinct promise,[10] but very few have been able to demonstrate significant and lasting success, with clear transfer of learning to other contexts. However, the CASE approach has done so, having been assessed at some length with KS3 science, across many schools. It has also been applied more recently to KS1 learners and shows promise in that setting, too. Rather than attempt to describe the whole of this complex project here, the aim will simply be to explain four particular features that are built into the design of each CASE lesson.

- *Concrete preparation*: introducing students to the technical vocabulary, the apparatus and the conceptual framework within which a problem is to be set. Clearly this helps with understanding.
- *Cognitive conflict*: introducing an event or observation that students find puzzling and discordant with their previous experience. This suggests to students that their existing knowledge is somehow not making sense of the problem and is thus inadequate. It alerts students to the need for restructuring of ideas.
- *Metacognition*: discussing with the students after the experiment what they found difficult and how they overcame their difficulties. This introduces a vocabulary to use in recognizing problems and reasoning about them. It encourages reflective thinking about thinking. It may help both understanding and applying knowledge.
- *Bridging*: connecting the ideas from the lesson explicitly to other similar problems in either school subjects or everyday problems outside school. This encourages students to generalize their new thinking across other problem contexts and is thus aimed at improving knowledge application. By making links between school learning and out of school experiences it may also help remembering.

These four CASE strategies for teaching will be illustrated via examples from their science lessons.

- An example of concrete preparation comes from a lesson in which the concepts of variables and relationships between variables were introduced. The teacher first displayed some books and asked 'In what ways are these different from one another?' Answers typically made reference to colour, size and hardback versus paperback. The teacher then explained that colour, size and material are three of the main ways in which the books vary and can be called variables. A collection of shapes, squares and triangles of different colours and sizes was then displayed and the students were asked 'What are the variables here?' Following this, the teacher moved on and encouraged the students to observe that, for example, all the squares were red whereas all the triangles were yellow, pointing out that here there is a relationship between the variables 'colour' and 'shape'. The same terms were then used during the lesson.

- An example of cognitive conflict comes from a lesson on density and floating. Students were introduced to a series of jars of different sizes, which either floated or sank when placed in water. Six of the jars (A–E) were the same size but had been loaded with different masses. Another six jars (1–6) were of different sizes but all contained the same mass. A table for recording results was prepared. The students were set to weigh the jars and then drop them into a large bowl of water, recording whether they sank or floated. As jars A, B and C float, whereas the heavier jars D and E sink, students usually argue that 'lighter things float, heavier things sink'. As the small jars 1 and 2 sink, whereas the larger 3, 4, 5 and 6 float, the students generally infer that 'larger things float, small things sink'. None of this offends their common-sense knowledge of such things as stones, pins and ships. Then jar X is introduced and weighed: it is as large as 3 (which floated) and as heavy as C (which also floated). The students confidently expect jar X to float, but it sinks! This surprise is intended to induce puzzlement, or cognitive conflict. The lesson moves on towards developing an understanding that floating and sinking depend not simply on weight or size but on 'weight for a certain size', or density.

- Metacognition means, broadly, thinking about thinking (and about learning and cognition in general). In CASE lessons it is introduced by teachers in student–student and teacher–student discussions. Thus one lesson involves a series of classification problems, using different materials such as animals, types of food and a range of chemicals. Groups complete a worksheet, which focuses on which classification activity was easiest, which was hardest, why they were easy or hard and why students think that classification might be useful. The teacher's role is then to draw out from the discussion general points about classification, its problems and its uses.

- Bridging to other contexts can be illustrated from a lesson on probabilistic relationships. Students first experiment with whether tea tastes differently if milk is added to. the cup either before or after the tea. One student tries tasting five cups of tea 'blind', saying 'tea first' or 'milk first' about each cup. Students then have to consider how many correct decisions would be convincing as proof of the taster's ability to discriminate. Typically the 11- and 12-year-old students consider that three or four out of five correct would be convincing. They next move on to an activity spinning five coins many times and recording how often five heads or five tails turn up simply by chance. This leads to conflict as they slowly realize that there is no single answer to the question 'How many is convincing?' Only a probabilistic answer can be given. Bridging then occurs through discussion of, for example, the relationship between smoking and lung cancer. Not everyone who smokes will get lung cancer; not everyone who does not smoke will avoid it. The idea of a probabilistic relationship is applied to different cases from everyday life.

The results of the CASE project are complicated but, very briefly, students who underwent 2 years of CASE science lessons showed significant gains, compared with control groups, in school science examinations and then in national GCSE science, maths and English examinations 2 years after the end of the programme. The apparent 'far transfer of learning' from science lessons to maths and English examinations is particularly interesting and suggests that significant numbers of these students, though not all, had somehow become generally more effective learners.

We cannot tell exactly which features, or combinations of features, of the CASE programme were influential but it is interesting that CASE emphasizes the need for arousing individual cognitive conflict and for the social discussion of problems and solutions, with attention paid to both metacognition and bridging. In sections 2.3 and 2.4 we saw how difficult it is to include restructuring and strategic application as regular task demands in lessons, but the design of the CASE project lessons seems to have attempted with some success to do this.

Looking at the problem of transfer, or knowledge application, other researchers[11] have suggested that there are two approaches that are likely to lead to success. One is the 'high road' of building up a good abstract understanding and management of some area of knowledge, through discussion, conscious learning and metacognition. The other is the 'low road' of frequent practice across many problems, leading to flexible automatic competence. As we have seen earlier, children's own metacognitive knowledge tends to emerge after long periods of practice, so the two roads may, ideally, converge. It is fashionable to argue that good learning depends on students engaging in lots of metacognition.[12] Although there may be some truth in this, I prefer to point out that good metacognitive awareness is probably a sign and outcome of thorough learning.

8.5 The Power of Practice

The active strategies for getting children thinking that are illustrated by CASE need to be supported by effective practice, if the three central challenges of remembering, understanding and applying are to be met. Practice is particularly important to all those varieties of learning in which routines or subroutines of thinking or skilled movement are involved. Thus swimming, playing a musical instrument, handwriting, solving simultaneous equations and writing up science experiments all require extended practice. We might say, therefore, that practice is powerful when performance involves some kind of repetition, or routine problem-solving. But the role of repetition in learning is much misunderstood. The power of practice is actually about change.

Practice has two main consequences: firstly it allows us to eliminate errors from our performance; secondly it leads to skills being transferred from conscious control to a kind of subconscious automation. When, say, practising a piece of music on the piano, it is true that repeated trials will lead gradually to improved playing, but this is so not because each trial is the same as those which went before but precisely because each trial is a little bit different. On each trial the pianist should attempt not to repeat the previous trial but to improve on it. Exact repetitions scarcely exist in any case, but the point is to try to change the performance each time to make it more accurate, rhythmic and expressive. In this way it is profoundly true that we learn by eliminating our mistakes. This is why experience is not the same as learning (see the fallacy of experience (2.4)).

As for the second effect, the automation of skills, William James captured very well the strange shift in conscious attention that results from practice, when he remarked that 'consciousness goes away from where it is not needed'.[13] As we become more skilled, whether playing that piano piece, driving a car, typing or skiing, we can gradually pay less and less conscious attention to the details of our actions, as more and more of the performance is taken over by subconscious parts of the brain. As the skill becomes automated, it leaves our conscious span of attention free to attend to higher-level concerns, or sometimes perhaps just to gossip. At any rate, practice automates skills and frees up attention. Another general finding from psychology has been that shorter periods of practice, spaced out over time, tend to aid learning more than the same quantity of 'massed' practice, all at one time.

One way of looking for examples of really effective deliberate learning is to study exceptional individuals who have succeeded in a particular field. In the following example, practice has a central role.

Example 8.4 Expert performance and deliberate practice

In a thought-provoking account, Ericsson[14] has argued that expert performance, in such fields as sport, music and chess, is predominantly a function of particular kinds of deliberate practice. In chess, for example, even child prodigies, who are far superior to their peers at the game, show gradual and steady improvement over time, taking at least 10 years to reach international master's level. Ericsson reviews literature that suggests that much the same time-scale is true of experts in musical composition, sports, science and the arts. In comparison to the tiny group of elite performers, the vast majority of us take up an activity such as tennis or chess later than the young prodigies, practise it less frequently and give up any intensive commitment to it sooner. What seems to mark out the careers of elite performers is a set of circumstances, including first having their talent, or interest, recognized at an early age; then being given superior training conditions and expert coaching over a long period of time; and, finally, showing an intense dedication to concentrated practice. For Ericsson, talent is far less important than dedicated practice.

In a study of violin students at a music academy, Ericsson and his colleagues found that by the age of 20, the best group of musicians had spent some 10,000 hours on solitary practice. This was 2500 and 5000 hours respectively longer than the next two groups below them in terms of achievement. For this practice to be effective, however, expert musicians generally state that they need to be fresh and able to sustain a high level of concentration. Interestingly the same expert musicians often reported taking regular naps in the afternoon in order to retain their levels of energy and concentration. Tired, stale practice does not work at all well. Nor does too much intensive practice in the early stages of learning, which can lead to 'burn-out'. Instead, young players need a playful approach to practice, followed by gradually increased levels of training. This slow build-up of training seems to bring about a physiological adaptation to the increasing demands of sustained practice, probably regardless of age.

A further characteristic of the experts studied by Ericsson was that they resisted the tendency to relapse into automatic inflexible habits. Long practice often leads to a certain automatic level of skill, but the expert typically wants to go beyond this everyday level and does so by continuing to plan, mentally rehearse, prepare, reason and evaluate his or her performance across different problems and contexts. A high level of active thinking and the formation of many detailed memories prevent 'arrested development' of the skills involved and enable the expert to respond rapidly and flexibly to new situations. For example, expert pianists could, when instructed to do so, play only alternate bars of the music, play piano one hand at a time or transpose the same music into a different key. From their teachers and their deliberate practice, the expert musicians built up complex mental representations, for instance of a desired performance, so that they were able to continue to monitor their playing and identify ways in which it failed to satisfy them. This also depended on a capacity to continue listening intensively to their own playing, resisting any tendency to relapse into giving an unthinking, habitual performance.

The key features of effective deliberate practice appear to be:

- a long period of intensive learning;
- acquiring a large repertoire of rich and detailed representations (roughly, perceptions and knowledge) of the specific field or activity;
- maintaining mindful and reflective monitoring of current performance;
- persistently striving for ever higher standards.

Most of us, if Ericsson is right, are not less talented than the elite, we simply settle for less.

Whether or not Ericsson is right to downplay talents and innate abilities, his research makes a powerful case for deliberate practice. Perhaps, putting together all the examples in this chapter, we can come up with at least some of the key ingredients of successful deliberate learning. This would be learning that would survive changes of context, would be accurately remembered, well understood and thus available for application to different problems and situations in life. A list of such ingredients might be as follows.

- The teacher communicates clear goals for learning to the students.
- The teacher assists performance by using modelling, direct instruction and all the strategies of interactive teaching.
- Students receive regular feedback on their progress in a way that does not discourage them from trying hard (see also Chapter 15).
- Teaching is sustained through all the stages of learning (incremental, restructuring, problem-solving, practice and revision).
- The process of restructuring is helped by the use of powerful analogies and examples, by engendering cognitive conflict and by active discussion, including metacognition and bridging to other problem contexts.

- Sufficient time is given to the topic so that extensive practice, problem-solving and revision are possible, leading to high levels of student confidence in applying the relevant knowledge.

8.6 Easy and Difficult Learning: A Personal View

What lessons should we take from these three chapters on learning? For myself, one clear, though hard to accept, message comes across. Whether we like it or not, deliberate conscious learning, which leads to really effective knowledge application, is relatively difficult and effortful for all of us. It is far away from the kind of intuitive, informal, social learning at which humans are naturally so good (no doubt because evolution equipped us to learn in those ways). The reason for this is becoming increasingly clear.

The brain, at birth, is structured in particular ways. It is not a blank slate but a complex physical organ prepared during millions of years of evolution to equip its 'bearer' with the necessary means to survive on this earth. Language, memory, attention, vision and all the other perceptual channels are tuned and shaped in particular specialist ways to suit a specifically human way of life (albeit one from long ago, that of hunter-gatherers). Our innate drives and needs, too, are the result of this long history of becoming the species we are. It is true that besides our specialist mental equipment we have a phenomenal general capacity to learn all sorts of things, including concepts, facts, rules and principles. This is also part of our heritage. But this general learning capacity, as opposed to the specialist 'mental organs' for particular kinds of intuitive learning (like face recognition or speech comprehension) is quite slow and error-prone in its operations. It requires effortful concentration, perseverance and practice. We have to live with the brains we possess.

However, we do not have to accept defeat simply because of these by-products of our biological history. Robust effective learning is, of course, perfectly attainable. We simply have to be realistic and accept that it requires good teaching, students who are prepared to concentrate and plenty of time. Ericsson's research shows what is required if one wants to reach really exceptional standards of excellence, but such standards are far beyond what I am aspiring to here. I simply want school learning that is genuinely useful to students and to society, learning that can be remembered, understood and applied. We have to choose whether to teach a huge and ambitious school curriculum, which is seldom actually learned, or a smaller manageable curriculum for which we expect much higher standards.

The coverage of such a reformed curriculum might not actually turn out to be that much smaller than the current one, by the end of KS4, if only we were prepared to travel more slowly on the way, so as to produce a greater depth of learning. Nor need it be in any way boring: applying knowledge confidently in independent problem-solving, across different examples and contexts, gives students exactly the control they love to exert and the success in which they exult. As another writer put it: 'good teaching constantly asks about old understandings in new ways, calls for new applications and draws new connections'.[15] Knowledge applications allow all kinds of rich and imaginative projects to be carried out. Students who really know what they are doing can be allowed a good deal more freedom than students who are confused and bored.

In my opinion, in this area of deliberate learning, less is more. I do not believe that there are any shortcuts to really thorough learning, and yet only really thorough learning lasts and gets put into practice. Nor do I think that, after several hundred years of trying to improve schools, we are about to discover some magic new method of teaching that no one has thought of before. The new technology of ICT has promise, for example, but it has not revolutionized schools. The most successful of our schools tend to use rather traditional well-tried methods. We can aspire to do better but we should not ignore their success. This adds up to a terribly simple argument, but also unfortunately a deeply unpopular one. Teachers frequently complain that students arrive in their classes without knowing the 'basics' well enough. 'Just give them a sound grounding and we can take it on from there', they cry. University teachers blame secondary school teachers. Secondary school teachers blame primary teachers. Primary teachers blame playgroups and playgroups blame parents. Each Key Stage blames the one before it. This is probably because they all want to move on and teach more advanced and interesting things. But this very ambition may just lead to insecure shallow learning that does not survive the move to out-of-school contexts.

8.7 Questions

The following questions are designed to help you check your understanding of the chapter.

1 Why is school learning considered here to be a special case?
2 Describe how Vygotsky saw adults operating as mediators of learning.
3 What are the main features of reciprocal teaching?
4 What, according to this chapter, are the three main challenges to successful learning in school?
5 What might you argue against someone who suggested that learning facts is a waste of time?
6 To apply knowledge effectively, what cognitive processes need to be carried out successfully?
7 What did the CASE project mean by 'concrete preparation', 'cognitive conflict' and 'bridging'?
8 Name two main outcomes of practice, for learning.
9 Name as many suggested key ingredients of deliberate learning as you can.
10 **Discussion question:** direct instruction has been treated here as a vital part of the repertoire of teaching (see also Chapter 1). Yet some researchers and teachers would argue that direct instruction is too didactic and limited and that students

fare better when more actively and democratically involved in a 'community of learners', collaborating with each other and with teachers over what is to be learned and how.[16] Discuss the likely advantages and disadvantages of such an approach, pooling whatever evidence you happen to have about more unconventional classrooms.

NOTES

1. Vygotsky (1962, 1978).
2. Wells (1986), p. 65.
3. Tharp and Gallimore (1988).
4. Vygotsky (1978).
5. Palincsar and Brown (1984).
6. Le Fevre, Moore and Wilkinson (2003).
7. For example Good and Brophy (1991); Kyriacou (1995).
8. Desforges (1995b).
9. Adey and Shayer (1994); also Adey, Robertson and Venville (2002).
10. Nickerson, Perkins and Smith (1985).
11. Salomon and Perkins (1989).
12. A good example of this point of view is set out in Claxton (2002).
13. Quoted in Searle (1992), p. 139.
14. Ericsson (2002).
15. Sheppard (2001).
16. One such example is mentioned later in Example 10.4. See Brown and Campione (1998).

CHAPTER NINE

Human Motivation

9.1 Introduction

At the risk of moving a long way away from the setting of the classroom, an attempt will be made in this chapter to set the world of the classroom in the much broader context of human motivation, providing a brief sketch of the whole range of drives, desires, fears and values, which move us to act in different ways. The point of this will be to show the classroom in its broader human context and thus reveal some seldom mentioned aspects of motivation in school. Then we shall look specifically at motivation in the classroom in more detail in Chapter 10.

In the present chapter we examine motivation in terms of needs, drives, rewards, social motives and values. The part played by curiosity and a desire for knowledge and control is then added. This leads us back eventually to the motives of students in classrooms. We have already encountered the topic of motivation in the classroom in Chapter 3. Although clearly an over-simplification, it was suggested there that students in class are most commonly motivated by:

- a desire to maintain their self-respect in the eyes of others;
- a desire to win the approval of respected others;
- a degree of interest and engagement with the tasks of schoolwork.

All these common sources of motivation vary from lesson to lesson, class to class and day to day. Some students are very socially popular and confident, others nervous or rejected by their peers. Some students are conscientious and work hard to gain the approval of teachers, whereas others care little for school and its values. Each individual may find his or her studies intermittently interesting or boring, fascinating or repelling. The 'respected others' may include a teacher, or possibly other members of the class (the peer group).

Educational textbooks and government documents, such as the QTS Standards, have rather little to say about motivation. For some, the only important issue facing teachers is to plan interesting lessons, which will engage students and give them the feeling of success. If this can be done then, it is argued, all else follows easily: the students will increasingly find the work satisfying, want to learn and try to ignore distractions. But this is much easier to recommend than to bring about. It ignores the history of a class, which may have built up many sorts of resistance to 'interesting lessons'. Also, it ignores the ups and downs in other strands of interest and anxiety in the students' lives. Teachers can indeed do a good deal to optimize levels of positive motivation, but this claim needs to be tempered with a degree of realism: teachers' powers are limited and students have other sources of motivation, other matters that concern them. Nor, as we shall see (10.2), is easy success a recipe for lasting self-esteem.

9.2 Basic Needs and Drives

I shall use the term 'drive' for much of this chapter to stand for our desires and fears. There are problems with the drive concept, as applied to human motivation, but I shall ignore these until the end of the chapter. Let us start with the brute physiological drives and needs that we share, via our history of evolution, with other animals, or at least mammals. In fact, let us start with eating. Animals, including humans, have evolved many ways of keeping their internal environment in balance, or equilibrium, and food is an important contributor to this state of comfort or discomfort. Imagine a plate of your favourite food on a table before you. Whether you feel moved to eat it right now will of course depend on whether you feel hungry. But that feeling of hunger is itself produced in your brain by the summation of an extraordinarily complex set of processes throughout your body. Hunger is the drive, which signals a need for nutrition. Actual feelings of hunger are brought about by activity in centres in your brain, particularly the hypothalamus. These, in turn, respond to feedback from your nervous system about your regular eating habits, your blood sugar level, your level of body fat, your current body temperature, the relative emptiness or otherwise of your stomach, the taste of food and the level of other drives. (For example, hunger may be marginalized by acute feelings of danger, cold or fatigue.) The feeling of hunger is thus only the brain's method of arousing you to look for food. It knows more about what is going on in your body than you do.

When the body, especially the brain, prompts an animal to notice that it is too cold or hot, hungry or thirsty, it starts to move about to solve the problem. In the case of hunger, an important element is that when the animal is hungry, food begins to look and smell more inviting. For us, too, with hunger the reward value of food increases. That plate of food you have been imagining may look irresistible if you have not eaten for some time, but it is much less appealing if you have just eaten two similar platefuls of the same food already. Satiation with food can easily occur. It will also be less appealing if you are in urgent need of warmth or are feeling extremely hot and thirsty. At this lowest level of motivation we can easily see that a number of key needs of the animal are taken care of by drives such as hunger, thirst, temperature control and fatigue. Sexual arousal, too, behaves very like a kind of appetite, subject to a similar range of influences from the internal state of the body, to regular habits and to influences from the immediate context.

When these physiological (or homeostatic) drives get going, it is as if an internal regulator or thermostat is registering a need or desire and we are prompted to do something about it. Such 'appetitive behaviour', for instance looking in the fridge for food, is the result of our history of learning. We generally know how to find the means to re-set the regulator by satisfying our desires. Actually eating some food is called by psychologists a 'consummatory act' because it finishes off, or consummates, the cycle of motivation. Normally it re-sets the regulator. Putting on a warm top is another consummatory act if it ends a feeling of chilly discomfort. In summary, when our physiological needs are out of balance, a regulator in the brain prompts us to 'feel like' doing something appropriate (the appetitive behaviour) to restore bodily equilibrium. We then seek out the consummatory action, which will re-set the regulator to 'satisfied'. Through learning we develop habits of maintaining our levels of bodily comfort.

Notice, also, how even when our desire for food is low, in terms of the body's needs, a particularly enticing item, say some chocolate mousse, may still be rewarding enough to tempt us to eat. Highly rewarding stimuli may bring about behaviour that is not strictly in line with our needs. In contrast, strongly felt values, such as a desire not to become overweight, may inhibit our raw appetite for the chocolate. In order to survive, or maintain a state of well-being, we have to satisfy our needs, but there is an imperfect match between the objective needs of the body and the psychological desires and fears that move us to action.

Some needs, such as that for liquids to satisfy thirst, are strongly signalled by the brain in the form of the relevant desires (or fears). Others, such as a need for vitamin A or for iron, are not directly signalled at all. Needs are objective: they are what the body needs for its welfare. Drives (or desires and fears) are what our brains have evolved to tell us about our needs. For all species of animals there is a considerable overlap between needs and desires, for otherwise the species would not have survived. But needs are not by any means perfectly correlated with desires. Some of our desires, for example for sweet or salty foods, may even be harmful to us (but are well known to food manufacturers).

9.3 The Law of Relative Rewards

Animals that can learn, like us, learn to behave according to a subtle and complex pattern of overall reward that is generally adaptive for our survival. It is all a matter of repeating the behaviours that lead to rewarding consequences and avoiding the behaviours that lead to unpleasant consequences. Up to a point, humans follow this general pattern. We all act, much of the time, to try to bring about bodily equilibrium and other forms of satisfaction. We tend to be attracted towards the situations and actions which we find rewarding, in one fashion or another. Rewards and punishments in the environment attract and repel us according to our internal states and our history of learning. Learning is thus nature's way of sculpting our activities to fit a pattern that, so far as possible, satisfies our desires and is generally adaptive to our species.

Rewards and punishments of this hedonistic kind, which lead to pleasure or pain, comfort or discomfort, are very varied and, as already noted, they interact. Some drives in animals are prompted by factors such as the cycle of daylight and night (e.g. the hunting of nocturnal animals), some by hormonal cycles (e.g. sexual behaviour in many female species of mammal). Others are prompted by external sources, for example fear aroused by the presence of a predator. But all our feelings about rewards are relative. Our desire for any one source of reward, say food, is relative to all our other current states of fear and desire. If we are very fearful, we may lose interest for a while in food while we seek safety. If we are extremely thirsty, we may start to imagine satisfying drinks, even where none exist. To a poor person, a 5-pence coin on the pavement may be attractive enough to prompt them to pick it up. A richer person might not bother.

If there is little opportunity for reward, then the least chance of relevant appetitive activity may become much more attractive. Thus drivers stuck in traffic may seem to get an inordinate amount of satisfaction from lurching forward a few yards or from beating a traffic light before it turns red. Someone who has narrowly escaped death and thus the anticipated termination of all desires and fears may, for a time, find a wonderfully renewed taste for life, in which the most banal and everyday of experiences take on a wonderfully rewarding character. At the other extreme, people who seem routinely to have an excess of all the normal sources of comfort may seek for pleasure in more unusual pursuits, such as collecting antique cars or expensive paintings. The rewarding quality of any one activity or source of pleasure is strictly relative to our situation at a given time and place, and to the balance obtaining between all our drives and all the sources of reward or pain in our lives.

This tendency of all animals to learn behaviours that lead to rewarding results is known as the **law of effect**.[1] Given that hedonism is the pursuit of pleasure, we can call it a law of hedonistic relativity, operating for all creatures for whom learning is important. It tells us something very basic about motivation, namely that we seek out relatively rewarding events. Moreover, we distribute our energies among different activities and responses roughly in proportion to how much of our total reward we expect from each one. But the law of effect, though a powerful generalization, does not actually tell us what we find rewarding or how to obtain it. Although sometimes this is pretty obvious (as with the hungry person seeking food), at other times it is more obscure (as when a person travels hundreds of miles to photograph a small bird or another person starves themselves in a state of anorexia). What we find rewarding depends on our drives and, as we shall see, also on our values. For once we become aware of the way that our behaviour is being shaped by the prospect of a reward, or a punishment, we may consciously decide to override its influence, because our values suggest that we should. Our values get into the equation by becoming involved in our feelings of reward and punishment. The interplay between our psychological drives and our beliefs and values gives human life a special complexity.

Whereas hunger and thirst are drives that are internal (regulate equilibrium states within the body) there are also drives that have to do with matters that are outside the body. These have to do especially with safety, or dealing with external threats. As we cross a busy road, we look out to escape being run over. But we also avoid dangerous situations (eating unknown fungi, accepting advice from strangers) even in the absence of any immediate danger. We thus learn in a longer-term fashion to keep ourselves relatively secure. Safety drives seem strong in young children, who often like environments and routines that are familiar and reassuring. This is probably simply because a higher proportion of situations are unfamiliar and unsettling to them. For the most part, such 'avoidance behaviour' seems to follow the same pattern of the law of relative effect. In fact, with both rewarding and avoiding actions, animals, including people, seem to distribute their actions across their total range of behaviour so as to match each type of behaviour to the proportion of reward (or avoidance of pain) that they expect it will provide. However, if we take a person who is well fed, rested, comfortable and feeling secure, does it mean that he or she will be inactive? It does not: far from it. With the basics of physiological homeostasis and security taken care of, humans show a considerable desire for social contacts and for new information about the world.

9.4 Social Motives

Humans are strongly social animals. The specific drives that motivate us socially remain open to question, but it seems reasonable to make some cautious claims. Firstly we have a desire for company, for human contact. We live mostly in social groups and we regularly seek out the people we like to gossip, eat, drink and make plans together. Let us call this the 'positive social drive'. Robin Dunbar[2] compares the social patterns of humans with those of many different primates and monkeys, who also lead intensely social lives. Monkeys and primates spend much time peacefully grooming one another, in pairs. This relaxes them and seems to reduce stress within the group. Dunbar argues that humans have substituted gossip for grooming, finding relaxation in casual talk about ourselves and about other people who matter to us. This substitution of words for the physical act of grooming came about during evolution, Dunbar argues, because grooming started to take up too much time in larger groups. The solution was to chat instead. Talk is low in energy demands and can be shared in small groups.

According to Dunbar, some two-thirds of most conversations in human groups concern relationships and reputations, reports of who is doing what with whom, who is in and who is out and how we feel about this. When we are not gossiping with friends we spend a further amazing amount of time reading about the wider social scene in newspapers, watching soaps on television or reading about the fictional social worlds of characters in novels. All-male groups talk as much about social matters as all-female ones do and broadsheet newspapers contain almost as many words in total about 'human interest' stories as the tabloid press. (If there is more talk about intellectual ideas, art and current affairs in mixed sex groups it is probably because the males in the group are 'displaying' to the females by showing off their knowledge. Academics are particularly prone to this.) Average social group size in different primate species also correlates well with the relative size of the neocortex, that part of the brain that deals with planning, judgement and decision-making. A larger neocortex, relative to body size, goes along with life in a larger social group. Our large brain may have evolved to keep track of the relationships across our complex social world, rather than simply to cope with the physical one.

Beyond a basic desire for human company, it seems that we all want to be loved, to be valued and needed to some degree. Affection is generally rewarding to us and we value friendship and intimate relationships very highly. It is not clear how far this is simply due to an inborn craving for affection and how far it is mixed up with other motives to do with security, reciprocity, status and sex. But whatever the exact source may be, alongside this cluster of positive social motives there are some corresponding negative ones. The pleasures of company, of friends and family, bring with them some corresponding pains. Other people may irritate us, hurt us, take away what we wanted to have for ourselves, watch the wrong TV channel or generally prove bothersome. Like most other sources of reward, we can have too much of the social life and in crowded societies especially there commonly arises a strong desire for privacy or control over personal space.

When we consider the balance between the positive and negative social drives, the contending feelings that pull us closer together or push us further apart, a further generalization seems reasonable. This is that when we are feeling afraid or insecure we tend, as a species, to crowd together with our close friends and relations, our own kind. When, correspondingly, we feel secure and confident we tend to drift apart and lead more adventurous individual lives. Those who have lived through wars have typically reported that a strong sense of community is established by the sense of facing a common danger together. Thus the Blitz in London during the Second World War famously brought about a heightened sense of community among the people living there. Moreover we know that young pre-school children, when they feel secure and happy, will often explore their surroundings, moving away from the security of their mother's body. But they quickly return and cling to her when they are feeling insecure or afraid.[3]

It is a feature of contemporary life in affluent Western societies that the many kinds of insecurity that plagued all previous human lives have been to a great extent eliminated. We do not, typically, fear where our next meal is coming from; indeed obesity is more of a problem to us than hunger. Of course pockets of hardship and poverty remain, and should not be dismissed, but the simple fact is that for the comfortable majority there is somewhere to live, regulation of cold and heat, a vast choice of clothing, medical care, social insurance and other means by which discomfort and danger are held at bay. At the same time we have evolved a lifestyle that emphasizes individualism in all its forms. We are led to believe that exercising choice in pursuit of individual happiness is our chief goal, that we can indulge ourselves because 'we are worth it'. Families no longer spend their whole lives together and we are used to a high level of mobility, moving about the world to go to different homes, social occasions, jobs and holidays.

The fact that we can often explore the world alone and not feel afraid might suggest that we are feeling the negative urge to get away from it all more strongly than the positive urge to huddle together with our friends. Or it may be that we feel secure enough to be relatively adventurous. Only in times of crisis, such as that which occurred on 11 September 2001 in New York, does the balance suddenly and dramatically shift back towards the desire to be together with those we see as allies, and to have a greater fear of those who seem outsiders or potential enemies. The relevance of these thoughts for teachers and schools is this: the various forms of security offered by a school, together with the social opportunities it supplies, are actually central to its functioning. The positive and negative social drives are both at work there, and because the basic physiological and safety drives are normally routinely satisfied, the social drives take on a particular salience. Children are clear, when asked, that the chief pleasure (to most of them) in coming to school is that they meet their friends there. They expect schools to be generally safe places, at least when adults are in control, where individuals receive careful attention and respect. In this atmosphere of benign care, without responsibility to attend to the more basic problems of food, shelter or safety, students may feel relatively low levels of community allegiance and a strong wish to express their individual wants.

Although schools are generally safe places, where responsible adult guidance is routine and where there is strong adult disapproval of violence, there is a further human social drive that operates in a contrary fashion. This is the tendency for humans, as for other primates and social animals, to work out a pecking order, or dominance hierarchy, within any group. Chickens, baboons and wolves all live within a strict social hierarchy of power and influence. The strongest animals dominate the weaker ones and enforce their powers with physical and social messages, if need be with pecks, bites and kicks. Those at the top of the hierarchy also frequently reserve scarce resources for themselves. We should beware of too easily assuming that humans organize their lives just as animals do; yet there is evidence that dominance hierarchies of a kind also exist for human groups, in looser less structured ways than they exist for, say, chickens.[4]

Individuals have a relative status within any group along dimensions such as skill, good looks, control over valued resources and competence of various kinds. More broadly, in society status seems to function as a key underlying motive for human behaviour. The rewarding aspect of status is represented by the gaining of the respect and liking of valued others, by way of our achievements, actions or possessions. The punishing aspect of status is the anxiety or shame we may endure if we feel that others see us as somehow less clever, popular, good-looking, fashionable, trendy, witty or 'smart' than we aspire to be. As with the law of effect generally, it is relative value that concerns us. One irony of our current affluence is that it is not absolute wealth but relative wealth that seems to predict peoples' general happiness and satisfaction with life. Surveys have shown, for example, that Americans report feeling much the same overall degree of satisfaction with their lives as they did 50 years ago, in spite of their absolute wealth having increased vastly during that time.[5]

The more superficial forms of status have to do with wealth, glamour and celebrity. But although we may feel that we enlightened ones can ignore such vulgar values, further reflection will probably uncover other ways in which we hope that those whom we like and admire will at least respect, if not admire, us. Status for one person might be a showy house or car; for another it might be to do with being seen reading the right book or having backpacked to the right destination. For still another, status will come from having a photograph of a rare migrant bird, to show off to fellow 'twitchers'. Few of us do not care in any way at all about how we appear, dress, speak and behave before others. The good opinion of others whom we respect is generally a powerful force in our lives, whether we are aware of it or not. We thus need to add status to the list of common human motives that already includes the basic physiological drives, feelings of safety and security and the warmth of some satisfying degree of social contact, including being loved.

There is evidence, to be further explored in Chapter 12, that the opinion of the peer group is extraordinarily important to human children and adolescents. One result is that classes and groups of students in schools normally exhibit an informal 'pecking order' of social status, and sometimes of dominance. Males may be more likely to resort to threats of force and physical domination, whereas females may operate on one another more via insults, threats to reputation and other forms of social control. In any event, the subculture of the teenage group provides a potent context not only for the operation of the two opposing social forces of attraction and repulsion, but also for the operation of status, influencing student behaviour in many ways. Nor are students usually mature or informed enough to realize consciously that these various forces are at work.

Bullying can be seen, in the light of these rather unwelcome facts, to be more a normal feature of human social life than we might wish it to be. It can be seen simply as the tensions of the dominance hierarchy being visited upon the weakest members of the group. We shall return to this subject, and our response to it, in Chapter 13. Meanwhile, let us note that the two common sources of motivation listed at the beginning of this chapter, the desire to maintain self-respect and the wish for social approval, take on a different light if we view them as rooted in relations within the peer group, rather than in relations with the teacher. Tensions between teacher and taught will be moderated by many values that are in operation in what we have called the 'ethos' of the class. It is to a consideration of values, then, that we next need to turn.

9.5 Values

So far we have considered motives under the heading of drives and needs, but humans also pay much attention to values. Let us define values, for now, as those actions and goals approved of by a social group. The !Kung people, a group of hunter-gathers who live in the Kalahari desert, have been studied in great detail.[6] Among the !Kung (the exclamation mark stands for a click sound in their language) a prime value is that all food should be shared. Every animal killed by hunters is carefully shared out according to a well-defined system of kinship rules. The same thing is true of the BaMbuti pygmies studied by Colin Turnbull[7] (see Chapter 6). Anyone breaking this rule, or even being suspected of breaking it, is subjected to constant harassment and social disapproval, with the ultimate threat being exclusion from the group. In their world, no individual can stand up against such social pressures for long. The alternative to life within the group is simply a slow, or perhaps even a quick, death.

Although the !Kung simply see sharing food as the 'right thing to do', it is clear to any observer that the system acts as a very effective kind of insurance policy for everyone in the group. A hunter who kills an antelope cannot eat it all himself. If he tries to hide the body for later consumption, it may rot or be stolen by other predators. Much better to take it back to camp and share it out according to rules, which everyone knows. Tomorrow he may not be so lucky in the risky business of the hunt, but then he and his family will be entitled to some part of the meat brought in by another hunter. There are few possessions and few sources of inequality in this way of life and the sharing ethos not only protects everyone in the long run but also lowers the possibility of jealousy and conflict within the group.

In our own society, values have become many and complex, and there is far from complete agreement about what they should be. The common backbone of our society's values might be said to be defined by our system of laws, but outside of this formal system (and our disagreements about it) there are many informal family, friendship, religious and other groupings that promote particular positive aims in life and ways of attaining them. Taking the simple example of a business, it employs people to work in order to provide others with either goods or services. It aims to make a profit, which generally signals that it is succeeding in providing something that people want (satisfying some drive and/or need) at a price they are prepared to pay. The money earned by the business is divided up between the people working for it and any shareholders or other creditors. This money acts as a token of value, which can be exchanged for the necessities of life (needs) or for pleasures (the objects of drives). Such goals as efficiency, consistent quality and expanding profits operate as the values of the business, which overlap to some degree with the needs and drives of employees and customers. The value of profitability may, however, sometimes be in tension with broader social values of honesty, fairness or threats to the environment and conflicts will then no doubt result. In general, the point is that values radiate from social institutions and overlap to some extent with individual needs and drives.

For an individual, say an !Kung hunter, we can now imagine motivation as a set of three overlapping circles. One circle stands for his objective needs (in order to stay alive and viable), and this overlaps with a second circle that stands for his psychological drives (what he wants and what he fears). Then there is a third circle, which represents the values of the social groups or institutions with which he is involved.

These vary across his different social roles of hunter, husband, father and so forth. The two circles representing the individual's needs and drives may overlap with the third 'values' circle almost completely or not at all. In the case of our hunter, staying healthy might be an aim that fits into the overlapping section of all three circles. The value of staying up all night dancing, in contrast, may fulfil one of his own desires and may also be valued by his group, but might not fit the 'need' circle if it threatens his ability to find food or avoid predators. The value of accepting that another hunter owns a kill that both of them were stalking may fit the group values circle (unselfish honesty as a hunter) but be outside his own drives circle (it is hard to concede a valuable resource to a rival).

We can predict that if a society's values conflict strongly with the drives of its individual members, there will be strong social tensions. If a society's values conflict strongly with the needs of its members (let us say by recommending a disastrous war or failing to prevent a health epidemic), it may not even survive at all in the long run. Thus social institutions survive by ensuring that their values overlap sufficiently with their members' needs and drives. They also routinely reward individuals who keep to their values and punish those who break them. Values, including our feelings of self-respect and status, thus become incorporated into the general web of anticipated pleasures and pains that we have labelled the law of relative effect. Social values are an attempt to redirect our drives and sometimes they succeed.

There is no simple means of predicting how conflicts between individual drives and social values will be resolved. We all know the conflicts that go on in our own minds as we attempt to follow a value (say slimness) that is in conflict with a drive (the desire for pleasurable foods). Sometimes we resolutely stick to our long-term goals, perhaps using social allies to reinforce our successes in resisting temptation and to police our behaviour in the lunch queue. Sometimes we persuade ourselves, in some strange way, that we do not really care that much about slimness after all, and certainly not enough to turn away from one small chocolate biscuit that otherwise would go to waste. It is as if there is a society of different agents within our own minds, which discuss, argue and elbow one another out of the way as they try to take over our attention and get control of the executive parts of the brain. In the end, one gains control and we act. Sometimes we probably even deceive and cheat ourselves, in these internal negotiations, without being aware of how we do it. Much of the internal discussion is likely to concern long-term goals versus short-term pleasures.

In our relations with other people, we also negotiate a pathway through life that includes enquiries, discussions and conflicts over what we should and should not do. When we meet our friends, we often spend much of our time telling anecdotes about our own lives in which we rehearse and celebrate the values that we share. We revisit past experiences, sharing our triumphs, commiserating with one another over our disasters and discussing our troubles (often value conflicts). More generally, if our needs, drives and values overlap well, we probably have some sense of moving forward with a coherent and satisfying lifestyle. If, on the other hand, they seem to be being pulled apart, we are likely to experience emotions such as uncertainty, anxiety, frustration or even shame and guilt. Our emotions can be thought of as the brain's way of telling us how our current situation matches up with our values. They are a guide to how we feel (in terms of drives and values) about what is happening to us and what we are planning to do about it.

Turning to children, it is extraordinary to realize how quickly they become involved in these tensions between values and drives. It is not uncommon to come across a 2 year old doing something naughty, such as pulling the petals off a flower, while saying to herself 'No! Bad girl. Lisa not spoil flowers!' By the age of 4, children can understand all the principal emotions and values that colour a story such as Cinderella or Jack and the Beanstalk. Love and hate, sorrow and joy, hope and despair, kindness and cruelty are comprehended from very early on, without any explicit teaching. This is one (powerful) reason why stories work so well for early teaching. As for children's broader development of values, their gradual emergence as moral agents, with feelings of approval and disapproval both towards others and themselves, it is clearly a long and complex journey. It is partly a matter of a shift away from control being operated solely from without towards control operated mostly from within. At first, young children are mostly regulated by the instructions, rules, sanctions and controls of their parents, older siblings, and others more powerful than themselves. Piaget[8] called this 'heteronomy', which simply means rule by another. With moral development, children become to some greater or lesser extent 'autonomous' or rulers of themselves.

Vygotsky gives us a clue about this process when he remarks that when children play they make rules for themselves, and in doing so start to practise self-control. 'Thus,' he says, 'the essential attribute of play is a rule that has become a desire.'[9] In so far as our rules become our desires, our values circle is bound in to our drives circle. We simply want to do what we think is right. Some of our drives, our desires and fears, are thus learned. To the degree that we act in accordance with our own thought-through moral principles, we can claim to be autonomous moral agents. To the extent that we bow and sway under temptations, social pressures and threats, we remain to a degree heteronymous. How autonomous a person becomes is thus one of the key aspects of character and the ability to self-regulate is itself prized as a value in our culture.

9.6 Knowledge, Curiosity and Control

We have almost completed our quick survey of human motivation. Humans, it has been argued, respond to their drives: their fears and desires. These drives are partly shaped by needs, transmitted to the brain by evolution, and partly by social values, including moral principles. But we are also information gatherers and processors, creatures who use symbolic knowledge to adapt to the world and solve the problems that face us. And, like other creatures, we attend mostly to the things that inform us about our special concerns, the things that we find rewarding or punishing and the conditions that predict their occurrence. If we are not getting new information about something we care about, then our attention tends to shift elsewhere. It is true that primates, monkeys and humans all show a good deal of general curiosity about the world, especially when young. Harlow showed long ago that monkeys in captivity would learn to solve mechanical puzzles just for the intrinsic satisfaction it gave them, without success being linked to any other reward.[10] Observing children's spontaneous play also quickly reveals how they, too, will explore and manipulate materials for the intrinsic satisfaction of so doing. But children in school are by no means constantly curious about the world; would that they were!

We need students to develop new interests, as well as learning about what already interests them. A great deal of learning in school is not intimately connected with either the students' immediate interests or with their present concerns, which is a major reason why motivation in the classroom is a problem. It is no doubt why we spend a good deal of time and energy attempting to convince children that long-term goals in life will be promoted by success in school. It is also why teachers often use forms of social influence, notably approval and disapproval, to persuade students to work harder. There remains something of a paradox, however, in that sometimes children are intensely curious and sometimes they are not.

The resolution of the paradox may come from realizing that curiosity is always a kind of desire, and its satisfaction generally involves the extension of one's control over the world. We may try merely to keep control, mounting a defence of our own existing resources, or we may try to gain control over extra resources, in competition with others. Control may be either a matter of physical mastery or manipulation, or some degree of power over another person or over resources. Alternatively, it may be the potential control that comes from greater understanding and knowledge. If I explore a new territory, I am adding a kind of potential to my capacities, an extension of where I might go and what I might do. A good musician controls, in this wide sense of the word, both his or her instrument and also a repertoire of music he or she can play. A mathematician controls a domain of knowledge about numbers, shapes or theorems. A doctor strives for control over diseases. A monk or nun may strive for control over the self. People sometimes characterize an individual as a 'control freak', meaning that they try to exercise rigid control over events or people in a neurotic manner. But perhaps we are all control freaks, in as much as we have an intrinsic desire to be, in this broad sense, in control of our lives. We may not consciously want to manipulate anyone or anything, but merely to control the resources, skills and knowledge that, in a given context, seem desirable. And having got control over one domain, we may want to reach out for another.

However, to desire knowledge in this way we have to feel that it comes within our range of interests; that it counts as what Margaret Donaldson has called a 'locus of concern'.[11] This requires a developing sense of what might be interesting. And this, in turn, is a result of learning. Eventually it may reach a level of generalized awareness, which allows us to view all knowledge as at least potentially interesting. As teachers we have to look therefore at a 'zone of proximal development' of our students' interests. One of the key features of children's spontaneous play is that it is under their own control; otherwise it is not play. The rule must become a desire, as Vygotsky said. Assisting them to desire something new is therefore one of the great challenges to a teacher. We have to persuade them that a task is connected to some existing desire, such as curiosity about a story or about a surprising phenomenon (the jar that did not float), or that it offers some longer-term pay-off.

One way that this can come about is via interesting and challenging intermediate goals. One may learn about the life of Marie Curie and learn all sorts of things about radiation in passing. Making a slide for marbles may teach one about gravity or how to build stable structures. A second way is via the influence of a respected (high status) other. If one's elder brother or an admired sixth-former says that, say, logic can be interesting, then one may be prepared to, as it were, go on a blind date with logic, to find out about it. (After all, smoking is often acquired in this way, even thought it is quite nauseating to the novice at first.) In one way or another, curiosity itself, as a drive or desire, needs to be developed by education from its origins in immediate novelty towards more generalized topics, puzzles and problems.[12]

So far I have talked of human desires and fears as 'drives' in a fairly uncritical manner. However psychologists have been criticizing drive theories of motivation for almost as long as there have been such theories to criticize. If one thinks of a drive only as some kind of response to deprivation, like hunger, which must be reduced, then while such a concept seems to fit the basic physiological drives quite well, it will not account for many human activities. Infants who stand up and learn to walk, tottering about for the first time under their own guidance, do so with evident delight. Some motives can be self-sustaining; they can grow by what they feed on. Extending our knowledge as a form of control over our world may continue to motivate us for as long as we live. Adults who have their basic comforts satisfied do not sink back and do nothing. Many of them learn new skills, practise hobbies and generally make use of all their capacities as humans in a way that suggests that this very use is itself rewarding. To do so, to make the effort to learn, they must believe that the outcomes will be more satisfying than the costs. These outcomes may have to do with mastery, status, material advantage or perhaps with a more general intrinsic desire for greater knowledge.

This intrinsic satisfaction, of finding out more about the world, is perhaps merely another form of potential control, or power (as Nietzsche argued); or perhaps it is rather a matter of having more meanings to play with and thus with the acquisition of a richer inner life. At all events, we have travelled far enough by now to have a sense of our students as humans who have desires, fears, needs and values, like anyone else. If deprived of basic needs such as warmth or security, we can expect them to be seriously distracted from learning by their internal 'regulators'. Beyond this level we expect them to be hungry for social contact, for attention, for status and affection, although also needing privacy at times. And beyond the immediacy of such social motives, we can expect them to be intellectually curious, but only to the extent that their curiosity has developed beyond its simple beginnings, in playful exploration of novelty in the world around them. Our motives are influenced by our values, as we have seen, but also by our beliefs. In the next chapter, we return to a focus on the world of the classroom, and see that beliefs, particularly beliefs about the self, have an important influence on motivation.

9.7 Questions

The following questions are designed to help you check your understanding of the chapter.

1 What is the difference between a 'need' and a 'drive'?
2 What is the law of effect?
3 What does Dunbar believe humans have substituted for mutual grooming?
4 Under what kinds of circumstance is the positive social drive in humans likely to be increased?
5 What do children usually identify as the chief pleasure of attending school?
6 How are our values linked to the anecdotes we tell our friends?
7 How is it argued here that values are linked to emotions?
8 How might a desire to learn be linked to the idea of 'control'?
9 **Discussion question**: how is it that people sometimes want to sacrifice their own needs and desires in order to help others?

NOTES

1. Brown and Herrnstein (1975), chapter 2.
2. Dunbar (1996).
3. Ainsworth (2000).
4. Brown and Herrnstein (1975), chapter 4.
5. Pinker (1997).
6. Lee and De Vore (1976).
7. Turnbull (1984).
8. Piaget (1932, 1965).
9. Vygotsky (1978).
10. Harlow, Harlow and Mayer (1950).
11. Donaldson (1992). This concept is further discussed in Chapter 11.
12. One of the few authors to write about this in depth is Kieran Egan (1990, 1997). Egan's work is discussed again in Chapter 11.

CHAPTER TEN

Influencing Student Motivation

10.1 Introduction

In order to return our feet firmly to the ground after roaming around human motivation in general, we will now consider how students tend to think about their own learning in school and how they respond to the different kinds of feedback and influence that teachers actually have at their disposal in a classroom. In the last chapter we saw how curiosity and a desire to extend our control, via adding to our knowledge, can potentially be important motivators for learners. In this chapter we shall examine social–cognitive research on motivation, which looks at the beliefs and theories that we build up about our learning and ourselves. It emerges that such beliefs and theories can have a powerful influence on our pattern of motivation and effort, especially on our likely response to situations involving difficulty or failure.

Such **self-theories**, as they have been called, have implications that reach out to many linked areas that will be touched on in this chapter. These include the part played in academic achievement by self-esteem and confidence, the kinds of reward that operate in school and the effects of different kinds of praise and feedback. They also lead us to a consideration of the expectations that teachers have of their students, the place of competition and collaboration in the classroom, and the motivating effects of group work. Throughout the chapter the common link running through all these topics is that students' motivation can be strongly affected by the implicit theories they hold about their abilities and self-worth.

10.2 Hope for Success and Fear of Failure

We saw, in Chapter 9, how humans are concerned with status and how others perceive them. We all, to some degree, want significant others to think well of us and indeed we want to think well of ourselves. However people differ quite profoundly in how they reason about experiences of success and failure. This is a subject with quite a long history in psychology. As far back as the 1930s, researchers were interested in the tendency of some students to be confident and hopeful of success when faced with challenging situations, whereas others seemed to fear failure and to avoid risks and challenges. McClelland and Atkinson developed a theory of 'need for achievement', in which they postulated a kind of drive for success that was held to be stronger in some people than others. In one experiment,[1] children were challenged to throw a ring over a peg some distance away. They were allowed to choose how far away from the peg they stood, but won more points for a successful throw if they chose a greater distance. The children had previously been tested on a 'need for achievement' task so that high scorers could be compared with low scorers in their response to the ring-tossing game. Children with a high need for achievement tended to choose a moderate distance from which to throw. This balanced a reasonable chance of success against a reasonably high reward for success. Children with low achievement scores, in contrast, tended to stand either very close to the peg or far away from it. They seemed to opt either for certain success but a low reward, or for almost certain failure but a failure that would not cause them any 'loss of face'.

McClelland and his colleagues felt more generally that how hard students will work on a task depends (i) on their estimate of the probability of success, (ii) on the reward value (or incentive) that is on offer, and (iii) on the person's inner level of achievement motivation (or drive). Later Atkinson, in particular, came to think that a separate tendency to avoid failure had to be included in the equation. That is, he thought that performance might come to be dominated by the hope of success or, alternately, by the fear of failure. There was also some evidence that whether hope of success or fear of failure came to dominate children's attitudes to their school work was linked to the way they were socialized by their parents. Much later, Noel Entwistle[2] came to link these patterns of motivation with two contrasting styles of studying, both at school and university. He argued that there may be a link between fear of failure and a superficial way of studying, one that concentrates on reproducing material rather than understanding it properly. This 'surface' approach to study seems to relate to worries about the *extrinsic* consequences of work, such as getting good or poor marks or looking good or bad in front of others. Other students, with a more robust set of attitudes, care more about a 'deep' approach to learning, in which they are genuinely motivated to understand what they are studying. Their *intrinsic* interest in the subject, and in making progress, are more important to them than marks or reputation.

From this early research came a tendency to argue that what teachers and parents should do is to give anxious children plenty of (easy) success and also praise them for it. It was thought that children who had too great a fear of failure needed their self-esteem and confidence boosted as much as possible, so that they would feel better about themselves and be generally more prepared to risk failure. Such beliefs were boosted by findings that indicated that successful students in school tended to have higher self-esteem than students who were failing. Unfortunately, as so often, this cluster of beliefs has proved to be an over-simplification, which has taken a long time to unravel. It was certainly possible to find students who exhibited low self-confidence and who also showed a sense of helplessness in the face of failures. If they did badly on a test or could not solve some difficult problem, their reaction was generally to blame themselves for being stupid, to feel depressed and to try to avoid further contact with the task. It seemed that they felt they could not do anything to help themselves; indeed, this pattern of response came to be called **learned helplessness**. Such students responded to failure in a way that actually led to them doing worse and worse. Their self-denigration and lack of persistence made it less likely that they would overcome their problems. The question then was: can one change such patterns of avoidance and fear of failure?

Example 10.1 Re-training in responses to failure

One such study was published in 1975 by Carol Dweck.[3] She identified a group of 11– 12 year olds who showed a strong 'learned helpless' response to failure. First, she gave them a series of maths problems over several days until they were showing a stable and high level of success. Then she slipped some unusually difficult problems into the work without any warning. The students, unsurprisingly, were upset by these problems. Not only did they fail to solve them but their performance on subsequent problems deteriorated sharply, even though these were exactly the same type of problem as those at which they had previously succeeded. (In similar studies, contrasting 'learned helpless' with more resilient students, the resilient students found the new problems difficult but quickly returned to their former level of success on the later problems.)

Dweck now set out to try to effect a change. The 'learned helpless' students were divided into two new equivalent groups, one of which was given a series of training sessions emphasizing success, whereas the other group received the same number of training sessions that emphasized effort in the face of failure. Thus, the first group were given timed sets of maths problems at which they regularly succeeded and were praised for their success. The second group were taught a new attribution for their failures. The work was manipulated so that they failed two or three problems out of every fifteen, within the time limit. They were then told how many they needed to get correct and were instructed that they needed to work harder in order to reach the target. Dweck made sure that this effort paid off by the end of the session. After 25 training sessions, the original assessment situation was reinstated, with stable performance on routine problems suddenly inter- rupted by a series of much harder problems. This time, the group who had been trained with routine success actually did even worse in their reaction to failure. However, the attribution re-training group, who had been taught that effort was an adaptive response to failure, did significantly better. They even improved their scores after the difficult problems, rather than letting their performance deteriorate.

Dweck came to feel that simply praising students for easy successes did little to improve either their long-term self-esteem or their response to failure.[4] Such praise might make students feel good about themselves in the short term, but it did nothing to help them cope with difficulty. Nor did it teach them a resilient approach to studying. Dweck found in her studies over a number of years that some 15% of students, chosen across ages from 11 to 22, did not show a strong tendency towards either resilience or learned helplessness. Of the other 85%, however, about half fitted each of the two main patterns. She also identified groups of intellectually bright girls, in particular, who unexpectedly showed a strong tendency to denigrate themselves and give up when they faced failure or an unusual challenge. Bright boys, in general, seemed less prone to this problem (see also 14.3). In fact the 'helpless orientation', as Dweck came to call it, was independent (rather surprisingly) of both a student's estimated academic ability and their self-esteem. Many less academically successful students showed the contrasting resilience, or **mastery orientation**, in the face of challenges.

A number of similar studies by Dweck and her associates showed that it was possible to predict a 'helpless' or 'mastery' orientation by using students' responses to a questionnaire and then demonstrate that these two distinct groups would respond in very different ways when confronted with unexpected difficulties or failures. The 'helpless' group were critical of themselves, looked around for ways out of the situation and became depressed. Their performance on subsequent (easier) problems deteriorated. The 'mastery' group seemed to relish difficulty and responded to it by increasing their efforts. Even if they failed on difficult problems, they did not let the failure worry them and quickly resumed their successful ways. Sometimes their efforts actually led them to solve problems that were supposed to be too hard for their age. The same contrast between 'mastery' and 'helpless' orientations was shown to predict similar behaviour in real situations in both classrooms and universities. But what had led to the orientations in the first place?

10.3 Seeing Intelligence as Fixed or Changeable

As she continued her research, Dweck made two further interesting discoveries. The first was that the 'helpless' orientation went with a mind-set that emphasized **performance goals** over learning goals. That is, these 'helpless' students not only reacted badly to failure but also had a strong tendency to see the main goal of school work as 'doing well' in terms of marks, grades or competition with others. They wanted to look smart, no matter what. The 'mastery' group, in contrast, mostly had goals that concentrated on learning, effort and improving their competence. Unfortunately, the emphasis on performance goals led the 'helpless' students to avoid challenges which might make them look bad or stupid and to choose easy tasks from which they would not learn much. The 'mastery' students, with the goal of improving their learning, would risk a challenge and would choose moderately demanding tasks, from which they expected to learn. Now, sometimes performance does matter; we need to get good grades or pass exams to reach some goal in life. But the point is that if we concentrate on these extrinsic signs of success too much, they can lead us into sacrificing valuable opportunities to learn something useful, because of our fear of showing ourselves up, both to ourselves and to others.

Dweck's second breakthrough was to discover that behind both the 'performance goals' and the 'helpless orientation' lay a certain implicit theory of intelligence. These performance-oriented students, who cared so much about their relative status and superficial successes, turned out overwhelmingly to favour a view of intelligence as a fixed entity, something you are born with. One of them defined intelligence as 'inborn ability to learn and evaluate complex ideas. I don't believe it can be learned from books.'[5] The students with a 'mastery' orientation and stronger learning goals generally held an incremental view of intelligence, as something that can develop and change. One of them defined intelligence as 'The amount of knowledge one possesses and how they use it.' Probably most of us are somewhat unsure of how fixed, or malleable, intelligence really is. There is an enormous amount of evidence, of varying qualities, on each side of the picture, as we shall see in Chapter 12. However it is clear that holding an **entity theory**, at least one that is too inflexible, can have a number of highly damaging consequences.

With this insight, Dweck was able to piece together a general picture of how learned hopelessness comes about. If you believe that intelligence is simply some 'thing' of which you have either 'a lot' or 'a little', then you will be likely to see your academic performance as directly reflecting your inner ability on each occasion it is tested. Feeling that your performance, good or bad, simply shows up how smart or dumb you are, you come to care about that performance and particularly how your results compare with those of your peers. If you find that work is difficult or impossible, it just indicates that you are not very bright. Thus an episode of failure reflects directly on your perceived ability and worth. Basically it shows you that you are not intelligent. In consequence you denigrate yourself, feel depressed and try to escape from the situation. The entity theory of intelligence thus leads to an emphasis on performance goals and to a 'helpless' orientation. Failure means that you are obviously no good at whatever it is that is being tested. Compare this with the attitudes of someone who has an **incremental theory** of intelligence. Failure to this person simply means that they did not have the right knowledge or strategies to succeed at this point in time. All the more reason, then, to acquire them through further efforts. Since performance and learning are both improved by working hard, you will probably see that as the way forward. Incidents of failure may be depressing, but they do not make you feel badly about yourself, for why should they? They have little to do with your inner self. Hence an incremental theory tends to go along with an emphasis on learning goals and a mastery orientation.

Example 10.2 Theories of intelligence and goals of learning
A group of Hong Kong Chinese researchers[6] working with Carol Dweck showed how these linked clusters of beliefs could affect academic choices in real life. In the University of Hong Kong, at the time, all courses were taught in English. New students were tested for their language proficiency in English and success in courses was crucially dependent on the use of that language. The researchers gave a group of new students a survey, which revealed whether they tended towards a belief that intelligence is a fixed entity or a developing set of knowledge and skills. They also had access to these students' scores on the test of proficiency in English. The new students were reminded how important the use of English would be in their future courses and asked if they would like to sign up for a remedial English course, if it was offered. Those whose language scores were high in the

*first place were not much interested in the proposed course. Those with low scores, how-
ever, only said they were interested in such a remedial course if they had 'incremental'
views on intelligence. The low scorers with 'entity' theories were no more interested in
taking the course than were the students who had high scores. Perhaps they did not want
to confront their difficulties, or perhaps they feared that such a course would show them
up as failures. In any event, they passed up an opportunity that might have helped
them significantly.*

*The same researchers, in a linked study, used a pair of vividly written psycho-
logy articles to manipulate students' theories about intelligence. One article was strongly
supportive of an entity theory of innate intelligence, whereas the other argued equally
strongly that high intelligence is a result of environmental opportunities and learning. The
articles were convincing enough to persuade graduate students in psychology that they
were genuine. The Hong Kong students were divided into two groups and given either the
'entity' article or the 'incremental' article to read. They then all answered a series of questions about the article they had read. Next they all took a test of non-verbal reasoning.
They were given false feedback on the results of the test, either to the effect that they had
done better than most other students on the test or worse than most other students. Lastly,
they were offered a special tutorial, with the advice that it 'was found to be effective in
improving performance on the test for most people'. Who would take this offer up? In fact
students mostly signed up for the tutorial if they had been told they had done better than
most. It seems that entity theorists are prepared to try some further learning if it does not
threaten them with failure. But in the group of those who were supposed to have done
worse than most, only those exposed to the 'incremental' theory opted in numbers (73%)
to take the tutorial. Among those exposed to the 'entity' theory, a much smaller proportion (13%) wanted to take the opportunity to improve.*

In these studies, a belief, temporary or longer lasting, that intelligence is a fixed
asset is shown to influence people who have concerns about exposing themselves to
failure, even if it means passing up an opportunity to learn more. Dweck has also
shown that such students tend to devalue effort in any case, as they tend to believe
that having to work hard just shows that you are not very bright in the first place.
Those who believe that intelligence is incremental, being tied to our learning and
skills, see that effort and learning are the way to become smarter. Failure has a
different meaning to them: it is simply feedback showing that they do not currently
know enough. It does not attack their underlying sense of ability or worth. An
optimistic outcome of these studies, both those with the schoolchildren and those
with the university freshmen, is that at least in the short term our beliefs about the
malleability or otherwise or intelligence seem quite easily to be altered. This shows
that it is a complex issue, on which it is difficult to hold 'final' views, and that
teachers have a good chance of working with students who have a 'helpless' orientation, to teach them to have more adaptive and useful attitudes to their learning.

In Dweck's work, confidence is shown to be rather less important than was once
imagined. It remains true that confidence about academic work does tend to follow
in the wake of success. The more important question, however, is whether it can
be maintained in the face of difficulty and failure. When students hold too rigid an

entity theory, then past success and present confidence is not enough. It crumbles quickly in the face of evidence that the student interprets as showing that he or she is not very bright after all. The kind of self-esteem that goes with a 'mastery' orientation and a resilient attitude to learning is not something that can be 'given' to students, by parents or teachers. It is not so much something that you 'have' or 'do not have' but rather something that you experience or do not experience. It is encountered, for example, when one is experiencing the satisfactions of working hard, making progress and using one's abilities to the full.

10.4 The Ladder of Reinforcement

Teachers have a range of ways in which they can try to influence student behaviour. One can imagine these methods set out as a ladder, with a number of rungs. On the bottom rung are material and physical **reinforcers**, such as pleasurable hugs, toys or food on the one hand, and painful blows or shouts on the other. These operate as rewards or punishments if, and only if, students will work to acquire or avoid them. In the past, physical punishments were commonly used in schools but our society has turned its back on them for principled reasons. We no longer regard it as morally acceptable to use pain and fear as reinforcers in schools. Of course what works as a reward or punishment for one student may not be effective for another. Some children, for example, enjoy seeing adults get angry. In fact such crude material reinforcers are seldom used in schools, although parents are often prepared to use them.

On the second rung of the ladder come activity reinforcers that use one activity, say playing a computer game, as a reward for another, say writing. Teachers do quite frequently use activities as rewards or punishments and as such they can be effective. The chief disadvantage is that some kinds of activity are being implicitly labelled as unpleasant 'work' and others as pleasurable 'play'. Such uses of an **extrinsic reward** can undermine children's nascent intrinsic interest in the work itself. The third rung of the ladder takes us up to various symbolic rewards and punishments, such as stars, certificates, team points and so forth. These may be used on their own or, in some situations, as a kind of currency, as tokens, which are exchangeable against activity or material reinforcers.

Symbolic and token rewards can be used flexibly in order to signal approval to a child in a form they may find easier to understand than words. Some teachers are happy to use these in a pragmatic way, especially in the early years of school, but others dislike their manipulative character. In general, teachers prefer to think that education is a desirable thing in its own right. Also 'inflation' can be a problem, in that the value of particular incentives tends to decrease with use. Students habituate to them, as to everything. I recently heard a neat comparison of such rewards to fireworks: they are both effective only so long as they are a novelty. And we need to bear in mind that we do not want our students only working for the reward, and then stopping. A material or symbolic reward should be a temporary motivator, signalling an achievement we approve of for its own sake.

The fourth level of the ladder concerns social approval and disapproval communicated directly, whether verbally or non-verbally. This is the level probably used more than any other by teachers. Because we use social influence in many subtle ways in all our relationships and interactions, it seems quite natural in the classroom; it is an extension of our normal manner of interacting with friends and family. But it is still a particular form of influence and we need to recognize that it is not effective with all students. For many students the approval or disapproval of a teacher is a powerful motivator, but clearly not for all. Also, for some students, a word of encouragement in private is more effective than recognition given in front of classmates. By and large, such social reinforcement from an adult is more powerful for younger than for older students.

If praise or disapproval is used, at any age, it should be directed at the behaviour rather than at the child. Dweck's research shows that praise and disapproval should be aimed at specific achievements and qualities of the work, rather than at the whole child or their intelligence. Thus 'That shows a real improvement in your choice of words, Sean' is likely to be more helpful than 'You're a great writer, Sean'; 'It's good to see you enjoying that new music, Emma' is preferable to 'I'm so proud of your achievements, Emma.' In some circumstances, too much emphasis on praise for outcomes or products seems to backfire and make students actually less willing to try hard. Students with a tendency towards a 'helpless' orientation may start to worry that they will lose their high status because they do not deserve it. For them, you are only as good as your last performance. Praise thus works best when it is contingent on good work, specific to what is good about it and credible to the student.

The fifth and final rung on the ladder concerns intrinsic reinforcement. Here, students work (or avoid work) simply because they find the work itself intrinsically interesting (or boring). This, for teachers, is ultimately the only really satisfactory level at which to work. The satisfaction of work is an end in itself and requires no other reinforcer. It is also the means to genuine self-esteem. The five levels of reinforcement, or means of influence if you prefer, are deliberately ordered from the least desirable (material) to the most desirable (intrinsic). In my view we should always work with the highest level of the 'ladder' that is actually effective. Whenever we can operate at the intrinsic level we will do so. Frequently, however, students do not see life this way and require at least social reinforcers to motivate them. Sometimes it is necessary to descend to lower rungs on the ladder, at least as a temporary measure.

10.5 Punishment and Exclusion

Punishments, once so commonplace, have become less and less acceptable in our schools. We prefer to emphasize the positive in our relationships with students. The punishments that remain, such as 'time out' and detentions, are variations on the theme of activity reinforcers. The term 'time out' is short for 'time out from all forms of positive reinforcement'. It substitutes neutrality, or lack of stimulation, for the normally reinforcing social world and works as a mild punishment. It can work well if carefully set up and supervised (see also 4.6). Detentions use enforced activity at schoolwork as a deprivation from free time. Again, as activity reinforcers, they have the disadvantage that this sends a message suggesting that schoolwork is a kind of punishment and should be avoided if possible. However, most well-adjusted students probably understand the trade-off perfectly well, without being damaged for life.

Schools are societies in microcosm and teachers, too, may occasionally face violence and find themselves in difficulties over how to respond. I have in mind not so much violent attacks against teachers, though these do sometimes occur, or even violence between students, but rather the occasional defiance of a school's rules by students who simply ignore all sanctions directed against them. Teachers have (rightly, I think) almost entirely given up physical threats and punishments, but they have to work out what they will do if a student defies their authority and threatens the peace and safety of other people in the classroom or school. Democracies ultimately need to be defended. Generally, senior staff and head teachers manage to contain such situations, avoiding extreme responses and using negotiations with both students and their parents to reach an outcome acceptable to all parties. If this does not work, however, students may, in the end, be suspended or excluded from the school.

Since local authorities have a responsibility to provide education for all children of school age, such students are not infrequently traded from one school to another. Sometimes they are found places in special schools, but this has two disadvantages: first, such placements are extremely expensive and, secondly, there are often problems re-integrating the student into his or her home area, and school, later. More recently, where such students can be shown to have special educational needs, extra funds have more often been channelled into mainstream schools to meet their needs and provide assistance to staff. Such students frequently have serious problems in relating to other people and in feeling positive about themselves (see also Chapter 13). They undoubtedly cause teachers many problems, but a concerted and determined school-wide policy to avoid exclusions can be effective.

Example 10.3 Seeking to avoid exclusions
One primary school attempted to find policies that would prevent or avoid excluding disaffected students.[7] *These policies included the following.*

- Staff meetings reviewed the school's behaviour policy to discuss problems and to improve on consistency of practice.
- Staff also met to agree on students 'at risk' of serious confrontations and disciplinary problems. Each of these students was given a 'personal tutor' who met with them regularly, discussed their lives and set them achievable targets for improved behaviour. They made a special point of talking about emotions and ways of avoiding disruptive and aggressive behaviour.
- A 'behaviour book' was placed in each classroom and in the dining hall and play-ground, in which all incidents of bad behaviour were recorded. This was first discussed with the Y5 and Y6 students. The head teacher used these records to monitor patterns of behaviour and progress made.

- **Circle time** was instituted in every class each week and used especially to discuss problems with relationships, bullying and school values in a relaxed atmosphere, in which students could put their own point of view.
- Where students were behaving badly on a regular basis, staff carried out a special review of their academic problems and then provided extra support to help with these.
- Use of a safe 'time out' room was combined with counselling of students who were sent there. In these sessions the students were encouraged to talk, in order to gain insight into their understanding of what had happened and how they thought their difficulties were being dealt with.
- Students who were in danger of exclusion were warned of a 'six strikes and you're out' policy. Parents were involved with such discussions and formal warnings. Meanwhile, the head teacher was privately determined that no student should ever reach 'six strikes'.

If classrooms are to be genuinely peaceful places, in which students all have an opportunity to learn, and if they are to remain safe, then minimal standards of behaviour have to be upheld. It seems reasonable that all teachers should have the power to exclude a child from a class who, after fair warning, persistently defies agreed rules. The teacher should be firmly supported in refusing to have such a disruptive individual in the room, but efforts should also be made to understand why such events have occurred. Any such temporary exclusion should of course be subject to due process, with safeguards for both students and teachers. Head teachers should decide how quickly such an individual might return to the class, given an undertaking to respect the rules in future. The school would also have to provide a safe place for such students to be while excluded, and decide what should be the resources to which they might still have access. Parents would have to be called in for consultation.

This ability to defend minimal standards of behaviour within classrooms represents, for me, the essential power that society must hand over to teachers. Only then can teachers uphold standards that respect the welfare of others and allow learning to go on. If they do not have this power, the danger is that compromises are made, standards are eroded, and other students then lose out. Seeing a school system failing to defend its own culture and ethos adequately is in itself, I believe, a corrupting experience for children. Having (rightly) ruled out the use of force against children, we have to face up to the implications. It is worth reiterating that the best way to motivate students to work is to provide them with a positive and supportive environment, with interesting challenges and good enthusiastic teaching. Almost all students respect teachers who persist in the face of difficulties and do a good job. And teachers who are trusted and liked do have a great influence on those they teach. Moreover, one can actively teach students to have better attitudes towards their own learning.

10.6 Teaching the Values Behind Effective Learning

The kind of deliberate conscious learning that is the speciality of schools is, as we saw in Chapter 8, relatively difficult for all of us, whatever our level of ability or knowledge. Guy Claxton has pointed out that the more effective learners among us have developed a set of values, based on their experiences, which help them through the hard times.[8] In many ways, his work is an extension of that of Carol Dweck on the 'mastery' orientation (10.3). In particular, Claxton argues that effective learners have learned the difficult lessons that (i) feeling stuck is normal and (ii) persevering through difficulties leads to satisfaction and heightened self-esteem. More generally, these kinds of 'lessons about learning' have to do with the following.

- *Teaching resilience*: learning to tolerate the frustrations of learning, persevering with problems, managing distractions, getting absorbed in tasks.
- *Teaching resourcefulness*: asking good questions, imagining, reasoning, getting help from others, capitalizing on strengths.
- *Teaching reflectiveness*: making a plan, monitoring progress, discussing how learning is going, revising, distilling learning into short pithy summaries.
- *Teaching reciprocity*: learning to imitate skilled others, listening, collaborating, developing empathy, sharing problems and celebrating successes.

Example 10.4 Designing a community of learners

Ann Brown and Joseph Campione[9] worked with teachers to design a new form of communal science education for 11–12 year olds. The project did not set out to teach metacognition directly, but instead designed an environment in which metacognition of various forms could and would flourish. It built on the principles of reciprocal teaching (see Example 8.2) and involved a high degree of student involvement and decision-making. One biology unit looked at changing populations of animals, which were categorized in five groups (extinct, endangered, artificial, assisted and urbanized). Five 'research groups' of students were formed and each was assigned one of these subgroups of animal. They had to research the topic and also prepare teaching materials for the other students. This involved a great deal of reading, writing, computer use and discussion. There was an emphasis on setting goals and priorities and on sharing information.

The teachers designed the unit, supplied the resources and also led regular whole class 'conferences' to monitor progress and set goals for learning. There were many opportunities for the teachers to make points about metacognition and good attitudes to learning during these conferences. They also used a 'jig-saw' approach to group work, whereby the students were reorganized into five new groups in which each member of a group was an 'expert' on one of the subgroups of animals. The role of the experts was to teach the others in the group about their category of animals and also to design test items for an assessment that the whole class was to complete on the unit. This way of working placed considerable responsibility on the students, who had both to collaborate and take on important individual responsibilities.

Individual children developed expertise in particular aspects of the curriculum in which they took a special interest and were deferred to by the other students as 'experts'. Discussion, questioning and criticism were common features of classroom discourse. Assessment of the unit indicated that the students taught in this fashion for a year outperformed control groups on reading comprehension tests involving facts, inferences, summaries and reasoning by analogy. They also did better than controls on short-answer tests of the biology content studied. Measures of the use of causal explanations, support of explanations with evidence and the use of varied forms of argument also showed improvements. (The authors are imaginative in the forms of assessment they used as well as in the design of the learning environment.)

This example reminds us that the whole person is very much involved in classroom learning. What might once have been described as 'character building' would now be more likely to be seen in terms of teaching positive attitudes and strategies for learning. As such, this is still very much the province of all teachers, of all age groups. Such teaching can use the same 'normal' teaching methods of demonstration, direct instruction, interactive teaching and setting up independent problem-solving as with ordinary curriculum content. A simple example, at the level of strategy, is the kind of list that teachers in primary schools often make with, and for, young readers, listing all the ways of reading a difficult word. Items on the list might include:

- try sounding it out;
- see if you can break it down into syllables;
- try re-reading the whole sentence and thinking about what it means;
- read on to see if the meaning becomes clearer;
- use the pictures to help;
- ask a friend to help you.

Using Claxton's longer-term attitudes, skills and strategies of resilience, resourcefulness, reflectiveness and reciprocity (which we might call the four Rs), it is possible to explain them, demonstrate them by sharing with students one's own attempts at learning, give direct advice about them, discuss them, design posters about them, include them in lesson aims, assess them and regularly make them an explicit part of your class's curriculum. They are not a substitute for learning the content of the curriculum, but they can have a dramatic effect on both class ethos and student attainment. Although they are currently fashionable, they are not altogether a new concern. Dr Thomas Arnold, the famous nineteenth-century headmaster of Rugby School, once remarked that he became 'increasingly convinced that it is not knowledge, but the means of getting knowledge which I have to teach'.[10]

10.7 The Influence of Expectations

There is a large body of educational research on teachers' expectations and the ways in which they may be communicated to their students. At one time, it was widely believed that if teachers held unduly low expectations of students a kind of self-fulfilling prophecy would come to pass, as the students came to internalize the same opinion of themselves. However this risk has probably been exaggerated. In one summary of the field, a respected researcher wrote as follows:

Most [effects] are more accurately construed as student effects on teachers rather than teacher expectation effects on students. Most differential teacher expectations are accurate and reality-based... Although the potential for teachers' expectations to function as self-fulfilling prophecies always exists, the extent to which they do so in typical classrooms is probably limited...[11]

The same writer considered that such limited effects (of the order of 5–10%) were more likely to consist of the effects of unreasonably rigid, low expectations depressing student achievement than of high expectations improving achievements. However most teachers had turned out to be realistic in their expectations and were also open to correcting them when new and surprising evidence turned up. The realism and accuracy of teacher's expectations has also been confirmed by more recent research.[12] Nevertheless, the suspicion lingers that expectations may be one vital ingredient among many others in motivating students to do well.

One possibility is that teachers naturally come to form expectations about individual students, based on their day-to-day work with them, and then tend to react towards individuals differently in such a way as to maintain their relative achievements. On the other hand, there is other evidence that many teachers work harder to help low-achieving students and that most teachers are prepared to modify their initial views, given new evidence. Another complication in this field is that whatever the expectations and behaviour of teachers may be, they have to bring about their hypothesized effects via the thoughts and actions of their students. Yet individual students are likely to respond in quite variable ways to the same teacher behaviour. Perhaps a more significant finding, in the end, is that research on schools that are particularly successful in raising the standards of their students in basic subjects (usually English and maths) has persistently reported that successful schools have, among other qualities, high standards for their students. Colin Rogers[13] reviews some of the thinking behind this claim.

It seems likely that teachers form a view of a normal, or typical, rate of progress in their classes. They then judge particular individuals as faster or slower than this 'norm'. It seems reasonable to infer from this that schools which have in fact been successful in terms of examinations, or national assessments, will tend to form relatively high expectations of the norm and judge their students accordingly. Now, if this causes them to communicate those expectations to the students and if the general culture (ethos) of the school is such that these high expectations are general, it may lead both teachers and taught to work hard to bring the standard of work up to the norm. In short, expectations may lead on to useful action. Equally, a school that didn't expect its students to achieve much might not go about trying to change that state of affairs. To this extent, high expectations may lead to people actually doing relevant things, such as appropriate teaching and learning, with rigorous standards, which then lead to good results.

It is also worth pointing out that 'high' in this context means high relative to existing attainments. A teacher may expect all his students to get good grades, but this may be a 'low' expectation if they are already performing at a very high level.

Conversely, a teacher faced with a seriously under-achieving class may have 'high' expectations in simply expecting them to reach the average national level by the end of the school year. It is the **value added** by teachers and schools that should be the relevant measure of their achievement.

Example 10.5 Communicating high expectations
One secondary school[14] improved its overall student examination results dramatically, following a campaign to instil a 'culture of achievement'. This programme included special efforts to motivate groups of disaffected boys, who were felt to spread attitudes that worked against the school's aims. Initiatives included the following.

- A fortnightly newsletter, reporting on current events and also celebrating achievements.
- Effective use of local media links to publicize the school's successes.
- Clear and regular communication with parents about the school's general aims and also specific aims for individual students.
- Assessing incoming students' academic 'potential' via both National Curriculum test results and cognitive tests. Targets were then set for progress to mirror that made by successful past students with similar profiles. Regular monitoring of progress then identified individuals and groups who seemed to be under-achieving.
- High-profile end-of-term assemblies, which celebrated academic as well as other achievements.
- Special 6-week achievement programmes for selected students at key periods of the academic year, with specific targets to tackle under-achievement. These were accompanied by involving successful older students as role models, by parental involvement and by giving small prizes for success.
- Senior staff undertook to sit in on lessons where poor discipline was reported as a problem.
- Intensive programmes for revision before examinations were instigated, with study packs, voluntary 2-day residential revision periods and individual tutoring.
- Voluntary summer schools for boosting literacy and numeracy were set up, with student teachers from a nearby university helping to staff them.

10.8 Competition, Collaboration and Group Work

Competition in many forms is prevalent in our society and this can lead to a hostile reaction to it from many people, who wish to encourage a more caring, cooperative ethos, at least in schools. The educational literature has many examples of writers persuaded of the advantages of collaborative learning and the pitfalls of excessively open competition between individuals.[15] Meanwhile, rather ironically, many schools in the private sector quietly continue to encourage competition between students, believing that this has a strong effect on their performance. I fully agree that the ethos of a school classroom should generally be one in which the participants try to help one another. Yet I think that competition is not always necessarily harmful. It is certainly difficult to eliminate, given the readiness of most children to compete in all kinds of ways. In fact it is so easy to get children to compete with one another that research has tended to concentrate on how we might get them to stop.[16]

Children will frequently try to compete with one another, in almost any valued activity, provided they think that they have some chance of succeeding. Gender may play a role here, with boys perhaps being more motivated by competition in general than girls. Boys may also be more likely to compete physically with one another, whereas girls often turn to more socially oriented forms of competition. It seems likely that this everyday feature of childhood has to do with their striving for status within the peer group and with estimating their own competence. It does not imply that they will always compete over academic work, since they may not value it, but competition is very easily observed, certainly at KS1 and KS2. Children are, of course, often encouraged to compete in all kinds of games and sports. The question is whether, as teachers, we should ever tap into this strong tendency of children to compete or should we always play it down? Can competition ever be 'healthy competition'?

The ethos of a whole school needs to be taken into account when considering this issue, rather than the views of a single teacher. In many lessons the question scarcely arises, since competition would not be in any way helpful to learning. No art or science teacher is likely to ask children to compete at painting or at carrying out an experiment. (However, I have regularly seen KS2 children trying to turn a science experiment into a competition, as in who can build the strongest bridge, find the strongest magnet, etc.) It is in the area of routine practice and revision that competition might be thought more relevant. If the same individuals tend to win and lose, of course, then the malign effects on the losers' motivation are not hard to guess. Most schools, I think, allow and encourage some competition, generally in situations in which it seems fair and not too hurtful to the losers. Thus few teachers would pit the best spellers against the worst in a spelling test. If they did decide to have two teams compete in a quiz about, say, mental arithmetic, then they would be sure to try to match the teams in order to make it a close (and fair) contest. If teams are set up to compete, there is at least the opportunity for collaboration within each team.

The competitive urge is clearly one that teachers need to harness with care. Competition is ubiquitous in childhood and can be a powerful source of motivation. It may make more sense to channel this force constructively than to try to avoid it altogether. Of course the fact that something is 'natural' does not automatically make it good. But if competition can motivate good work, without harmful side-effects, it is worth considering. Taking part in fair competitions and learning to win or to lose with a good spirit can itself be seen as a useful lesson for students. However, Dweck's emphasis on the harmful consequences of concentrating too much on 'performance goals' also needs to be borne in mind (10.3).

Getting children to work together in groups has long been a strategy for improving their engagement with the curriculum. It is usually justified as a strategy for learning but it will be discussed here mainly from a motivational point of view. Originally, work in groups was mostly recommended as being a productive 'halfway house' between an ideal of individual teaching and the reality of whole-class teaching.

Evidence that it actually improved standards of attainment, however, was hard to come by. One problem, especially in primary schools, was that although teachers routinely sat children in groups, they often then set work that was essentially individual in its nature. Working collaboratively on the same task was actually a rare event.[17]

In secondary schools, work in small groups was recommended mainly as a means of involving students more actively in thinking about the ideas being targeted in a lesson. 'Active' discussion was promoted over 'passive' listening to a teacher. The importance of developing oral language has also been widely promoted for its own sake. Teachers realized, however, that setting groups to work actively on a task carried the twin risks that (i) they might drift off-task and discuss their own social lives and (ii) that some members of the group might opt out of learning, allowing themselves to be carried along by the work of others. Such students became known as 'easy riders'. In more recent times, the power of good whole-class teaching has come to be more appreciated and group work has often been justified on a different basis: as a means of teaching smaller clusters of students at about the same level of attainment. In this form, it becomes a kind of differentiated teaching, as in group reading and group writing within the 'literacy hour'.

'Groups' have often been assumed to consist of between three and six students working together, but groups of this size actually assume considerable sophistication in the management of communication and work within the group. Adults, let alone children and adolescents, find it hard to work well in groups of more than about four. It is arguable that the most natural and productive human 'group' is actually a pair.[18] Pairs of students can often work productively, with both members taking an active part and without difficulties over shared communication overshadowing the task. For this reason I would advocate almost always starting group work with pairs, unless you are teaching a whole group yourself. Pairs may then, sometimes, get together in fours, before feeding back to the whole class.

The idea of 'jig-saw' groups can also work well, at least for some tasks involving the gathering of specialist information (Example 10.4). Here each original group of four or five sends a member to a second 'specialist group'. The specialist groups carry out reading or research into just one aspect of the general problem, sharing the work between them. Each 'specialist' member then returns to his or her original group and has the responsibility of advising the others on their specialist topic. The original groups may then work together to put the four or five specialist pieces of the jig-saw together into a complete response to the problem. The whole class can then compare the different responses or products.

Group work has two main benefits of a motivational kind. Firstly, it taps directly into students' desire to interact socially with one another. It is clear that although this interaction can lead to argument and strife, students mostly report that they enjoy working with one another. It may be necessary, however, for the teacher to keep control of the membership of the groups and take steps to train a class actively in how to work productively together. Secondly, talk and work with others can make students engage more actively with the concepts and facts of the lesson than they do when listening to the teacher instruct. Group work, in other words, can provide a relief from the effort of listening to long periods of teacher talk. Listening to one speaker for longer than a few minutes requires good effortful concentration (11.2). It is all too easy to find one's attention drifting. During group work, in contrast, students are likely to have to commit themselves to views and work out differences in their points of view. The confrontation of different views may itself be a powerful means of encouraging the restructuring or modification of one's ideas (2.1, 2.2, 2.3).

If a group enables each individual to work in a mentally active way, articulating concepts and ideas for themselves, then each is more likely to learn and remember, as well as to enjoy the activity. The risk, of course, is that the talk in groups will drift off-task or communicate misconceptions. It is thus important that teachers set up clear purposeful tasks, with outcomes that can be reported back to the whole class.

10.9 Exercise and Questions

As an exercise, choose one example from each of the four Rs (see 10.6) that seem particularly appropriate to the students you are teaching. (Alternatively, if you are not currently teaching, choose four aims that you think you could profitably apply to your own learning.) Now plan and teach (or apply to yourself) these four 'aids to good learning' in some fashion in your next four lessons. Keep it simple at first. Remember you can start from concrete examples, talk about your own learning, ask your students to talk about how they feel when learning is going well or badly, involve them in writing their own list of advice (e.g. on what they do when they feel stuck) or include relevant discussion in the final part of a lesson. This dimension of motivation is something that can be learned. It is also affected by the nature and quality of assessment that a teacher uses, an issue that will be taken up in Chapter 15.

The following questions are designed to help you check your understanding of the chapter.

1 Why may 'entity' theories of intelligence lead to 'learned hopelessness'?
2 Why does building up students' confidence, through success and praise, sometimes seem ineffective?
3 If material reinforcers are on the first rung of the ladder of reinforcement, what are on the next two rungs?
4 What is meant by 'intrinsic' reinforcement, or motivation?
5 How are teachers recommended to use praise?
6 What does research suggest about self-fulfilling prophecies in schools?
7 List five ways in which schools have tried to promote a 'culture of achievement'.
8 What, according to this chapter, are the four Rs?
9 What are some of the advantages and disadvantages of group work?
10 **Discussion question:** 'Excellent schools are themselves learning places – the staff learn and develop, and the curriculum changes and improves over time.'[19] How might schools help their staff to 'learn and develop' and to be resilient in their own learning?

NOTES

1. This work is summarized in Entwistle (1981), chapter 9.
2. Entwistle (1981), especially chapters 4, 5 and 9.
3. Dweck (1975).
4. The following account of research comes mainly from Dweck (2000).
5. This and the next quotation come from Dweck (2000), p. 61.
6. Dweck (2000), p. 22.
7. This example draws from material in Cooper et al. (2000).
8. Claxton (2002).
9. Brown and Campione (1998).
10. Strachey (1918).
11. Brophy (1983).
12. For example Jussim and Eccles (1995).
13. Rogers (2002).
14. Example paraphrased from the Standards website: www.standards.dfes.gov.uk/
15. For example Watkins et al. (2002); also Slavin (1995).
16. For a classic study, see Sherif (1966).
17. Galton, Simon and Croll (1980).
18. Dunbar (1996).
19. DfES (2003), p. 1.

CHAPTER ELEVEN

The Developing Mind

11.1 Introduction

There is no doubt that the subjective experience of teaching is strongly coloured by the age group one teaches and also by the subject one is teaching. Students in the age groups 4–6, 7–11, 12–14 and 15–17 are so different in physical size, maturity, knowledge and interests that they present a teacher with totally contrasting social worlds. Teaching music is also quite different from teaching language, or science or history, if only because of the subject matter knowledge, materials and tasks that each subject involves (see Chapter 16). This book has deliberately concentrated on the generic aspects of teaching and learning, those things that remain largely unchanged across subjects and age groups. Now, however, it is necessary to deal with at least some of the differences of age and I propose to do so in terms of what we have learned about the developing mind.

Education in schools has to pursue two rather different aims: the preparation of students for life as citizens in a technologically advanced democracy, and the development of the powers of the individual mind. But what is meant by the development of the mind? Its general shape, at least, needs to be sketched out and clarified. For a teacher, the point of understanding something about the general ways in which human minds develop is that it helps one to recognize how developing knowledge can best be tailored to the developing mind. It provides a kind of map, alerting one to the main zones of proximal development, and proximal interest, that characterize milestones on the intellectual journey that we all embark on when we go to school. Such milestones can be linked, to some extent, with particular age groups or Key Stages. This mapping process can (potentially) be taken further in particular school subjects, to alert the teacher to likely areas of difficulty and progress in learning.

To explore the developing mind, I shall follow the elegant scheme worked out by Margaret Donaldson[1] in combination with the framework of developing educational understanding devised by Kieran Egan.[2] Donaldson provides a way of describing cognitive and emotional development in terms of the expanding 'modes' of thought that become available to us. Egan links these to the intellectual tools that we master and the levels of understanding to which they give rise. The chapter starts by considering how the advent of going to school changes a child's intellectual world. It then follows the general course of cognitive development, along with the development of associated emotions and values, chiefly using Donaldson's framework. Cognitive development is seen to involve a gradual 'unpacking' of various increasingly specialist powers of the mind, or modes of thought. It is not a simple 'stage' theory, in which new stages of more powerful thinking replace older weaker ones. Rather, it suggests that we can broaden the repertoire of kinds of thinking we use for different purposes as we develop. Some of the more advanced modes are closely associated with schooling (or similar learning carried out elsewhere). The account of the developing modes of thought is accompanied by a second description: that of Egan's stages of educational understanding. These two theoretical frameworks have been chosen because they are coherent, complementary and seem to me particularly well suited to understanding educational progress.

11.2 The Impact of Schooling

Schooling presents children with a profound change in the mode of operation that is expected of them. In school we deal primarily with representations of the world: with talk and books and pictures, with blackboards and whiteboards and videos and computer screens and models and role-play. We can import bits of the 'real world' into the classroom and we can explore real people and places on outings from school, but then we revert to normal 'school ways' of doing things. We take the material back to school and we talk about it, write about it, draw it and make graphs of it. We make representations and we operate upon them, in order to learn. (For most children schooling also involves, of course, a break from the emotional security of the home. However, the fears and uncertainties that this involves are often, happily, quite rapidly overcome and I shall not say more about them here, important though they are to the work of Reception teachers.)

Some school lessons do include real practical problem-solving, as in craft and cookery lessons, science experiments and music making, but even here the point of the practical activity is generally to learn something general from the particular things that are being done. Art subjects have a perennial difficulty in deciding how far they are about making art and how far about studying art. Science, also, is caught in the tension between encouraging students to engage in first-hand discovery versus learning about the vast store of discoveries made by others. In maths, also, personal investigations have to live alongside the learning of an established body of mathematical knowledge.

Young children mostly like doing things; they are oriented chiefly towards action. Evolution has fitted them to move, to explore, to interact and to try things out in a practical way. The Science Museum in London is a good place to observe this propensity. What children chiefly like to do in the Science Museum is to press buttons, turn wheels, pull levers, run about and generally try things out. This tendency towards exploring the world by acting upon it affects all children of primary school age. If sat for too long in a school assembly, for example, Reception and Y1 children actually start to writhe about physically, in a manner they cannot control. If let loose in a playground after lessons, they typically run about, twirl around, jump and shout, at least at first. These simple facts, familiar to all who spend any time with children, are for some reason seldom mentioned in psychology books. One implication, however, is that children will have limited patience and perseverance with classroom activities that demand long periods of inaction, of listening rather than speaking, and of attention only to the slender 'thread' of a teacher's spoken language.

All primary teachers intuitively know that tasks involving some form of making or doing are initially likely to be more popular than tasks involving listening, silent reading or writing. (Stories are our main way of getting children to edge beyond this difficulty.) By KS3 the pattern is set but there remain many students who are happier practising life than dealing with representations of it. No doubt, at times, we all have this urge to shrug off the second-hand nature of classroom experience in order to plunge into life itself, to become participants rather than observers. But we also know, as teachers, that there are richer and more varied ways of relating to life than those typical of the cheerful pandemonium of a school playground.

Initially, perception, action, thought and emotion are bundled closely together in children's mentality and are gradually, and partially, disassembled during development. Thus babies seem to perceive, act, feel and think all at once; they cannot separate thought from feeling or feeling from action. As they get older, children gradually learn to look without touching, then to think and talk without acting, even about things they cannot see. Perception, thought and action are gradually disassembled. Finally, they may learn to put feelings to one side in the process of dispassionate enquiry. Of course we also know that in schools even 5 year olds, or most of them, can learn to sit quietly on the carpet and take part in a 'literacy hour' or some other relatively formal lesson. School is the place, par excellence, where we learn to look and think and speak in a context where the problem at hand is represented symbolically, and where approved behaviour mostly consists of sitting still and concentrating on the manipulation of representations.

School latches on to the fact that children come to school able to use oral language (except in a few exceptional cases who require exceptional help). The dominant mode of early schooling tends to consist of talk (and craft and art making), followed by reading and writing, rather than physical exploration and active manipulation. To this extent it is 'unnatural' in a sense, from the child's point of view, and many children will find it irksome, at least from time to time. Even in physical education, movement is taught and regulated rather than spontaneous. We might call the initial bundle of perception, action, thought and feeling all acting together the 'manifold'. As we develop our minds, the manifold gradually gets unpacked into more specialized forms of mental activity.

11.3 The Core Modes of Mind

In the first months of life infants, so far as we can tell, are mentally focused almost entirely on their current purposes, perceptions and actions. They think and feel as they see, hear and act upon the world. Donaldson calls this initial mental way of being the *point mode*. Sensations and purposeful movements are typical of mental life at this point and it provides us all with a kind of somatic, or bodily, 'common sense', a familiarity with what it feels like to be a human, with a human body, human senses and human feelings. Egan refers to the same level as 'somatic' (i.e. bodily) understanding. (We can all operate within the point mode, even when other modes have opened up to us. For example, I think of the immediate sensations and movements involved in diving into a swimming pool.)

Then, from about 8–10 months of age, infants seem to start to remember the past and to imagine what lies ahead. They begin to have hopes and fears, anticipations and recognitions. Their mental states reach out into time past and future, as an extension of what they are currently trying to do and be. This is still a personal past and a personal future, bound up with the desires and wishes of the self, as it articulates for itself its place in the wider world. It involves the first attempts to make sense of the past and to plan for the future. Donaldson calls it the *line mode*. Our ability to represent the world to ourselves is also gradually transformed by the acquisition of language, roughly between the ages of 1 and 5, which provides us with words, our first abstractions, with which to think about the world.

We do not leave the point and line modes behind us; they always remain important ways in which we can function. The point mode limits our frame of attention to the here and now; the line mode limits our mental operations to specific events and people related in some way to our own experience and to ourselves. Within the limits of the point mode I may choose to concentrate on threading a needle, or brushing my hair or conveying food to my mouth. In each activity I am absorbed, for a moment, in the here and now, all my attention focussed on my own purposes and actions and reactions. My perceptions, my emotions, my thoughts and my actions are all focused on one concentrated point. Within the limits of the line mode I may have all sorts of different foci for my interest and attention, moving away from the present moment to contemplate the past and future, but I cannot easily escape the context of my own personal world, my desires and fears. Nor do we leave behind the early 'somatic' knowledge of sensation and movement that was our very first, pre-linguistic, knowledge. Our intelligence is always embodied and we never lose the sensations of inhabiting our (changing) bodies and of using our perceptual senses as we engage in intentional actions and reactions.

Example 11.1 Emmy's monologue
A verbally precocious child of 21 months is talking to herself in her bed as she goes to sleep. The bed is a new one, bought as part of arrangements for the arrival of a

new baby in the house. Her speech is being recorded by a cassette recorder under her pillow.[3]

> Make my bed. Probably when I wake up and probably my sleeping liking this bed. And Emmy felt the bed so good. Emmy saying Emmy felt the good bed. Emmy didn't like it [?]. Emmy, when Emmy fell down the bed and bring [?] and sometimes and make new bed for Emmy. And that be now [?] up. That [?] bed me. And new bed for me. And new bed for baby. Make new. And after make new bed for baby. I [?] and make new bed for the for the my little baby. Maybe. I like that book. Mommy that book. I don't know.

According to her mother, this rambling stream of thoughts, on the edge of sleep, concerns not only Emmy's own life and circumstances but also her memories of a story that had been read to her a few weeks before. In the story a father makes a bed for a new baby. The passage seems to show how, in the newly acquired line mode, Emmy can think about her own life and feelings. She is reflecting, in a simple way, on both past and future. The thinking is accompanied, we can guess, by quite strong emotions, by worries and longings. This is all very typical of human ways of carrying on, as we reflect on our lives.

When she was a little older, perhaps around 3–4 years of age, Emmy would have expanded her mental deliberations beyond the line mode into what Donaldson calls the *core construct mode*. This shift takes a child beyond a concern with specific personal happenings and towards more general questions and answers. Thus a toddler may show a great interest in when some jam tarts are ready to eat and not too hot. A 4 year old may pause and ask 'Why do jam tarts get hot in the oven?' To give another example, a 2 year old encountering a dead bird in a field might ask what it is and comment 'Bird dead.' A 3 or 4 year old will sometimes follow up with a question: 'Why do birds die?' In this momentous shift, the child is seeking for knowledge of a very general kind, about how the world works. At this age children also observe, listen (sometimes!), try things out, play and argue. In all this, emotion and thought generally go hand in hand. Children's acquisition of knowledge is bound up with their hopes and fears, their excitement and disappointment, joy and grief. Emotions are understood in this scheme to be 'value-sensing', i.e. as indicating to us in different forms, which are felt in the body, how important the object of our thought is. If something does not matter to us at all, typically we feel no emotion about it. If it is of great significance, then we feel correspondingly profound emotions. Often children are still pursuing their own immediate concerns, as we all do, for much of the time but the point is that they can now occasionally change gear, mentally, and undertake a more general kind of enquiry, which takes them beyond matters of self-interest towards a concern with the general nature of the physical or social world. They are able to do this particularly because they can use language, to construct an initial web of understanding. Language enables us to communicate not only about what is happening to us now but also about what is absent, what lies in the past or future and about generalities.

Example 11.2 James and the oven tray[4]
James, age 5, comes into the kitchen just as his mother has taken some cakes out of the oven. There is a loud metallic 'crack'.

James: Who did that?
Mother: I expect it was that tin contracting.
James: Which tin?
Mother: The one with your pastry in.
James: Why did it make that noise?
Mother: Well, when it was in the oven, it got very hot and stretched a bit. I've just taken it out of the oven, and it's cooling down very quickly, you see, and that noise happens when it gets smaller again and goes back to its ordinary shape.
James: Oh! Was it a different shape in the oven?
Mother: Not very different. Just a little bigger.
James: Naughty little tin. You might get smacked – if you do it again.

In this example you can hear James moving into the core construct mode, as he comes to grips with the unusual sound and his mother's explanation of it. His questions show a real curiosity about the world, but his thoughts and emotions are still closely bound together and linked with his current (line mode) concerns. Donaldson argues that the core construct mode remains one of our most common modes of thought. In it we can think and feel in very general ways about the world, using oral language, but always in relation to some familiar context. The context may be the one we are in and can perceive, or it may be one that we imagine or recollect. But thought and its accompanying emotion, guiding us towards what we find significant, relate to some real world, or even fantasy world, that we comprehend. In early childhood, in the ways already described in previous chapters, we learn to build up a picture of how the world is, a 'model of the world in our heads' that is our constant reference point for making sense of experience.

In our everyday use of language we make use of this ability to contextualize words in order to make sense of them all the time. Take a remark such as the following: 'It must be quite an effort, going that way.' The meaning is ordinary enough but its sense is unclear until we have a context. Let us say the context is that the speaker is looking at a picture of a man on skis apparently making his way up the steep slope of a snowy mountain. Immediately the sense of the comment would click into place. It takes an unusual mind, like that of the philosopher Wittgenstein, to look at such a picture and ask (as he apparently did) 'How do you know he's not sliding down the hill backwards?' The answer is that normally people try to climb slopes forwards and not slide down them backwards: Wittgenstein's idea is logically possible but we would not ordinarily entertain it. If Peter says 'I've finished cutting the grass', we fill in various bits of background knowledge automatically, to make the remark fit our understanding. We would not think that Peter had cut the grass with a knife, on his hands and knees, or that the grass covered a thousand acres of prairie, or grew under a bed. The words allow these bizarre interpretations but our background understanding contextualizes our sense of meaning.

We can all use the point mode, the line mode and the core construct mode. Development does not consist of leaving modes behind, or replacing them, but of:

- adding modes to the repertoire;
- broadening our competence within each mode; and
- improving our management of thinking and feeling within a mode, to fit our purposes.

If the point mode is about the 'here and now' and the line mode is about 'there and then', the core construct mode is about 'sometime, somewhere'. It permits a very general interrogation of the world and allows our thoughts to travel far away from our immediate experience. It is typical of much of the thinking we ask students to do in school, at all ages.

When they first come to school, children are still making sense of the world in terms of simple ideas that often form pairs of global opposites: good/bad, male/female, large/small, hot/cold, domestic/wild, safe/dangerous. Even faced with quite non-stereotypical objects and events, they may draw them and talk about them in quite stereotyped ways, as in their first drawings of houses and people. Egan argues that they also have a liking for fantasy creatures and objects that inhabit the spaces between the global opposites. Thus between 'life' and 'death' we get the idea of 'ghosts'; between humans and animals we get talking rabbits in stories, who wear clothes and drink tea out of cups. Fantasy is exciting partly because it lives on the edge, just out of sight of the normal everyday world. It also allows the child, who has relatively little power, to identify with powerful characters, who can go on adventures and do naughty things.

With their global concepts, young children can understand myths and folk tales, which are full of such 'in between' creatures, including giants, witches, ghosts and goblins. They enjoy stories partly because they identify with the main characters, sharing with them the vicissitudes of the plot. They share their thoughts and emotions, their perils and victories. But stories not only excite because their characters get into, and out of, danger but because the story teaches us how to feel about the events portrayed. We know that Cinderella is good and kind and that the Ugly Sisters are mean and horrid and we exult in her triumph and their downfall. Such threats to, and confirmations of, core human virtues are satisfying and reassuring. Perhaps a second equally profound reason for the popularity of simple folk tales is that they retain the entire manifold – the totality of mind and body in action – in the actions of their characters. Perceptions, feelings, thoughts and actions are all closely packed together. They thus represent humans, or other characters, as entire and undivided, albeit now represented in the form of oral or written language. So with stories, children are back in the 'home world' they understand best, but dealing with it at one remove, via language. The best stories are at the same time both excitingly new and also reassuringly familiar.

For Egan, this ability to understand and enjoy story and myth is dependent on the oral language that is a young child's chief intellectual tool. It allows a 'mythic

understanding' in which magic and fantasy mix with reality to provide a comprehens-
ible world, including storybook disruptions of normality, accompanied by thought,
emotion and evaluation. Although they are developing their knowledge of how
living things differ from non-living things, and how plants differ from animals and
animals from humans, they happily explore 'animistic' ideas, such as trees or pigs
or tin trays that can 'behave' and talk and generally have the attributes that truly
belong to human minds. Even tin trays may be 'naughty' and need a smack from
time to time. The curriculum in the early (pre-school and KS1) years sensibly taps
into these themes of mythic understanding to tempt children to learn.

11.4 Developing Beyond the Core

In the core construct mode, thought and emotion still go hand in hand. Children
do much of their early thinking in the rush of experience, as the situation and their
feelings demand. To ask 'Why do birds die?' is an intellectual move, but it may be
accompanied by strong emotion. Such general enquiries into the nature of things
arise out of the current interests of the child. What young children find it harder
to do is to 'turn their minds' to a consideration of some topic that is essentially
arbitrary and unconnected with what they are doing. Yet this is exactly what they
are trained to do in school. Teachers in the early stages of schooling take great care
to find a story, game or other agreeable context for introducing new knowledge;
they know that the children need to understand and identify with the context first, in
order to make the most of their cognitive resources. (Remember the Russian painter
in Chapter 1, who introduced the painting of a wood in autumn via a story about an
old woman, a babushka, going for a walk.) More generally, students thinking in the
core construct mode need to be able to imagine a context for their thinking. The
closer the topic is to something familiar to them, that they have often experienced
for themselves, the easier they find it to construct the imaginative context that helps
them to think. Clearly this is a matter of great relevance to teachers, who must try to
establish such contexts and also link them, one with another.

   According to Egan, the core construct mode is greatly aided in its development by
literacy. Learning to read and write enables us to look at ideas written down, and to
think about them. It encourages a very detailed 'mapping' of the world in terms of
explicit words and it provides a huge aid to memory and to the recording of events.
Not for nothing do the earliest histories, which consciously try to separate true facts
from myths, come from literate cultures such as that of the ancient Greeks. The
explicit and detailed recording of ideas, events and happenings all seem to provoke
the general question 'What is really true?' And then the question of truth is differentiated from myth and rumour. The mapping of reality, aided by writing, thus leads
to a concern with realism as opposed to magic and myth. Whether Egan is right about
the specific influence of literacy, it certainly is the case that children, around the age
of 7, start to become much more sceptical about such ideas as Father Christmas
and the Tooth Fairy. They start to develop an altogether harder-headed view of life.

Playfulness is by no means left behind, but a new realist 'take' on the world is evident in a search for the limits of the real, the boundaries that separate the actual world from the world of fantasy and storybook. Even in their fantasies, these older children, aged from about 7 to 11, like realistic details of people, machines, planets and processes. Superman's special powers have to be explicable in pseudo-scientific terms.

Egan refers to this important phase, which accompanies KS2 but lingers on well into KS3, as *romantic understanding*. This is chiefly because it is characterized by a romantic liking for people and events that are real but special. His argument is that the exploration of reality is both exciting and threatening. One way of dealing with threat is to associate with powerful allies. Thus children at this age have a great liking for heroes and heroines who embody real human qualities, such as strength, beauty and courage, or sporting excellence, but in exceptional forms. (Sport seems to lend itself to a mythology of action, recapturing the world of the manifold, in which thought and feeling always go together with action.) Such heroes, who in our culture are typically footballers, singers, explorers or princesses, are at one and the same time real and unreal, human and superhuman. They have to battle with realistic challenges but do so at a heroic level. Popular films such as the *Indiana Jones* and *Terminator* series tap into this kind of romantic world of the strange, the exotic and the heroic. At the same time, children appreciate new knowledge that is presented in a context of the lives of real human individuals, great scientists, kings and queens, generals and poets. Science is more palatable in the context of a Pasteur, struggling against the prejudices of his time; history is enjoyed most in terms of narratives about conflicts, heroic resistance and intrepid journeys.

The ability to 'turn one's mind' to any subject at will is one that requires thinking that is to some degree separated from ongoing motivation and emotion. A related ability is what Donaldson refers to as 'dispassionate thinking'. To do this we put our wishes and fears on one side and try simply to think objectively. This might involve listening to the presentation of arguments for and against some proposition, or trying to gather scientific data to test some hypothesis. Emotion is not absent altogether, for we may still be motivated by curiosity, uncertainty or some other strong feelings, but we think 'dispassionately' in order to get the thinking (or observations or judgements) right. We try to put aside any feelings that might distort or bias our thinking. Giving priority to thought in this way (bracketing off unhelpful emotions) is typical of a subdivision of the construct mode that Donaldson calls the *intellectual construct mode*. It can be expected to develop, starting from about the age of 4, especially in situations in which children can concentrate on a problem without their immediate goals and interests being engaged. It continues to expand throughout the years of schooling.

Little children, undertaking science experiments such as 'floating and sinking', often get so personally involved in the activity that they want one outcome or another to take place and will even cheat to make sure that it does. It is not easy to be objective. Nor is this kind of problem confined to KS1. I once set university students to prepare arguments about one of a set of well-known moral issues (capital punishment, vegetarianism or abortion). First they had to say which side of the argument they favoured themselves. I then made them prepare the case for the opposing side, arguing against their own convictions. At first they found this extremely difficult but also, eventually, enlightening. They told me they had never tried to do such a thing before. It forced them, for a short while, to imagine another point of view and also to separate dispassionate argument from strong emotions and values.

Another, related, ability contributing to the intellectual branch of the construct mode is to be able to pay close attention to the words of a statement, or proposition or text, and to distinguish between 'what is meant' and 'what is actually written'. Again this can be seen as a kind of splitting off of the object of thought from its context; in this case meaning is split away from its normal context of the speaker's intentions. Like Alice, we have to learn that to say what we mean is not the same as to mean what we say. It is an ability that is almost certainly greatly aided by learning to write, as well as to read, for in writing one's meaning has to be generated by the written words alone, without any helpful accompanying context.

Example 11.3 What is said and what is meant
Astington and Olson[5] told teenagers a story in which a character, Barbara, wants to sneak out of the house and buy Adam a present, without him knowing. In the course of the story, Barbara says, 'We're out of milk. I'm going to the store.' After hearing the story, the participants were asked which of the following correctly describes what Barbara did when she uttered that sentence.

Barbara means that she is going to buy milk.
Barbara concedes that she is going to buy milk.
Barbara asserts that she is going to buy milk.
Barbara implies that she is going to buy milk.

Very few 12 year olds could get this right. This example is indeed a difficult one but similar research shows that only in middle childhood do children distinguish clearly between the (easier) cases of asserting, predicting and promising. In general, the difference between what people actually say and what they mean (their communicative intention) is hard for young children to understand.

Four characteristics of intellectual construct thinking have now been highlighted.

- The ability to ask very general questions, unrelated to one's own immediate interests and concerns.
- The ability to turn one's full attention to a problem when it has nothing to do with one's own immediate ongoing problems or goals.
- The ability to set aside unhelpful emotions so as to think dispassionately.
- The ability to distinguish between what is said and what is meant, implied, asserted, etc.

Donaldson is keen to emphasize that emotion, too, can be developed beyond its core mode. She points out that there are many contexts in which we use our emotions, as value-sensing guides, to explore beauty or ugliness, suffering or salvation, in ways which go beyond our own personal interests and goals. We can, in the contemplation of a work of art or in meditating on human suffering, follow the guidance of our emotions while temporarily putting critical thinking on hold. There is thus a *value-sensing construct mode*, a subdivision of the core construct mode, to go alongside the intellectual one. The development of a disinterested sympathy for others, a sense of the value of some remote historical event or the joy of watching a skilful dancer, are all examples of this kind of stretching of the emotions away from the mundane contexts of our own well-being. They are an important contributor to our education, especially in such subjects as English literature, history and the arts. This is not a case of raw passions being irrationally unleashed. The particular emotions we feel are always related to our (cognitive) interpretation of what is before us. A light in the darkness may signal to us hope if we are in need of rescue, or fear if we are trying to evade capture. But although thought is still present (as emotion was still present in the intellectual branch), it is controlled so as to allow us to explore our feelings for someone else's predicament or to sense the feelings aroused by a scene of beauty. Emotion here is empowering; it is not cut off from understanding but nor is it assimilated to thought.

All these developments will take place gradually in a child's life across the school years and will be helped by the kind of deliberate learning in which schools specialize. All rely, also, on the thinker being able to generate a background context of sense, for understanding. In summary, development of the modes and levels of understanding so far described are shown in Table 11.1. Clearly the age levels suggested are somewhat rough and ready. We need to remember also that for both Donaldson and Egan the new ways of operating do not wholly replace what went before. We can all operate in the point and line modes; we can all indulge in mythic or romantic levels of understanding. (The tabloid press, by and large, never seems to reach beyond them.) However, besides using the intellectual construct mode, some children, towards the end of the primary phase of schooling, begin to be able to make an occasional shift away from the usual dependence of construct thinking on a context that can be seen or imagined. They begin to take an interest in very abstract patterns of relationships, generally using symbolic notation. This takes them beyond the ordinary intellectual construct mode.

Table 11.1 Development of the modes and levels of understanding.

	Infancy (0–1)	Early childhood (2–6)	Middle childhood (7–11)
Modes	Point mode	Line mode	Intellectual construct mode ↗ Core construct mode ↘ Value-sensing construct mode
Forms of understanding	Somatic	Mythic	Romantic

11.5 Advanced Modes and Levels

Donaldson talks of giving children sets of coloured counters, or objects, of say four or five different colours and asking them 'How many pairs can you make, so that each pair contains a different combination of colours?' Typically, children can make sense of this task but they do so largely via unsystematic trial and error. As a result, after collecting a number of pairs, 7 year olds may think they have found all the possible pairs, but have no strategy for checking whether they have missed some. Between 7 and 9 years, children may be uneasy as to whether they have definitely found all the possible pairs, but are still unlikely to know how to make sure. From about the age of 9, some children attack the problem more systematically, for example by setting out a matrix of rows and columns recording the colours. Or they may take one colour and match it with each other colour, then take a second colour and so forth, setting out the results systematically. They may be able to show why they are sure that they have found all the combinations. What is more, some children may even be able to find the general pattern of numbers of combinations which results from combining things two at a time, from sets of different sizes.

At this point the child may not require the counters at all. He or she begins to operate within the world of mathematics, in a way that transcends any particular instantiation of the actual world. As Piaget put it, the actual world comes to be thought of as simply one among many possible worlds. This kind of move beyond the actual world to investigate quite abstract systems of relations is rare at KS3, let alone KS2. But it is a kind of thinking that becomes very important in science and mathematics, and probably in other contexts too. This kind of rather advanced thought is not to be confused with abstract thinking in general. It is often thought that abstract thought is beyond young children but this is not the case. Any child who can understand the concepts 'tomorrow', 'pretend' or 'kind', which most 3 year olds can, is doing abstract thinking. But now we are thinking of problems that are purely symbolic, such as 'How could we find out which of three independent variables has a causal effect on a given dependent variable?' Our problem has been abstracted away from any single context, although it can be applied to many. Its relevance transcends (goes beyond) any particular time and place we can imagine as a context. Donaldson therefore calls it *intellectual transcendent* thinking.[6]

Work towards this kind of systematic and quite abstract thinking usually depends on the use of some kind of notation, as in maths, logic, music or chess. A familiarity with the notation gradually seems to provide its own familiar symbolic context. It is as if the symbolic world of signs begins itself to operate as a context, rather like a theatre of characters, rehearsed in one's mind. Donaldson also mentions the importance of sticking with the exact problem set. If one is asked to investigate parallelograms, it is no use looking only at squares or rectangles. If one is asked to consider the political and religious problems facing Queen Elizabeth I on her accession, it is no good spending lots of energy writing about the economic conditions or about her personal relationships. The idea of 'relevance' comes to be central to all effective intellectual work.

In English and the humanities generally, the close reading of texts also becomes central to advanced work. Here the intellectual transcendent mode may possibly consist mainly of reading at different levels of meaning, and relating them to one another. Thus a historian will read at the levels of literal meaning (the actual words of the text), inferential meaning (what the words imply) and evaluative meaning (what interpretation might be placed on the meaning historically). In looking for some singular feature that characterizes all work, right across the curriculum, at this level, I am tempted to suggest that it has to do with finding very general patterns of relationship (in meanings, mathematical functions or physical variables) and testing the 'truth' of the patterns by trying to find counter-examples. This generally involves both analysis (breaking things down into significant parts) and synthesis (putting parts together to make significant wholes).

Unless one is regularly involved with intellectual problems at this level, it is unlikely that one will use this kind of intellectual transcendent thinking much if at all. It is not typical of everyday life, and yet it is central to various intellectual disciplines. Putting Donaldson's ideas together with my own additional speculations, it seems that its development is aided by:

- abstracting away from a perceptual context towards a focus on relationships between variables;
- having a firm sense of 'relevance' for a particular problem, so that its precise wording and conditions are stuck to, rather than some vaguer more convenient question or set of circumstances;
- being able to set about the investigation systematically, probably using a written record of some kind;
- having a fluent grasp of some system of notation with which to think about the relationships;
- looking for patterns and testing them by finding counter-examples;
- using analysis and synthesis to continually try to differentiate (find further distinctions) and integrate (find further connections).

Going back a little in the developmental story, some earlier research on adolescent thinking shows that as students develop the intellectual branch of the construct mode, they only very gradually improve the quality of responses and explanations they can produce when faced with complex situations and problems.

Example 11.4 Complex explanations[7]
Some years ago, E. A. Peel presented to adolescent students of varying ages the following text, as one of a series of similar problems. The student had to read the text and then answer two questions.

Only brave pilots are allowed to fly over high mountains. This summer a fighter pilot flying over the Alps collided with an aerial cable railway, and cut a main cable causing some cars to fall to the glacier below. Several people were killed and many others had to spend the night suspended above the glacier.

The first question asked 'Was the pilot a careful airman?' and the second 'Why do you think so?' The students' responses could be categorized as belonging to one of three classes.

1 Restricted: these showed irrelevant, fabricated or inconsistent reasons and explanations, for example 'Yes, he was brave', 'Yes, the cable shouldn't have been there', 'No he was a show off.'
2 Circumstantial: these showed a focus on one part of the text as decisive, for example 'No, because he hit the cable', 'No, because if he was careful, he would not have cut the cable.'
3 Imaginative: these showed a concern for extenuating circumstances, for example 'You can't tell, it depends on the weather/state of the plane.' More generally at this level the student took account of the different facts presented (which usually pointed to opposing conclusions) and went beyond them, pointing to the need for further evidence to settle the question.

The average quality of the responses rose steadily across the years of KS3 and KS4. A student of Peel's tried a similar study by reading short poems to students aged 11–17. He then asked the individual students 'What does this poem mean to you?' The most primitive responses showed either complete incomprehension or simply repeated fragments of the poem or its meanings. More satisfactory answers provided some kind of affective reaction, sometimes with tenuous reference to the text, or showed some understanding of a single part of the content. Mature responses united thought with feeling and explained the poem's impact by relating it to wider human knowledge or experience. Most of the 11 year olds' responses (85%) fell into the most primitive category. The majority of 12, 13 and 14 year olds' responses fell into the second (more satisfactory) level, whereas about 4–11% at ascending ages managed mature responses. Only at 15 and 16 did some 45% of the students manage a mature response and even at these ages some were still providing 'primitive' answers.

Another investigator tried a similar study of adolescents' understanding of a series of geographical problems, one of which was represented by a map showing the seasonal migrations of Masai cattle farmers. The map showed that the farmers moved their cattle each year from the north-west highlands to the base of the Rift Valley in the south-east. In the highlands there were permanent waterholes and also nearly 125 centimetres (50 inches) of rainfall per year. In the valley floor annual rainfall was less than 50 centimetres (20 inches) and waterholes were temporary. The map showed that the Masai moved their cattle twice to the highlands (in July and December) and twice to the valley (in February and September), between two periods of heavy rainfall (March–June and October–November). Students aged between 11 and 15 were asked to explain this pattern of migration.

To understand the pattern, it is necessary to understand both the need to conserve water and forage and the best months for moving from one area to the other. The 11 year olds, for the most part, could not effectively interpret the information supplied. They found the map hard to understand and tended to fix on the heavy rainfall in the highlands, arguing for example that the farmers had to move to avoid being flooded. Older students gradually produced better answers, trying to combine descriptive information about the rainfall and movements of cattle, as in 'they move therefore one month before the rainfall'. At 15, some students were able to combine the information given and use it to formulate an explanation:

The Masai migrate twice a year . . . to get the best seasonal rainfall they can . . . [movement details] . . . The reason why they keep moving is that the waterholes in the valley are non-permanent, but the waterholes in the mountains are. Another reason for their task is that when they are in the valley using the grass and water, the grass and water in the highlands is building up. This means that when they return to the highlands, the water and food is there for them. This method keeps repeating.

In each of these studies we see a gradual development during the secondary-school years of the ability to combine information about complex events and to formulate an appropriate explanation, which is both relevant and supported by the evidence. General patterns are conjectured to exist and detailed evidence is related to them. Although this research emphasized responses at different ages, teachers need to remain aware that knowledge is more important than age. Within each age group there were marked differences between the most and least effective respondents. Some children develop highly elaborate systems of expertise about special interests, which they have studied at length. Relating these problems to Donaldson's modes of thought, we can see that the intellectual construct mode, let alone the intellectual transcendent mode, requires many kinds of strategic mental ability, especially a clear grasp of the concepts embedded in each problem, a willingness to accept uncertainty (in that not all evidence points one way or is available) and the ability to proceed carefully and systematically. It also requires an ability to articulate responses and explanations in fluent language.

None of these studies, incidentally, represents any ultimate limit to what teachers may be able to achieve; they simply illustrate studies of particular school samples, at a given point in time. They show how difficult and slow the building up of effective deliberate knowledge can be. In relation to this, Donaldson has clearly stated her own beliefs:

> a question then arises that should be faced directly but is often evaded. Can the kind of spontaneous education that works so easily in the early core modes serve equally well for learning in the advanced modes? . . . The conclusion seems inescapable: the core modes 'come naturally' in a way that the remainder do not.[8]

Such a view will not come as a surprise to any reader who can remember the main themes of Chapter 8.

For Egan, the crucial move from the earlier romantic level of understanding comes when adolescents become able to grasp abstract theoretical systems. He notes that this tends to occur in later adolescence, if at all, from about the age of 15 years onwards. He calls it *philosophical understanding*, because it is typified by a systematic rational approach as found in the work of Aristotle and other ancient philosophers. Such thinking tries to understand problems by relating them, as instances, to some general theoretical system, which might for example be religious, scientific or even historical/economic (as in Marxism). What were appreciated as bright interesting details at the level of romantic understanding are now welded together into explanatory wholes. In ancient Greece we can trace the beginnings of such systematic theorizing, as applied to medicine, science, history, mathematics, philosophy, legal trials and political debates, among other topics.

Clearly there is a close similarity between Egan's philosophical understanding and Donaldson's intellectual transcendent mode. In each case we have quite general abstract systems, often using notation or a specialized vocabulary. We also have an attempt at dispassionate enquiry, searching for the truth, as warranted by consistency of reasoning and relevant evidence. There is a concern with explicit reasoning and with an exact use of language (or mathematical terms). Particular cases or instances are explained under general laws or theories. New conjectures are tested against empirical or conceptual standards. All logical possibilities are considered, quite apart from actualities. Contingency is distinguished from necessity. Such are the general characteristics of intellectual work in the academic disciplines.

Egan in fact articulates one final level of understanding, the *ironic*, which comes to criticize all general systems of explanation, using a new reflexivity about self and language. The ironic thinker appreciates the humour behind such self-defeating statements as 'all generalizations are false'. But this level, which has been so important to post-modernist thinkers, must remain a topic to be explored outside this book.

In all the examples so far given of developing intellectual power, the difficulty for young children arises from having to abandon a perfectly normal and natural orchestration of perception, action, thought and emotion acting together (that I have called the manifold). Gradually, modes of thought become available that are not immediately linked to perception or action and in which unhelpful emotions are screened out, so far as possible. We need to remember also that this sort of rational critical thought is not the only viable or indeed valuable kind. Donaldson is careful to re-instate a sensitive attention to the emotions as a relevant way in which we come to appraise our values. Guy Claxton[9] reminds us that there are also slower, more hidden kinds of thinking, as in brooding reflectively over an idea, or letting the brain do its non-conscious work on a creative problem as we go for a walk or doze or daydream (6.7). Sudden flashes of insight sometimes occur quite unexpectedly after such periods of 'incubation'. These subconscious modes are important for creative thinking and sometimes for working out personal dilemmas related to conflicting values. We are still learning how best to combine the subconscious creative powers of the brain with our deliberate, reasoning, conscious brain.

11.6 Summary

In Donaldson's scheme, we have various different modes of thought available to us. The first three, in order of development, are the point mode, the line mode and the core construct mode (Table 11.2). We develop these one after another but we keep them all in our repertoire. The first two relate to our own interests and ongoing lives and the third one (core construct) opens up general enquiries about life, based on our existing model of reality. Children coming to school can manage all these modes,

Table 11.2 The modes of thought

Components	Locus of concern			
	Here and now	There and then	Sometime, somewhere	Out of space and time
Perception, action, thought, emotion	Point			
Thought, emotion		Line	Core construct	
Thought (emotion)			Intellectual construct	Intellectual transcendent
Emotion (thought)			Value-sensing construct	Value-sensing transcendent

Source: After Donaldson.[1]

although they may not use the core construct mode very often at first. However it is a mode especially practised in schools. The kind of learning we do in school helps us develop the intellectual branch of the construct mode, which is just like the core mode but more impersonal and objective. It does not replace earlier modes, it just adds to them. The intellectual transcendent mode is more advanced and it is not clear how many students use it with any frequency or fluency. It moves us on from actual to possible worlds, represented not by some imagined context but by the abstract patterns of linguistic and mathematical (or other) symbols.

Egan, meanwhile, pursues an essentially parallel course, emphasizing the gradual mastery of intellectual tools, as in oral language, literacy and then general abstract theories. Where Donaldson describes each mode as having a 'locus of concern', in time and space, Egan is concerned to say more about such 'loci of concern' by attending to the typical areas of excitement and uncertainty that seem to characterize each of his levels of understanding. He thus manages to link thought with value and motivation, with ideas about what matters most to students at each level. This is particularly helpful to teachers for it provides a 'way in' to think about the difficult question of how to interest children in the curriculum (Table 11.3).

A large field has been covered at high speed in this chapter. My hope, obviously, is that the overall framework provided will provide a helpful background to the practical tasks of planning lessons and schemes of work, as well as in pitching teaching at the right level and in gaining some clues about assessment. For this, I acknowledge, the general map needs relating to much more detailed ones in particular subjects.[10] My purpose here is partly to indicate that the intellectual journey through childhood and adolescence is a long one, albeit one that can be taken much further in adulthood. Teachers need to realize this and be sensitive to the difficulties

Table 11.3 Egan's levels of educational understanding

Level	Preponderant age	New intellectual mastery of	Typical loci of concern
Somatic	0–2 years	Imitation and gesture	Pre-linguistic, exploration via sensation, perception and voluntary movement
Mythic	2–7 years	Oral language	Pairs of global binary concepts, fantasy, magic, the intuitive abstractions of words, metaphor, rhyme, rhythm, story and myth
Romantic	7–15+ years	Literacy	Plotting the limits of reality, facts and details, the strange and exotic, archetypal figures and heroes, knowledge with a human face
Philosophic	15 years	Abstract theoretical systems	General systems of explanation, the realm of the possible, systematic rational thinking, second-order questions, the lure of certainty
Ironic	Not known	Reflexivity applied to language and self	Irony, scepticism, multiple perspectives, refined sensitivity to the limitations of our conceptual resources

Source: After Egan.[2]

and confusions of travellers who have temporarily lost their way. Beyond this I hope that any reader who does some teaching will feel curious enough to test some of the ideas presented here and take them further, by practical investigations with children and by further reading.[11] Finding out more about the details of this journey of the developing mind is one of the lasting satisfactions of teaching.

11.7 Questions

The following questions are designed to help you check your understanding of the chapter.

1 What, for teachers, is the main point of understanding how the mind develops?
2 What natural characteristic of young children may schooling frustrate?
3 What four basic components were said to make up the manifold of mental life?
4 Explain the main differences between the point and line modes.
5 How does the core construct mode go beyond the line mode?

6 What, for Egan, characterizes mythic understanding? How do teachers tap into it?

7 What are some of the new powers of the intellectual construct mode?

8 What aspects of the intellectual transcendent mode can you recognize in your own specialist subject?

9 What kinds of thought might we value in addition to rational critical thought?

10 **Exercise and discussion question**: two problems[12] are listed below. Choose one of them and try to solve it (alone or in a group). Then discuss what kinds of thinking you used and what difficulties you encountered. If you can, try to relate the types of thinking you used to the modes covered in the chapter.

(a) A man, a woman, a boy and a girl want to cross a dangerous river. None of them can swim and they only have one canoe. They can all paddle the canoe, but it can only hold one adult or two children (*not* an adult and a child together). How do they all get across? What is the minimum number of crossings required?

(b) Imagine a matchbox with its eight corners labelled A, B, C and D on the top side and E, F, G and H on the bottom side. A fly is sitting on one corner of the box. The fly walks only along the edges of the box from the starting point (A) to get to the corner farthest away from it (G). The fly never moves upwards and never walks along the same edge twice on any journey. How many different routes can the fly take? Sort the routes according to the number of edges the fly uses. See what you can find out about the distance walked.

NOTES

1. Donaldson (1992).
2. Egan (1997).
3. Nelson, quoted in Donaldson (1992), p. 60.
4. Wells (1986), p. 59.
5. Astington and Olson (1990).
6. Donaldson also develops her scheme to include a value-sensing transcendent mode, but details of this must be sought in her own work (see note 1).
7. Taken from chapters by E. Lunzer, E.A. Peel and W.T. Rhys in Floyd (1979).
8. Donaldson (1996).
9. Claxton (1997).
10. The levels of attainment for particular (UK) National Curriculum subjects are a very helpful stab in this direction, though they are not based on research.
11. Both Donaldson's and Egan's schemes are more complex, and are supported by more evidence than I have been able to indicate in this chapter. It will probably be clear that in order to use either scheme you would need to read about it in more detail in one of the references given above.
12. The puzzles may be found, for example, in Burton (1984). Both have legitimate solutions.

CHAPTER TWELVE

Individual Differences

12.1 Introduction

When faced with a class of students in school for the very first time, one can be almost overwhelmed at first by their individual personalities, appearances and habits. They can seem to be so different from one another. This chapter considers both how different and at the same time how similar they actually are. We start off with one of the most controversial and difficult dimensions of difference: intelligence. This will involve quite a wide-ranging look at intelligence tests and the question of the heritability of intelligence. This leads on to a consideration of other, possibly more productive, ways of thinking about the concept of intelligence as it applies to work in schools. There follows a section on personality and temperament and a final section on the relative influence of parents and the peer group on developing children and adolescents.

12.2 Intelligence: the Dog that Doesn't Bark

A curious thing has happened to the concept of intelligence. When I first entered teacher training, a little over 20 years ago, it featured prominently, as an obligatory part of the curriculum for all teachers in training. There were compulsory lectures on IQ tests and their limitations and there were readings, seminars and essays devoted to what intelligence really was, and was not, all about. Debates about 'streaming' versus 'mixed ability' grouping for teaching were also in full flood. Since then, however, intelligence has slipped silently away until it has become a ghost at the banquet, seldom mentioned at all, except to be criticized as an outdated, or unhelpful, concept. From being a highly fashionable and visible topic it has achieved a sort of intellectual pariah status. Yet teachers very commonly talk about the 'ability' of students. And, during the same period, research has largely firmed up a picture of the nature of measured estimates of intelligence that is not so different from that already established years and years ago. Like the dog in the Sherlock Holmes story, which was important because it did *not* bark, the absence of intelligence from current debates on teaching and learning deserves our attention.

As detectives, pursuing the explanation for this strange disappearance, let us start by noticing what a sensitive subject it is. Primo Levi, the great Italian writer, once observed that both poets and chess-players have a reputation for being touchy and irritable. He put it down to the fact that members of each group have rather little excuse for their failures, which stem all too clearly from their own mistakes or limitations of mind. He went on to write:

> It must be added that poet and chess player work only with their brain, and when it comes to the quality of our brain we are all very touchy. To accuse another of having weak kidneys, lungs or heart, is not a crime, on the contrary, saying he has a weak brain is a crime. To be considered stupid and to be told so is more painful than being called gluttonous, mendacious, violent, lascivious, lazy, cowardly: every weakness, every vice, has found its defenders, its rhetoric, its ennoblement and exaltation, but stupidity hasn't.[1]

I think this is a shrewd insight. It may be associated with a related fact, namely that academics, who in their own teaching denounce IQ tests as more or less the work of the devil, can sometimes be heard talking in off-guard moments about their own individual students as 'bright', 'dull', 'quick', 'basically rather thick', 'brilliant' and so forth. Common sense is immovably convinced that individual persons are more or less clever by nature, but reluctant to apply the terms to any well-known friends. Teachers talk a good deal about 'ability' but are extremely reluctant to label their students in this way. We are all touchy about intelligence.

Another reason that the topic of differences in intelligence is such a touchy subject is that it forms part of the 'nature–nurture' debate, the enquiry into how far inherited characteristics shape us as individuals.[2] To those who resist any notion that we are partly who we are because of the particular set of genes we inherited, any mention of evidence about the heritability of IQ acts as a red rag to a bull. I think this is misguided. In the end, the fuss over IQ is unimportant largely because it does not have many, if any, important implications for teaching and learning. I say this while acknowledging that in the past it has sometimes had an influence on educational policies that has not always been (in my view) for the good.

12.3 IQ Tests

Some of the problems in this area can be laid at the door of psychologists and their tests; others are due to misunderstandings of these same tests.[3] Tests of IQ (intelligence quotient) are at the same time quite powerful and reliable and yet, paradoxically, almost useless to a teacher, as we shall see. The powerful and reliable tests are rather few in number. They consist of the Stanford–Binet (the oldest), the Wechsler range of tests (the most common, including the Wechsler Intelligence Test for Children, or WISC) and the British Ability Scales (the most recently designed and a UK-based product). Each of these is an individual test that must be administered by a trained psychologist to a single child and takes about an hour to complete. The complete test in each case includes about ten subtests covering such topics as vocabulary, verbal analogies, remembering strings of digits, arranging pictures in a logical sequence, finding the logic of visual patterns and mental arithmetic. Such tests are very seldom used on ordinary students in schools, unless as part of a research project. They are arranged so that an average score, for a given age, is 100 and varies (normally) by a standard deviation of 15. This means that about two-thirds of the population will score between 85 and 115 (100 ± 15). Similarly, roughly 95% of the population will score in the range 70–130. The scores virtually cease to have meaning outside the range 50–150.

At first sight the tests seem rather rough and ready, a hotchpotch of items, verbal and non-verbal, involving memory or not, timed and untimed, dependent on general knowledge to a greater or lesser degree. They have been designed pragmatically with great care, however, so as to provide the statistical virtues of discrimination, reliability and predictive validity. They offer up an individual score and a profile across the subtests, which can be compared with the large population on which the test was originally standardized. Thus version III of the Wechsler Adult Intelligence Scale (WAIS), published in 1997, was standardized on 2450 people in the USA aged between 16 and 89. The sample was chosen so that by sex, region, ethnicity and educational qualifications the members were representative of the general population.

Male and female samples produce the same average scores (thank heaven, and thanks to the test constructors). Scores start to be statistically reliable from about the age of 7 years and as children grow older the raw scores rise steadily until about 18 years of age, when they level off. Statistical manipulations change raw scores into positions on one and the same scale so that comparisons are easy. Learning to use the test involves learning to give carefully standardized instructions, so everyone gets the same treatment, and to use precise rules on how to score different responses. There are also many shorter group tests of intelligence, usually involving just verbal and non-verbal reasoning. These are simpler but not as accurate or informative as the 'proper' individual tests and should not be confused with them.

Advantages

The main strengths of IQ tests are as follows.

1 They produce pretty reliable results. Studies of people tested and then re-tested up to 12 years later show **correlations** between their scores of around +0.8, which is about as good as psychological tests ever get. (For an explanation of correlations see note 4.) In one fascinating study, Ian Deary and colleagues[5] persuaded 73 brave Scottish people, aged 77, to re-sit a Moray House reasoning test that they had all originally taken in 1932, when they were aged 11. Although this was not a full IQ test and no fewer than 66 years had gone by, the overall correlation

between the two sets of scores was still a little above +0.6. In other words, people had mostly not moved far from their original position in the order from lowest to highest score. (Scores were higher overall at age 77 than they had been at age 11 and in general it seems that although performance tends to fall off after about the age of 30, the decrements are mainly due to those items that measure speed of information processing. General knowledge and verbal abilities are remarkably stable.)

2 Whichever IQ test is used, it turns out that scores on all the subtests, although their various items seem so different, show positive correlations with one another. People who are good at one of them tend to be good at most or all of the others. If this surprises you, think of a school sports day. Children who are very good at some of the athletics events tend, by and large, to be good at others. Conversely, children who are poor runners are often also poor jumpers and discus throwers. It is not unreasonable to think of a general 'athletic' ability, although there will be individual exceptions. With IQ tests one can extract a general factor, which psychologists call g (for general intelligence), that accounts for about half of all the variability between different peoples' scores.

3 Scores on the subtests tend to cluster together in groups, which seem to be tapping recognizable abilities or 'factors'. Typical group factors have to do with verbal ability, numerical ability, working memory, perceptual organization and speed of information processing. (In our school sports day analogy, one could probably also find clusters of associated events such as sprints, distance running, jumping and throwing.)

4 The tests do manage to assess abilities that most people associate with the term 'intelligence'. They combine abstract thinking and reasoning, problem-solving and a capacity to acquire general knowledge.

5 The tests predict academic achievement quite well (with typical correlations between +0.5 and +0.8). This is scarcely surprising, since the tests are quite similar to many pencil-and-paper type school tasks. They also provide as good an indication as careful structured interviews of how well people are likely to perform at many skilled jobs, such as in the civil service. The only better selection method is actually to try people out at a particular job.[6]

Disadvantages

Now let us look at the main weaknesses of these same tests, from a teacher's point of view.

1 Although the results are stable when one looks at large groups of people, any individual child will on a given day produce one score, which is only a sample of her intelligent behaviour. It is not necessarily the child's 'exact' or 'true' score. In fact the statistics indicate that the tests typically have a standard error of measurement of ±5 points. In plain English this means that if one tested the same child over and over again (heaven forbid), one would expect her scores to vary around

a mean score, with two-thirds of the scores obtained lying within 5 points either side of that mean and with a few odd ones even further away. Remember that most people (68%) will score in the central range of the test (85–115) anyway. If our hypothetical child scores say 95, then all we know is that the test is indicating a 'true' score between 90 and 100. This is rather vague and all we can say is that the child is scoring very slightly below the mean but still within the average range for her age. True, one is only likely in practice to want to test unusual children. For example, a score of 75 may indicate that a child will need extra help to survive in a mainstream school; a score of 130 indicates a bright child, probably in the top 2% of the population. But no greater precision is obtainable.

2 Although one does indeed obtain a profile of scores for a child, across the range of subtests, the profile is not terribly informative. Sometimes there is a marked difference, say between verbal and non-verbal subtests or a weakness in perceptual organization, which may be of interest. But such profiles seldom tell us much about the child's ability to manage any given subject on the school curriculum. Thus IQ test results only indicate a fuzzy range within which an individual's true score lies and a range of subscores which, though sometimes interesting, seldom help the teacher with planning schoolwork.

3 There is a more basic objection to calling these tests evaluations of human intelligence. A little thought will probably suggest that such things as imaginative thinking, perseverance, good judgement and particular talents (e.g. shrewdness in dealing with people) are also relevant to real-life instances of 'intelligent behaviour'. Going back to our sports-day analogy, success at a limited range of track and field events may predict rather little about a child's success at other unrelated sports such as swimming, tennis or show jumping. The 'intelligence' being tested is thus of a rather restricted kind.

In connection with this, Howard Gardner[7] has argued that we would be much better off with a concept of multiple intelligences. He suggests a list of different types or dimensions of intelligence, including physical/kinaesthetic (sport and dance), interpersonal (social skills), intrapersonal (much like metacognition), musical, linguistic, logico-mathematical, spatial and naturalistic (related to natural objects and processes). A 'spiritual' intelligence has also been considered as a candidate dimension, which perhaps indicates where the difficulty with this approach lies.

Gardner's approach is very attractive in its inclusiveness and for this reason, I suspect, it is popular. It certainly succeeds in getting away from a very restricted view of intelligence. However, when we look more closely at his list it seems partly to replicate the well-known group factors from IQ tests (verbal, spatial, mathematical) and partly to introduce other kinds of particular ability that only dubiously belong within practices that we normally call 'intelligent'. It is not as if intelligence has to cover every attribute that we happen to think is valuable. If a talent at music is to be included, then why not include a talent at sculpture, or photography, or drama? Intrapersonal and interpersonal skills are arguably better considered as dimensions of personality or as social skills in their own right. The physical/kinaesthetic dimension has to do with sport, dance and other such pursuits based on skilled movement. These are greatly to be valued, no doubt, but mixing this kind of bodily intelligence with the intellectual kind arguably muddles more than it clarifies. As for a spiritual dimension, that would surely better indicate an 'interest' or a 'commitment' than an 'ability'. Once the list is allowed to expand it is hard to see what limits it. Why not add a 'gardening' intelligence or a 'mechanical' intelligence? For these reasons, although agreeing that IQ tests are pitiably narrow in their range, I will say no more about Gardner's approach. I prefer to insist that we need to value a far wider range of kinds of human ability, especially practical ability, than merely 'intelligence'. In short, we need to put intelligence into perspective.

4 One can argue that the cultural effects of the tests are generally malign. It is easier to think of ways in which a child might be hurt by being labelled with a test score than ways in which such a score might help them.[8] Although they have the advantage of being objective and 'blind' to social factors such as class, ethnicity and gender (a fact that once was an enormous help to the cause of women's education), the tests may also suggest that measured intelligence is especially important. In fact there are many other equally or more important qualities that relate to worldly success, including hard work, reliability, expert knowledge and social skills. Nor is the possession of high intelligence an automatic passport either to success or happiness. Physical or mental illness, addiction, criminality and despair, for example, can all take their toll.

In an old but classic study, Louis Terman[9] studied the lives of a group of about 1500 Californian children who all scored 140 or more on a group IQ test in 1922. Contrary to the stereotypes that prevailed at the time, this group turned out on average to be better physically developed, healthier and better socially adapted than their lower scoring peers. Of the males, about 15% went on to obtain doctorates at university and many became prominent in business, politics, academia and the law. Together they wrote thousands of published books and articles, registered hundreds of patents, won many prizes and were typically rather wealthy. On the other hand, some individuals from the group were relative failures, in worldly terms, and some became alcoholics, suffered from mental illness or committed suicide. Moreover, two boys from the original sample who 'missed the cut' because their test scores were not high enough later went on to win the Nobel Prize for physics![10] Clearly we need to keep IQ scores firmly in perspective.

5 Another argument often launched against IQ tests is that they are culturally unfair. It is claimed that they are biased in favour of those who have had a better early education, who already know more. There is substance to this argument, in that general knowledge certainly does enter into many of the test items. Also some children will be more at home than others with the very idea of a test, of answering a bewildering string of arbitrary questions put by some stranger as if it really mattered. On the other hand, when relatively 'culture-fair' subtests (such as reasoning about the logic of visual patterns) are compared with blatantly culture-unfair subtests (such as vocabulary) the difference in outcome is often surprisingly

small and sometimes goes against the direction one would expect. Training can improve one's test score by about 6 or 7 points, but not much more. It is likely that highly intelligent children tend to pick up general knowledge quite quickly and that the tests reflect this.

It remains true that higher IQs are, on average, associated with stable home backgrounds, high parental incomes, small family size and living in an urban neighbourhood. (This does *not* mean that you will never meet a strikingly intelligent individual who comes from an enormous family of poor, divorced farmers.) Moreover, some cultures probably train children to behave more intelligently. Perkins[11] quotes figures showing that in the 1990s some 27% of the US population attended higher education, whereas for Jewish children the figure was 62%. Similarly, Asian families have the lowest school drop-out rates of any US ethnic group. However, this leads us to the further (upsetting) possibility that some of these groups, say with smaller families, higher incomes or Chinese-American family culture, may also have genes that favour high intelligence.

There are two issues intertwined here: firstly, is IQ subject to genetic influence? And, secondly, are there significant differences in the average IQs of different socially defined groups of people? I do not intend to deal with the second topic at all, partly because the evidence is so cloudy and difficult to interpret and partly because it is largely irrelevant to teachers anyway. Whatever group differences do, or do not, exist, they are irrelevant to the way we respond to individuals. This is both a moral and a practical point. We rightly feel it would be invidious to treat any individual as if he or she were a stereotyped member of some group. And even if we were insensitive enough to do so, we would very probably misjudge them as a result. Distributions for IQ in terms of large groups of people cover the whole range of scores and overlap much more than they divide. As teachers, in any case, we are faced with classes of individual students. No matter what their background, we simply want to make them effective learners and teach them as much as we can. Any large-scale group differences are thus irrelevant to our job, however they might be caused. The more relevant matter for teachers is to establish what each student knows.[12]

12.4 Heritability of IQ

Research on the degree to which intelligence might be innate, which relies entirely on using IQ tests as measures of intelligence, strongly supports the notion that there is a genetic underpinning to IQ. The main evidence comes from comparing groups who are more and less closely biologically related to one another and seeing how closely their IQ scores correlate. Correlations for IQ test scores are zero for totally unrelated persons but about +0.3–0.5 for siblings, who share half their genes. (For more information on the meaning of correlations, see note 4.) Adopted children living in the same family, who are genetically unrelated, have IQ correlations close to zero. Identical twins, who share all their genes, have correlations of about +0.88. This is almost as close as the scores of one person tested twice at different times. Fraternal twins, on the other hand, who have the same genetic closeness as siblings in general, have the same test correlation as siblings (0.3–0.5). There are also rare cases of identical twins reared apart from infancy. They have exactly the same genes but have been reared in different environments, so provide a particularly tough test of the genetic link. In the best study we have of such twins[13] their IQs still correlated very highly (+0.69), more highly than fraternal twins reared together.

These are very striking findings and unpopular with those who deny 'nature' any part in the story. There are some counter-arguments to the genetic case. One can argue that (i) all twins share one environment, namely the womb in which they developed; (ii) although different, the environments of the 'separated' twins may in fact have been quite similar; and (iii) one may share the same family home but be treated very differently as an individual child. Very briefly, researchers have tried to check all these possible complications, but they do not make any significant difference to the case for a strong genetic influence.[14] For one thing, both identical twins and fraternal twins share the same womb, yet their test correlations are very different. For another, adopted children are more similar to their biological parents, in IQ scores, than they are to their adoptive parents, who raised them from infancy onwards.

From these studies, scientists work out a figure known as heritability, which is the proportion of the total variance in a trait that correlates with genetic relatedness. There are several technical problems with exactly how these figures are calculated and they vary somewhat from one study to another, but overall they suggest a heritability of about 50% for IQ. To put this another way, about half of the differences in IQ scores between groups of people are attributable to their degree of genetic relatedness.

One important factor in these calculations is that heritability is basically a proportion, the part of variability that has to do with genetic differences, the other parts being to do with the environmental differences in the sample being studied and measurement error. Changing one proportionate part will leave more, or less, for the others. The 50% figure is an average, coming from studies done largely in North America and Europe. It might change if we looked at either a sample from very closely matched environments or a sample from wildly differing types of environment. Interestingly, if we studied groups of biologically related and unrelated children who were carefully raised in (so far as possible) identical environments, any differences remaining in their scores would be largely down to genetic factors, so the heritability would, just by the logic of the case, go up. Moreover, IQ tests are only suitable for use with cultural groups who share the broad culture of the test designers, so they are not of much use in cross-cultural studies.

It is important to grasp that genetic influences are highly indirect and do not rule out the important effects of experience. Even if the heritability of a characteristic is high, as it is for example for height, it can still be powerfully affected by the environment. Ceci and Williams[15] cite evidence about Japanese children whose grandparents had migrated to the USA. These second-generation Japanese children, raised in the USA, were estimated on average to be over 12.5 centimetres (5 inches) taller than they would have been if they had been raised in Japan. (This was presumably mainly because of diet.) Yet their heights still showed a heritability of 90%. Taller sons had taller fathers, on average, and shorter sons had shorter fathers. But overall the children were taller than both their parents and their grandparents.

If genes matter, and it seems that they do, they matter first and foremost because they make us all humans, with extremely similar brains, rather than say chimpanzees or wolverines. And if the tiny differences between our individual brains matter, as they sometimes may, it will be because hundreds and hundreds of different genes have made tiny subtle differences to an incredibly complex system of a billion developing neurones in the brain. To trace the routes of cause and effect among these minute potential influences is to explore a maze that will keep neuroscientists busy for the foreseeable future.

12.5 Revising the Concept of Intelligence

David Perkins[11] argues that the bad press that IQ tests generally receive comes from four misconceptions about the intelligence that they measure. These are that IQ is (i) really important, (ii) unitary, (iii) inborn and (iv) largely unchangeable. All these ideas are at least partly misleading, or overstated. IQ is arguably not all that important; it is simply one kind of test performance which bears a relation to success in schoolwork and any similar tasks. Even Louis Terman eventually decided that it did not much matter what score a person obtained over a figure of about 120. Very few children are ever tested for IQ in the UK because there is no good reason for doing so. In my opinion, the only really useful role for IQ lies in research, where it sometimes does have an important function.

There *is* a strong common factor (*g*) running through the subtests that make up an IQ test, but the common factor is just as likely to be an overlapping feature of the subtests as some kind of 'essence' of intelligence. Individual profiles can still vary quite widely, with some people stronger on visual problems, other people being highly verbal, others liking to work with numbers and so on. The question of innateness has already been considered but here we can state again that about half the variance in IQ scores is attributable to environmental influences of some kind. Poor children adopted into middle-class educated families, for example, have been known to show about a 12-point gain on the tests. As for its unchangeable nature, it is true that IQ scores are fairly stable over time, but this should not be confused with our knowledge and ability to solve problems, which can change radically.

If we take a broader definition of intelligence to mean 'potential problem-solving ability', then Perkins suggests we think of three crucial aspects of the intelligence that we bring to bear on any problem.

- Neural intelligence: the basic efficiency of our central nervous system.
- **Experiential intelligence**: our accumulated knowledge and skill.
- Reflective intelligence: the management of our own cognitive resources.

With regard to neural intelligence, psychologists and brain scientists continue to hunt for the 'holy grail' of the detailed physiology of intelligent behaviour, the actual brain-stuff that makes it work. Steven Pinker[16] reports on their progress but no simple answer can yet be given. We can also look after our brains well, or badly, in terms of such things as health, nutrition and lifestyle. Of course much more of the structure of our brains is the same than is different; in fact any differences are vanishingly small. Yet they could still be significant, if we knew what they were. The evidence from IQ tests and brain research remains consistent with the general hypothesis that brains, like every other part of our bodies, vary (a bit) at birth and that some of us probably have faster, less error-prone models than do others. It seems foolish to deny this, but to teachers it is probably the other two items on Perkins' list that are of far more interest.

The key point to grasp is that it is our knowledge and skills that are by far the most important ingredients we bring to the solution of most of our problems. Imagine a child of genius IQ who had never seen a car before and was asked to mend one. She would not have a chance! Similarly with literacy, science, languages, humanities and everyday life: what we generally need is the knowledge and skill relevant to a problem before we can solve it. In most lines of work it is far easier to spot the people who are really experienced, who know what they are doing, than it is to say which ones are more or less intelligent. Many a highly intelligent person has been reduced to impotent frenzy by not understanding how a computer (or oven timer or video recorder) works. And knowledge (together with skill) is something we can go on accumulating all our lives. Thus it is Perkins' second 'aspect', experiential intelligence, that is the most important in most contexts, including school.

Psychologists originally hoped to create tests that measured pure 'potential' for intelligence, uncontaminated with knowledge picked up along the way. However, this was an illusory goal. Uncoupling intelligence from knowledge does not really work. A newborn baby has huge potential but very little knowledge, and is virtually untestable. Humans make little or no sense when separated from their knowledge. This is the most important limitation of the concept of 'intelligence' as it developed within psychology. Funnily enough, the word 'intelligence' once stood only for information, as in 'What intelligence do you have of the enemy's position?' Thus it was once more or less synonymous with 'knowledge'.

The work of Carol Dweck, surveyed in Chapter 10, showed that an 'incremental' view of intelligence, based on the idea that we can improve our usable knowledge, is far more useful to students than is an entity view, which sees intelligence as something fixed and unchangeable. Students who actually believe in the potential power of their own efforts and learning to make a difference, you will remember, tend to have better attitudes towards setbacks and make better use of their cognitive resources. This implies that we would be wise to think of intelligence not as some kind of innate potential but as a current capacity for solving problems. The stability of IQ test scores is illusory, in a way, just because these tests use items which are relatively unaffected by prior knowledge. By trying to exclude experiential intelligence they miss one of the most important facts about humans: that their problem-solving ability generally depends on the knowledge they can bring to bear on a problem. Dweck's work on the impact of incremental versus entity views on students' attitudes and choices provides a link between experiential intelligence and Perkins' last category, reflective intelligence.

Reflective intelligence (the same concept as our 'metacognition') opens up the interesting possibility that we can learn to manage what intelligence we have far more effectively than many of us do. We have already looked at the potential of this area (10.6). As we saw there, the more closely we look at how effective learners operate, the more we are forced to take into account the whole person, with their attitudes, values and personality, rather than just their intellect. Motivation and attitudes, together with social skills, habits and strategies, all affect the resilience, resourcefulness, reflectiveness and reciprocity of learners. There is clearly much more to effective learning and problem-solving than raw 'neural' intelligence. I stop short of arguing that such intelligence is utterly unimportant, however. High neural intelligence is a scarce resource and should be nurtured and valued wherever it is found. I have to conclude that Perkins' neural intelligence does exist and is even important, in that some children generally learn more quickly than others. But to the teacher, knowledge, skill, good attitudes and motivation to learn are more important. As Lauren Resnick observes, your intelligent behaviour depends on 'the sum total of your habits of mind'.[17]

We need to lose our fear of intelligence, and put it into a sensible perspective. We also need to value other kinds of ability that contribute equally to our culture. The absurd veneration we feel for those who are clever at theoretical subjects such as astrophysics or pure mathematics needs to be toned down in favour of more even-handed appreciation for such sterling human qualities as imagination, physical grace, wit, practical competence, organizational ability, warmth in personal relationships, musical or artistic talent and moral courage.

12.6 Personality and Temperament

One of the ideas that we all tend to take for granted is that members of the same family often show physical resemblances to one another. They may be very strikingly similar, or hardly at all similar, but we are used to the general idea. We are also deeply imbued with the idea that our personality and values are largely the product of our upbringing, that parents in particular have a strong influence on their children. But we need to tread cautiously here. In the first place, parents and children resemble one another anyway, simply because they are genetically related. We are used to the shared physical features but not so much to shared mental ones. In the second place, we need to distinguish carefully between the kinds of things that parents do pass on to their children, culturally speaking, and the things they do not. We need to distinguish between personality, temperament, habits and values, at the least.

IQ, as we have seen, has a strong genetic component, but just thinking about your own family is quite likely to remind you that family members are still very varied in their intellects, as in most other things. The term 'personality' is so vague that it means rather different things to different people. It gestures towards the distinctiveness of individuals, without being clear about just what personal characteristics are supposed to contribute to it. 'Temperament' is a more manageable term, in that it suggests a long-term set of features of the mind, a kind of mental tuning or constitution, and I will stick mostly to that. Psychologists have looked at very many individual traits of temperament and the lists they come up with of the most important ones have varied somewhat over time. The current list of favourites is summed up by the acronym OCEAN, which stands for openness, conscientiousness, extroversion, agreeableness and neuroticism.[18]

- Openness: the degree to which one is curious, open to new experiences and imaginative, as opposed to incurious, resistant to new things and unimaginative.
- Conscientiousness: being dependable, organized and practical, as opposed to impulsive, careless and irresponsible.
- Extroversion: being sociable and enjoying being the centre of attention, as opposed to being reserved and socially withdrawn.
- Agreeableness: being good-natured, sympathetic and warm, or quarrelsome, unfriendly and cold.
- Neuroticism: linked to anxiety, emotional instability and irritability, as opposed to having low anxiety, stable emotions and low reactivity to stress.

It is unfortunate that so many of these traits have one pole that is attractive (curious, dependable, good-natured) and another that is not (unimaginative, irresponsible, cold). We need to remind ourselves that, as with IQ, most of us are somewhere in the middle range of these traits: extreme values on any of them are quite rare. Also the social context of our behaviour is extremely important: we are all capable of being unfriendly, irresponsible or anxious. We can learn to be more responsible, organized and sympathetic. The point is that, in terms of our natural temperament, we may be starting from rather different places.

Research similar to that done on IQ, using twin studies and adoption studies, has revealed that roughly 40% of the variance in these traits is correlated with genetic relatedness. Identical twins are more alike, as measured by questionnaire responses, than are fraternal twins, even when the identical twins were reared apart. Adopted children are more similar to their biological parents than to their adoptive parents, not only in IQ scores but also in their temperament.[19] Apart from genetic influences, it has proved difficult to pin down the source of the remaining variance. It may even be largely 'noise' from the rather unreliable method used whereby people fill in questionnaires about themselves. However, as with the heritability of IQ, we need to remember that high heritability does not imply that environmental influences may not also be powerful. A given pattern of temperament may 'play out' very differently in different cultural settings and situations. In fact there is widespread evidence that personality and temperamental traits can be affected strongly by situational factors. Self-theories and values, also, are likely to play an important role in leading us to behave as we typically do.

We might think of nature and nurture as affecting the individual person's actions rather as the tides and the wind affect a rower, trying to row a boat in a particular direction. If we liken innate factors to the tide or to underlying ocean currents, we need to figure out if we are rowing with or against their force. If cultural norms and influences blow at us like the winds, then we will have to row that much harder if we want to move our boat against them. Our choices and actions, like the rower's efforts, can potentially move us in any direction, but it will be easier to row with the wind and tide than against them. Educational debates always have, swirling beneath them, assumptions about how easy or difficult it is for people to change and develop. The evidence considered in this chapter is compatible with a moderately optimistic view, namely that people certainly can develop and change, through learning.

In so far as temperament is a style of mind, a set of currents that flow beneath the conventions and rules of everyday life, it surfaces in the manner in which we do what we do and how we react to events. In school, it is generally only students with rather extreme temperaments who run into difficulties. They may be so anxious as to find the stress of school life almost intolerable or they may be so shy that they never really make friends. In other cases an unfortunate temperament, such as a ready temper and liking for being the centre of attention, gets them into trouble frequently. Introverts who are high on anxiety (neuroticism) are likely to react to difficulties in school by withdrawing and becoming defensive. Extroverts high on neuroticism are more likely to 'act out' their frustrations in an aggressive outgoing manner.

We all have to learn to recognize and adjust to our own strengths and weaknesses of temperament and teachers can help us to do this, while remaining sensitive to our individual natures. I can imagine that using the OCEAN list of traits to describe a class of students one was teaching, rating each individual on a five-point scale for each trait, could be an interesting exercise in assessment, always provided that one remained open to the possibility that one had got it wrong. The local culture and context would, of course, influence the ways in which such traits were being expressed. The results of such an exercise, though clearly fallible, might help teachers to highlight certain problems that a student has socially, or in learning, and suggest ways of countering them.

12.7 Socialization: the Home and the Peer Group

Given that temperament can be thought of as a kind of fine-tuning of the nervous system, with some being more highly strung than others, I have not myself been surprised to learn from the research that genetic factors contribute to this tuning. What is more surprising, at least to me, is to discover how little effect parents may have on how their children turn out. The researcher who more than any other has forced us to reappraise this issue is Judith Rich Harris.[20] Harris reviewed all the evidence that suggested that the 'socialization' of children by their parents was crucial to their adult personality and found it lacking. With courage and humour she has since taken on the large establishment of 'experts' who make a living telling parents (and sometimes teachers) how they should treat children so as to have successful well-adjusted offspring, and, in my opinion, has largely won the subsequent argument.[21]

Let us be clear about what is being argued. It is not being claimed that parents are of no importance to their children; on the contrary a happy and successful childhood is very much the result of caring, sensitive parenting. Nor is it being claimed that parents do not influence their children at all; on the contrary they strongly influence their behaviour at home, especially in the early years, and they pass on all kinds of knowledge, skills and values. No child should be neglected, unloved, treated cruelly or with indifference. Every child should be loved and taught how to get along both within the family and with other people outside it. Rather, what Harris is pointing out is the following:

- Similarities in temperament or behaviour between parents and their offspring may be caused by inherited similarities, rather than by socialization.
- Parents are not the only influences on their children: siblings and the peer group also play powerful roles.
- Children sometimes have an effect on how parents behave, rather than vice versa.
- Although attitudes, values and interests may be learned partly at home, along with general knowledge and skills, these are not what IQ tests or personality questionnaires mostly tap.
- When children are away from home, they start to learn new ways of doing things, to the extent that this is necessary.

Harris suggests that we compare the advice given to parents in the UK and USA 100 years ago with the advice given over, say, the last 20 years. It is dramatically different, to say the least. Whereas formerly parents were exhorted not to spoil their children or draw too much attention to them, now parents are often advised that self-esteem must be nurtured and built up by lots of sensitive praise and attention (but see 10.3). Formerly it was considered a duty of parents to spank their children if they were naughty; now all forms of corporal punishment are rejected as cruel and as dangerous models of violence. Once parents were taught that 'over-stimulation' could be harmful to the brain; now parents are encouraged to stimulate children's minds in every way. At one time parents were warned against showing too much overt affection; now parents are advised to give their children all the hugs and kisses that are going. Harris's simple question about all this is the following: are children turning out better now than then? Are they happier and better adjusted? Are they less aggressive? Less anxious? Nicer? Hmmm.

Imagine watching a mother saying goodbye to her young son at the start of the school day in a Reception class. The small boy cries bitterly and clings to his mother. She clings back and is nearly in tears herself. The teacher who is watching and has seen this situation many times before, kindly tries to distract the child, leading him off to play with some toys, reassuring him that mother will return by and by. Then the teacher spends more time reassuring the mother that all will be well. In a few minutes he will settle and be as right as rain. In this case, let us imagine that the child is not convinced, but continues to wail and protest all morning. The mother is reluctant to depart and, when she finally does so, is clearly herself in tears. The teacher knows that it is perfectly natural for mothers and children to have this kind of reaction, but this pair is a little extreme.

The teacher is quite likely to assume at this point that this mother has taught this child to be rather too dependent and 'clingy'. The mother needs to learn to let go and her son needs to learn a little more independence, and all will be well. Perhaps she is right, but then again perhaps not. The teacher might just as logically say to herself that possibly both mother and child are relatively high scorers on the neuroticism scale and thus both are unusually prone to separation anxiety. Or she might remind herself that the mother's anxiety may well have been not the cause but the effect of her son's frequent tears in public places, together with her natural empathy for his misery. There is more than one way for these things to come about.

When children emigrate to foreign lands with their families, they take time to adjust to the new culture but, if they are still young and provided they start to mix with children of their own age, they rapidly learn to talk the local language and often learn new games, habits and attitudes too. In fact it is the parents who are generally slower to learn the new language and to let go of the culture of their old homeland. The children, as they grow up, usually try their best to fit into the new culture and often distress their parents deeply by so doing. They may retain some of the habits and skills they learned at home (for example to do with religion, cooking and food) but only if their life away from home allows this without any stress. Even parents who move from one region to another within the UK can be startled to hear how quickly their children start to pick up the local accent and identify with local heroes. To be a successful child, it is necessary to learn how to get along at home. But it is equally important to learn how to get along *outside* the home, to learn to do things right at school and in the society of other children.

Children are adaptable and they quickly learn that one uses different social moves, different games, different words and different forms of politeness when one is with an elder sibling, a teacher, a new friend, or Mum or Dad. They easily learn how to respond differently at their grandmother's house or to a new teacher in class. In fact they are experts at this business of social adjustment. Our language codes, for example, vary constantly across different social contexts. When the culture is exactly the same both inside and outside the home then of course children's behaviour has no need to change, and does not. But where there is a real clash between the culture of home and that of the peer group, the peer group wins almost every time. (Think about current attitudes to drugs, sexual behaviour, clothes, body piercing and music.) The painter Augustus John, a notable rebel, once said to a friend when they were both young adults 'We've become the people our parents warned us against!' He was, of course, triumphant about this.

In hunter-gatherer societies, our original environment of evolutionary adaptation, social groups are small and infants are kept in close physical contact with their mothers, and breast-fed mostly on demand, for 2 years or even longer. The child is then usually displaced at the breast by a new baby and has to join a small group of other children, generally of very varied ages. They play together about the camp and the older ones are mostly dominant. There is not a lot of aggression, typically, because the difference in size and strength between the leaders and the newcomers is simply too great. The young child learns how to join in with the group and gradually moves up the pecking order. In extreme circumstances, however, when normal family life breaks down completely, children form peer group gangs, hunting for food and living together, as can be seen today in most of the slums of the great cities of the world.[22] Children are equipped by evolution to survive and in the end that means surviving in the social world of your fellows. Children join the peer group and then nothing can shake its primacy in their lives. If the peer group rejects them, as it sometimes does, they are miserable, for nothing can really take its place, unless they team up with another rejected soul and make their own 'band'.

One great difference for children in the modern world, as opposed to that of hunter-gatherers, is that very large groups of children of the same age find themselves living together in schools. This raises the level of competition for status between them (and probably explains why small village schools are relatively peaceful places). It also leads to rival peer groups setting themselves up and to many opportunities for these groups to create their own generational subcultures.

I vividly remember leading a double life at school. I was not alone, however; we all lived double lives. We lived in one 'official culture' that was run by powerful adults and which had many, many rules. In that culture we mostly did exactly what we were told and we tried to keep out of trouble, for the punishments on offer were severe. But in our spare time we lived in our 'unofficial culture', which was partly inherited from older boys (it was an all boys' school) and partly invented by ourselves. This culture had totally different rules and aims and, like most adolescent subcultures, it had its own slang, its own language, its values and jokes. We could not share it with grown-ups either at home or at school. There were overlaps, of course, between the two codes, but in many contexts they were strikingly different. When there was a direct clash between the adult world and ours, we sometimes had to admit defeat on the surface, in one way or another, for 'they' were more powerful than 'we' were, but privately we judged everyone's actions by our own code of honour and loyalty and we did not forget betrayals. Now I see that this was a normal state of affairs.

Within peer groups the members are not clones of one another. Not only do they come from different homes and have differing temperaments and brains, they tend to differentiate their roles within the group. There will be leaders and followers, those with high status and those without. Sometimes status is acquired by becoming a 'joker' or by showing expertise at some particular occupation, or by demonstrating contempt for adult rules ('them'). Harris believes that these group identities sometimes mark their holders for life. Partly it is a matter of working out status in terms of clothes, language, nicknames and styles of behaviour. Students at university can find themselves doing much the same thing, as they sort themselves into groups. Where teenagers in a peer group need information about the adult world they now have at least three choices: they can watch how their parents and relatives go about things, they can watch TV or they can observe the styles of older children in and out of school. Parents will not always be the most influential source of ideas.

Just to emphasize a point already made, children will not need to change their behaviour greatly if the culture of their peers is much the same as that of their home. It is in cases of conflicting values that parents may lose out to peers. Also research is still coming up with ways in which parents may yet have long-term influences on their children. For example, Melissa Kamins and Carol Dweck[23] have evidence that parents who praise and scold their children with person-oriented words, implying that they are good, bad, smart or dumb as persons, have an impact in making their children develop worries about their basic self-worth. This anxiety is then developed, via the child's self-theory and associated beliefs, into an entity theory of human nature and an unhealthy preoccupation with performance goals and learned helplessness in the face of failure. On the other hand, parents who praise and scold the specific behaviour influence their children in the direction of having an incremental theory of human nature, a mastery orientation and a belief in their ability to grow and change.

Clearly this is an issue that will continue to attract research. Parents may be distressed to learn that they have, at least comparatively, less power than the experts once told them they had. But they may also be relieved to find, in their own case, that they did not turn out exactly like their own parents. And they have the consolation, in the light of this new theory of 'group socialization', that they are not responsible for all their children's mistakes, unhappiness or misfortunes. They remain responsible for what goes on at home and for the early years of childhood. As another writer has put it: 'Being wisely loved and regarded with respect at home is the best of all beginnings.'[24] Parents may, or may not, succeed in influencing which other children their children associate with. They may also set a good example and succeed in teaching their children all sorts of useful things. They may help to set up entity or incremental theories of intelligence and associated attitudes to learning and self-worth. But we may have exaggerated the extent to which the actions of parents shape the adults their children become. Having said this, parents can still often provide a safe haven for a child to return to, when life away from home gets too stressful.

12.8 Questions

The following questions are designed to help you check your understanding of the chapter.

1 Why is it claimed that intelligence is an especially sensitive subject?
2 Between what scores would you expect the results on an IQ test of the middle two-thirds of the population to fall?

3 What does g stand for?

4 In what ways is the 'intelligence' measured by IQ tests somewhat narrow?

5 What three aspects of intelligence did Perkins distinguish? Which is the most important in everyday life?

6 What does the acronym OCEAN stand for?

7 How might the environment (local culture and situation) affect the ways in which temperament and personality are expressed?

8 In what ways does Judith Rich Harris undermine the assumption that adult personality is a consequence of childhood upbringing?

9 **Discussion questions**: do schools, in general, encourage a particular type of personality? What sorts of personality, or temperament, might prove difficult for a student to manage in school? Can teachers do anything about this?

NOTES

1. Levi (1991), p. 133.
2. See Ceci and Williams (1999).
3. An excellent guide can be found in Deary (2001). Another good introduction is given in chapter 11 of Brown and Herrnstein (1975). If you are interested in measuring your own IQ, you can buy a book that will enable you to do this, provided you do not cheat! One well-known example is by Hans Eysenck.
4. A correlation is a statistical measure of how closely two variables co-relate, or vary together. If two variables are completely independent of one another (i.e. unrelated), then their correlation coefficient will be zero. If two variable are perfectly correlated, so that knowing the value of one would enable you to predict exactly the value of the other, then their correlation coefficient will be either +1 (as one variable increases in value, so does the other) or −1 (as one variable increases in value, the other decreases). In the social sciences, correlation coefficients of around ± 0.1–0.3 are generally regarded as 'weak', coefficients of about 0.4–0.7 as 'medium' and coefficients of 0.8 and above as 'strong'. The fact that two variables are strongly correlated does not necessarily mean that one caused the other; correlation does not imply causation.
5. See Deary (2001), chapter 2.
6. See Deary (2001), chapter 5.
7. Gardner (1993).
8. A possible exception would be the identification of highly intelligent children who are growing up in conditions of poverty and neglect. A high IQ score might help them obtain valuable resources or education. But then one might ask why other children, with somewhat lower IQ scores, would not also benefit from the same help.
9. Terman (1925, 1930, 1947, 1959).
10. The two were William Shockley and Luis Alvarez.
11. Perkins (1995).
12. If you wish to follow up the subject of group differences, try for example Sternberg (2000).
13. Bouchard et al. (1990).
14. See, for example, Deary (2001), chapter 3.

15. Ceci and Williams (1999), introduction.
16. Pinker (1997).
17. Quoted in Claxton (in press).
18. Bouchard (1999).
19. Loehlin (1992).
20. Harris (1998).
21. Harris (1999).
22. For a dramatic account of such a social breakdown, see Turnbull (1987).
23. Dweck (2000), chapter 15.
24. Donaldson (1996).

PART III

Extending Teaching

The third and final part of the book extends the coverage of teaching beyond the general principles introduced in Part I to consider some rather more advanced topics.

- Chapter 13, on special educational needs, is concerned with important differences between learners. The topics of bullying and child abuse are also included in this chapter because they both give rise to cases of special need.
- Chapter 14 is about gender and ethnicity, as dimensions of life in school. They are both characteristics that have attracted much attention in relation to equal opportunities for students and under-achievement.
- Chapter 15 is specifically about assessment, especially assessment for learning. Although this is an important aspect of teaching from the very start, it has been reserved for Part III, rather than Part I, because assessment has in the past proved to be a particularly difficult aspect of teaching to develop to high standards. The chapter also allows some expansion of topics addressed in Part I, such as the use of questioning and target setting.
- Chapter 16 is concerned with teaching a specialist subject and with what we know about how teachers learn and develop their expertise. It is also about what it means to become a professional teacher.

CHAPTER THIRTEEN

Special Educational Needs, Bullying and Child Abuse

13.1 Introduction

This chapter will introduce the challenge of teaching children with special educational needs (SEN). It also includes sections on bullying and child abuse. Bullying is a problem that plagues schools and results in victims who have special needs. Child abuse also results in cases of special need and teachers have important responsibilities in connection with its identification and prevention. Special needs are thus the unifying theme of the chapter. The chapter begins with some of the recent history of the treatment of SEN, to set current policies in perspective. It continues with an emphasis on good practice in schools and on the detailed role of the teacher. Many brief individual case studies are provided in order to indicate what an enormously varied range of special needs teachers may encounter. The chapter concludes with sections on bullying (and anti-bullying policies) and child abuse (and child protection).

13.2 Background to SEN Policies

Some 2–2.5% of children have needs that make it very difficult for them to thrive in mainstream schools without extra help. They have congenital or acquired impairments, physical, mental or both, which seriously affect their use of language, their mobility, their perception or their learning. Common examples of such conditions would include cerebral palsy (some degree of impairment of the brain, most commonly caused by lack of oxygen during birth), muscular dystrophy, Down's syndrome, autism and severe mental handicap of unknown origin. Many from this small minority of the population are assessed as having special needs long before they get to school age and some of them are subsequently educated in special schools, such as those for the severely physically handicapped, the visually impaired, the hearing impaired or children with severe learning difficulties. The advantages of such special schools are chiefly that they can provide:

- smaller classes and better funding;
- specialist equipment and resources (such as physiotherapy and speech therapy);
- specialist expertise in teaching and behaviour management;
- close links with both parents and potential employers;
- companionship with others sharing the same problems.

However, parents are not always happy to see their children go to special schools, which isolate them from the general culture and peer group to some extent. Rightly or wrongly, parents often see a special school, despite its extra resources and expertise, as a kind of second-best, an extra handicap for the child to carry. Partly because of this, an alternative policy has developed of including these students in mainstream schools wherever possible.

There also exists a far greater number of children, perhaps 10–15% of each age group, who have moderate learning difficulties or who present behavioural problems severe enough to make them stand out in ordinary classes as having special needs. A small number of these children have traditionally been educated in special schools, for example those for children with moderate learning difficulties, specific learning difficulties (dyslexia) and emotional and behavioural difficulties. The names and labels have changed, over the years, and are always somewhat misleading. Many children suffer from a combination of difficulties: they have learning needs which are soon accompanied by behaviour problems, or behavioural difficulties that before long give rise to learning deficits.

Physical and perceptual impairments, language difficulties, epilepsy, asthma and other forms of illness often combine in complex ways with family problems, social problems, neglect or abuse. Physical needs may combine with social disadvantage and both become tangled with learning difficulties or emotional needs. Some difficulties are severe and some mild; some are temporary and some permanent. Some children are 'on the margins' and might, once upon a time, have been placed in a special school in one area but in a mainstream school in another area. Children with Down's syndrome are a good example, a group with very widely varying abilities and needs, who have sometimes been placed in special schools and sometimes in mainstream schools. In 1978 the Warnock Committee delivered a landmark report, setting out its thoughts and recommendations on the whole field of what it chose to call 'special educational needs'.

The Warnock Committee estimated that some 20% of the school population had SEN at some time during their education. Most of these students were, and would remain, in mainstream schools. Although the committee recognized the qualities and expertise of many special schools, they were generally in favour of 'integration' whereby as many children as possible would have their special needs catered for in mainstream schools, by careful, individually tailored programmes of extra resources and support. The many and varied professionals dealing with such children and their families (including doctors, physiotherapists, teachers, speech therapists, educational psychologists and social workers) were exhorted to work more closely together and to help parents, in particular, to find their way through the complex network of health and educational provision. The 1981 Education Act put some of these recommendations into practice and children began to be 'statemented', a legally backed process of assessment that was to guarantee a proper level of funding to match the degree of need. A series of steps were defined by which SEN could be provided within a mainstream class, in special units in mainstream schools or in special schools.

Two of the problems underlying this wide-ranging and humane report proved very difficult to solve, however. First, little explicit thought had been given to money; that was up to the politicians to provide. But both the number of children who could or should be helped and the degree of extra funding that could or should be provided were extremely elastic. They constituted, in effect, virtually a bottomless well of need. Local education authorities were already strapped for cash and the process of statementing turned into something of a bureaucratic nightmare, a battle for scarce resources, effectively rationing them to the most needy and often taking months or even years to complete. Secondly, the SEN defined by the report did not (indeed were not allowed to) include the very large numbers of children whose parents were poor, badly housed, unemployed, in prison, insane, or suffering from all manner of educational and social disadvantages. Had this 'disadvantaged' population been included, the famous 20% of children with SEN might have risen to 35 or 40%. There was also widespread concern that especially gifted and talented children were often not provided in mainstream schools with the extra resources and challenges they needed in order to fulfil their potential. Then there were so-called 'clumsy' children, 'delicate' children, bereaved children, children failing to learn to read and children with phobias about school. There were children who were victims of bullying and social isolation. There were many children for whom the UK was a new culture and English a second language. There were travellers' children, still leading a semi-nomadic life. How could one exclude any of these groups, given that their needs were so glaringly obvious both to parents and to teachers?

In the years since the Warnock Report, governments, local education authorities, teachers and educationalists have continued to struggle with these problems. Funding has gradually increased. The most recent policies are enshrined in the Special Educational Needs and Disability Act 2001 and an SEN Code of Practice.[1] This Act strengthened the rights of all students with SEN to receive education suitable to their needs in a mainstream school, wherever possible. It also protects the rights of the disabled to fair and equal treatment. The code sets down in great detail the procedures for identification, assessment and provision for SEN, from early educational settings to transitions to adult employment. Interventions are divided into three main steps.

1 School Action: here existing SEN resources within the school are targeted so as to meet the special needs of a student, as set out in an **individual education plan** (IEP).
2 School Action Plus: here external expertise, advice, assessment or equipment are added to the school's resources, so as to meet needs which could not be met under 1. Again, an IEP sets out the immediate goals and means to reach them.

3 For a few students, where their needs are still not adequately met, a statutory
assessment and statement may be called for by the local education authority,
detailing the extra resources and strategies needed to meet the student's SEN.
This process has many requirements and obligations embedded in its procedures,
including careful communication and negotiation with the child and the child's
parents. It is intended to be completed within a time span of 26 weeks.

The Code of Practice outlines four key areas of educational need:

- communication and interaction;
- cognition and learning;
- behavioural, emotional and social development;
- sensory and/or physical impairment.

Interestingly, having English as one's second language, or speaking no English on
arrival at school, are not considered as special needs, although such individuals
may, of course, in addition to the linguistic challenge facing them, also have other
special needs.

There are currently a series of descriptive labels and acronyms that act as a kind
of shorthand for the main groups of students with SEN. The most important of these
are physically handicapped (PH); hearing impaired and visually impaired (HI/VI);
severe and moderate learning difficulties (SLD/MLD); emotional, behavioural and
social difficulties (EBSD); and autistic spectrum disorder (ASD). The main thrust of
policy is that all children should be educated in mainstream schools wherever possible, unless this would be incompatible with the efficient education of other students. It remains the case that a very small percentage of disabled and handicapped
children are educated in special schools. A far, far larger number are in mainstream
schools, with or without a statement of SEN, but hopefully with an IEP. The popular
image of an SEN student is probably still that of a child in a wheelchair, but by
far the largest groups, numerically, are students with MLD and/or EBSD. Integration
(or 'inclusion') has become accepted as the policy of first choice, although it has
not invariably been popular with parents, teachers or children. If adequate specialist
resources and teaching are not provided or if children in the 'mainstream' reject
children with SEN socially, then the results can be appalling. When the system works
well, however, it brings benefits to both students with SEN and all other students.

In a climate of extreme pressure on schools to improve their academic results, which
has now continued for some 20 years, there is a continuing suspicion that some
teachers and some schools would prefer to exclude children with SEN from their
classes and schools, in spite of government policies. Children with SEN, taken as a
whole, do not generally obtain such good academic results as 'mainstream' children,
although there are many exceptions. They also undoubtedly face teachers with extra
challenges, with new and worrying responsibilities and with extra work. Some teachers accept this with energy and enthusiasm, whereas others do not. It is probably fair

to say that schools vary in the reputation they have for SEN provision, from excellent to poor. In the last analysis, our determination to provide effective education, and later employment and other forms of support, for the whole SEN population is an index of the degree to which we care, as a society, for those who need our help. At the same time, it is important to try to ensure that help for SEN does not mean disadvantage to other 'mainstream' children, who after all are no less important. It is above all teachers who have to face this problem, head on, and try to cope with it.

There is an important difference between impairment, disability and handicap.[2] Take a child with a visual impairment: she might have *impaired* vision, but an effective pair of glasses may solve most of her problems, so her impairment does not result in *disability*. Another child, even with the best glasses available, may still have a disability related to sight and hence to moving about in a dangerous world. She might require special magnifiers, anti-glare blinds or Braille training to make sure her disability does not become a *handicap* in school. In short, impairment is a problem; a disability means that, in spite of help, the impairment still affects normal functioning; a handicap means that, in spite of all efforts to help, the problem remains at least partly unsolved. Our efforts must be directed to removing handicaps and minimizing disabilities.

13.3 SEN Provision in the Mainstream School

All schools have a policy on SEN provision and a special educational needs coordinator (SENCO). All Ofsted inspections carry out investigations into the quality of SEN provision. Some schools have specialist units or special resources or learning support departments within them. Others have developed links with local special schools. All class teachers in both primary and secondary schools can expect routinely to be dealing with a wide range of students with SEN. However, the range and variety of such needs is such that they cannot all be covered here in detail. Moreover, experience shows the truth of an important principle to grasp in this field, namely that students with SEN do not so much require a different kind of teaching as simply very good teaching. Almost all the advice routinely given to teachers on this subject is as applicable to the rest of the class as it is to those with SEN. It is true that the treatment of certain conditions requires specialist knowledge or special equipment, but by and large these will be supplied by SENCOs and/or by specialist advisers and teachers visiting schools. Parents are also a rich source of expert knowledge. Finally, there is no substitute for practical experience with particular children, whose individuality always outstrips their textbook image.

Example 13.1 Inclusive good practice[3]
One study of five secondary schools, which had good reputations for their practice in including students with SEN, highlighted the following successful policies and practices.

- A determination to include students with SEN in all aspects of school life, including extracurricular clubs and activities, drama, sport and visits out of school, with extra support given where needed.
- A firm anti-bullying policy, which helped make students with SEN feel secure and accepted. One commented that 'other people recognize my problem'.
- Teachers were encouraged so far as possible not to distinguish between 'special' and 'normal' students in their interactions.
- Extensive work was carried out liaising with parents of students with SEN regarding attendance, transport, homework and any problems.
- Detailed records were kept on academic and social progress.
- Challenging academic targets were set, including GCSE exams for students who, at other schools, might never have been entered for such exams.
- Extensive use was made of learning support, or teaching, assistants.
- Teachers were responsive to individual needs in planning lessons, differentiating tasks either by outcome or level of support.
- Learning support staff tended to be attached to subject departments rather than individual classes or students. They gained expertise in that subject and were routinely included in planning and evaluation meetings. This made them both more flexible and more useful in supporting a range of students.
- Learning support staff were careful to support a variety of students in any class rather than only one target student, using their time to support when necessary and also to encourage independence.
- Lunchtime clubs and after-school homework clubs were provided, as well as in-class support.
- Careful induction schemes ensured that SEN students were prepared for entry to a school by visits (accompanied by familiar teaching assistants), information and photographs about key people and places, and staff meetings planning for satisfying the student's needs.

An Ofsted report[4] on inclusion of children with SEN highlights similar policies and judged that success in this field depends on:

- whole-hearted commitment of staff, from the head teacher and senior management to every teacher and member of support staff in a school;
- high expectations for both academic work and behaviour, with careful target setting and carefully defined levels of extra support;
- appropriate adaptation of the curriculum, where appropriate;
- good-quality teaching, adapting to individual needs;
- analysis and monitoring of small steps in learning in key subjects;
- well-managed support, from specialist visiting teachers and advisers and from teaching assistants;
- skilful management of, sometimes difficult, behaviour;
- giving priority to the personal and social development of students with SEN;
- good liaison with parents and careful induction for new students.

Example 13.2 Instances of good practice
The following examples supply a range of instances in which students with SEN were enabled to take part in normal lessons and school activities, with greater or lesser adaptations to their needs.

1 A blind 5-year-old girl joined a mainstream primary school, with special resources devoted to her learning of pre-Braille skills. Initially she was considered to be babyish, refusing to sit up straight and screaming for attention. She was reported from home to have an eating problem but, with support, managed to eat a packed lunch regularly. She became keen to manage hanging up her own coat, making her own way to the toilet and helping to put a cover on the Braille machine. She was felt to be making good progress within a short time with her social skills, communication skills and mobility.

2 A primary student with SLD was able to take part in maths lessons, with the help of a teaching assistant. In one lesson involving pictograms of children's preferences for fruit the teacher used large, brightly coloured, cut-out pictures of different fruits, building up the pictogram piece by piece. This held the attention of the 'special' student, who was able to follow the lesson and quietly counted the numbers of fruit in each column.

3 Jack has behavioural difficulties and is at a large primary school where an adult support worker helps him. Mostly the class teacher treats him as 'just another member of the class'. Sometimes, however, if Jack does not respond to a quiet word, the support worker takes him out of the class. He is now her responsibility and she uses a range of activities and tasks to distract and calm him down. As soon as she can, she returns him to the lesson. Jack is responding by slowly showing better awareness and control of his own behaviour. He realizes that his support worker is now helping other students in the class and at first complained about this. His support worker reassured him that this was because he is making such good progress. Jack now says with pride that 'she can help other people now'.

4 In a primary school language unit, a student with ASD initially refused to turn around to face a whiteboard. He and a friend seemed to want to make an issue of this, but the teacher responded quickly, making one general request for the class to face the board and a second specific request naming the two boys and asking them to move to different seats. She communicated her expectation that she would be obeyed without fuss, in a non-confrontational way. At the end of the same lesson, the ASD student refused to give up some felt-tip pens as the student collecting them had not said 'please'. The teacher let this go, to avoid giving such a matter too much attention, but had a quiet word with the student at the end of the lesson, explaining the social aspects of the incident in a calm positive way.

5 A profoundly deaf Y9 student had been socially isolated on first coming to a school, spending most of his lunchtimes in the library by himself. Teachers and support staff encouraged him to join clubs and sporting activities, and he started to make friends. Before long he was playing in school sports teams and had developed a social network.

6 One Y9 student, Paul, was registered as blind and had learned touch-typing in primary school. He was learning Braille and in an English lesson was able to use a Braille version of the key worksheet, provided by a specialist resource base, working with the teacher. Blue blinds cut down the glare from windows and the boy also used a laptop

computer, fitted with a voice synthesizer, to answer questions. In a well-planned and structured lesson, which included pair and group discussion, silent reading, reading aloud and whole-class discussion, Paul was able to take an active part in all the activities. He had a friend sitting next to him, who helped with the organization of equipment when needed. Paul was observed to be a very confident learner.

7 A Y10 girl with learning difficulties was in a science lesson in which the class did some extension work on acids and alkalis, involving chemical formulae. This was considered inappropriate for the student with SEN who, instead, worked with a teaching assistant, reinforcing earlier work on coloured indicators, using a well-illustrated textbook and making drawings with annotations. At the end of the lesson she was able to answer the questions 'Can you tell me an acid you know?' and 'What turns the indicator red?'

In all these examples it seems that careful planning and good levels of resourcing are combined with sensitivity to individual needs and a good deal of common sense.

13.4 The Role of the Teacher

As a class teacher in a primary school or a subject teacher in a middle or secondary school, your first responsibility to students with SEN is to find out as much as you can about them. They should have an IEP designed within the scope of School Action or School Action Plus. A small number may have had a statutory assessment (statement) of their needs completed. For all of them, an IEP should exist that sets out their curriculum and the nature of any special help they are entitled to. IEPs should only contain material about additional or different provision from that provided for other students. In particular, the IEP should contain:

- three or four key short-term targets in core academic or social areas;
- specific teaching strategies, where relevant;
- the nature of additional or different resources to be put in place;
- dates for review and updating of the plan;
- success or 'exit' criteria, explaining a successful outcome.

These plans have to be reviewed at least twice per year and parents and the child should be involved with at least one of these reviews. Having read the plans, there are then three phases of your own teaching to consider: (i) advance planning, (ii) teaching and support, and (iii) assessment, recording and reporting.

Advance planning

If a student is new to the class or school, consult with the SENCO about induction and a likely series of priority aims. You should consider whether special equipment or modifications to the built environment are needed, and whether the normal timetable needs to be modified. If a teaching assistant is to be involved, you will need to plan with him or her. Think about whether you need to alert your class to this student's particular needs and ask them how they might help him or her to settle in.

Example 13.3 Edward
Edward transferred from a special school for EBSD students into Y7 of a mainstream school. When he was younger, he experienced some parental neglect and was eventually taken into care. He then frequently truanted from his primary school. There is also a suspicion in the record that he suffered from a middle-ear disorder (sometimes called 'glue ear'), which affected his hearing whenever he had a cold, which was frequently. This would have made it hard for him to hear and understand speech in a classroom and may have been one reason for his failure to make good progress in the early years. His placement at a special boarding school had been reasonably successful but now he was with new foster parents and hoped to adjust to a mainstream school. Records were sent from the previous school, detailing his behaviour difficulties, interests and levels of attainment in the core subjects of English, maths and science.

It was agreed at planning meetings at his new school that he should receive some support from a teaching assistant in ordinary lessons and should be withdrawn for some lessons in the learning support department in order to further develop the skills and concepts he needed for mainstream curriculum work. He was then included in a general induction week for all incoming students, so that he could learn about the school along with others and make new friends. On his first day a teacher he had already met greeted him on arrival and made sure he knew where to go. After his initial week, detailed targets were agreed with him for his personal, social and academic work. He was also assigned to a class tutor who took a special interest in his progress and was available to help him if a crisis arose. He settled in quickly and started to catch up with his peers, proving to have considerable ability in both maths and science.

Example 13.4 Natalie
Natalie was a visually impaired student approaching her GCSE exams. She had hoped to take 10 subjects but her mother became worried that she was spending every night on homework, since she needed extra time to complete almost every assignment. Negotiations were carried on and the school agreed, with Natalie and her mother, that it would be best to compromise. She was allowed to drop French as a subject, and to use French lessons to catch up on her homework in other subjects. The school expected her to get high grades in all her other nine subjects.

Teaching and support

When planning lessons, you need to decide what forms of differentiation might be needed to meet the needs of individuals in your class. This will usually consist of setting different tasks (*differentiation by task*), or the same task but expecting a different level of outcome (*differentiation by outcome*) or the same task but providing extra support (*differentiation by support*). Sometimes different equipment or materials might also be needed. Next, consider your seating plan, trying to ensure that any students with special visual or hearing needs are seated so they have maximal opportunity to see and hear. Keep students apart if they tend to misbehave or distract one another. You might consider seating them near you. Think about whether a 'buddy' needs to be assigned to help an SEN student with organization of materials or mobility, or to give some general support with learning. Consult with your teaching assistant, if you have one, over what her role is to be and what extra materials, or different tasks, might be needed.

Think about the objectives for learning that you have for the lesson as a whole and consider whether they need to be broken down into smaller steps of progress for any student with learning difficulties. Check that your lesson has plenty of variety in it and is designed to capture the interests of all your students. Try to avoid situations in which SEN students are ignored or given low level 'time-fillers' that do not really enable them to progress. Think about how you plan for them to participate and when you may need to give extra support to one or two individuals.

In your teaching make sure that all crucial ideas and instructions are understood by everyone, using questions to check on comprehension. Ensure that teaching materials are well prepared and easy to read. Remember to ask questions at different levels of difficulty, so as to allow different students to answer at their own level. Try not to single out students with SEN as 'different' but be prepared to give them some special help discreetly. Plan to stretch the talents of unusually able students at some point in the lesson, perhaps with extension work or greater independence. Remember the importance of finding positive things to praise, about work and behaviour, with students who are struggling. In plenary sessions, check that the main points of the lesson have been grasped by everyone. Keep records of key events and outcomes.

Example 13.5 Sally

Sally, a Y4 student, has learning difficulties but takes part in mainstream lessons in her local primary school. She may be subject to a statutory assessment but this has not yet been decided. Meanwhile her school has talked to her parents and set up some immediate steps to help her. Under School Action, the SENCO and class teacher have drawn up an IEP. The main extra provision is for a teaching assistant to work with Sally and two other students during the group and individual sections of literacy and numeracy lessons each day. Sally takes part in the shared, whole class, beginnings and endings to these lessons. Sally's assistant is very experienced at making teaching resources to help slower learners, often using visual prompts and a carefully graded vocabulary. She and Sally's teacher have made it a priority to try to make Sally more independent in spelling and basic arithmetic.

Sally also takes part in voluntary lunchtime and after-school 'booster' lessons in literacy and numeracy, which make extensive use of games and computer programs. She particularly enjoys working with Emma, a Y6 student, who has been assigned to Sally as her 'mentor' and helps her with her reading. (Emma is a volunteer and has had some training to do this work.) Sally's teacher keeps in close touch with her parents, often meeting them informally at the start or end of the school day. A home–school diary is sent home with a reading book daily, and Sally's teacher and her parents write comments to one another on her progress and any minor problems that arise from day to day. The school feels that Sally continues to find schoolwork difficult but that she will make reasonable progress, given consistent help and careful monitoring. They are currently worrying about how to help her to fit in socially, as she is finding it hard to mix with her peers and prefers playing with younger children, whom she can 'mother'.

Example 13.6 Ewan

Ewan is a Y8 student with Asperger's syndrome (a variant of ASD). During an English lesson, the class is working on practical criticism of a set poem. They work in pairs and groups, brainstorming ideas and reporting back to the whole class. This puts great pressure on Ewan, who has difficulty understanding all social and emotional interactions and communications. In this case he is being asked to empathize with the poet's feelings and consider how they are expressed in the language of the poem. He is also being asked to compare the poet's feelings with his own and to discuss these with his peers. At times, he is anxious and turns away from the rest of the class. He also uses his exercise book as a screen to hide behind. His teacher is aware of his difficulties but does not comment on them. Instead, she waits until he is looking more confident and then asks him a question, scaffolding his response skilfully by repeating and reflecting on the responses of other students. Ewan manages to answer and also to contribute to work with a partner, albeit haltingly. His response is not as good as those of most other students but his teacher notes that her target was for him to 'make a reasonable try at responding'. Ewan succeeds at this and manages to stay in touch with the lesson.

Example 13.7 Children's university

One primary school with a high proportion of ethnic minority children and children from disadvantaged homes decided it needed to make more effort to cater for the needs of exceptionally bright individuals. In addition to regular work in class, they organized a 'children's university advanced mathematics class' once a week, for 40 students aged between 7 and 10 years. ICT is a strength of the school and the advanced maths class makes extensive use of the Internet. Teachers were initially amazed at the progress made and the speed of the students' learning of new ideas. The students take a great pride in their work and enjoy the sessions. The school goes to considerable trouble to make sure that each student, including one profoundly deaf student, has access to a computer at home so that they can continue with their mathematical investigations. It is planned that some of the students will take GCSE maths in Y6.

Assessment, recording and reporting

Generally, the same assessment and recording system can be used with students with SEN as with others, except where there are specific requirements in connection with an IEP, related to additional or different provision (see also Chapter 15). Often small steps of progress in learning need to be noted for these students, who may for example be working towards National Curriculum level 1. If this is so, use can be made of the **P scales** of progress towards level 1 published by the QCA or a similar scheme. Reporting on progress to parents is particularly important in the case of students with SEN. Parents are also often key allies and helpers, who understand their child and can give advice to the school.

Example 13.8 Robert

Robert is a Y4 SLD student at a mainstream primary school. The school's SENCO helps the class teacher to prepare detailed targets for Robert in the core subjects. A normal school record sheet is used, on which broad aims and objective assessment data are filled in. These include QCA 'P' scales of work towards level 1 for core subjects, with the previous term's assessments shown for comparison. These broad aims are then broken down into a more detailed IEP, which the class teacher uses to plan her lessons. Targets are agreed for each half term and some strategies for teaching are suggested for both the class teacher and a teaching assistant. Key skills and priorities cover both academic and social priorities for Robert. The targets are reviewed by the SENCO half-termly. She also prepares a single sheet for Robert, with three star shapes on it, each containing a key target headed English, maths and 'Me'. She goes through this with Robert, who signs it. Robert's parents also see these records and discuss his progress with his class teacher at the end of each term.

13.5 Recognizing Individuals

Teaching students with SEN can be wearing for teachers and they sometimes worry, particularly when behaviour is a problem, about the effect of one difficult student on the rest of the class. One group of researchers[5] put forward the following framework of pairs of values to consider:

Fairness: treating all the same	↔	Fairness: recognizing difference
Collective rights and responsibilities	↔	Individual rights and responsibilities
Need for correction	↔	Need for understanding

In each case two values are in tension with one another. We know that fairness by a teacher normally consists in equal treatment of all students, but we also know that there can be individual differences that should be recognized. Perhaps the key is to ask oneself: am I discriminating (recognizing a difference) on a basis that is relevant to the decision I am making? Our general rule should be 'no discrimination without relevant differences'. If a child is known to have recognizable problems with controlling emotions and behaviour, such that he or she is unable to regulate them as another child of the same age could, then arguably we have a relevant difference, which needs recognition. Similar arguments apply to the tensions between collective and individual rights and the need for understanding versus correction. Other students in the class, depending on their age and maturity, will probably also recognize, if you discuss it with them, that different treatment is sometimes justified for special cases. A general rule of thumb for teachers and schools is not to allow their policies or ethos to be dominated by either the left-hand set of values (only strict, tough-minded) or the right-hand set of values (only forgiving, tender-minded).

Example 13.9 'Rhinos'

Not all the troubled individuals in a school will cause overt trouble in class, however. Another school[6] decided that they should take a closer look at passive but unhappy students, who were under-achievers and who did not seem to participate very much in school activities. They called them 'rhinos', which stands for 'really here in name only'. They were able to single out a number of such students of different ages. Interviewing them produced a profile of frustration, difficulty in getting attention and feelings of being at odds with the general culture of the school. The research group concluded, however, that there was no general remedy: the key to success was to recognize the private agenda of each individual and to try to help with it. Thus, for one student a reporting system was introduced to improve standards of homework. Regular correspondence was entered into with the student's mother and, as a result of the scheme, which the student accepted and supported, considerable progress was made. A second student wanted to study drama. After correspondence with his parents a link was set up with a local drama group. Later, a work experience placement was found with a local theatre and eventually the student started work with a visiting youth theatre group.

Example 13.10 Simon

Simon is a student with mild ASD attending a secondary school. The school recognizes his difficulties and 'bends' the school rules so that he is allowed, for example, to carry a set of familiar objects around with him, which provide feelings of security. They also prepare a special visually attractive timetable for him, tailored to his need to know where he is supposed to be at all times. His occasional vagueness and odd social behaviours are often tolerated and ignored, by both staff and students, although efforts are also made to increase his social skills.

Example 13.11 Russell

Russell, who is in Y5, is dyslexic. He has always found written text confusing to understand and he has continuing difficulties with both handwriting and spelling. This affects his work in maths as well as English, and makes written work difficult across all subjects. In spite of his special needs, Russell takes part in the daily 'literacy hour', which has been a considerable help to him. He likes shared reading, in particular, where the reading of all the class supports his own efforts. Russell was lucky, in that his problems were recognized by his parents before he came to school and he was shown to have 'specific learning difficulties' at the age of 6 years. Since then, a careful programme of reading and writing has been planned for him, and supported from home. Russell is now reading at a level only one year behind his chronological age and his teacher thinks he will reach National Curriculum level 3 at the end of Y6. 'Multisensory' teaching has been used by his teachers and teaching assistants throughout his time at the school. That is, he has been taught to look at words, sound them out syllable by syllable, and then spell them out letter by letter, often tracing them out in a sand tray. Tracing over enlarged letters, while saying the word aloud, is a form of practice he feels helps him to remember words.

His teacher believes that word processing will be a considerable help to Russell, and his withdrawal from the class for extra help with literacy is now targeted at teaching him keyboard skills. He enjoys the satisfaction of seeing his work tidily printed out. His teacher often allows Russell to give oral answers or to answer in note form, so that his progress in other subjects is not constantly frustrated by his difficulties with writing. The school's SENCO believes that Russell is making good academic progress generally, but also thinks that he will continue to need extra support in secondary school with his writing. She intends to use Y6 to target more advanced reading and study skills, at which Russell is weak, and to teach him rigorously to check important examples of his writing, once for spelling errors, once for grammatical confusion and once for general meaning and coherence. Russell accepts that he has special needs but is generally cheerful and confident at school.

13.6 Bullying

Bullying was mentioned in Chapter 9 as an enduring feature of peer-group competition and striving for status in middle childhood and adolescence. Victims are those who, for one reason or another, are 'scapegoated' or rejected by their group. But to recognize its common roots is not to shrug one's shoulders and accept it as a fact of life. On the contrary, as one student put it: 'Bullying is not an unpleasant fact of life. People can do something about it.' In the last 10 years or so, anxiety about the prevalence of bullying in schools and about the awful suffering it can cause has led to research, vigorous national campaigns, and anti-bullying initiatives in the UK. Where once it had a low profile as a problem, it is now the subject of government policies. It is obligatory for all schools to have an anti-bullying policy in place and there is now a government anti-bullying charter, which all schools must sign, and which is linked with Ofsted inspections. A great deal of advice on tackling bullying is available in book form and on the Internet.[7]

Bullying can be defined as aggressive or insulting behaviour by an individual or group, often repeated over a period of time, which intentionally hurts or harms. It can undermine confidence, induce feelings of worthlessness and result in misery and social isolation. It can also lead to withdrawal from school activities and truancy, with consequently bad effects on academic progress. Serious and long-term harm may be done to an individual's social and emotional development. Yet firm action by schools can make a significant difference, reducing incidents of bullying and supporting victims through recovery.

The incidence of bullying remains difficult to pin down, partly because it shades imperceptibly into more minor kinds of teasing and banter and partly because children and adolescents are loath to admit to it or talk about it to adults. However, we do know the following.

- It can happen in any school, even the least likely.
- It is rather more common in secondary schools, with Y7 students being most at risk.
- There is a difference between the sexes, in that boys are more often physically hurt whereas girls suffer more from verbal and psychological attacks.

- One survey found that 10–20% of respondents reported having been victims of bullying within 6 months of the survey. Of these, 9% reported bullying which had gone on for a year and a further 13% reported bullying over several years.
- Schools have to remain constantly on the alert for this problem, never becoming complacent about it.

Schools with a good record on preventing bullying are reported by Ofsted[8] to have the following characteristics.

- A proactive rather than reactive attitude to bullying.
- Strong leadership from the head teacher, with a positive approach to building a good social atmosphere and confident relationships in the school.
- A clear policy that is followed through with day-to-day alertness and good procedures to reduce incidents, support victims and deal with perpetrators.
- Planned lessons and tutorial time focused on bullying and how to deal with it.
- Setting up of safe play areas or a quiet room, which is supervised.
- Efficient monitoring by staff or senior students of the school site, especially of toilets, secluded areas and lunchtime queues.
- Close supervision of students coming into, or leaving, school.
- Prompt and thorough investigation of any reported incidents, with provision for discrete reporting of bullying and staff available to listen and respond to victims.
- Punishment of perpetrators, combined with measures to understand their needs and communicate with their parents.
- Follow-up work with both victims and perpetrators to prevent further incidents and to repair damage.
- Training and use of peer mentors, 'buddy' systems, 'circle of friends' systems or outside agencies who can listen and help.

These successful schools admitted that they could never take their good record for granted. It was always necessary to maintain a high level of alertness and to make sure that written policies were actually working. Many schools undertake anonymous questionnaire surveys to see if bullying is a problem and accept that students may be more prepared to talk to an independent outsider, a senior student or a particular teacher rather than to just any member of staff. Mixed-age tutor groups, in secondary schools, and the use of trained peer mentors have been successful strategies. Primary schools have often used a 'circle of friends' approach, in which a group of peers is trained and encouraged to include either a victim or a bully in social activities and games. Fear of social isolation can sometimes be a cause of bullying as well as a result of it.

Teachers need to be alert to signs of bullying (as of signs of abuse), which can include unusual non-attendance, sudden depression or anxiety, reluctance to join in playtimes, torn clothing, or reports of thefts or damage to property. Sometimes scratches, cuts or bruises are a give-away sign. If students tease or use 'put-downs' of one another in class, it is important that the teacher does not passively accept or condone them as this can seem like acceptance of the practice to the students. Tacit acceptance of bullying by bystanders is often part of the problem. Verbal bullying includes teasing, name-calling and text messaging. When accused of bullying, the bullies will commonly protest that 'we were only having a laugh' or 'I was only teasing'. Primary-aged students are more likely to tell their parents about bullying, whereas secondary-aged students are more likely to tell a friend. In secondary schools, in particular, name-calling can have sexual, religious or racial overtones, which are especially hurtful and potentially damaging to the community. Teachers may find this hard to deal with but it must not be ignored. As a junior member of staff, be prepared to ask for advice from senior colleagues.

Many minor incidents verging on bullying are successfully resisted by the intended 'victim'. Successful strategies include resilience (laughing it off), assertive replies or finding new friends. About half the students who bully are reported to have been bullied themselves. Bullies also have their problems and needs; they can emerge from any social background and any level of ability. They sometimes bring family feuds into school or may be reacting to distress in their own lives. Sanctions against bullying can range from a sincere apology to withdrawal of privileges or membership of school teams or, in serious cases, fixed-term or permanent exclusion from the school. Parents of both the bully and the victim need to be told of incidents and interviewed. Unfortunately, parents of victims are often extremely angry and may even be in search of revenge, whereas parents of perpetrators sometimes refuse to believe that their child could do such a thing. Getting at the truth can be very difficult.

Teachers should deal explicitly with friendships, rivalries, teasing and bullying in lessons and tutorials, or circle time. English teachers can use examples from literature of resistance to isolation, intimidation or abuse. History teachers can use incidents from the past of persecution and oppression. In each case students need to try to empathize with those involved and try to understand their motives and suffering. Drama lessons can also be a powerful way of living out the issues in role-plays or simulations. Bridging can then be done to look for connections between the lesson and the students' own relationships. In the end, bullying needs to be seen in relation to the whole ethos of a class or a school. A strong and positive ethos is probably the best preventive, but we also have to recognize that bullying arises out of perennial peer-group rivalry and conflict and is unlikely to go away entirely. The good news is that effective teachers and schools can make a huge difference.

13.7 Child Abuse and Child Protection

The protection and welfare of children must always be a priority for schools. All teachers need to be alert to any signs that a child is being abused, either at home or at school. Worries or fears that children bring into the classroom should not go unnoticed. All schools have a designated teacher to whom reports of suspected abuse should be made, and a child protection policy that you will need to read and understand. More child protection referrals, to social services and the police, come from schools than from any other source. The Children Act of 1989 currently provides the legislative basis for child protection. The definition of child abuse usually distinguishes between four main varieties.

- *Physical abuse*: physical injury that is knowingly inflicted or not prevented. Indicators include bruises, lacerations, burns, unusually frequent or unexplained injuries, or confused explanations for injuries.
- *Emotional abuse*: persistent or severe emotional ill treatment or rejection. Indicators include excessive dependence, attention-seeking, anxiety, social withdrawal, signs of depression.
- *Sexual abuse*: involvement of immature children or adolescents in sexual activities that they do not truly understand and to which they do not, or cannot, give informed consent. Indicators include signs of pain (e.g. in walking or sitting, tummy pains), regression to enuresis (bed-wetting), sexually explicit drawings or writing, inappropriate sexually provocative behaviour, indiscriminate friendship, attention-seeking, social withdrawal, furtive or secretive behaviour, signs of blood or discharge on underclothes.
- *Neglect*: negligence by carers resulting in impairment of health or development, or failure to thrive. Indicators include inadequate or poorly washed clothing, hunger, poor growth, apparent deficiency in nutrition, dirty or smelly presentation, lassitude or fatigue.

What you should always do as a teacher

- You should always know the name of the designated teacher for child protection in a school.
- Look for posters in the staff room providing contacts for other child protection agencies.
- Read the school's child protection policy and note its procedures. Study the guidance provided on www.teachernet.gov.uk/management/childprotection.
- Know the main varieties of child abuse and their common indicators.
- Find out whether the school has a policy relating to physical contact, i.e. touching students.
- In a primary school, check the school's arrangements for KS2 children changing for PE lessons. This can be a sensitive area for children, parents and teachers. If you are recruited as a member of staff at a school, consider whether you need further training in this area and, if so, ask for it.

What you should do if a child reports abuse to you

1 Your initial role is as a listener. Listen carefully and ask questions to clarify what is being said, but not leading questions which might distort the account given.
2 Talk to the child/student in a way that takes their age and understanding into account. Reassure that help can be provided but do *not* promise confidentiality.

3 Record the report in writing. Include the date, time, place, who was present and what was said. Make sure you are objective and base your report on evidence not opinion.

4 Report the incident to the designated teacher or to a senior member of staff. Do not gossip about it.

5 Understand that you may be required to take part in a subsequent investigation or assessment or a child protection conference. You may also need to help monitor the welfare of a child who is placed on the child protection register.

6 Understand that there are procedures for any allegations of abuse made against members of school staff.

7 If you think you may be called on to give an account of a child, for example at a meeting, make sure you have secure and confidential records that cover such matters as attendance, educational progress and attainment, behaviour, participation, relations with adults and other children, and appearance (where relevant).

Child protection in the curriculum

Awareness of child protection issues and strategies should be a normal part of personal, social and health education. It should cover such matters as:

• recognizing different risks in different situations, and how to behave responsibly;
• judging what kind of physical contact is acceptable or unacceptable;
• knowing where and how to get help;
• recognizing when pressure from others threatens safety or well-being;
• using assertiveness techniques to resist unhelpful pressure;
• developing skills for coping with emergencies.

A final word

Allegations of abuse are not always justified or true, but they all need to be taken seriously and not 'swept under the carpet'. As teachers we are in a position of trust. We owe it to all children, and to their parents, to take good care of them at all times.

13.8 Questions

The following questions are designed to help you check your understanding of the chapter.

1 What did the Warnock Report set out to achieve?
2 What does School Action Plus mean?
3 What does the abbreviation EBSD stand for?
4 Distinguish between impairment, disability and handicap.
5 What are the main features of schools that are successful with students with SEN?

6 What kind of advance planning would you undertake, as a teacher, for a student with SEN who is newly transferring to your school?

7 What are the main different sorts of differentiation?

8 What are 'P scales' and why do they matter?

9 How would you, as a new member of staff, judge a school's anti-bullying policies and practices?

10 If a child reports some form of abuse to you, what steps should you take?

11 **Discussion question**: could a strong positive emphasis within a school on students with SEN have detrimental effects on the welfare or progress of other students? How might this come about? What warning signs would you look for?

NOTES

1. DfES (2001).
2. Bayliss (1995).
3. Florian and Rouse (2001).
4. Ofsted (2003a).
5. Cooper et al. (2000).
6. Sprowston High School, Norwich; see www.gtce.org.uk/research, positive alternatives to exclusion: case studies.
7. For example Smith (1999) and DfES (2000; revised edition 2002).
8. Ofsted (2003b).

CHAPTER FOURTEEN

Gender and Ethnicity

14.1 Introduction

There are some tendencies of human nature that give rise to recurrent problems. One of these is our weakness for superstitious ways of thinking and reasoning, finding sympathetic and mysterious patterns in the world for which there is no good evidence. Another is animism, the treating of non-human things such as trees, rivers and crystals, as if they had minds like us. Then there are sources of social conflict, including the tensions that exist between the two sexes and the hostility that regularly erupts between different social groups and different cultures.[1] In all these cases, one can trace the same, or similar, errors and conflicts afflicting humans throughout history. And in each case, education turns out to be the main source of a solution to the problem. One implication, however, is that these educational solutions will be needed in every generation; the problems will not just disappear. In this chapter we will look at how issues arising from differences in gender and ethnicity have had an impact on education in schools. (Although gender and ethnicity are treated here as sources of 'problems', we need to remember that they are also sources of a diversity that enriches our lives in many ways.)

The chapter begins with gender, reviewing some of the past attempts to improve equal opportunities for boys and girls and looking at psychological differences between the sexes. Some of the recent work on raising the attainments of boys is then reviewed. In the case of ethnicity, I look especially at Afro-Caribbean boys and at the work that successful schools have done to boost the achievements of their black students. The chapter ends with some thoughts about how schools try to reconcile cultural diversity with inclusion, along with teaching about global citizenship.

14.2 Gender and Schooling

For someone approaching this topic for the first time, there may be something of an Alice in Wonderland quality to the discourse of the past 30 years or so. Following a widespread conviction that women were being systematically discriminated against in almost every dimension of British society, including business, politics, education and family life, the rise of feminism in the 1960s and 1970s led to a wave of research and interventions aimed at improving the educational opportunities and achievements of girls.[2] In fact, as the researchers conceded, girls were already doing rather well at school, their examination performance at 16 being ahead of boys in most subjects, although they were not maintaining their lead in higher education at that time. However, with equal opportunities as the main focus, it was argued that girls were being discouraged from following subjects such as mathematics, the sciences and engineering and were frequently being corralled into narrow cultural backwaters to do with domesticity and children. One chapter summarizing the state of affairs in the mid-1990s makes almost no mention at all of boys having educational problems.[3] By 2004, however, the Gender and Achievement section of the Government's Standards website confronted one almost entirely with information about attempts to boost the achievements of boys.[4]

There is nothing actually contradictory about these efforts, which are universally well intentioned, but they should alert us to the way in which cultural and intellectual fashions can blow us this way and that. In the 1950s and 1960s, equal opportunities concerns in the UK focused almost completely on social class differences in attainments. Then they shifted to gender and ethnicity. But social class differences still exist![5] Moreover, there is an underlying assumption in much gender-related work that the only correct situation would be one in which every major educational subject and form of employment showed an exact fifty-fifty match between the success of males and females. However this is a fallacy, if one is prepared to grant that there are some enduring psychological differences between the two sexes.

Perhaps we should test each outcome that is not fifty-fifty just in case prejudice and ignorance lies behind it. But we should not be surprised if, at the end of our efforts, we find that more women in general want to be nurses, primary teachers and administrators and more men want to be fire-fighters, pilots and engineers. Exceptions to such general trends should also, of course, be both expected and tolerated, not to say welcomed. When my own university, in the 1990s, happened to hold a graduation ceremony for engineers and primary educators on the same day, it was sobering to see how one side of the hall was composed of about 95% male engineers and the other side of about 80% women primary teachers. This was after at least 20 years of active striving to reduce or eliminate such differences in vocational choices. I now think the imbalances simply reflected broad enduring preferences. There is no incompatibility between being a feminist and accepting that men and women are psychologically rather different, in the average case. This could not be said in polite company until recently, but research (much of it by women) is increasingly bearing it out.[6]

14.3 Sex Differences

Bearing in mind that we are once again dealing in huge generalizations, with many individual exceptions, there is evidence that, right across the world, the sexes differ in the following ways. Boys are more vulnerable to almost all kinds of genetic and prenatal problems. More male embryos are conceived (120–150 to every 100 females) but more are spontaneously aborted. About 105 males are born for every 100 females, but the greater vulnerability of the male continues, with higher rates of birth injury (perhaps related to greater average size) and of congenital and early illnesses. Problems related to the X chromosome are also more likely in males because they possess only one copy of the X chromosome, which allows any deleterious genetic defect to be expressed, whereas females, who have two copies of the X chromosome, will not show recessive defects by virtue of having a second normal allele. Male embryos begin to secrete the male hormone testosterone from around 6 weeks after conception and this, and other, hormones affect the development of genitalia, body shape, maturation and even brain structure. Visual problems are about equally distributed between males and females but hearing impairments and speech defects are more common in males. Learning difficulties, emotional and behavioural difficulties, hyperactivity, reading problems and delinquency are all more prevalent in males. Boys are more than four times as likely as girls to be excluded from school. Boys are also more often referred for psychiatric help than girls. Almost the only category of psychological problem where girls have higher rates than boys is that of anxiety and depression during adolescence (twice as common in girls than boys). Women, of course, have a greater overall life expectancy than men. Overall, the female sex seems more physiologically robust than the male one.

Crime remains an overwhelmingly male problem, although currently women in the UK seem to be doing their best to even things up. In 2003 only about 6% of the UK prison population (of a total of around 70,000) were women. Men are much more aggressive and violent than women, in all cultures. They commit far more homicides and are much more likely to make or own weapons and to fight in wars. There is no known culture as yet in which men do nearly as much caring for babies and children as women do.[7] In the realm of cognitive abilities, girls and women consistently have a slight advantage in language and literacy. Boys and men do somewhat better than their female counterparts in spatial reasoning and quantitative problem-solving. In a cross-cultural comparison of childhood in six cultures around the world, boys were consistently found to be more egotistical and aggressive and girls more altruistic and nurturant.[8] Boys are more rough and aggressive in their play and probably more competitive, at least in physical contests. These differences, and other more minor ones, interact with cultural differences in the ways boys and girls are raised. They then spill over into vocational choices and preferences. For example, in the UK in 2002, 90% of those following GNVQ foundation courses in health and social care were female, whereas 81% of those choosing foundation courses in ICT were male.

Example 14.1 Talent and preference
Steven Pinker[9] cites one study of a sample of American seventh-graders (approximately 13 years old) who were talent-spotted in a nationwide search for students gifted in mathematics. All were sent on special summer programmes in maths and science and were generally encouraged by their parents to pursue their special talents. Once at university,

however, the young women in the sample chose a wide range of arts, humanities and science courses to follow. The young men mostly stuck to maths and science. Fewer than 1% of the women pursued a doctorate in maths, physical sciences or engineering, whereas 8% of the men did so. In general, the women went into medicine, law, the humanities and biology instead.

One study does not substantiate a general case of course, and if smoke is by now issuing from your ears, let me reiterate that to recognize quite minor cognitive differences between men and women is not to reduce by one iota one's determination to root out unfair discrimination against either sex. One's membership of one sex or the other, and one's sexuality whatever it may be, should quite simply not count when it comes to life chances or opportunities. Nor should the recent efforts to help boys do better at school prevent us from working to eliminate prejudice against women. It is also true that in our culture we tend to treat girls and boys differently, from birth onwards, but similar arguments apply here as given in Chapter 12 about parents and socialization. Cultural differences are not all arbitrary: they can arise from biological differences, and they can operate causally from child to adult as well as from adult to child. It remains true, however, that gender can be 'played out' and expressed in a multitude of ways within and between cultural groups. As with ability and temperament, our innate biology exists, but it does not dictate how we should live our lives.

As a final attempt to wrest this issue from the realms of prejudice, let us also be clear that the complex reality of sex and gender differences does not boil down to the kind of crude sexism that is still used in many places to oppress women. However this may be, at present, it is boys in our schools who seem on average to be doing badly. There seems no good reason why this should be so, and therefore both teachers and schools are trying to find out why they are failing and investigating ways of reducing the 'gender gap'. Rather than being motivated solely by moral concerns for equality, however, this interest in raising achievement by boys may have more to do with the search by schools for ways to further improve their academic success rate. The quickest way to boost one's position in an exam results league table is to spot under-achievement and remove it. Perhaps, by the time you read this, schools will have largely succeeded in closing the gender gap in examination attainments.

In the primary years, girls currently tend to be better at English whereas boys just maintain an edge at maths and science. In 2002, GCSE results at 16+ showed girls holding a strong lead overall, with 58% of girls obtaining five or more A–C grades compared with only 43% of boys. In English, girls are ahead of boys at all Key Stages, their lead increasing from around 5% at KS2 to 18% at KS3. Boys have an advantage in maths and science at all Key Stages but it is smaller than that of girls in English. But is this an area where we should expect exact fifty-fifty outcomes? This seems to be the underlying assumption of the Standards website, but it is probably wrong. Girls will most likely continue to show a slightly greater interest and ability at English (and languages generally) wherever they have a fair chance, whereas boys will probably do somewhat better at maths and science, provided they can be persuaded to do some work![10] At university, the female lead in educational achievement now continues, with women generally performing better than men except in the proportion who obtain first-class degrees. It does not seem easy to pin down statistically, but there has for a long time been a suspicion that females are generally more reliable in their academic performance whereas males are more erratic, appearing more frequently in both the highest and lowest scoring categories.

It is also worth remembering that in Chapters 3 and 10 research was cited in which it appeared that attitudes towards responsibility for learning often differ between the sexes. Girls may have a tendency to blame themselves when they do badly and yet attribute their successes to good teaching. Boys, on the other hand, seem more prone to blaming failures on poor teaching and attributing success to their own efforts. This might be a side-effect of underlying differences in beliefs about intelligence, learning orientations or patterns of response to failure (10.2, 10.3). These differences, like many others between males and females, may largely disappear if we can get our teaching right.

My own attempt at expressing, at a very general level, the main differences in world-view of males and females, culture notwithstanding, would be to say that males are more aggressive and show more interest in the physical and technical world, whereas females are more nurturant and show more interest in the human social (and animal) world. It is crucial to remember, however, that these are merely average trends across huge numbers of males and females. In the individual case we should assume nothing until we have some solid evidence. Some men make excellent nurses, psychotherapists and novelists. Some women are brilliant mathematicians, electricians and steeple-jacks. Neither sex should be discriminated against in education.

Having said all this, it does seem less than satisfactory that boys should be lagging behind girls so badly in their examination results at 16. So, what are schools doing about it?

14.4 Raising Achievements in School

As in the case of students with SEN, we need to be careful that our efforts to help one group are not at the expense of another. In this instance, efforts to make the curriculum more 'boy-friendly' must defend themselves against the possibility of making some things 'girl-unfriendly', a hole we have been trying to dig ourselves out of for the past 30 years. We also need to realize that gender tends to interact with other social variables, notably social class, ethnicity and local regional traditions.

Example 14.2 School campaigns to close the gap
One secondary school,[11] *concerned about boys' under-achievement, held widespread staff discussions and came up with a variety of measures.*

- Students were seated in boy–girl pairs in most classes. This was aimed at improving the behaviour of the boys and the risk-taking of the girls.
- Teachers in some departments asked questions in class alternating between boys and girls.
- Single-sex assemblies were started so that the boys could be challenged to do as well academically as the girls (tapping into male competitive motives).

- Individual under-achievers were interviewed about their progress and given new targets for progress.
- Sixth-form boys were asked to become mentors and role models for younger boys.
- Teachers agreed to set shorter tasks in class and structured homework with clear outcomes, as these seemed to help boys.
- Writing frames were more widely used to help boys structure different genres of writing.
- To combat their impulsivity, boys were taught to plan first and then act, rather than acting first and only then evaluating the results of their action.
- Single-sex humanities lessons were held for Y10.
- More male teachers of English were recruited (surely the most controversial move).

Perhaps the most interesting feature of this case is that the various measures were introduced after an outside speaker had made a case for significant male/female differences in learning style, a talk which clearly divided the staff deeply, some agreeing and some disagreeing. Given the gap in achievements between the sexes, however, the head teacher was determined to push the policies through. In the first few years of implementation the gap did start to close, but then expanded again. The boys' achievements had risen substantially, but those of the girls had risen even further.

In a primary school, a similar drive to close the gap in attainments between boys and girls in reading succeeded in reducing a 14% lead by the girls (in the numbers attaining level 4 in their reading SATs) to only 5% in a single year. The school went about this in the following ways.

- Parents were involved from the start, with letters being sent to explain the school's new policies on reading. Parents of boys were asked to complete a 'reading interview', which aimed to raise the profile of reading at home and alert parents to their sons' progress and reading interests.
- Teachers used the results of the reading interviews to guide boys' choices of reading materials.
- A 'Boyzone' was created, which contained lively displays and specially purchased new books, appealing to boys' interests.
- Teachers instituted a scheme called Fiction Friday and Magazine Monday to broaden the reading experience of boys towards more fiction reading and girls towards more non-fiction. All were encouraged to talk and reflect on their reading (a skill at which the boys were relatively weak). Boys were paired with girls to discuss particular stories and characters. All were challenged to try to get a letter accepted for publication in a magazine (and several succeeded).
- Three fathers agreed to attend school assemblies to talk about the importance of reading in their work.
- Teachers instituted a check on boys' reading records and looked for ways to broaden interests and improve weaknesses. They also made sure that boys remembered to take a book home with them every day.

The school considered its campaign a success. It was well led and resourced and also imaginative. The attainments of the girls did not decrease, whereas those of the boys increased. The campaign appears to have succeeded in persuading boys that reading is both 'cool' and enjoyable.

Sometimes in interviews female teachers have said they prefer teaching boys to girls because they find them more interesting. Some male teachers seem to prefer teaching girls. One finding that has relevance to all teachers is that male students tend to gain more attention from their teachers, both male and female, than females do.[12] This may be partly because they misbehave more and partly because they are more prepared to take risks in answering questions. There is more than one way in which males may choose to 'display' in the classroom. You may find it worth observing the male/female pattern of interaction in lessons where you are observing or assisting, and also in lessons where you are the teacher.

14.5 Ethnic Differences and Schooling

We all have a tendency to identify with an in-group of 'people like us' and to be suspicious, or at least less friendly, towards 'outsiders' and 'foreigners'. Psychologists call this *ethnocentrism* and it is universal to all human cultures.[13] Although we tend to see it in terms of 'black versus white', skin colour is mostly irrelevant, except in so far as it acts as a distinguishing mark identifying a group. In India, Indians are frequently prejudiced against Africans. Africans, at least in some countries of Africa, are often prejudiced against Asians. In China, the Chinese are often prejudiced against both Europeans and Africans, and so on. Although some social scientists believe that racism is largely a fault caused by structural imbalances of power within societies, there is little doubt that ethnocentrism also plays a part. We all have a tendency to bond together in families, to give preference in treatment to our parents, children and siblings over unrelated people. To some extent, ethnic groups, although genetically diverse, are somewhat like large extended families. But their genetic likenesses and differences are largely irrelevant. It is cultural differences that matter.

The idea of separate human ethnic 'races' has long been abandoned by scientists and, although they differ in their detailed accounts of the history of humans and their spread around the world, the scientific consensus currently favours the 'Out of Africa' hypothesis, which argues that all modern humans are related to an original group of *Homo sapiens sapiens* who emerged in Africa about 100,000 years ago.[14] Globalization is now increasing the contacts of all ethnic, cultural and national groups. To the extent that we speak a common language to one another, we are becoming a 'global village'. This carries with it risks of all kinds, including the threat of cultural and linguistic homogenization, but it also brings opportunities and hope.

A character in Russell Hoban's novel *Turtle Diary* contemplates some green turtles swimming in a pond at London Zoo. A sign explains their scientific name and adds that they form the ingredients for turtle soup. He thinks to himself that, come to that, we could be said to form the ingredients of human soup. I like to think that, as globalization continues, with intermarriage between individuals from different ethnic and cultural groups, mobile patterns of work and leisure, and growing cultural exchanges, we will increasingly come to see one another simply as varied members of the same 'human soup', which, as it says on so many of our tins, is 'made from ingredients from more than one country'. Meanwhile, Britain is a multiethnic and multicultural society, striving to find ways of valuing our various cultural histories and traditions and also of living together under the same law. Schools are, perhaps more than any other institution, in the front line of this process, as our children grow up.

Example 14.3 Schools committed to making a difference
School attainments for different ethnic groups in the UK are very varied and interact in complex ways with gender, social class and features of home background. One group that has consistently given rise to concern comprises black Caribbean boys. However, a recent Ofsted report[15] *on the achievement of black Caribbean students makes it clear that individual schools, once again, can make a significant difference to outcomes. Based on data from 2000, 129 secondary schools in England and Wales have 10% or more students of black Caribbean origin. Overall, in this sample, 37% of black Caribbean boys and 45% of black Caribbean girls achieved five or more A–C grade passes at GCSE in 2001. This is well below the national average (45% for boys and 55% for girls in that year). In the six secondary schools visited by Ofsted, however, attainments were higher than the national average, with 53% of the black Caribbean boys and 62% of the black Caribbean girls attaining five or more A–C passes in 2001.*

The ethos of these schools was committed to valuing all individual students, having high expectations of them, giving them strong personal support and tracking individual progress intensively. The schools had all achieved strong credibility with parents and the local communities. Parents, in their turn, spoke out strongly for a 'morally supportive environment' and some spoke of their fears that a struggle was going on for their children's futures, with the schools on one side and 'street culture', with local criminal gangs often involved in drugs trading, on the other.

Even where teachers and students might deny the reality of racial prejudice, it was clear that there were strong sensitivities about the issue on the part of many black students, who suspected the existence of both prejudice and disrespect. The response of the schools was to put emphatic anti-racist policies in place and to follow them up in vigorous day-to-day work. They combined strong academic policies with intensive support for students and regular contact with parents. Typical measures included the following.

- Early identification of students at risk of failing, with target setting, mentoring and monitoring of progress. Parents were frequently involved in this process.
- Saturday and holiday support classes for under-achieving students.
- An emphasis on 'one-world' global issues in the curriculum.
- A purposeful and businesslike but relaxed and sociable atmosphere, in which staff addressed students in a straightforward way but used humour and were able to talk to students about their interests out of school.

One parent spoke eloquently both about the way that racism had blighted his own life and then about his anxieties for his son:

My boy is like Daniel in the lion's den. He is in constant danger of being sucked into illegal activities when money is short. Our communities are being undermined by poor employment opportunities. Some parents' supervision of young people is poor and they can't cope. People have to work long hours at times when they need to be at home with their children. When they don't have good support from family and friends they are on their own. You see them struggle to keep their children off the street but once the child knows that fast money can be made from criminal activity especially related to drugs, it becomes hard to hold the line for the rest of us.[16]

Where relationships with parents were good, they were based on a willingness to listen to parents' concerns, to be honest and open with them and to work with them at resolving problems and differences.

The black students, for their part, spoke of the way they were treated sympathetically and sensibly by most of their teachers. One student put it like this:

We have lots of teachers in this school that handle you right. When they deal with you they listen to your point of view and don't jump in. They don't shout at you, or poke you and stuff like that. They don't accuse you of things, they talk to you about it and if they get it wrong apologise. They treat you with respect.[17]

These were popular schools, with strong leadership and a culture of hard work and achievement. Staff worked very hard and persisted in their efforts, although acknowledging that they were not always successful. The schools used data on progress in sophisticated ways, using ethnic and gender classification to identify groups at risk of under-achieving and then putting policies in place to tackle the problems.

In a parallel Ofsted report[18] on three primary schools, which also have a track record of success with black Caribbean students, the general messages are very similar. 'The Schools have not invented anything new, comment the inspectors, it is just that they combine strong leadership, good teaching and a caring ethos, backed up by a great deal of hard work. It may be, however, that a certain degree of stability, of the teaching staff, of school policies and of social and economic conditions in the local community, were providing a supportive environment. These are also successful schools, both socially and academically, and to some extent success breeds confidence and further success. The schools all take a firm stand on racism, as an extract from one their policy documents illustrates:

The staff at [X] Primary School are opposed to racism in any form. We are committed to the principle that all children should be given equal opportunities to fulfil their potential. We condemn discrimination against people because of skin colour and cultural background because it is offensive, illegal and wrong. Our school is multi-cultural and multi-racial and we value this cultural diversity. Every member of the school should feel their language, religion and culture are valued and respected. In order to achieve this we will use what children know and understand about themselves in our teaching.[19]

Work with parents is constantly emphasized. This takes the forms of welcoming parents, listening to them, keeping in good contact with them and responding quickly if things seem to be going wrong. Past students are encouraged to return to the schools and talk about their careers. Students are taught what prejudice means, how racial discrimination occurs and how they can take a stand against all its forms. Attendance, punctuality and academic progress are all analysed, by ethnicity as well as other variables. In the curriculum, each subject has a policy, thinking through how it can contribute to the general school policy of improving students' understanding of cultural diversity. Assemblies are used to communicate both the schools' core values and their high expectations. Any racist name-calling is logged and dealt with firmly. Parents are called in, if necessary, and addressed on the subject of the school's values. By and large, the parents are very supportive and appreciative of the schools' efforts.

One student, Craig, joined one of these schools in Y3. At his previous school he felt that 'Black kids got blamed for everything.'[20] When he first arrived he had low self-esteem and was suspicious of staff. He made poor eye contact with adults and tended to give one-word answers. He refused to read to his teacher. His behaviour was immature; sometimes he laughed on 'inappropriate' occasions and was resentful when reprimanded. The school responded by talking to him individually and laying down very clear goals for his behaviour, especially in relation to playing with other children without being violent. They persevered even when progress was slow. Craig had to see the head teacher on a number of occasions when he got into trouble. The head backed up the class teacher with an approach that was firm but sympathetic. Teachers did not merely get cross with Craig; they taught him what he was doing wrong and showed him what he should be doing instead. His confidence slowly grew and his behaviour and work improved. After 18 months at the school, though not a model student, Craig was making good progress. He himself commented that:

> I like this school because it's fair . . . If you tell the head the truth he doesn't shout. I think he's fair. He gives you a chance. He's strict but I like him because he's kind and fair. The teachers are all nice and helpful.[21]

Another black Caribbean student at one of the other schools visited stated that 'Our school is good because there are lots of different races and cultures here. That's good because you can learn from each other. It widens your understanding.'[22] This seems an excellent summary of how education can gradually transform ethnocentrism.

14.6 Reconciling Inclusion and Difference

The problems and opportunities involved in teaching students about ethnic and cultural diversity may not seem as obvious and pressing in those areas and schools where few people from ethnic minorities live. However, the need to educate students to understand and appreciate diversity and to oppose racism is just as acute. Where there is little opportunity to mix with other ethnic groups there is exactly a context where ethnocentrism may thrive and lead to racism. Besides the multicultural and religious tolerance and awareness that has been part of the curriculum in most British schools for a generation, there is now an increasing enthusiasm for teaching 'cultural diversity and global citizenship'.[23] This rather grand title will turn into different forms in different schools, but it supplies a useful umbrella heading under which a number of important curricular themes and a general openness to the world can be pursued. These include:

- political education, about citizenship and democracy;
- environmental issues such as sustainability and pollution;
- cultural diversity;
- the worlds of the rich and the poor;
- community understanding and involvement;
- social and moral education.

The lack of any form of political education has been an obvious and worrying gap in the British curriculum for far too long. Citizenship was at last included in the revised National Curriculum of 1999 and has a variety of learning objectives attached to it. A set of 'key virtues' is identified as a means of providing a common moral core to this otherwise pluralistic approach, namely truth, honesty, justice, trust and a sense of duty. Here we see a sensible attempt to map out some cultural common ground. For multiculturalism has its limits; we have to evolve a common moral framework for children in school as well as a common law of the land.

The optimism that stems from reading about the work of successful schools, which construct an ethos, a curriculum and a set of procedures for ensuring that diversity is appreciated and that all individual students and staff are valued and respected, should perhaps be tempered with a note of caution. The best work in this area on behalf of one age group can be undone by another. For example, adolescent peer groups may move towards ethnic identities and, as we saw in Chapter 11, the power of the peer group may undermine the efforts of well-intentioned adults almost overnight. Or the advent of adult worries, say over employment or housing, can change the context so harshly that what seemed well learned in school is quickly forgotten or overlaid by new fears and aggressive demands. Education can overcome ethnocentrism, but not all learning takes place in school. Much will depend on the ethos and practices of other institutions and of the wider community. Nonetheless, schools have a key strategic role in combating all forms of prejudice and must play it with all the energy and imagination at their disposal.

Inclusion has been a theme of both this and the previous chapter. As a society we want to both include and yet respect difference. As well as appreciating and exploring the very varied traditions of the world's religions and cultures, and the backgrounds and knowledge that students bring with them, schools have to evolve a set of common rules to live by. Multicultural richness and diversity are indeed to be celebrated, but at the same time schools have to nail their moral colours to the mast and try to live up to them. We cannot be moral relativists and still live together because moral principles are exactly those rules that we feel we should apply equally to ourselves and to all others in similar circumstances. This means being prepared sometimes to argue against particular cultural practices that offend against human rights (or indeed the rights of animals). Diversity has, in the end, to be balanced against fairness and equity. Special educational needs, gender and ethnicity have provided the definitions of 'difference' that have been examined in these chapters, but bear in mind that other social categories, including age, nationality, social class, sexuality and even physical appearance, may also become relevant.

14.7 Questions

The following questions are designed to help you check your understanding of the chapter.

1 'The only acceptable educational outcome would be equal results in every subject for both males and females.' Do you agree?
2 In what ways are males the more vulnerable sex?
3 In which areas in school are boys currently under-achieving?
4 How have schools recently tried to improve boys' attainments in literacy?
5 What is meant by ethnocentrism?
6 How might work with parents help a school develop effective anti-racist policies and practices?
7 How would you begin to tackle multicultural issues in your own subject specialism?
8 How might respecting cultural differences sometimes lead to moral conflicts for teachers?
9 **Discussion question**: in France there is a long tradition of secular state education, although arguably Christianity has in fact enjoyed a privileged status. Recently, after fierce debates, the wearing of the *hijab*, a traditional headscarf, by Islamic girls was banned in French state schools. Do you think this was the right decision?

NOTES

1. See, for example, Pinker (2002) and Brown (1991).
2. See, for example, Delamont (1990).
3. Weiner (1995).
4. www.standards.dfes.gov.uk/gender.
5. Perhaps we should think more in terms of 'educational classes' these days.
6. For example Konner (1982), Geary (1998), Bee (1989), Hausman (1999) and Gottfredson (1988).
7. As I write, experts in the field of childcare work are debating how best to meet 'ambitious' government targets to increase the proportion of men working in childcare jobs in the UK from 3 to 6%.
8. Whiting and Whiting (1975).
9. See Pinker (2002), p. 356.
10. Interestingly, results for the QTS skills tests for would-be teachers in 2001–2002 show that men were slightly more likely to pass the numeracy test at the first try whereas women were slightly more likely to pass the literacy test at the first try. In the ICT test, however, there were (sound the trumpets!) no significant gender differences.
11. A case study from the Standards website on Gender and Achievement.
12. For example Galton, Simon and Croll (1980).
13. Brown (1991).
14. See, for example, Bryson (2003).
15. Ofsted (2002a).

16. Ofsted (2002a), p. 13.
17. Ofsted (2002a), pp. 14–15.
18. Ofsted (2002b).
19. Ofsted (2002b), p. 3.
20. Ofsted (2002b), p. 21.
21. Ofsted (2002b), p. 21.
22. Ofsted (2002b), p. 24.
23. See Clough and Holden (2002).

CHAPTER FIFTEEN

Assessment for Learning

15.1 Introduction

The first four sections of this chapter concern classroom assessment for learning. Sections 15.5 and 15.6 survey some of the broader issues relating to standards and the external assessments of schools. Good-quality assessment by teachers is crucial to learning in school. Yet teachers and student teachers have found it one of the most difficult features of their professional practice to put into effect. There were signs, however, at the start of the twenty-first century that something of a revolution was underway in British schools, with formative assessment or 'assessment for learning' becoming at last a central and welcomed part of classroom teaching.[1]

15.2 The Case for Formative Assessment

The revolution stemmed partly from a lengthy review of research on assessment and learning carried out by Paul Black and Dillon Wiliam[2] at the end of the 1990s, which came to three main conclusions.

1 Improving formative assessment had repeatedly been shown to raise standards of learning in schools.
2 There remained plenty of room for further improvements, since formative assessment was not at that time well established.
3 There was evidence suggesting how to go about improving the quality of formative assessment.

The evidence they surveyed suggested that, by improving formative assessment, quite dramatic improvements could be made, especially for low-attaining students. Good assessment generally resulted in a narrowing of the range of outcomes of teaching, with the least successful being pulled up nearer to the standards of the most successful. For these authors, formative assessment 'is at the heart of effective teaching'.[3]

A second background reason for the new-look approach to assessment in schools was that the National Curriculum, with its descriptions of performance in each subject at different levels, had made it much easier for teachers to 'benchmark' progress and set targets. The criteria for ascending grades at GCSE offer a continuation of the 'levels' for KS4. A third reason was that government agencies, together with the Internet, had begun to provide comparative data on educational attainment on a scale never seen before and these were being used by schools to plot their development.

Until these changes, good practice in formative assessment had proved elusive. In their annual report for 2000/2001, Ofsted stated that they had judged the quality and use of formative assessment as 'good or better' in only 37% of the schools they had inspected. This contrasts with figures of 74% 'good or better' judgements for planning and 90% for standards of general professional knowledge. The same report also mentioned that although most parents were very satisfied with their children's schooling, the quality of school reporting to home was a weak area, with many parents complaining that reports were too often bland and uninformative. Ofsted have also regularly reported that student teachers are weak in using formative assessment in the classroom and receive too little help and support in this area from their class teachers and mentors. Yet when formative assessment works well, it is not only effective in terms of learning but also popular with students, as a more recent Ofsted report[4] suggests: 'Where the school handles assessment sensitively, thoroughly and honestly, the students are overwhelmingly in favour of the approach and usually respond very well.' Or, as one Y9 student put it:

> I transferred here from middle school – nobody had told me what to do to improve my work. Now I know exactly how to improve my grades. I know the criteria for particular marks in an assignment, and it's my fault if I don't do the work.

15.3 Some Basic Distinctions and Principles

Educational assessment consists of making observations and judgements. The *observations* may be of:

- a student's behaviour (is she paying attention and working?);
- a student's oral answers (does he understand this point?);
- a student's product of work (does this piece of writing show that the writer can use evidence to support an argument?).

The *judgements* compare the observation with one of three things:

- the same student's past performance (has she made progress this term?);
- the performance of other students (is this above average?);
- some objective standard of performance (does this writing include grammatically complex sentences?).

Assessment may be relatively informal, as when a teacher enters into dialogue to see how much is being remembered and understood, or relatively formal, as in a GCSE examination. The assessment may be carried out before teaching begins (to establish students' level of existing knowledge), during a lesson (to assess progress) or at the end of a scheme of work (to estimate how much has been learned).

When assessment occurs before or during a course of work it is called **formative assessment**, for it helps to form what happens next. When the assessment occurs at the end of a course it is called **summative assessment**, no doubt because it summarizes the position reached. Formative assessment is assessment *for* learning, whereas summative assessment is assessment *of* learning. Both teachers and learners tend to prefer formative to summative assessment yet it has been the summative variety that has generally been imposed on schools by government agencies. This is because assessment of teachers and schools, in terms of their results, has become a favoured means of quality control.

The basic strategies for assessment are:

- observing students as they work;
- asking questions;
- discussing work with students;
- looking at samples of work or performance.

Following on from the review by Black and Wiliam, referred to above, an Assessment Reform Group was organized that made proposals for the reform of school assessment in England and Wales. These proposals were eventually accepted by the chief government agencies, including the DfES, Ofsted and the Qualifications and Assessment Authority (which coordinates policy on school assessment). The Assessment Reform Group proposed 10 principles for good 'assessment for learning', namely that it:

1 is part of effective planning;
2 focuses on how students learn;
3 is central to classroom practice;
4 is a key professional skill;
5 is sensitive and constructive;
6 fosters motivation to learn;
7 promotes understanding of goals and criteria;
8 helps learners know how to improve;
9 develops the capacity for self-assessment;
10 recognizes all educational achievement.

The fundamental idea of formative assessment is that learners need to know how to get from A to B, where A is their present level of performance and B is the next realistic goal for their learning. Having identified this 'gap', the teacher and student need to work together to close it.

15.4 Making Assessment for Learning Central to Your Teaching

In order to help you make assessment for learning central to your teaching, this section provides an extended 10-step guide.

Step 1: plan for assessment

Researchers studying formative assessment have argued that it is not enough to assess informally, when the mood strikes you. Instead, opportunities for 'assessment incidents' have to be built into planning and given time during lessons.[5] Too often, in the past, teachers have subordinated assessment to instruction and it has faded from view. Typical of such planned assessment incidents would be:

- a series of planned questions asked around the class to judge levels of existing knowledge and awareness;
- a small group task looking at examples of work and comparing their qualities against criteria (standards) for different levels of quality;
- dialogues between teacher and individual students as the teacher circulates and monitors work;
- a short quiz or test of recall of recently taught material;
- a discussion in the plenary session to evaluate what has been learned.

Step 2: link assessment to objectives and success criteria

A basic feature of good assessment for learning is that it is linked with both objectives for learning and criteria for success. This relates back to points made in Chapters 3 and 5 about making the goals of learning really clear to students. Two common features of lessons that fit this model are that the teacher puts the main goals for learning in writing and shares them with students at the beginning of the lesson and that she also talks through the criteria for success at the task. Many teachers represent the success criteria by writing them on the lines of a graphically represented 'success ladder'.

Example 15.1 Sharing objectives and success criteria

1 A KS2 teacher started a science lesson by sharing a written objective: 'our learning intention is to be able to make a circuit that will be able to make an electrical object work'. After discussing the task, she followed up by saying 'What I'm looking for is that you know what you need in the circuit, the parts, and that you can use these parts to make the light or the motor work.'

2 A KS3 teacher of French explained that 'students are issued with a recording grid so that they can track their own progress in each attainment target; this is linked

to a self-assessment sheet, completed twice a year and discussed individually in class.'

3 In some situations, oral statements of the goals of learning are more practical. A KS4 teacher of team games was coaching a class in hockey. He focused the lesson on 'triangles', explaining that the player with the ball needed team-mates to move into space, so as to give at least two options for a successful pass. A third option of a player upfield would make the situation even better. Two students were detailed to watch the subsequent short practice games, recording points for players who moved into space as part of a triangle, or received a pass. Periodically the teacher stopped the game and the observers fed back the points gained to the players. At the end of the session the teacher discussed with the students how the strategy could be further improved.

This open approach to teaching students exactly what they need to do to succeed may come as quite a 'culture shock' to students who are not used to it. A teacher who had worked through the process commented that afterwards: 'They told me they hold the success criteria in their minds as they work. I see a big difference.'

Step 3: teach your students to self-assess

Sally Clarke[6] warns that careful training over a period of at least 2 weeks may be needed to teach students how to become involved in self-assessment of their learning. This teaching might include:

* clarifying what assessment for learning means;
* relating it to learning objectives and giving examples;
* describing self-assessment strategies, linked to clear success criteria;
* explaining how self-assessment will feed into conversations with the teacher and then into future targets and plans;
* discussing examples of work and showing how a teacher would mark them.

Students need to understand that it is all right to make mistakes; that recognizing mistakes helps us to move on; that feedback gives help; that asking for help is essential for learning. In plenary sessions, encourage students to recognize that learning can occur:

* by listening or observing;
* by imagining and visualizing;
* by doing, handling, examining;
* by talking and asking;
* by reading or writing;
* by memorizing and recalling;
* by practising and applying;
* by thinking about different options;
* by answering questions.

In the plenary discussion at the end of a lesson, ask them to think about the following.

- How would anyone know if this work was good? What would they see?
- If you were to do this all over again, what would you do differently?
- What was easy and what was hard about that work?
- Do you remember the objectives for learning today?
- What do you think you need more help with?
- Have you noticed any progress you have made?
- How would this help you in the future?

(This kind of discussion links with the 'lessons for learning' discussed in 10.6.)

Step 4: provide sensitive feedback

Clearly, talking to students about their progress, strengths and weaknesses is a delicate task, requiring a fine blend of honesty and tact. It is all too easy to convince low-attaining students that (i) they are doing badly, (ii) there is little they can do about it, and (iii) they therefore might as well abandon efforts to overcome their problems. Able students, too, may feel ashamed if their successes undermine their status in the peer group (see also Chapters 9 and 10). On the other hand, sensitive teachers may too often in the past have disguised their honest opinions so as not to hurt students' feelings and self-esteem. In this way students, not to mention their parents, may build up a false picture of how they are doing in school. Ways of sensitizing your feedback include the following.

1 Use 'sandwich' marking in written feedback, with a positive comment on either side of a suggestion for improvement, as in:

> What I liked about your letter, Simon, was that:
>   it was well phrased and interesting,
>   it used a wide vocabulary, including some polysyllabic words.
> You could improve this by:
>   using a dictionary to check the spellings of longer words,
>   using re-drafting to make improvements, e.g. looking for small errors and
>   improving the flow of your writing.
> I enjoyed the bit about the cat!

2 Not all oral feedback needs to be given in public. Take opportunities to talk quietly to individuals or give feedback during individual 'tutorial' sessions. Use journals or learning diaries to correspond with your students privately.
3 Do not postpone assessment until it is too late to improve the work! One KS2 teacher instructed her class: 'Read your partner's work and then on a post-it note mark two ways they could improve it.' A KS3 student said about his geography

lessons: 'Before we give work in we always check it with each other.' A middle-school student commented on humanities work: 'When we're working towards a big piece of work the teacher marks our work along the way so that we can improve it before the final piece.'

4 Consult your students on how they like your written comments to be made. Some students feel that their written work is spoiled if a teacher writes all over it. Others may not mind. See if it is best to write in the margins, on a separate piece of paper, or on a post-it note. Try including the student's name in your feedback, to make it personal.

5 Think about how you respond to incorrect answers. A simple 'no' may not be the best way forward. Instead, with younger students, you might say 'Nice try, but not quite right' or 'Are you sure about that?' or 'What do other people think?' With older students you might try counter argument, as in 'Well, let's think. If you're right about that, then it would suggest that . . .'

6 Beware of extrinsic rewards such as smiley faces, marks, house points or activity reinforcers getting in the way of clear feedback about what is *good* about a piece of work. If progress is recognized, it may be reward enough. Remember to stick to comments on the quality of the work rather than making judgements or evaluations of the worker (10.2, 10.4).

7 Think about how you react to assessment of your own work. Do unto others . . .

Step 5: use targets to link assessment with planning

A common problem in the past has been the tendency for teachers to think and plan mainly in terms of the tasks they set, and to talk mainly about tasks to students. It is a further step, as we saw in Chapter 5, to look for the learning behind the task, especially if we also attempt to analyse the kinds of learning demands being made (as in incremental, restructuring, problem-solving, practising and revising; see Chapter 2). If clear and unambiguous objectives for learning can be defined, then it is much easier to ask oneself the question: how will I know if these objectives have been reached? What evidence do I need? Not all aims for learning are suited to precise objectives, however. Sometimes we have to include vague but important aims (e.g. make students more independent, encourage collaboration, develop a capacity to take realistic risks).

Schools increasingly use data from the previous Key Stage to set initial expectations for students. Thus secondary schools, looking at a new intake to KS3, examine results for KS2 assessments; often they will add data from a cognitive ability test, using the results to group students for teaching. In the process, grouped data for gender, ethnicity, mobility, English as an additional language and SEN will be analysed where relevant. Targets for KS3 will be set in each subject. These targets relate not only to the individual student's past attainments, but also to the school's own development plans for 'adding value'. Subject teachers take the initial targets on and link them to initial classroom assessments, in order to set students more detailed short-term goals for each attainment target in each subject.

Example 15.2 Instances of good practice

1 One Y7 student was able to tell an interviewer: 'My target is to get a level 6 for science in my Y9 assessment.' The same student had targets for each subject. For English he had a log for each module he was taking, listing skills to be addressed in each one and with a few more specific short-term targets for improvement, such as 'learn to use imagery in writing poems'.

2 A Y10 student, who was better at science and maths than at English, had a teacher who was trying to raise all the boys' achievements by using the language of skilled trades in his target setting, writing of 'quality of workmanship' and 'jobs completed'. This boy was working towards a predicted C/B grade in English GCSE and his current targets were focused on building up arguments in writing, making good use of evidence and linking sentences effectively. He was able to talk about his progress, showing evidence from the marking of his recent assignments. He understood how the same targets could help him make progress in history. For both subjects he had the relevant level descriptors to consult when necessary in his folder or books.

3 In another secondary school, one personal, social and health education lesson at the start of each half term was used for 'setting and review', with form tutors working to review individual programmes and progress and encouraging self-assessment tasks. Students wrote an action plan related to their targets. The targets were adjusted in this lesson for the next half term and then reviewed more briefly at weekly intervals. Targets were a meeting point for communications between teachers, parents, support staff and students. One Y9 student with an IEP had its details worked out as part of exactly the same process and said simply 'I feel the same as the other girls.' Sometimes a student in difficulties might have targets re-written or dropped. A student commented: 'The subjects that gave me the most targets were science and geography. I had to think about the areas I was doing badly in. I am happy with all my targets as they are targets I can work on.'

Target setting is not always easy. Some aims are far less easy than others to define clearly or assess objectively. The language of National Curriculum criteria has to be translated into user-friendly language appropriate to students of different ages. Some KS1 teachers write targets for their students as speech bubbles, attached to drawings of cartoon characters. Others print them out on colourful animal-shaped cards. Some targets are set as group or class objectives, but most relate to individuals. The main problems of target setting appear to be:

- writing targets that are both challenging and yet achievable;
- tying specific targets into broader aims for progress in a subject;
- keeping track of progress, especially for younger students, who find it difficult to assess their own progress against criteria;
- failing to break progress down into small enough steps;
- making sure a target is clear enough so that students can recognize when they achieve it;
- avoiding leaving students with 'dead targets' for too long without review;
- making sure that one teacher follows through with monitoring and reviews of each student's profile of targets across all subjects.

Some teachers experimenting with target setting at KS1 found that it helped to discuss social targets for the whole class (e.g. taking turns, getting resources ready) during circle time and to write them up on a 'Golden Rules' notice board. Some also found that wall charts, tracking individual progress, were helpful for motivation at this age. Targets can have a focus on learning ('I am learning to use a thesaurus to find alternatives to the word "said" ') or attitude ('I will have go at spellings without worrying about mistakes') or can simply operate as an aide memoire ('I am going to put a full stop or question mark at the end of each sentence'). For many targets, students can record their own successes. Teachers may judge that three, or five, 'hits' are required before a target is considered to be met. Older students can relate targets to criteria for Key Stage assessment levels or GCSE grade criteria. In a subject like English, it would be important to balance targets at word level with others at sentence and text levels in order to avoid a fragmentation of the subject.

Powerful though they are proving to be, targets are not a panacea. They may give the illusion that all learning can be broken down into bite-sized morsels and dealt with one at a time. But teaching is more than 'painting by numbers'. Teachers need to keep specific objectives in perspective, alongside broader more elusive aims such as 'writing with imagination', 'taking on the point of view of other people' or 'understanding that more than one interpretation can be supported from the evidence'.

Step 6: adjust teaching to follow up assessment

Good formative assessment assumes that teaching will change as a result of feedback on learning. This means that teaching plans have to be adjusted and even distorted in order to give extra time to problems and areas of confusion and uncertainty. Building up trust with students demands that teachers not only set targets but also provide the support necessary to achieve them.

Example 15.3 Instances of adjusting teaching

Brian Dockrell[7] and his team investigated formative assessment as it was being developed in some secondary schools. At that time, the teachers were compiling their own lists of core learning outcomes that they wished to assess. With the help of researchers, they designed written tests, performance measures, observation schedules, essay marking scales and attitude questionnaires to gather evidence of different kinds. One group of geography teachers prepared a test of six core concepts relating to a project on environmental education. From the results they found that some of the concepts were significantly more difficult than others for the students to understand and remember. They followed up the test with remedial teaching for different groups and individuals, depending on their test profiles. Then the test was re-administered, with the result that an initial total of 54 failures to understand concepts (across the whole class) was reduced to 26. A revised version of the test and of the remedial activities were then tried out with classes in several other schools. Overall, of 500 students who failed on the first test, 44% showed success in the post-test.

Another group of geography teachers, also studied by Dockrell, carried out a short diagnostic test of a series of lessons on 'settlement'. Again the results were very informative: some concepts had been grasped by almost all the students, others only by a small minority. This prompted the teachers to reconsider what should count as 'core' learning outcomes. There were five teachers and twelve Y9 classes involved and the variation between teachers and classes was initially striking. One teacher had a success rate of 77% on the concept of 'optimum site' with one class and 0% with another! She was able to work out what had probably gone wrong and, as with all the teachers, was able to take remedial action. Another group of teachers wanted to find out if they had changed their students' attitudes towards developing countries as a result of their teaching and used a questionnaire, involving simulated choices of donations to a range of charities, to find out. A surprise result was that although attitudes did improve as a result of the teaching, they had actually been very positive to start with. To some extent, the teachers found that they had been preaching to the converted. They were able to consider how they might use their time more effectively.

Step 7: use questioning skilfully

Questioning is a prominent part of the teacher's role and a vital part of formative assessment, as we have already noted in previous chapters. Yet it is worth pausing to ask ourselves if perhaps we ask too many questions. Research has shown in the past that the most common questions used by teachers (up to 60%) are **closed questions** asking for the recall of facts.[8] These are questions to which there is only one correct answer, as in 'How many sevens make 21?' or 'Who was it who came to the throne in 1837?' A further proportion of teacher questions (12–30%) are about the management of behaviour, as in 'Are you getting on with your work?' and 'Would you please sit down?' Only some 5–10% of questions make challenging intellectual demands on students, requiring them to think. This is in spite of the fact that teachers typically ask an average of 43 or more questions per hour. The reasons for these patterns of questioning probably relate partly to the difficult circumstances of negotiating learning in classrooms (see Chapters 3 and 4). However, they may also reflect the fact that as teachers we tend to slip into unconscious habits, with mannerisms of speech and fixed routines of questioning featuring strongly among them. Clearly we ought to try to avoid such traps. We should try to introduce variety into our teaching, rather than dull predictability.

Closed questions have their place, for example in arousing recall of a previous lesson or quickly revising some facts. But it seems likely that teachers should at least balance them against more open questions. Open questions are open-ended: they prompt thought. Some good open questions might be:
How did you find that answer?
Why do you think it happened?
What are the alternatives?
What would we like to find out?
Where could you find another example?
Can you tell me more about that?
Could you summarize Jean's answer for us?
What else do we know?

If you simply want to get to know an individual or a small group, as when you meet them for the first time, it is worth considering whether asking questions is the best way to proceed. Questions tend to be 'controlling' moves in a conversation, steering the topic one way or another. The response of children, and indeed some adults, may be to be wary of saying too much. If the teacher asks 'Did you like that story?' and the child replies 'It was OK', then the conversation stalls until, as likely as not, the teacher asks another question to fill the silence. A more productive strategy might be to say 'What I liked about that story was the way it surprised us in the end . . .' If you offer information, the other person may be prepared to offer something in exchange.

When using questions, think about what you are using them for. It might be to:

- find out what students already know;
- keep attention focused on the work at hand;
- test recall of an important fact or idea;
- encourage many students to take part;
- reach different levels of attainment across the class;
- check understanding of an important idea;
- push students' thinking further.

The last of these reasons deserves more attention. But before we consider it in more detail, note that you may need to plan some key questions, which are important to check understanding. These may be the questions that help students to restructure ideas and make connections between old and new knowledge.

Example 15.4 Planning key questions
A KS2 teacher, planning to teach a history lesson on the evacuation of children from London in the Second World War, had as general aims (i) to help students understand what evacuation meant to those involved and (ii) to show that situations like this are open to interpretation and are not clear-cut. In order to challenge her students' thinking, for this lesson she prepared detailed questions to ask them during the lesson.

- Why was evacuation considered so important to the war effort? (Relieving stress? Economically? Morale?)
- Using evidence, what can you deduce about how it felt? (To be an evacuee; to have your children evacuated; to receive an evacuee.)
- What were the drawbacks to evacuation? (For evacuees; for their families; for those who hosted them; for the Government.)
- What alternatives might there have been? What would you have done if you had been a politician at the time?

Clearly, this level of detailed planning would not be possible or necessary before every lesson, but in selected cases it could be a powerful means of raising the intellectual challenge of your teaching.

To push students' thinking further, it is useful to keep in mind that questions that start 'Why' and 'What . . . for' generally make more demands on thinking than questions that start 'What' or 'How'. Questions can also be used strategically to make progressively greater cognitive demands (2.4), as the following hierarchy (from simpler to harder questions) suggests.

- Recall questions: 'Who was . . . ?' 'What did . . . ?'
- Comprehension questions: 'What does . . . mean?' 'What does it mean by . . . ?'
- Application questions: 'What would happen if . . . ?' 'How would you . . . ?'
- Questions requiring analysis: 'What evidence can you find for . . . ?'
- Questions requiring synthesis: 'So, what conclusion does that suggest?'
- Evaluative questions: 'Can you say which is better, and why?'

Step 8: teach students to improve their work

Some students are hard to reach, but so far as possible teachers should do whatever they can to make sure that their students are 'doomed to succeed'.[9] This is likely to involve teaching them to recognize success.

Example 15.5 Instances of good practice

1 A KS3 geography class had completed a lesson involving making a decision on the location of a new leisure centre. In the next lesson the teacher brought in several alternative answers. Students were asked to work in groups to rank these answers in terms of their quality, using a list of criteria. They realized from this exercise that there was a significant difference between simple descriptions and attempts to explain and analyse the information given. The students were then asked to re-examine their own answers, comparing them with the examples they had worked through and seeing which seemed the best match. Finally they worked on analysing the strengths and weaknesses of their answers and highlighted how they could improve them.

2 A KS1 class (Y1) were having their first dance lesson, which was based on the picture book 'Mr Gumpy's Outing'.[10] The main aim of the lesson was to teach the students to express in movements the way children are when they are happy. Key questions included 'When you're happy how do you move? Are you fast or slow? Strong or light? Do you skip? Do you jump for joy? Are you on your own or usually with your friends?' As the lesson progressed the teacher commented on individuals: 'I love the way you're skipping, Ellie, with high knees and lots of bounce!' 'Who is showing me a happy face as well as happy movements?' After stopping the class, the teacher asked individuals to show how they had interpreted the task: 'Ellie, show us how you used skipping to show your happiness.' Other individuals also modelled their dance movements. The teacher then held a talk on the different ways that happiness can show in movements. Finally the movements were tried out again.

3 A Y2 class were asked to design a very simple telescope and then write simple instructions for Y1 students to use in making the same telescope. The Y1 students provided them with some very clear feedback, including that some words did not make

sense and that some instructions were in the wrong order. The Y2 class set to work to revise their instructions but first produced a 'success ladder' for the teacher to use in marking their work. They were then set further instruction-writing tasks, such as instructions for changing for swimming (which they had noticed caused much noise and confusion in the Y1 class next door). They tried to use their 'success ladder' but found it no longer fitted the task. They revised it, as a group product, and it read:

Important words stand out and are easy to read

Illustrations help the writing

Clear neat handwriting

Short sentences

Instructions are in the right order

Each instruction is clear and understandable.

Step 9: use marking and feedback to teach

With younger students, feedback mostly needs to be oral and immediate. As students grow older, they can use more delayed feedback from marking and written comments. It is generally a good idea to comment on successful aspects of work and also to highlight specific ways in which it could be improved. Comments that are too vague are likely to be unhelpful:

KS2 student: I could do better if I was told what could be better.

KS3 student: Comments like 'use paragraphs' are useless – if I knew how to use them I would have done.

Helpful feedback is focused on manageable improvement:

Teacher: Check to see if you can replace 'and' by other words, such as 'since', 'although', 'as if', 'after', 'before'.

Teacher: This would reach level 5 if all the commas, speech marks and apostrophes were correct; check where I have marked.

Marking takes up a great deal of teachers' time. It should therefore contribute as much as possible to student progress. Useful pointers include the following.

- Make sure you know the school's policy on marking. For example, are all spelling errors to be pointed out, or only a proportion which stand a chance of being corrected and learned this time around?
- Use a simple code to communicate messages such as 'Here is an error to put right', 'Look along this line to find an error', 'Discuss this one with me', 'I have put this error right for you to learn from' and 'This was exactly what I was looking for'.
- Give students time to go through written feedback, make corrections and try to improve their work.
- Give students practice in marking one another's work, using the criteria external markers would use.

- Give students practice in evaluating work orally in pairs, giving each other balanced feedback on strengths and weaknesses.
- Teach them to put a wiggly line in the margin if they are unsure of what they have written and would like some help.
- Teach your students that some work will be quickly read through and acknowledged with a tick, whereas other pieces will be marked in detail.
- Use marking to check and revise targets for progress.
- Try to follow up marking with oral or written dialogues on key ideas.

Step 10: use recording and reporting effectively

It is difficult to give detailed advice on record keeping and reporting. It varies widely across subjects and Key Stages and schools all have their own systems that you will have to learn to use. Some general points can be made, however. Recording for students might include use of target sheets and cards, checklists, wall charts, displays, log books and planners. Recording and reporting for other teachers will probably use forms supplied by the school and will involve using National Curriculum attainment targets and criteria. Recording and reporting to parents might involve home/school diaries, handbooks, newsletters, entries on a school website, letters, dialogues at parents' evenings and official written school reports. In general you should try to implement the following:

- Only record what will actually be used by someone.
- Be aware of the audience for whom you are writing.
- Respect confidentiality where appropriate.
- Experiment with your own notes and records to find a system that is practical and useful.
- Try to be as specific as possible so as to encourage clear perceptions about what needs to be done. For example, 'She could improve her anticipated grade to an A* if she practises sketching graphs from equations' or 'He needs to extend his background knowledge by using secondary sources of information to extend his notes.'
- Use A, B and C subcategories to summarize current levels on attainment targets, where for example 4A indicates strong level 4, 4B average level 4 and 4C marginal level 4.
- Collect different sorts of evidence to support judgements, including samples of work and self-assessments.
- Use your records to look for under-achieving individuals or groups.
- Check that your records are feeding back into your planning.
- Be clear about whether you are recording for formative or summative assessment purposes.

The aim of this extended section of 10 steps has been to integrate formative assessment into all the main phases of teaching, from planning, through teaching to record keeping and reporting. Its potential for contributing powerfully to learning should now be clear. In the following section we shall turn briefly to summative assessment.

15.5 Summative Assessment

In Chapter 3, I introduced Walter Doyle's view that students tend to shape their work to fit their perception of the assessment regime operating in a class. School can degenerate into an exchange of 'work' for grades. Teachers, too, may find that an externally imposed assessment regime is shaping their priorities and determining to a large extent what they teach. The previous section has tried to show how to use formative assessment to avoid these problems and to drive real learning forward. However, assessment also operates to evaluate teachers and schools. Teachers have to be accountable to parents, to local authorities and, ultimately to the society that funds their work. Society, in its turn, needs to respect the difficult work that teachers do and provide them with the necessary conditions and powers to carry it through properly. To those in positions of authority it is appealing to try to exercise control over teachers by insisting that they examine and report on how well their students are learning. The authorities can then set targets for improvement. Indeed it does seem reasonable that there should be *some* quality control over the system for the benefit of all concerned. However one important question is: how much? Assessment has costs as well as benefits, in terms of time, material resources and (not least) energy.

External authorities tend to be concerned with 'standards'. In assessing, we make judgements based on observations. The judgements almost always compare the observed evidence to some standard. Take as an example a piece of narrative writing at KS2. We might compare this to the set of descriptors for levels 3 and 4, in the National Curriculum for English, to see which is the best fit. When teachers engage in what they call 'levelling' they are seeing whether a piece of work reaches the standards, or criteria, defining a given level of attainment. This kind of assessment is called **criterion-referenced assessment**. Other examples of criterion-referenced assessments include the driving test, in which the candidate has to reach carefully defined standards for knowledge and performance in driving a vehicle, or swimming standards, where two lengths of breaststroke may win you a badge or some other honour. The standards for achieving QTS are yet another example. The key question in criterion-referenced assessment is: has the work, or performance, reached the defined criterion (singular) or criteria (plural)? If it has, then it is successful at that level. Criterion referencing is most suitable when we want to estimate what a person actually knows or what level of competence has been achieved.

Instead of comparing our written narrative with the criteria for some level of attainment, we might be more interested in seeing how it compared with this student's former efforts in the same field. To compare a student's work with his or her own previous work, to see whether progress has been made, is called **ipsative assessment** (from the Latin *ipse* meaning 'same'). One problem with this is that if one only looks at the progress in one person's work, it is difficult to judge whether they have made enough progress to be deemed satisfactory. How much progress counts as enough? Therefore teachers tend to compare one student's progress with that of other students. The key question tends to be: has this individual done better or worse than the average?

In the case of exceptional students, for example those with SEN, ipsative assessment may be very important indeed, comparisons with others being to some degree irrelevant. More generally it is comparisons of one student's performance against that of others that interests us and this is called **normative** (or **norm-referenced**) **assessment** (a norm being what is normal or typical for a population). Normative assessment is especially suitable when we want to put people in rank order, from best to worst, in order to select some of them, as when a university looks at A-level grades as part of its efforts to select the best undergraduates for a course.

15.6 Criteria, Norms and Standards

These three kinds of comparison, criterion-referenced, ipsative and normative assessment, are generally held to be different and independent of one another. However they are, in practice, closely linked. In GCSE and university degree level awards it is even difficult to discover whether they are 'really' criterion- or norm-referenced, as the two become fatally entwined. Ipsative assessment, too, becomes linked to normative assessment whenever one asks: is this student's progress sufficient to satisfy me? One can only answer this question by looking at the student in comparison with others, in other words in comparison with norms of some kind.

Normative assessment becomes linked to criterion-referenced assessment as soon as one tries to compose a test or examination. If all the questions in a test are so easy that all students obtain full marks, then it is said to show a 'ceiling' effect; the best students are bumping up against the ceiling and are not able to demonstrate their greater knowledge. If all the questions are so difficult that no student can answer them, then the test is relatively useless, for no one can even reach its 'floor'. The goal of test constructors, therefore, becomes to design a test that enables the best student to get almost full marks and the worst student to score some marks. Such a test is said to discriminate well between the best and worst students. But it does so by setting its criteria for success at the right level, around the norm for the population. Thus criteria become inevitably linked to norms.

If a university department sets final examinations and all its students end up with first-class degrees, other departments will be sure to complain. In theory all the students *might* reach the criteria for a first-class degree; but human nature being what it is, members of other departments will think that the exams are failing to discriminate and will complain bitterly that standards are falling. Degree standards may look as if they are criterion-referenced but actually they become (roughly) norm-referenced. In the National Curriculum tests at KS2, and in GCSE awards, the same problem exists. If the number of students gaining level 4 in the National Curriculum tests continues to rise, people become suspicious that level 4 is being 'dumbed down'. If more and more students get A–C grades at GCSE, or A grades at A-level, it appears, on the face of things, that standards of education are rising. Yet the press and public draw exactly the opposite conclusion: the exams must be too easy. Educational standards are falling! In theory, these public examinations are criterion-referenced: a given grade should correspond to a given standard of work. In practice, the public (and most teachers) tacitly accept that they should be norm-referenced: only a fixed proportion of students should be awarded the top grade. This, in turn, reflects an entrenched view that any large cohort of students will be of differing ability, and that each generation of students will be much like the previous ones (see also Chapter 12).

This confusion, caused by the fact that criteria have to relate to norms and norms can only be established via criteria, is widespread in educational debates. It also becomes tangled up in ideas about improving standards. An increase in students reaching levels 4 and 5 in the National Curriculum tests at KS2 is unambiguously a sign of progress, but only provided that the criteria and difficulty of the tests remain constant. Hence the constructors of these tests have to proceed with a care and caution that would do credit to a team of people handling the reprocessing of nuclear waste.[11] Improved A-level results have been subjected to this kind of doubting scrutiny for years. In comparison, the fact that running a mile in under 4 minutes is now commonplace for elite athletes, whereas it was once a unique world record, is accepted because, drug-enhanced performances aside, the criterion is seen to be objective and unchanged.

In fact, if a large proportion of a cohort does reach some 'high' educational standard, the predictable result will be demands that the standard should itself be made more difficult to achieve. This is perfectly logical, if we accept that tests need to discriminate between students. But, arguably, this kind of discrimination is only relevant if we need to use the test to select some candidates and reject others. Selection may be a legitimate function of assessment, as when a government decides that it only has the resources to educate some proportion of its population, say at university level. Selection is relevant in choosing the people best fitted to do particular jobs and in cases where scarce resources need to be devoted to those who can make best use of them. Since comprehensive secondary education was introduced in Britain, however, selection has not been needed within the primary and secondary school system in relation to students. Instead, it is being used to discriminate between schools.

Originally the National Curriculum sought to escape from the long tradition of norm-referencing of public examinations, which was seen to label any less than average student as a failure. It seemed far less socially divisive, as well as common sense in motivational terms, to allow everyone, potentially, to succeed. The answer was sought in criterion-referenced levels, levels that any student might attain, and this was indeed how the National Curriculum levels were originally set up and presented.[12] However, within a very few years, in spite of these good intentions, the press and politicians had started to label level 4, at age 11+, as the 'required standard'. It was around the average level of attainment for the age, at the time, and therefore anything below it became seen as 'below standard'. Hence norms were swiftly imposed on (originally neutral) criteria. Soon the figure of 80% to achieve

level 4 or above was set by the Government as the goal to reach in the three core
subjects of English, maths and science.[13] If and when this goal is reached, the predictable response will be either to make level 4 harder to attain or to make level 5
the new 'standard' of acceptability. The people who lose out in this ratchet-like
process are those who progress more slowly than the average, which is by definition
(leaving distinctions between means, medians and modes aside) half the population.
The debate about how best to make summative assessment compatible with good
formative assessment for learning seems likely to continue for some time to come.

15.7 Questions

The following questions are designed to help you check your understanding of
the chapter.

1 What three kinds of comparison form the basis of most educational assessments?
2 What distinguishes formative from summative assessment?
3 How might you build assessment into a lesson plan?
4 What questions during a plenary session might help to tune your students into
   self-assessment?
5 Should formative assessment usually occur at the end of modules of work?
6 What are some of the main difficulties with effective target setting?
7 How might you use questions to increase cognitive challenge?
8 Why do criteria tend to become entangled with norms?
9 When is criterion-referencing most appropriate? When is norm-referencing most
   appropriate?
10 **Discussion question**: could we give up all forms of summative assessment? Give
   reasons for your answer.

NOTES

1. An excellent source of information on this topic is the QCA website www.qca.org.uk/.
   I have used examples from this site throughout this chapter, drawing in particular on work
   done in Suffolk and Gillingham schools. See also Torrance and Pryor (1998).
2. Black and Wiliam (1998).
3. Black and Wiliam (1998), p. 1.
4. Ofsted (2003c).
5. McCallum (2000).
6. Clarke (1998).
7. Dockrell (1995).
8. The figures in this section come from the Suffolk schools case study on the QCA Assessment for Learning website (see note 1).
9. I owe this splendid phrase to Sean Cameron, of the Portage Project and the University of
   Southampton.

10. I owe this example to Sue Chedzoy of the School of Education, University of Exeter.
11. I discovered this for myself from a presentation given by NFER staff at the United Kingdom Reading Association conference at St Catherine's College, Oxford in 1999.
12. Task Group on Assessment and Testing (TGAT) (1987).
13. Interestingly, the original KS2 criteria and tests were written without the benefit of research evidence. One unintended result was that the National Curriculum tests for science were almost certainly easier than those for English, with maths in between. The 'standards' are to this extent completely arbitrary.

CHAPTER SIXTEEN

Developing as a Professional Teacher

16.1 Introduction

In this final chapter of the book we shall be thinking about what it means to be a teacher, to be a professional and how teachers learn about and develop their own practice. The emphasis is partly on what we know about the development of teachers' knowledge and partly about teaching as a career. Becoming a professional is usually bound up with becoming a specialist subject teacher in one or more subjects. Up until this point, the book has concentrated on generic processes of teaching and learning, taking examples from different Key Stages and different subjects, as if what you are teaching and to whom does not make much difference to the discussion. In the next section, however, the tacit assumption that subjects do not make much difference will be dropped. In later sections the personal nature of teaching, as an occupation, will be examined, together with what is meant by being a 'professional'.

16.2 The Psychology of Teaching Academic Subjects

There is not the space here to attempt to consider each and every school subject in detail, so instead we will look at what aspects of subjects need to be researched by their teachers and why. At KS3 and KS4 the importance of specialist subject knowledge is perfectly clear, because teachers mostly teach only one or two subjects. At KS1 and KS2 it is far less clear, since the balance between being a general class teacher and being a specialist in one or more curriculum subjects has shifted to and fro over the years, and may yet change again. It will be assumed, however, that developing a subject specialism will remain part of the repertoire of all teachers.

For many years in the latter half of the twentieth century, educational research was dominated by 'subject-neutral' accounts of teaching and learning, but this had not always been the case. In the early part of the century, when educational psychology was first becoming established, it was not uncommon to view educational research in terms of the teaching of different subjects. However, by the 1970s, debates about the curriculum were swinging in the opposite direction, often claiming that the division of knowledge into separate disciplines and school subjects was to some extent arbitrary and anyway of little relevance to everyday life. Primary schools, especially, experimented with cross-curricular projects and different groupings of subjects.[1] Such speculations were put to rest for the foreseeable future by the arrival of the National Curriculum in 1988–89, which was organized in traditional subject form. Educational psychologists might yet have continued mostly to ignore subjects were it not for the fact that Lee Shulman[2] and other researchers brought them back to prominence. Shulman pointed out that teaching always involved teaching something to someone. The 'something' was normally a subject and the 'someone' was a student of a particular age. Together, as researchers were to demonstrate, they made a great deal of difference to what actually went on during teaching and learning. Connecting the 'something' to the 'someone' turned out to be what made teachers experts at their craft.

Shulman argued that teachers need a great deal of subject matter knowledge in order to teach effectively. In addition to this, they need to know how to represent the content and processes of a subject in order to communicate it to students in a way that will promote learning. The academic subject has to be transformed, for this purpose, into suitable tasks, activities and explanations. This representation of subject matter knowledge, centred on classroom tasks and activities, is generally called **pedagogical content knowledge**. It includes knowledge of all the following:

- Representations of facts, concepts and methods in the subject, using metaphors and analogies to connect with more general knowledge.
- Tasks that are productive for learning, including the relevant resources, their organization and health and safety issues.
- Examples of key ideas, rules and problems which link the particular to the general and thus promote understanding.
- Students and their existing levels of understanding and skill in the subject, including common misconceptions and errors.
- How understanding in the subject typically advances from one level to another.
- Productive locations for out-of-school work.
- Knowledge of research that supports teaching and learning in the subject.

All professions are identified with some kind of specialist knowledge or skill and here we have the speciality of teaching. Pedagogical content knowledge is an awkward term, but what it represents lies at the heart of the specialist knowledge that provides the foundation of teaching as a profession. Building up one's pedagogical content knowledge is extremely basic to learning to teach and it continues to be an important area of research.[3] It connects the subject, via the teacher, with the minds of students. However, in spite of its importance, it has proved quite difficult to pin down. This is because it is a rich web of interconnected knowledge and skill, partly conscious, partly intuitive, which relates to particular students, particular contexts and particular curriculum knowledge. It is further complicated by being strongly influenced by a teacher's values.

Initial teacher training has always involved some tensions between generic and subject-specific kinds of knowledge for teaching. One school of thought tends to argue that the skills of good classroom management (especially planning, organization, control and assessment) are central to all teaching and can be taught across subjects (see, for example, Part I). The opposing school points out that if a lesson is not well planned in terms of the 'fit' between the subject matter, tasks and students, then no amount of expertise at classroom management will save the day. In truth these are not so much opposites as a complementary pair of insights, each on its own a necessary but not sufficient condition for overall success.

16.3 Teachers' Subject Matter Knowledge

Shulman's work inspired researchers to explore two main areas: the extent to which teachers, especially in the primary school, had adequate subject matter knowledge to teach right across the school curriculum, and the ways in which teaching was actually different in different subjects. In connection with the first of these questions, a cartoon once showed a young woman with a worried face sitting down in the famous black chair of the *Mastermind* quiz programme on television. The question-master asks her: 'Name?' She replies, 'Sally Smith.' 'Occupation?' She replies, 'Primary teacher.' 'Specialist subject?' She replies, 'The universe!'

In fact, the development of a National Curriculum, with core and foundation subjects, levels of attainment and corresponding QTS standards, has gradually led to a much clearer view of exactly what knowledge is required by teachers at each Key Stage. Since all teachers currently train to teach across two Key Stages, and are expected to be several levels above their students in their understanding, it remains a challenging goal to have satisfactory subject matter knowledge for teaching. It will be especially challenging if it is some years since you studied some, or even all, of these subjects at school yourself. Teachers at KS3 and KS4 will normally have degree-level knowledge of their specialist subject but this is often far removed from the knowledge making up the school curriculum.

In Britain, the first strand of the research about subject matter knowledge led eventually, and indirectly, to the setting up of QTS skills tests for competence in literacy, numeracy and ICT. Passes in all these tests, though not necessarily at the first attempt, are now required by all teachers in order to obtain QTS. In addition, the standards for the award of QTS section 2 (knowledge and understanding) set out a very detailed account of pedagogical content knowledge, both within particular subjects and across them, for the various Key Stages. Although this must be a daunting prospect for student teachers, faced with a mass of overlapping requirements in all directions, it has also probably made qualified teachers feel more confident of their professionalism. Primary teachers, in particular, once tended to identify themselves mostly as creative people with sound general knowledge and a deep understanding of children. Now they are more likely to identify themselves with very extensive knowledge of both subjects and children. Their professional status has thus, arguably, been given firmer foundations.

16.4 Uses of Subject Matter Knowledge

So, why should subject matter knowledge make such a difference to teaching? The undergraduate trainee teachers with whom I used to work were sometimes addicted to the practice of brushing up on the immediate content of lessons just before they taught them. Understandable though this strategy is, it is not sufficient in the long term, as we shall see. Reports from school inspectors have, for some years, argued that subject matter knowledge is vital to good primary teaching. Thus a 1997 Ofsted survey of KS2 teaching had this to say:

> The quality of teaching of subject specialists is almost always better than that of non-specialists. In virtually all lessons where high standards are achieved, teachers have sound or good knowledge of the subject they are actually teaching.[4]

Concerns of this kind surface mainly at KS2, where specialist knowledge first comes to the fore. KS1 teachers need more than anything to be specialists in the teaching of early literacy and numeracy.[5] By KS3 there is little disagreement about the need for specialist subject knowledge, although there may be violent disagreements about exactly what knowledge is relevant. But at KS2 there are tensions between teaching as a specialist and as a generalist class teacher. To bridge this potential gap the range of knowledge required is considerable.

One research study showed that student teachers in training were generally better at teaching their own specialism at KS2 than were other, non-specialist students.[6] However, simply knowing a good deal about an academic discipline at an advanced level, say via a degree in maths or English, is not enough in and of itself to make for good teaching. This is because the subject as it is studied in universities is simply too remote from the school curriculum. Rather, what is required is a conception of the subject, its core concepts and its procedures for advancing our knowledge that can all inform pedagogical content knowledge.

Good teachers use their deep knowledge of a subject in a number of ways.[7]

- They can ask good *questions* of students and also spot when a student's question, or even an error, is a productive one. (For example, when a student said that the number 6 'was both odd and even' because it had 2 and 3 as factors, one good maths teacher, instead of just saying he was wrong, was able to deepen her class's understanding through encouraging a long discussion about odd and even numbers, in which they sought to pin down exactly why this was an error.)
- Such teachers feel more secure both about *demonstrating their knowledge* and being able to *respond to questions*. They are not tempted to 'play safe' in order to

avoid areas where they are themselves unsure of what they are teaching. (One primary teacher, for example, found that a course on electricity and magnetism improved her confidence in monitoring and supporting her students' investigations of electric circuits. She was better able to ask challenging questions and to encourage fruitful lines of enquiry.)

- They can produce helpful *examples and analogies*, but also keep an eye on when these may actually mislead. (A maths teacher used ideas about a lift going to floors both above and below ground level to illustrate positive and negative numbers. She then switched to an alternative analogy, of having or owing money, to explain how numbers changed sign when moved to the opposite side of an equation.)
- They can judge when an investigation is leading in a productive direction and focus on *key ideas or processes*, which are central to a subject. (Thus a history teacher seized on a student's chance observation about church-going in Tudor England to explain the power of religious institutions at that time and their political influence.)
- They use the *language* and *concepts* of the 'parent' discipline with authority and can explain them clearly. (A skilled music teacher was able to explain different rhythms and their notation, as well as illustrating them via clapping activities. Her knowledge was especially critical in pushing students to reach higher levels of rhythmic accuracy and precision.)
- They are more *critical of published texts and software*, using them only in the context of their own broader curriculum knowledge. (An effective teacher of literacy used published 'writing frames' as a resource but was also able to write such frames herself to suit different circumstances.)
- Even their ability to *assess learning* is generally superior, because they have a better sense of what counts as authentic progress in a subject. (A poetry teacher, who was himself a poet, had great insight into the signs of poetic progress in his class's poetry writing, which went well beyond National Curriculum level descriptors.)

However, one of the great problems in this area is that what counts as 'worthwhile knowledge of a subject' is often contested within the subject itself. In particular, 'subject matter' and 'subject thinking' are often very different in everyday uses than they are in academic uses. In mathematics, for example, everyday calculations and measurements depend on applying sound, but repetitive, knowledge of number bonds and arithmetic routines. This is nothing like the work of professional mathematicians, who live with great uncertainty and highly abstract concepts, making conjectures about possible relationships and searching for counter-examples or pathways towards proofs.

In science, everyday knowledge of materials and technologies used around the home has rather little to do with experimental method or with advanced computing skills, both of which are crucial to professional scientists. In English, some teachers are persuaded that their key role is to teach an appreciation for the greatest literary masterpieces of their cultural heritage, whereas others are convinced that functional uses of literacy and critical judgements about messages in the mass media have a higher priority for their students. Art teachers disagree about the relative importance of art-making and art appreciation, as well as about the importance of skills such as drawing. Subjects can thus be represented in the classroom in more than one way. All we can say here is that at least a well-informed teacher is better able than an ignorant one to reach a thoughtful and balanced position about teaching a subject in the light of such debates.

16.5 Instructional Explanations

Gaea Leinhardt[8] has extended our understanding of how subject expertise affects teaching. She has studied effective teachers of maths and history in the USA to find out how their subject matter knowledge, together with pedagogical content knowledge, actually inform the kinds of explanations they give to students. Their explanations started from their aims and were followed through into the tasks they designed for lessons. They were then expressed especially through the talk that went on around these tasks. The subject matter and its nature thus became woven into the very texture of lessons. (You may remember from Chapter 5, for example, how a lesson plan about lino cuts for book illustrations would naturally have led the teacher into talk about drawing quality, mark making and the tools appropriate to lino-cutting.) History teachers were especially concerned with explanations for historical events and Leinhardt shows how their instructional explanations included three different kinds of historical elements, at rather different levels of difficulty.

At the first level, these history teachers talked about events in terms of a narrative of temporal sequences and causes. Historical events were thus explained in terms of actors, their purposes and motives and the consequences of the actions. This kind of explanation is close to our common-sense explanations of events and to stories in general. It is thus fairly easy for students to understand. Secondly, however, the history teachers would discuss social structures and institutions and relate them to events. Thus, to give an English example, the English Civil War would involve talk about the powers of the monarchy and the emergence of the New Model Army. Such structures develop and change and need to be analysed, rather than simply being 'told' as a story. This was more difficult for students to follow. At a third level, more general historical themes were talked about, such as freedom, political struggle, power or wealth. Talk, for example about the power of Charles I in his struggles with Parliament, would naturally lead to links being made between many different events and structures in order to illustrate this general theme. At this level, general historical interpretations and hypotheses (e.g. the weaknesses of Charles as a monarch) came to characterize history lessons. Such themes might crop up many times across a series of lessons and represent the manner in which history is composed not only of people and events but also of what we make of them. Historians build cases and arguments and these teachers were doing the same in their classes.

Good mathematics teachers, in contrast, used instructional explanations that focused on questions such as 'How can we . . . ?' and which used operations, functions and iterations, on entities such as numbers, shapes or graphs. Problems were often solved in steps or stages. Some of their lessons made use of concrete representations, such as blocks or paper cut-outs, and instructional explanations were then partly constrained by the nature of these concrete materials. Other lessons concentrated on mathematical ideas embedded within problems, in which case the talk took on the entities of the problem world. At still other times, maths teachers talked directly about mathematical concepts.[9] They also made great use of examples and analogies and these can make a difference to the way the maths concepts are understood. If, for example, fractions are understood by way of an analogy with pieces of a pie, cut up into slices, then the multiplication and division of fractions becomes mysterious, as one cannot easily visualize dividing one piece of pie 'into' another, or multiplying one 'by' another.

General rules were sometimes investigated by Leinhardt's maths teachers, with talk about counter-examples and proofs. Notation and its uses was another characteristic feature of maths lessons, as was the attempt to resolve the nature of errors. There is thus, in maths, a constant search for patterns and rules, for consistency and for sense making, as students try to advance their understanding while keeping intact the links with their everyday knowledge. Characteristic questions included 'How would you convince someone else of what you are saying?' and 'Is there another way of finding a solution to this problem?' General **heuristics** taught by these teachers included trying to simplify problems, to look at extreme cases and to look for the convergence of different approaches to the same problem.

At their best, instructional explanations make links in two directions: towards examples and applications in everyday life and towards authentic features of the 'parent' discipline. Explanations that fail to link with the parent discipline may mislead students in the long run, whereas failures to make links with students' existing knowledge may lead to a breakdown in their understanding. Everyday knowledge of maths suggests that it is mostly a set of rules (or **algorithms**) for solving arithmetic problems. But maths is, or becomes, far more than this. The Chinese-American researcher Ma[10] compared the knowledge base of 72 Chinese and 21 American mathematics teachers in elementary schools and found that the Chinese teachers taught with a far more powerful 'knowledge package'. In effect they appear to have had a more refined understanding of pedagogical content knowledge than their American counterparts, and it in turn was founded in a deeper understanding of the underlying discipline.[11] Ma calls this 'profound understanding of fundamental maths'. The Chinese teachers' ideas on teaching maths made use of:

- key ideas that 'weigh more' than others in the subject;
- sequences of tasks for developing ideas;
- concept 'knots' that link together crucial related ideas.

In Japanese elementary schools, to take a related example, teachers appear to be comparatively successful in teaching both maths and science. There is a tradition for Japanese teachers to meet together to discuss particular 'research lessons', comparing detailed representations, examples and forms of organization.[12] As in the case of Ma's research, we glimpse here a world in which teachers seem to have a very firm tradition of pedagogical content knowledge, which they largely agree upon and which they can continue to refine and share through their own practice. It may well be that developing and sharing better, more detailed accounts of pedagogical content knowledge, linked with demonstrably successful learning outcomes, is a key strategy for improving teaching and learning. It may also be important to establish more clearly that well-connected everyday knowledge (core construct knowledge, to use the terminology of Chapter 11) is properly the focus of concern during KS1 and probably for most of KS2. Knowledge that reaches more towards the authentic parent discipline is (I assume) properly the concern of KS4. However, the balance in KS3 between the everyday and the academic remains uncertain and perhaps needs to be determined more clearly.

In summary, although 'pedagogical content knowledge' is an awkward name, it seems to be central to successful teaching. As a developing professional you will need to spend time researching this and building up your own repertoire in your own specialist subject or subjects. It is one of the main ways in which expertise as a teacher is acquired and it takes time. Although official documents insist that all kinds of 'competence' should be achieved in very short order before QTS can be awarded, it might be wise to accept that the development of subject expertise is a longer-term process. (The task of compiling a Career Entry Development Profile and the work carried out during your induction period as a teacher should both contribute to this development.)

16.6 Teachers' Knowledge and its Development

Good teachers make teaching look effortless and this makes the nature of their underlying knowledge and skill hard to pin down. Their expertise is hidden beneath the surface of their interactions with their students and they may or may not be good at talking about it. However, looking at the practice of expert practitioners, useful though it is, does not tell us *how* they became experts. Researchers are united in their recognition that teaching expertise is a rich contextualized mixture that has to do with subjects taught, with learners and with the school system. Lee Shulman[13] considered that it could be divided up into seven main strands:

- subject matter knowledge (especially content and methods);
- pedagogical content knowledge (see above);
- general pedagogical knowledge (this book's speciality);
- knowledge of the curriculum (and, we might add, its assessment);
- knowledge of learners;
- knowledge of educational contexts, such as schools;
- knowledge of educational ends, purposes and values.

Having separated these many strands, we have to accept that in practice they are woven back together in complex ways in living, working teachers. While actually teaching, events arrive and decisions have to be made far too quickly for the luxury of any prolonged deliberation. The knowledge used in action has to be immediate and practical rather than propositional;[14] it is contextualized, situated and applied. Few people, if any, believe that teachers first learn some theoretical principles and then go off and 'apply' them in practice. Rather, it seems to be the case that most of us plunge into some form of teaching, acquire a certain degree of routine competence or skill, and then attempt to make better sense of our experiences in terms of more general ideas and research findings.

A number of researchers have argued that beginner teachers develop their practice through a series of recognizable stages.[15] These stages are defined in terms of dominant concerns.

1 Survival concerns: focus on becoming sufficiently competent at teaching to satisfy both external assessors and one's own standards of professional adequacy.
2 Task concerns: consolidation and extension of mastery of the core processes of teaching.
3 Impact concerns: new focus on developing longer-term influences over either students or other teachers, or both, via posts of greater responsibility.

Jennifer Nias,[16] in an insightful study of a sample of 99 primary teachers over a period of 15 years, found that this 'stage' picture was a slight simplification. Each of the three successive phases of concern could indeed be identified in her sample but each could be seen as related to these teachers' unchanging determination to defend and preserve a core of educational values, identified closely with an inner 'self'. This idea will be taken further in the next section.

There is little doubt that the early stages of teaching are challenging because they raise basic questions about the self's adequacy and suitability to succeed in a chosen field of work. For some teachers, the battle to survive the early years seems to lead to a defensive and inflexible approach to teaching, in which institutional realities ('this is how we do it here') swamp any more idealistic or rational aims. Other individuals successfully make the transition to 'task concerns' without losing their ability to change and develop within the job. 'The phrase "Learning to Teach" rolls easily off the tongue, giving the impression that this is a straightforward, easily understood process. In fact we do not have well-developed theories of learning to teach. . . .' So wrote two authors[17] pondering the way in which novice teachers learn to become experts. But research has made it clear that teachers draw on many experiences, going back to their own childhood and career at school, as well as lessons learned in training and from colleagues, in learning how to teach. They also make their developing knowledge explicit in a number of different ways, including via telling anecdotes, interpreting cases, justifying decisions and referring back to critical incidents.[18]

In fact there is no reason to suppose that the many varieties of learning surveyed in Chapters 6, 7 and 8 do not all apply to teachers. The problem is more that we are not sure which varieties are most important at which stages of an apprenticeship in teaching. Many teachers report that they have modelled their practice on that of one particular experienced colleague, in whose practice they saw their own educational values being brought to life. The craft knowledge of teaching has been likened to a kind of 'teaching sensibility' in which background moral values, understanding of a context and empathy come together to infuse practical judgements and actions. Practical arguments are likely to be given later, in retrospect, to justify practical reasoning that was embedded in action at the time.

Both practical arguments and practical reasoning surface in teachers' planning and evaluations. But we have seldom been able to validate such expert craft knowledge, by showing that it actually and reliably leads to superior results in terms of learning. Hence it is important to continue trying to build up a body of research on effective teaching, which is grounded in particular practical contexts and yet is general enough to inform other teachers and other contexts. There are difficulties in moving from the particular to the general, as well as from the general to the particular. Yet we know that teachers do learn and change. Initially, imitation and practice (with feedback) may be the most important modes of learning. Later, observations and reflections may lead teachers to interpret and question their own practices, in the light of their underlying aims and values. Such reflections may lead to discussion, to the reading of research and to practical attempts to develop practice in planned directions.

Several researchers have found that student teachers' core assumptions and values are actually very hard to change, by way of either university-based courses or teaching practices. However from the same sources there is also evidence that allowing teachers to collaborate together in groups, on longer-term projects focused on enquiry into their own classrooms, does lead to changes in both their beliefs and practices.[19]

This raises a basic question about the usefulness of the present book and of others like it. Can teachers learn from the experiences of others in this indirect way? No definitive answer can be provided, but it seems reasonable to argue that an introduction such as this can (i) provide an orientation towards important issues for beginners, (ii) continue to supply a series of 'signposts' or 'landmarks' giving teachers a sense of direction in navigating through their everyday work, and (iii) provide the experienced teacher at least with an argument, or series of arguments, with which to engage in some critical thinking.

Practical experience will no doubt shape the meanings that teachers read into research, but without research teachers may find it hard to see beyond their most immediate, short-term, practical problems. Research seems especially helpful in enabling teachers to reframe the puzzles of experience, to use the language of Donald Schön.[20] If student teachers are plunged too quickly into intensive teaching practice, facing large classes and the regular curriculum, they are likely to focus their minds exclusively on short-term planning, classroom management and practical resource issues. Allowing them breaks in which to think about such early episodes of teaching, using both discussion and writing to make sense of them, seems more likely to lead to a thoughtful approach to teaching that looks beyond mere survival.

An alternative view of learning to teach, which sees teaching as a set of definable skills or competences to be learned exclusively via practice, has sometimes seemed to underlie official views of teacher training. In this view, competences are either present or absent, rather like a switch that may be on or off, and practice is simply a matter of defined standards and hard work, plus feedback from more experienced teachers. There is something to be said for this simple view, especially in its determination to make practical experience an essential priority, but in my view it underestimates four facts about teaching.

- Even skilled teachers actually fluctuate in their performance, across both time and subjects, between barely adequate and high levels of skill and effectiveness.
- Teaching is too complex to be reduced to a simple set of skills; it involves no less than an investment of the whole person in a process of gradual development, guided by values and open to change.
- Teaching is too unpredictable to allow for mere practical training on the job in one or two contexts (vital though that practice is).
- We cannot yet say exactly what the skills or competences are that reliably lead to effective learning at different ages.

Donald Schön, in his influential book *The Reflective Practitioner*,[20] contrasted professional practices that fit a model of 'technical rationality', where well-established scientific knowledge can be applied to well-defined problems, with those professions that grapple with uncertainty, uniqueness, instability and value conflicts. In the latter cases, 'rigorous' applications of technical knowledge are not as apposite as 'relevant' applications of experienced artistry. As he put it:

> In the varied topography of professional practice, there is a high, hard ground where practitioners can make effective use of research-based theory and technique, and there is a swampy lowland where situations are confusing 'messes' incapable of technical solution. The difficulty is that the problems of the high ground, however great their technical interest, are often relatively unimportant to clients or to the larger society, while in the swamp are the problems of greatest human concern.[21]

Even in the 'major' professions of medicine or engineering there are areas in which technical rationality is a real possibility and other areas that more closely resemble the swampy lowlands. In education, the swampy lowlands have always been the dominant terrain and consequently the intuitive knowledge, or artistry, of experienced professionals has been highly valued. Schön was writing 20 years and more ago, and now perhaps we can claim to be emerging from the swamps to rather better-drained educational meadows, but technical rationality will still not answer as an adequate or complete approach to teaching. Craft and artistry remain important, as do personal qualities.

16.7 The Teacher, the Person and the Self

In the first one or two years of teaching, many highly motivated and skilled new teachers come up against serious problems in the forms of various practical obstacles, institutional inflexibility and student unwillingness to change (3.4, 3.5). During this period it is particularly easy to allow all previous knowledge and experience to be 'washed away' by the day-to-day realities of the current situation. Faced with a new environment, physical fatigue, long hours, recalcitrant students and (sometimes) unhelpful colleagues, not to mention illnesses contracted from the many new viruses encountered in a school, it is scarcely surprising that some newly qualified teachers feel dispirited and even hopeless.

No amount of training seems altogether to prepare one for the challenge of a first year's full-time teaching. Among other things, one needs to become physically 'fit' for the job. It is to be hoped that the professional support of more experienced staff, particularly designated mentors, will provide newly qualified teachers with the support and practical assistance they need at this time. However, for the primary teachers studied by Jennifer Nias,[16] albeit some time ago, it was not always the professional 'help' provided which counted for most. Often her teachers relied on informal reference groups, either within or without the school, to keep their hopes and even dreams alive. Such reference groups were made up of people, sometimes only a solitary person, with whom an individual teacher shared core values about education and professional standards, who 'saw things the same way'. They talked to these people, in person or by phone, during the school day or during evenings and weekends, and described these contacts as 'what kept them going'. If the reference group did not include colleagues within a school, the teacher often moved, eventually, to another school which provided a more sympathetic setting. Those who survived the early years and moved on to 'task concerns' had usually found a setting in which they felt they could 'be themselves'.

Nias argues that teaching, as work, makes heavy demands upon the individual, as a person. Most teachers see their work as more than 'just work' and have a commitment to their students that demands a high level of investment of time and energy. It is neither improper nor sentimental to suggest that many teachers show what amounts to a form of love for those they teach. Since teaching involves the building up of relationships and the working out of an ethos (1.6), teachers feel both vulnerable and personally engaged in what they do. This sense of personal engagement is often reinforced by the context of their work, in that many teachers have little contact with other adults during the day but live, effectively, shut up with their students in classrooms. These facts, at the same time, make the mutual support of teachers for one another vitally important to the effective and happy running of schools.

Teachers also gain part of the satisfaction of their work from a sense that it involves the expression of their own very particular talents and skills. They want sufficient autonomy and control over their own work to be able to feel that in their teaching they are communicating their own values and personalities. Nias argues that, despite wide individual differences, self-image is important to all teachers. Her analysis of the 'self' concludes that as well as being constructed of a 'me', which is largely a product of social interaction with others, the self includes an 'I' that is elusive, creative and a reservoir of inner self-regard. This complex 'self' can give rise to powerful emotions and to the building up of strong defences against threats to its core values. This has already been alluded to when we looked at the ways in which teachers and students defend their dignity and self-respect in the classroom (3.5). It comes up again in the present context because it is linked to the development of personal identity, of coming to 'feel like a teacher'.

The teachers Nias studied had virtually all freely chosen teaching as an occupation. Yet, interestingly, very few of them actually saw themselves as teachers, even five or more years after they had begun to teach. They said things like 'I'm still not convinced that this is for me' and 'I don't yet see myself as a teacher, though I'm beginning to see my way to becoming one.'[22] For a small minority, identification of themselves as teachers stretched all the way back to commitments originally made in childhood, but for the great majority identification with the role took place only very gradually, if at all, as a consequence of a long immersion in the realities of the job. This identification of the self as a teacher tended to emerge only after the initial phase of concern with 'survival' was completed, when they had moved on and were consolidating their mastery of teaching. Those who did not feel they could identify their core selves with the task of teaching, or who failed to find a sympathetic context in which they could 'be themselves' as teachers, frequently sought another job or left teaching to start a family. A further small, unhappy, minority found themselves trapped by financial and other commitments, staying on in a job that they had come to find essentially uncongenial.

Those teachers in Nias's sample who went on to identify themselves as teachers, and who stayed on in the profession for a decade or more, often moved on to concern themselves with 'impact' or influence on others, by taking on positions of greater responsibility. They were relaxed in their role as teachers and had found ways of continuing to develop as persons within the job. Thus, as Nias puts it:

> It seems, therefore, that the personal concerns of teachers do develop but that in a fundamental sense, they remain the same. The heart of this paradox is the notion that the substantial self is the core of both person and teacher. In other words, although teachers can and do develop, they will not change professionally unless they also change as people. It is, inexorably, the person who takes up and carries out the job – and people . . . are characterized by a stable sense of self, imbued with values and beliefs which are powerfully self-defining.[23]

The self inside the person needs to come to terms, in one way or another, with the person who is the teacher. Some teachers come to blend their professional work with their private lives and interests, so that there is hardly a barrier between them. Many, for example, marry other teachers and work, and talk about their work, frequently at home. Others keep their lives in more separated compartments, reserving some of themselves for their lives outside school. Both kinds of adaptation seem viable.

16.8 Teaching as a Profession

The term 'professional' was once restricted to a few occupations, notably medicine, law and the church, which all shared certain characteristics. They were founded on a systematic body of specialist knowledge and they provided services that were widely valued in society. They required lengthy periods of both academic education and practical training and they defended their professional rights and privileges by way of a code of ethics and a system for rejecting those who failed to live up to the code. These (largely male) enclaves preserved a high degree of self-governing autonomy, justifying this by arguing that it was essential for the forming of independent professional judgements. Most of this small privileged world has now been replaced, with governments increasingly funding and regulating the operations of the old professions and with many other occupational groups now claiming professional status.

Teachers, along with nurses, architects, engineers, town planners, actors, accountants, bartenders and athletes, all lay claim to the now rather tarnished and dubious label of 'professional'. In the case of teachers, relatively low pay and low status has always threatened their self-esteem. Conscious of fulfilling one of the most arduous and valuable roles in society, they have felt widely undervalued, at least in the Anglo-Saxon world, by the general public. Nor are they a unified group, with university and further education teachers having little in common with either one another or primary or secondary teachers. Professional associations sit uneasily beside trades unions and a small privileged private sector exists alongside a much larger state system. There seems little left of the status and value once associated with the term 'professional' and little to convince the impartial outsider that teachers are a united profession.

Since Nias completed her study at the end of the 1980s, teachers in Britain have been inundated by a deluge of externally imposed reforms, which have removed from teachers any control they once might have claimed to exert over entry to the profession, the content of the school curriculum, its assessment or even approved methods of teaching. A once diverse system, with a diffusion of power and control across many central, regional and local institutions, has been transformed into a highly centralized state system, tightly controlled by a hierarchy made up of the Prime Minister, education ministers, DfES, Ofsted, QCA and TTA. Yet the Standards for the Award of Qualified Teacher Status still speak of 'professional values and practice' and 'professional development'. The list of documents making up the relevant legal framework for teachers' work and conduct, of which teachers have at least to be 'aware', runs to over 25 government circulars and Acts of Parliament, without counting either the National Curriculum or the QTS standards themselves. Clearly 'professional' does not mean what it once did. On the other hand, as was claimed earlier, the gradual codification of the knowledge now required of all qualified teachers has probably strengthened at least one sense in which they feel themselves to be a unified group of professionals.

'Professional' now seems to mean (i) paid a salary and (ii) subject to extremely detailed and widespread regulation. There is an irony here, in that professionalism, and in particular professional development, traditionally implied a degree of authority over, and responsibility for, one's own developing professional knowledge. It still implies some personal commitment to, and ownership of, change. Without this personal commitment, teaching would probably be painfully reduced in its influence and effectiveness. Insisting on compulsory 'professional development' is thus almost a contradiction in terms. In relation to this, I remember once noticing among primary teachers in the beleaguered inner city schools of a London district a strong atmosphere of autonomy and personal confidence. This surprised me at first, until I reflected that these teachers knew very well that no one was likely to want them to stop doing their highly valuable work, and that no crowd of alternative candidates was queuing up to take over their jobs. They, and especially their hard-won professional experience, were not only valuable but also valued. They were, essentially, irreplaceable and they knew it.

I would not wish to give the impression that the professional development of teachers is anything but highly desirable. Nor should it depend merely upon the whims and local leverage of particular groups of teachers. Yet the tensions between teaching as a public service, controlled from above, and teaching as a valued profession, demanding a high level of personal investment, will continue to reverberate until the responsibilities are matched by corresponding rights. The responsibilities and duties of professional teachers should be matched by corresponding levels of trust in their judgements. They need the power to ensure that learning can progress, unhindered, in their classrooms and they need at least a degree of autonomy over the direction of their own professional and personal development. They should be listened to and should participate in the development of the curriculum and its assessment. They should have a large part in the training of their own successors. But to do these things they will need to keep their own knowledge base up to date.

The long-term satisfactions of teaching come largely from the intrinsic qualities of the work itself. They come from enjoying the company of children or older students, from the satisfaction of helping others to learn and from exercising personal talents and abilities. There are many ways in which these satisfactions can be frustrated but, when the conditions are right, teaching can provide not only a sense of competence but even of wholeness and fulfilment as a person. It seems only sensible that the large investment that our society makes in training teachers should be protected by making sure that subsequently they have the conditions of work in which to thrive and develop. This would be good both for teachers themselves and for the wider society they serve and influence.

16.9 Questions

The following questions are designed to help you check your understanding of the chapter.

1 Explain what pedagogical content knowledge is and why it matters.
2 How does deep subject matter knowledge tend to affect teaching?
3 How do 'everyday' uses of your own specialist subject differ from 'academic' uses?
4 Why might pedagogical content knowledge feature in your Career Entry Development Profile?
5 Why is it suggested that what is learned on a course of initial teacher training may often get 'washed out' by the first few years of teaching?
6 What features of teaching make it difficult to learn in the form of a list of definable skills?
7 Why were 'reference groups' important to Nias's young teachers?
8 Why is the self so engaged and challenged by teaching?
9 Are there good reasons for insisting that all teachers should continue working on their professional development?
10 **Discussion question:** why be a teacher?

NOTES

1. See, for example, Barnes (1982).
2. Shulman (1986).
3. See, for example, Richardson (2001), chapter 19 etc.
4. Ofsted (1997), paragraph 18.
5. In fact, of course, QTS standards require them to have more specialist knowledge than this, but this remains the highest priority in my personal view.
6. Bennett and Turner-Bissett (1993).
7. Shulman and Quinlan (1996).
8. Leinhardt (2001).
9. These different levels of representation in mathematics no doubt give rise to many occasions for possible misunderstandings of the subject. For example, when working with concrete representations, it is easy to confuse the search for mathematical proof with empirical enquiry.
10. Ma (1999).
11. In Ma's original study, for example, she gave the problem $3/4$ divided by $1/2$ to her teachers to solve mentally. Only 9 of the 21 American teachers got this right, whereas all 72 of the Chinese teachers did.
12. Lewis (2002).
13. Shulman (1986).
14. The distinction here is between propositional knowledge, which can be stated explicitly and may be true or false, and skilled practical knowledge, which is implicit in action and articulated with difficulty. A very similar distinction is often made between 'knowing that' (also called declarative knowledge) and 'knowing how' (also called procedural knowledge); see also 5.6.
15. For example Fuller and also Nias, described in Munby, Russell and Martin (2001).
16. Nias (1989).
17. Feiman-Nemser and Remillard (1996), quoted in Munby, Russell and Martin (2001).

18. Munby, Russell and Martin (2001).
19. Richardson and Placier (2001).
20. Schön (1983).
21. Schön (1983), p. 42.
22. Nias (1989), p. 39.
23. Nias (1989), p. 79.

Analysing a Complete Lesson

The following transcript provides a complete lesson to analyse, as a follow-up to Chapter 1. You should try to recognize examples of as many of the generic processes of teaching as you can, including the different kinds of teaching that go on, the teacher's strategies for engaging the motivation of the students and any examples of metacognition and ethos that you can spot. As an exercise in extending and assessing your own understanding, after reading this lesson you should try to write your own brief analysis, in note form, and then compare it with my analysis, which is given on pp. 277–80. To make it easier to refer to the transcript, sections have been numbered.

Example 1.4 The Frog Prince: KS1 English[1]

(1) It is 10.55 a.m. on a cold day in February. In Caroline Lawson's KS1 class there are 27 children this Wednesday morning. Although this is not a large class, she faces the challenge of teaching three different age groups in the same room. Eight are in their Reception year (aged 4.5–5.5), having started in the autumn, and one little boy (aged 4.5) is in his first term at school. Another eight children are in Y1 (aged 5–6) while ten children are in Y2 (aged 6–7). The building is over a century old, but the furnishings of the classroom are modern. Small tables and chairs are grouped around the room and there is a rich variety of books, resources and displays of the children's work on view.

(2) The children come into the room chattering, full of excitement from their playtime. They sit down on a carpeted area in front of their teacher, who is seated. 'Sit down here, Mark,' Caroline says to the smallest boy, indicating a space near her. 'Oliver, move away from Mary, find your own space. Hannah, stop fussing. Everyone's eyes this way! Oliver! Your head is round the wrong way . . .' The children quieten down and wriggle into more or less comfortable positions.

(3) 'Can you show me your fingers?' asks Caroline, quietly. The children hold up their hands and, rather to the observer's amazement, there is immediate and complete silence.

(4) 'We've been looking at poems by . . . who?'

'Shirley Hughes!' say many voices together.

'And we found some of her poems in this . . . what kind of a book is it, do you remember?' The children aren't sure. 'It has a special name, this kind of book, which has poems by several poets collected all together . . .'

A hand shoots up from a Y2 child in the back row, then two more hands.

'Sharon?'

'Anthology.'

'That's right, it's an anthology. Now let's have a look at these two poems . . .'

(5) The two short poems are printed as enlarged texts, on an easel, which can be seen and read by everyone. They start a shared reading of the first poem. Every child in the class, at this point in time, is attending and taking part in the reading. Two minutes have passed and the lesson is under way.

(6) Caroline is a teacher in her forties. She has been teaching the KS1 class in this village school for 6 years. She has been a primary teacher for 20 years. She is smartly dressed in a long skirt and dark green jersey and sits up in her armchair with a straight back. She is a rather undemonstrative teacher, quiet in her manner and showing little emotion. She is calm, unthreatening and yet confident. As the lesson proceeds she is remarkably persistent in a number of ways: she insists that things are done correctly and she consistently expects that children will work hard and answer challenging questions. Not very many 6 year olds know what an 'anthology' is, for example, but several children in this class did. The children, in their turn, show a remarkable confidence, both in their contributions to the lesson and in the way they respond courteously, but without fuss, to the observer, whom they have not met before. They appear committed to their work and enthusiastic; they seem to be good with words.

(7) After the shared reading of the poems the younger (Reception) children move to a table where they put on headphones for a listening task and are supervised by a classroom assistant, a woman in her late twenties with several years' experience at the school.

(8) The older children read another enlarged text all together, part of a story that they have been writing as a group and which Caroline has word-processed and spiral bound. It concerns a frog named Thomas, who lives in a small pond. The language is full of alliteration and the story is full of magic spells, as well as facts about frogs.

(9) A small multicoloured model frog, made of a beanbag, sits on the arm of the teacher's chair. He is wearing a golden crown made of cardboard.

(10) 'I'm going to underline some words.' Caroline underlines the adjectives on the page. 'Some of these words are used to describe other words,' she explains.

(11) 'Like "deep" makes it more describing,' says a boy, without being asked.

'That's right. What other words could have been used to describe the pond?'

(12) 'His crown's fell off!' The frog's crown has been dislodged by the teacher's arm and has fallen on the floor. Several children giggle.

(13) 'Oh yes, right.' She stoops and picks up the crown. 'What other words might we have had to describe the pond?'

(14) The children look back at Caroline and offer 'tiny', 'shallow' and 'big'. Caroline writes them on a whiteboard beside her. It is a little awkward for her to reach the board sideways.

(15) 'My writing's not very neat this morning,' she comments. There is a small, appreciative laugh.

(16) She asks for more describing words and receives 'massive', 'enormous', 'blue'.

(17) 'Now, look how Thomas is described in the story: "shiny", "light-green". How else might we have described him?' There is a pause. Then words begin to come: 'slimy', 'smooth', 'bumpy', 'tough'. Caroline kneels on the floor to reach the board more easily and writes them all down.

(18) 'How about "wrinkly"?' she asks.

(19) After a few more minutes she asks a child to bring her some cards from another table. They have riddles typed on them. Each one ends 'What am I?' The sentences all contain adjectives. Individual children are asked to read them out, one at a time.

(20) One boy, Johnny, gets stuck. 'Help him out, you others,' says Caroline. They do. 'Now you know how it goes,' she says to him, 'can you read it again, in a big voice?' This time Johnny's reading is much more fluent.

(21) 'Now, you can choose someone to guess what it is.' The boy hesitates about his choice.

(22) 'Are you with me?' Caroline asks a boy who is staring into space. He re-orients to the class.

(23) Three riddles are read out, one at a time, and 'guessed'. The answer to each one is an animal and the children guess quite easily, pressing forward, kneeling up, thrusting arms in the air, groaning with their desire to be chosen. Where there is a doubt, Caroline re-reads the card, to make its sense clearer.

(24) The Reception children, meanwhile, have moved on to a new activity, still supervised by the classroom assistant, involving writing sentences.

(25) Caroline introduces a new task, which is especially for the Y1 children. She has 18 adjectives, typed out on individual cards and stuck with Blu-tack to a blackboard.

(26) They read all the words out, together ('squishy', 'gleaming', 'sad', 'glossy', 'crinkly', 'cuddly' . . .).

(27) 'What does "glossy" mean?' she asks, when they reach this word. The children try to explain and she gives examples of the word used in context.

(28) She then produces a teddy bear and asks them which of the words on the board accurately describe him. As each suitable word is agreed upon, a child is asked to go and fetch it from the board, which of course involves picking out the correct word from the others.

(29) 'Last one . . . no, I know you haven't all had a turn, but we'll be here for ever and a day. This'll be the last.'

(30) Next Caroline returns to the beanbag frog. She reminds the children of how the frog is supposed to have started off life in a pond.

(31) She sends individuals off to collect a series of pink cards from surfaces around the room. The children crane their heads to see what is on the cards. Each has a message on it, which they read together.

(32) 'Help! Help! I can't swim!' 'Please help me, I don't like living in this cold pond.' 'Beetles and flies give me indigestion.'

(33) 'Is he really a frog?' Caroline asks them.

'I think he's really a prince,' says Hannah.

'Why is that?' asks Caroline. Hannah supplies a rather long-winded answer, which makes reference to traditional stories and to their own story.

(34) 'Why was he in the pond, Jules, can you remember?' asks Caroline. The memories of different children turn out to vary. The Y2 children are patient as the Y1 children also offer their suggestions.

(35) 'OK, I'll tell you what I want you to do now . . .' Caroline explains the task for the Y2 children, which is to write a 'wanted' poster for a missing prince.

(36) She has an example and starts various posters off with them: 'Wanted! One prince wearing a golden crown.' 'Missing! Have you seen this man?'

(37) She explains how they will have to describe the missing prince carefully. 'It's your choice. I'm not going to write this for you. It's up to you.'

(38) She further explains that the Y1 children are to write a sentence for each of the adjectives describing the teddy bear.

(39) The Y2 children are to work on the 'wanted' posters for the prince. The instructions as to what to do take quite a time, but Caroline persists, working through an example sentence with the Y1 children, for describing the teddy bear, using the adjective 'enormous'.

(40) Finally she says 'Does everyone understand? You're all very fidgety. Do you all understand? Do Year Ones understand?' There is a chorus of 'Yes!' 'Do Year Twos understand?' A further chorus of 'Yes!'

'Does Jules understand?' Jules nods his head. He does.

'Right, off you go.'

(41) The children disperse to different tables. Some start writing immediately. Others chat to one another and examine their books. Caroline circulates around the room, settling them down and interacting with individuals.

(42) 'Right! How are we doing? A gloomy pond; where was the gloomy pond? . . . What letter goes on the end of that? Yes, it does, doesn't it.' Five minutes pass.

(43) 'Who's done two sentences? Come on, Richard, have you chosen another word? . . .

(44) A tall what? What's tall? . . . What do you have at the end? Full stop, well done . . . Johnny that's really, really good.' She reads some of their efforts aloud and comments on them, giving praise quietly but freely.

(45) She moves around the class quite rapidly, visiting each table and also monitoring the work of the Reception children.

(46) After some time she pauses and speaks in a louder voice, reaching across the whole room. 'How are we doing? Have we got more than one sentence? Richard, have you gone to get a second card from the board? Well I think you should, don't you?'

(47) She continues to circulate and to speak to individuals. 'He was lost in 1897? That's a long time ago . . . No, that's all right, he could have been lost in the pond for a long, long time.'

(48) The younger children start to bring their work up to her, for her to read and praise, which she does for a few moments.

(49) Then she checks her watch. 'Right! Who's finished?' She goes and sits in her chair. 'As soon as you get to a point where you can leave your writing, can you come over here, so we can talk about it.'

(50) The children arrive piecemeal and she takes their books and reads out their work. Again she finds something to praise in every one. 'You got that right all on your own, Sally, good girl!'

(51) Some children persist in writing, until finally Caroline says 'Can you leave it as it is, please, and come and join us? Bring your work!' She waits for them all to be ready before proceeding.

(52) 'Now, I've read some really interesting "missing" posters. We haven't got time for many but don't worry, you'll have an opportunity later. Come on then, Nicola, let's hear yours.'

(53) A lively and detailed description of the missing prince is read out, ending 'he was wearing crocodile-skin shoes'. Another includes 'he was lost in 1897'. A third ends 'he had a gun in his pocket. He is . . .'

(54) 'I've got to write "dangerous" next,' explains the writer. Caroline asks them to spell 'dangerous'.

(55) Several more posters are read out. Almost all the children listen eagerly. Caroline is clearly amused by their efforts. She points up the adjectives they have used.

(56) 'Now come on, Year Ones, any of you got some really exciting sentences? You've got nine? You've got three describing words in one sentence? Well, let's just have the best . . .'

(57) She turns to an individual: 'If you were looking this way you could help!'

(58) Sentences are read out. Caroline comments on every one. 'The triceratops is really enormous. Where did you get that spelling from? From the dictionary, I see.'

(59) 'Well, that's all we have time for, now. You two, collect up the books, please, and put them on the table . . .

(60) Some of these posters will be going into our story. I wonder how this prince went missing? You've had a lot of ideas today. So, was it difficult, or easy? Quite easy, was it? Right. I'm pleased that some of you tried hard with your spellings on your own.

(61) Right, sitting up straight, please! If you've got blue tights on . . . go to dinner . . . Shoes done up with Velcro . . . off you go.

(62) Jules you have to listen or you won't get it. No that's not Velcro.'

(63) The children listen keenly, wanting to be chosen. 'Buckles! . . . right, laces!' the last children walk off to their dinner.

(64) It's two minutes past twelve. Caroline collects up the cards and books and chats with her class ancillary.

This lesson took exactly 60 minutes. The shared reading and the word-level work on adjectives, including the frog story, the riddles and the teddy bear, took 29 minutes. The writing activities took 20 minutes and the final 'plenary' sharing of the writing took 11 minutes. The Reception children followed a somewhat different course for the middle 35 minutes of the lesson.

Analysis of Example 1.4

I shall use the numbered sections for reference. This lesson can be divided up into quite a large number of different subepisodes. Overall, however, it follows the prescribed shape of the 'literacy hour' in that (i) whole-class teaching (shared reading and word-level work) is followed by (ii) group teaching (guided reading and writing), then (iii) independent work (writing), and finally (iv) a plenary session (sharing and evaluating written work).

In terms of the *repertoire of teaching*, Caroline uses interactive teaching for most of the lesson. We can also note the occasional use of direct instruction (e.g. 10) and demonstration (14–18). The independent work (writing) counts as independent practice and problem-solving. We can notice examples of prompting (in 4) and prompting and coaching (in 20). In fact (20) offers an example of contingent instruction, or scaffolding, employing other children as the helpers. There is some discussion, following an open question, in (33) and (34).

Metacognition does not feature much, but is touched upon in (37) and (40) and is clear in (60).

Motivation is richly embedded in many aspects of this lesson, including:

- children's love of traditional stories;
- pride in producing their own storybook of the Frog Prince;
- their pleasure in toys such as the model frog and the teddy bear;
- competing and enjoying the game of guessing the riddles;
- the mystery element introduced by the finding of messages apparently from the Frog Prince;
- (possibly) the satisfaction of producing a piece of original writing;
- the celebration of the children's writing in the plenary;
- Caroline's frequent, but discriminating, use of praise;
- the children's general desire to please their teacher.

Ethos can be seen being communicated in many ways, including the following.

- Caroline's use of inclusive language: 'we' and 'our', 'are you with me?' (22), etc.
- The press for hard work and quality work: 'a big voice' (20), 'really interesting' (52), the whole of (46), 'really exciting sentences . . . well let's just have the best' (56), 'you have to listen or you won't get it' (62).
- Caroline's subtle management of order, which combines firmness with reason and humour: 'your head is round the wrong way' (2), 'if you were looking this way you could help' (57), etc.
- The emphasis on helping one another, e.g. 'help him out, you others' (20).
- Sensitive attention shown to individuals, e.g. in (34), (44) and (50).

Teacher's knowledge: Caroline has in-depth knowledge of the English curriculum, of children's literature, and of spelling, punctuation and word classes. She was comfortable doing work on adjectives and is herself highly literate.

Planning of this lesson had been meticulously thought out, in terms of:

- fitting into the school's curriculum plan;
- being designed to appeal to children's interests at this age;

- having clear goals for the children's learning;
- being adapted to the needs of different groups within the class;
- having clear goals for the teacher's various roles in aiding learning;
- including means of monitoring the children's progress (means which in this case included marking the writing afterwards).

Resources: in this lesson a great deal depended on the preparation of word cards, messages and posters. Caroline worked with her classroom assistant and together they made almost all their own teaching materials. She admitted that it took up much time, but felt that it was a worthwhile investment. She had typed and bound the children's frog story so that it already looked an almost professional product. Before enlarged texts ('Big Books') were widely available she had made her own, from simple materials. Her word cards were smartly word-processed and had transparent 'sticky-back' coverings, for durability. Each year group had access to its own card index of home-made core vocabulary cards, with alphabetical dividers, as well as to simple dictionaries. The little model frog, with its special crown, and the teddy bear came from a well-used stock of such props. The riddle cards and messages from the Frog Prince were specially produced for this lesson, but would also be used again.

Seating: Caroline varied the seating arrangements to suit different episodes of the lesson. She made much use of the carpeted area and her armchair for whole-class teaching, which encouraged perceptions of the class as an intimate group, working together. She was meticulous over placing individual children. The older Y2 children sat at the back, so that the younger ones would easily hear their more fluent reading. Several individuals were kept apart, though with no overt criticism.

Some further notes on the teaching

(2) Pre-lesson procedures: coming in and settling down. The children are very used to such routines. Simple routines are great aids to orderly lessons.

(3) Procedural introduction: a commonly used signal ('show me your fingers') is given to which the children immediately respond, out of habit. Repetition has trained them in this routine. It enables teaching to begin rapidly and without fuss.

(7) Younger children are withdrawn to another task and supervisor. Classroom assistants are a highly valued resource at KS1, but their presence also means that the teacher must become an organizer and manager of other adults, a skill in itself.

(38)–(40) Further preparation for independent work: instructing each year group on their next task. Note how Caroline is prepared to spend much time making sure that every child knows exactly what to do in the independent work. This is a 'cost' in terms of time and pacing, but she felt it was worth it.

(41)–(48) Independent work: writing (individual). Caroline chooses to circulate and monitor work (rather than teaching small groups, as recommended in the original 'literacy hour' guidelines). But note that this monitoring includes much detailed instruction, as well as supervision, assessment and evaluation. At (43) and (46) we see Caroline putting some pressure on the children, in terms of the need to produce adequate work. She is conscious of time and not prepared to let individuals drift.

(49)–(51) Procedural instruction: preparation for plenary. Caroline is sensitive here to the need for children to finish their writing.

(52)–(58) Plenary session: sharing and evaluating writing. Here Caroline includes more practice in reading, some evaluation, some more instruction and there are opportunities for informal assessment (e.g. in 58).

(59)–(63) Post-lesson procedures: getting ready for dinner. Caroline varies this routine in order to prompt attention and observation, and to teach vocabulary. Allowing the class to depart in small groups also eases the pressure of their arrival at the toilets and dinner hall.

Overall evaluation

To the observer perhaps the most striking features of this lesson were:

- the very warm and friendly relationships which characterized the interactions between teacher and students;
- the way in which the flow of work was smoothly managed;
- the way in which the children seemed enthusiastic and keen to work, with virtually no exceptions.

It was not surprising to discover that KS1 National Curriculum test results for English are excellent for this school.

NOTE

1. Example 1.4 comes from a lesson observed by the author.

Analysis of Example 2.6: Maximum Box

This analysis refers to the example given at the end of Chapter 2. In this case there is no teacher present. The basic teaching mode is thus independent practice and (group) problem-solving, which has been set up by the teacher. The original text-book problem is about the capacity of a box, which the pupils have to construct. The demand on the learners is pitched at the level of problem-solving. They have to apply existing knowledge and skills to construct the cuboid from card and calculate its capacity. (More accurately, one or more of the group have to do this, which raises the issue that some members of the group could be 'coasting' and not answering any task demand at all. However, all the girls do seem to be attending to the problem.)

Emily, on whom the extract focuses, seems to be confusing the concept of capacity with that of area. She cannot see how the capacity of the box can be greater than the initial area of the card it was made from. Neil Mercer, in his original commentary, remarks on how easy it is for pupils to spend lots of time in school calculating areas, volumes, angles, and so on, on paper, and so never have to consider how these concepts relate to the real world. Faced with a real card container and a practical task, Emily's weakness in distinguishing between area and volume (or in this case capacity) is brought out into the open. In terms of the learning demand on Emily, therefore, a problem-solving task reveals an underlying need for some restructuring.

The four girls have a discussion about Emily's initial objection to their answer. Pupil A draws Emily's attention to 'all this space in the middle'. This is the equivalent of interactive teaching in the form of dialogue, or discussion. Pupil A, and to some extent pupils B and C, try to explain their understanding of the three-dimensional nature of capacity. The quality of the extract comes largely from Emily's determination not to let go of her perception that the proposed answer must be wrong. Possibly, Mercer suggests, had a teacher been present, Emily would not have defended her view so vociferously. She might have kept quiet and hidden her con-fusion. Thus the practical nature of the task, together with the learner-led discussion, was probably instrumental in bringing about some restructuring of her concepts by

Emily. Mercer adds that Emily's sudden realization ('Oh yeah') is quite apparent from the tape recording.

Had a teacher been present, how should he or she have tried to help Emily? Some probing of her understanding and some prompting might have been needed. A clear explanation, or reframing of the incident, would probably be called for. One hopes that a teacher would have articulated the problem (area versus capacity; two versus three dimensions) more clearly than these pupils do. But we should remember that it is the relative difficulty of the concepts, for them, which leads them to speak rather imprecisely. They could all do with some further tuning of the language of maths.

Glossary

accommodation A term used mainly by Jean Piaget to describe the manner in which a learner modifies his or her understanding, or actions, to fit new experiences. If a child tries to imitate an animal, for example, she will accommodate her movements or voice to try to match that of the animal. A baby who tries to crawl up stairs has to accommodate his crawling strategy to fit the demands of the rising treads. See also **assimilation.**

accretion The acquiring of new information in a first meeting with new experiences, words, ideas, skills or values.

advance organizer A brief overview of a lesson, offered to students at the start to help them understand what is to come.

algorithm An effective procedure, or series of instructions, for solving a given type of problem. Named after the Arab mathematician Mohammed ibn-Musa al-Khwarazmi, who pioneered written solutions to arithmetic problems as opposed to solutions using an abacus.

analogies Comparisons made between one thing and another. Analogies, like metaphors and similes, help teachers to link new knowledge to old. They are an important form of representing knowledge, by which teachers can support the learner in accretion and restructuring. For example, a teacher may try to help pupils understand the concept of 'electric current' by comparing it to the flow of water along a pipe. However, as this example should show, analogies can be both helpful and, potentially, misleading. See 7.7.

apprenticeship Originally a formal period of training in a craft, but in education used as a metaphor for the process of learning the way of life within a culture. See 7.6.

assimilation The process of absorbing into a system. Used here to indicate the absorbing of experiences into the categories of existing knowledge, with minimal new learning, or restructuring. Jean Piaget argued that all new experiences involve learners coming to terms with the situation partly by assimilating it to their existing knowledge and partly by accommodating (changing) their knowledge to fit the new situation.

assisted performance The process of learning with the help of a more knowledgeable other.

basic processes of learning Learning is analysed, initially, into three separate processes: accretion, restructuring and tuning. These can and do occur together, but tend to change in their dominance at different stages of the cycle of learning. To these we also added **strategic application** and **revision**. (Other ways of describing the processes of learning are elaborated in Chapters 6, 7 and 8.)

bridging The process whereby a teacher makes links between new ideas and familiar ones, for example by using **analogies** with familiar objects or events, or by suggesting how school knowledge might be applied to other school subjects or to problems or situations out of school.

circle time An organizational format in which personal, social and moral education is carried out with students sitting in a circle, usually involving interactive games and discussion.

closed question A question with a single correct response. (What is the capital of Hungary? How many degrees are there in a complete rotation? What is the difference between a metaphor and a simile?)

coaching A subvariety of interactive teaching, in which the teacher provides verbal feedback or instruction to aid the learner.

concept, conceptual learning Refers to ideas and their learning. More technically, a concept is a class (e.g. animal), containing elements (e.g. aardvark, ant, antelope, etc.) that share one or more similarities (being living organisms capable of sensation and voluntary movement). Concepts are frequently, but not always, words (verbal concepts). To 'have a concept' or to 'grasp a concept' implies the existence of an abstract or symbolic representation in the mind. Concepts are abstractions from perception and experience, from which they derive their content. In the framework of this book, concepts can be acquired, elaborated, restructured, extended and applied during learning.

constructivism A view of learning, based on the metaphor of constructing knowledge. It originated with Piaget and has been extended by the work of Vygotsky and others. Its main insight, perhaps, is that learners cannot simply be 'given' information or new ideas, but must do active mental work in order to understand them.

contingent instruction The process of matching the level of instruction to the level of dependence or independence of the learner. Our principle of contingent instruction states that when a learner gets into difficulty with a task, immediately offer more help; when a learner succeeds at a task, with a given level of help, reduce the level of help next time around. This is clearly an easier thing to do with one pupil than with several together.

correlation A statistical measure of how closely two variables co-relate, or vary together. If two variables are completely independent of one another (i.e. are unrelated), then their correlation coefficient will be zero. If they are related then they will correlate. If they are perfectly correlated, so that knowing the value of one would enable you to predict exactly the value of the other, then their correlation coefficient will be either +1 (as one variable increases in value, so does the other) or −1 (as one variable increases in value the other decreases). In the social sciences, correlation coefficients of around ± 0.1–0.3 are generally regarded as 'weak', coefficients of about 0.4–0.7 as 'medium' and coefficients of 0.8 and above as 'strong'. The fact that two variables are strongly correlated does not necessarily mean that one caused the other; correlation does not imply causation.

craft knowledge The knowledge that all experienced teachers acquire intuitively from their own trial and error experience or from observing, or talking to, other teachers. It is very valuable indeed, but stays at a practical, pragmatic level of 'what seems to work'. In particular, it is usually justified by appeals to general experience rather than references to systematic research.

criterion-referenced assessment   Assessing performance in relation to a standard or criterion. See 15.5.

declarative knowledge   Knowledge that can be consciously expressed in terms of a proposition, as opposed to **procedural knowledge**, which is implicit and embodied in a practice or skill. Sometimes referred to as 'knowing that' as opposed to 'knowing how'. Thus I may know *that* Beethoven wrote string quartets, whereas I know *how* to tie a bowline knot (but could not easily describe how).

deliberate practice   In Part I, this has been used to refer to conscious deliberate practice in becoming a teacher. As such, it is seen as essential to becoming a competent professional. It is further elaborated as a general concept in Chapter 8.

demonstration   A means of teaching that involves demonstrating or showing pupils how something should be done. It is sometimes also referred to as 'modelling'.

dialogue   A subvariety of teaching in which the teacher enters into discussion with one or more pupils, so that the pupils are given some control over the topic, over who speaks and over who asks questions or evaluates contributions. (More accurately, therefore, it should perhaps be called a 'multilogue'). When participants are genuinely equal partners in such a discussion we can call it a conversation.

differentiation   A term used in education to refer to the varying of teaching to meet the different needs of individuals. See 5.5.

direct instruction   Teaching via talk that directly introduces pupils to new topics, problems, ideas or skills. It usually involves some combination of informing, describing and explaining.

educational research   Systematic published research bearing on life in classrooms.

eliciting   This is one of the common, or generic, processes of teaching, in which the teacher attempts to get pupils to demonstrate their knowledge or simply to participate in a lesson.

engagement   A process whereby the attention of learners is attracted and maintained. Without attention, learning will not occur. Engagement is thus often the first task a teacher needs to address.

entity theories   These are personally held implicit or explicit beliefs and theories about such matters as intelligence and personality (or temperament) that see such traits as innate and fixed. Inflexible entity theories can lead to an over-emphasis on performance goals and maladaptive responses to failure or difficulty. See also **incremental theories**.

episodic memory   Tulving, a psychologist, has suggested that our memories can be divided into two sorts, in terms of their contents. Episodic memory is personal, having a content referring to a specific experience in place and time (e.g. what you had for breakfast). This is opposed to **semantic memory**, which contains information about our stock of organized knowledge (e.g. what a square root is).

ethos   Any way in which the participants in schooling communicate their values and attitudes to one another. It is particularly important in the relationships formed between teachers and their pupils and also in pupils' moral education.

experiential intelligence   A term introduced by David Perkins to describe the knowledge and skill underlying the ability to solve problems. See 12.5.

extrinsic reward   A reward that is added on, from the outside, rather than being inherent in the nature of an activity or task. Extrinsic rewards (such as sweets, pats on the back or prizes) are contrasted with **intrinsic rewards**, such as the satisfaction of getting a problem correct or enjoying a book, which are internal to the activity in question.

facilitating learning A rather facile phrase which nevertheless is useful for describing in a very general way what the central task of teachers is, namely to aid learning.

fallacy of experience The mistake of assuming that because a learner has some kind of experience then new learning will inevitably take place. If the learner merely adapts to the experience by applying existing knowledge, then learning will not occur, at least not beyond the level of tuning.

formative assessment Assessment that shapes or informs the process of learning. Generally contrasted with **summative assessment** that attempts to sum up learning after it has occurred. See 15.2.

generic processes of teaching This refers to common kinds of teaching, such as **direct instruction, interactive teaching** and **independent problem-solving**, which apply across different age ranges of pupil and different school subjects. The term can also be used to refer to the many common 'moves' made by teachers, such as **eliciting**, initiating, questioning, **recapping**, etc.

guided participation The process of learning by taking part in an activity under the guidance of a more knowledgeable person. See 7.6.

habituation The process whereby humans (and other animals) adapt to repeated stimulation, or experience, by reducing the intensity of their response. (The reverse process is dishabituation.)

heuristic Literally, serving to discover. It originally meant finding out by trial and error, where no algorithm (effective procedure) was known. It is sometimes used to refer to some strategy or rule that provides the initial step in solving a problem.

implicit learning Learning that occurs without the learner being able to verbalize what has been learned explicitly.

incremental task One that requires the learner to acquire new knowledge, via accretion.

incremental theories Personally held implicit or explicit beliefs and theories about such matters as intelligence and personality (or temperament) that see such traits as malleable, or changeable, as a result of experience and learning. They are associated with mastery goals and with resilience in the face of failure.

independent problem-solving One of the basic varieties of teaching, in which the learner, or learners, are set to solve problems on their own, without constant support from the teacher. The teacher is still often actively involved in organizing opportunities to learn, supervising and monitoring progress, responding to requests for consultation and evaluating outcomes.

individual education plan (IEP) A plan setting out learning targets and related specifications for resources and teaching, generally for a student with special educational needs. See 13.4 and 15.1.

interactive teaching One of the main varieties of teaching in which the teacher engages one or more pupils in interaction. It allows a wide variety of teacher 'moves' to be made, e.g. confirming, reminding, checking, prompting, correcting, encouraging, elaborating, reframing. Subvarieties of interactive teaching include prompting, coaching and dialogue.

intrinsic reward See extrinsic reward.

ipsative assessment Assessment that compares a student's progress with his or her own past progress. See 15.5.

IRE (initiation–response–evaluation) pattern A common pattern of interaction in classrooms around the world. The teacher initiates interaction by asking a question (e.g. 'How many sides has a rhombus?'), the pupil, or pupils, offer a response (e.g. 'four') and

the teacher evaluates the response (e.g. 'right'). Remember that different questions, and indeed evaluations, can make radically different levels of demand on the learner.

law of effect A generalization at the heart of behaviourist learning theories, which states that actions or responses resulting in pleasurable consequences are likely to be repeated and learned. See 9.3.

learned helplessness A learned response to failure or difficulty that includes feelings of loss of worth, of inadequacy and of inability to overcome problems. See also **performance goals** and **entity theories**.

mastery goals (or orientation) An orientation towards learning that sees the goal of learning as improved competence and knowledge, attained largely through effort. Such learners are relatively unimpressed by grades, marks and comparisons with others. They are focused on greater mastery through learning. See also **performance goals**.

maturation The process of (genetically controlled) growth and development of the body and the brain, dependent only on normal healthy conditions of life. It is often contrasted with learning, which results from specific experiences with, or in, the environment.

mediation The process whereby one person acts as an intermediary for another. In education, it has come to refer to the role of parents, teachers or others who act as guides for children to a culture and its constituent knowledge.

metacognition Simply stated, this is 'thinking about thinking'. More generally it refers to the vital area of a person's awareness and self-regulation of thinking, remembering, learning and problem-solving. Its development is vital if learners are to become truly independent.

monitoring The processes of watching, listening or checking up on pupils' work and progress. Note that it can be a relatively passive matter of making sure that pupils are engaged in their work or a more active process of interacting with them to teach them, or to evaluate their learning.

motivation A psychological term that refers to the causes of, or reasons for, actions. It is elaborated in Chapters 9 and 10.

norm-referenced assessment A form of assessment that compares one student's performance with that of others in a general population. A norm is what is typical. See also 15.5.

open question A question that has no single correct response. (What do you usually do after school? What sort of character is Mr Micawber? What colours should we use to paint the sky?)

overlearning The process of learning something beyond the point where it can be perfectly recalled. Overlearning may lead to the further automatization of skills, algorithms, etc. and may prevent forgetting. See 8.4.

pace Refers to different aspects of the speed with which various things occur in a lesson, for example speed of questions and answers; frequency of introduction of new ideas, problems or challenges to the learner; time allowed to complete a task.

pedagogical content knowledge The knowledge, generally centred on tasks and activities, that teachers have relating how to teach a particular subject to particular classes of students. See 16.2.

performance goals An orientation towards learning that sees the goal of learning chiefly as obtaining good grades, marks or qualifications, without much regard to underlying competence or usable knowledge. Such an orientation can lead the learner to anxiety about failure and to a surface approach to learning.

plenary Meeting of teacher with all members of a class, generally at the end of a lesson, in which discussion, evaluation and further teaching may occur. It forms a part of the standard format of lessons in both the literacy and numeracy strategies.

practice task One that requires the learner to apply well-learned knowledge or skills to routine problems so as to produce tuning in speed, accuracy and economy of effort.

predictable breakdown in learning Part of the logic of the classroom situation, namely if a teacher fails to make certain demands on learners, then associated processes of learning are most unlikely to occur.

problem-solving task One that requires the learner to apply existing knowledge in an insightful and appropriate way to new problems. Note that the degree of difficulty and novelty of the problems can vary greatly.

procedural knowledge See **declarative knowledge**.

prompting The process of helping a learner by supplying some part of the answer or completing some part of the task on the learner's behalf. Prompts can be verbal or physical.

P scales Steps of curriculum learning, published by QCA, which precede level 1 of the National Curriculum. See 13.4.

Qualified Teacher Status (QTS) The general qualification required in order to find employment as a teacher in a British state school. Programmes of study approved by the Teacher Training Agency lead to QTS, as set out in the QTS Standards (see TTA website).

recap A common term used to describe the summary of a lesson, or part of a lesson.

reframing Teachers often describe a series of shared events or ideas by re-interpreting them, or reframing them, to the pupils so as to bring out their educational potential. The teacher may select what is most relevant, highlight important concepts or problems, or make use of appropriate technical vocabulary.

reinforcer A stimulus or event that follows a response, as a consequence, and makes the response more likely to occur. Often used to refer to rewards or punishments, the terms 'reinforcer' and 'reinforcement' originated in behaviourist learning theories.

repertoire of teaching The range of types of teaching at which all professional teachers should be competent. In this book they are referred to under the headings direct instruction, interactive teaching and independent practice (see 1.5).

representation Teachers use words, images and sometimes patterns of sound or movement to represent knowledge to their pupils. Choosing apt representations, including good examples, analogies, stories and images, is a key process in planning and teaching. Good representations help to **bridge** knowledge across contexts and aid **restructuring**. Pupils also need to be able to move between different representations of the same concepts.

representational redescription A term used to describe the process whereby we become consciously aware of items of knowledge, or mental representations, which have previously been only grasped intuitively. See 6.6.

responsibility for learning The general proposition that when teachers teach pupils, successful learning is always a joint responsibility. This means that both teacher and learner have to play their part if learning is to succeed. One implication of this is to make the matter of accountability for learning problematic.

restructuring The process of transforming, or reorganizing, our knowledge so as to invent, construct or understand new ways of knowing and solving problems.

restructuring task One that demands that the learner reorganizes knowledge or restructures it, in applying new facts, concepts or skills to essentially familiar problems.

revision task   One that requires the learner to recall knowledge learned some time in the past and apply it to familiar problems. This should contribute to tuning and to the stability of learning.

scaffolding   A term much used to describe the process of supporting the learner in interactive teaching, by doing that part of the task that the pupil cannot yet manage for him or herself. It has also been called 'assisted performance'. Jerome Bruner uses the term in a rather more specialized sense, in which scaffolding refers to the steps taken to *reduce the degrees of freedom* in carrying out some task so that the child can concentrate better on the difficult skill she is in the process of acquiring.

schema (of learning)   Used in this book to refer to any organized unit of perception, knowledge or information represented in the mind. The similar terms 'scheme' or 'schemata' are sometimes used with the same, or related, meanings. See 2.2.

scheme of work   A term used conventionally to describe a series of lessons, or episodes of teaching, that are thematically linked, typically spanning half a term or a term.

self-theories   Describe systems of belief about the self, which can have significant motivational power and may be linked to self-relevant goals and feelings of self-worth. See 10.1.

semantic memory   See episodic memory.

strategic application   The process of selecting appropriate knowledge from one's existing repertoire and using it to solve new and unfamiliar problems.

summative assessment   Assessment that attempts to summarize, or sum up, the learning achieved in a lesson, module or course. See 15.5.

task demands   Teachers typically set their pupils tasks to perform, involving different sorts of problems to solve. Such tasks vary greatly in the demands they make on the learner. The demands have been associated in Chapter 2 with basic learning processes.

time out   A mild form of punishment consisting of removing a person to a place where there is little to experience. It is an abbreviation of 'time out from reinforcement'. See 4.6.

transfer   In an educational context, this refers to the extent to which learning can be 'transferred' or generalized across different problems and contexts.

tuning   The process of gaining in fluency and accuracy in using some form of knowledge through practice. It includes the swift and accurate recall of facts, the smooth application of appropriate concepts and the successful enactment of controlled sequences of skilled movements.

value added   In the context of schooling this generally refers to the attempt to assess how much learning has occurred in a given lesson, class or school, over and above what a student had on entering that context.

zone of proximal development   A term originating with Vygotsky, who used it to refer to a range of performance, at any task, that is within a student's grasp if he or she is appropriately helped or supported. It thus lies between the level at which the student can perform independently and the level at which the student fails even with help. It is thus an ideal level at which to aim teaching.

References

Adey, P. and Shayer, M. (1994) *Really Raising Standards*. London: Routledge.

Adey, P., Robertson, A. and Venville, G. (2002) Effects of a cognitive acceleration programme on Year 1 pupils. *British Journal of Psychology*, 72, 1–25.

Ainsworth, M. (2000) Infant–mother attachment. In: W. Craig (ed.), *Childhood Social Development: The Essential Readings*, chapter 1. Oxford: Blackwell.

Alexander, R. (2000) *Culture and Pedagogy*. Oxford: Blackwell.

Astington, J. and Olson, D. (1990) Metacognitive and metalinguistic language. *Applied Psychology: An International Review*, 39, 77–87.

Barnes, D. (1982) *Practical Curriculum Study*. London: Taylor & Francis.

Baron-Cohen, S. (1995) *Mindblindness: An Essay on Autism and Theory of Mind*. Cambridge, MA: MIT Press.

Barrett, L., Dunbar, R. and Lycett, J. (2002) *Human Evolutionary Psychology*. Basingstoke: Palgrave.

Bayliss, P. (1995) Teaching for diversity. In: C. Desforges (ed.), *An Introduction to Teaching*, chapter 12. Oxford: Blackwell.

Bee, H. (1989) *The Developing Child*, 5th edn. New York: Harper and Row.

Bennett, N. and Carre, C. (eds) (1993) *Learning to Teach*. London: Routledge.

Bennett, N. and Turner-Bissett, R. (1993) Knowledge bases and teaching performance. In: N. Bennett and C. Carre (eds), *Learning to Teach*, pp. 149–64. London: Routledge.

Bennett, N., Desforges, C., Cockburn, A. and Wilkinson, B. (1984) *The Quality of Student Learning Experiences*. Hillsdale, NJ: Lawrence Erlbaum Associates.

Berliner, D.C. and Calfee, R.C. (eds) (1996) *Handbook of Educational Psychology*. New York: Macmillan.

Berry, D. and Broadbent, D. (1984) On the relationship between task performance and associated verbal knowledge. *Quarterly Journal of Experimental Psychology*, 36A, 209–31.

Black, P. and Wiliam, D. (1998) Assessment and classroom learning. *Assessment in Education*, 5, 1.

Bouchard, T. (1999) Genes, environment and personality. In: S. Ceci and W. Williams (eds), *The Nature–Nurture Debate*, chapter 7. Oxford: Blackwell.

Bouchard, T.J., Lykken, D.T., McGue, M., Segal, N.L. and Tellegen, A. (1990) Sources of human psychological differences: the Minnesota study of twins reared apart. *Science*, 250, 223–38.

Brophy, J. (1983) Research on the self-fulfilling prophecy and teacher expectations. *Journal of Educational Psychology*, 75, 631–61.

Brown, A. and Campione, J. (1998) Designing a community of young learners: theoretical and practical lessons. In: N. Lambert and B. McCombs (eds), *How Students Learn*, chapter 7. Washington, DC: American Psychological Association.

Brown, A.L. and Reeve, R.A. (1987) Bandwidths of competence. In: L. Liben (ed.), *Development and Learning: Conflict or Congruence?*, pp. 173–223. Hillsdale, NJ: Lawrence Erlbaum Associates.

Brown, A., Kane, M. and Echols, C. (1986) Young children's mental models determine analogical transfer across problems with a common goal structure. *Cognitive Development*, 1, 103–21.

Brown, D. (1991) *Human Universals*. New York: McGraw-Hill.

Brown, R. and Herrnstein, R.J. (1975) *Psychology*. London: Methuen.

Bruner, J.S. (1969) On voluntary action and its hierarchical structure. In: A. Koestler and J.R. Smythies (eds), *Beyond Reductionism*, pp. 161–79. London: Hutchinson.

Bryson, B. (2003) *A Short History of Nearly Everything*, chapter 29. London: Doubleday.

Burton, L. (1984) *Thinking Things Through*. Oxford: Blackwell.

Carey, S. and Spelke, E. (1994) Domain-specific knowledge and conceptual change. In: L.A. Hirschfeld and S.A. Gelman (eds), *Mapping the Mind: Domain Specificity in Cognition and Culture*, chapter 7. Cambridge: Cambridge University Press.

Ceci, S. and Williams, W. (eds) (1999) *The Nature–Nurture Debate*. Oxford: Blackwell.

Chen, Z., Sanchez, R. and Campbell, T. (1997) From beyond to within their grasp: the rudiments of analogical problem solving in 10- and 13-month-old infants. *Developmental Psychology*, 33, 790–801.

Clarke, S. (1998) *Targeting Assessment in the Primary Classroom*. London: Hodder & Stoughton.

Claxton, G. (1997) *Hare Brain, Tortoise Mind*. London: Fourth Estate.

Claxton, G. (2002) *Building Learning Power*. Bristol: TLO.

Claxton, G. (in press) Learning is learnable (and we ought to teach it). In: Sir John Cassell (ed.), *Ten Years On*. National Commission on Education Report.

Clough, N. and Holden, C. (2002) *Education for Citizenship: Ideas into Action*. London: Routledge Falmer.

Cockburn, A. (1995) Learning in classrooms. In: C. Desforges (ed.), *An Introduction to Teaching*, chapter 4. Oxford: Blackwell.

Cooper, P., Drummond, M.-J., Lovey, J. and McLaughlin, C. (2000) *Positive Alternatives to Exclusion*. London: Routledge Falmer.

Craig, W. (ed.) (2000) *Childhood Social Development: The Essential Readings*. Oxford: Blackwell.

Deary, I. (2001) *Intelligence: A Very Short Introduction*. Oxford: Oxford University Press.

DeCaspar, A. and Fifer, W. (1980) Of human bonding: new-borns prefer their mothers' voices. *Science*, 208, 1174–6.

Delamont, S. (1990) *Sex Roles and the School*, 2nd edn. London: Routledge.

DeLoache, D., Sugarman, S. and Brown, A. (1985) The development of error correction strategies in young children's play. *Child Development*, 56, 928–39.

Desforges, C. (1993) Children's learning: has it improved? *Education 3–13*, 1–8.

Desforges, C. (ed.) (1995a) *An Introduction to Teaching*. Oxford: Blackwell.

Desforges, C. (1995b) Learning out of school. In: C. Desforges (ed.), *An Introduction to Teaching*, chapter 5. Oxford: Blackwell.

Desforges, C. and Fox, R. (eds) (2002) *Teaching and Learning: The Essential Readings*. Oxford: Blackwell.

DfES (2000, revised edition 2002) *Don't Suffer in Silence.* London: HMSO. Available at www.dfes.gov.uk

DfES (2001) SEN Code of Practice. London: HMSO. Available at www.dfes.gov.uk/sen

DfES (2003) *Excellence and Enjoyment,* p. 1. London: HMSO. Available at www.dfes.gov.uk

Dockrell, B. (1995) Approaches to educational assessment. In: C. Desforges (ed.), *An Introduction to Teaching,* chapter 17. Oxford: Blackwell.

Donaldson, M. (1992) *Human Minds.* London: Penguin Books.

Donaldson, M. (1996) Education and the scope of the mind. In: D.R. Olsen and N. Torrance (eds), *The Handbook of Education and Human Development,* p. 337. Oxford: Blackwell.

Doyle, W. (1986) Classroom organisation and management. In: M.C. Wittrock (ed.), *Handbook of Research on Teaching,* 3rd edn, pp. 392–431. New York: Macmillan.

Drage, C. (ed.) (2002–3) *Primary ICT Handbook Series.* Cheltenham: Nelson Thornes.

Dunbar, R. (1996) *Grooming Gossip and the Evolution of Language.* London: Faber & Faber.

Dweck, C. (1975) The role of expectations and attributions in the alleviation of learned helplessness. *Journal of Personality and Social Psychology,* 31, 674–85.

Dweck, C. (2000) *Self-theories: Their Role in Motivation, Personality and Development.* Philadelphia: Psychology Press.

Edwards, D. and Mercer, N. (1987) *Common Knowledge: The Development of Understanding in the Classroom.* London: Methuen.

Egan, K. (1990) *Romantic Understanding: The Development of Rationality and Imagination, Ages 8–15.* New York and London: Routledge Books.

Egan, K. (1997) *The Educated Mind.* Chicago: University of Chicago Press.

Entwistle, N. (1981) *Styles of Teaching and Learning.* Chichester: John Wiley & Sons.

Ericsson, K.A. (2002) Attaining excellence through deliberate practice. In: C. Desforges and R. Fox (eds), *Teaching and Learning: The Essential Readings,* pp. 4–37. London: Blackwell.

Eysenck, M. and Keane, M. (1995) *Cognitive Psychology: A Student's Handbook,* 3rd edn. Hove: Psychology Press.

Feldman, D.H. (1980) *Beyond Universals in Cognitive Development.* Norwood, NJ: Ablex.

Flavell, J.H. (1985) *Cognitive Development,* 2nd edn, p. 16. London: Prentice Hall International.

Florian, L. and Rouse, M. (2001) Inclusive practice in English secondary schools: lessons learned. *Cambridge Journal of Education,* 31(3), 399–412.

Floyd, A. (ed.) (1979) *Cognitive Development in the School Years.* London: Croom Helm.

Galton, M., Simon, B. and Croll, P. (1980) *Inside the Primary Classroom.* London: Routledge.

Gardner, H. (1993) *Frames of Mind: Multiple Intelligences.* New York: Basic Books.

Geary, D. (1998) *Male and Female: The Evolution of Human Sex Differences.* Washington, DC: American Psychological Association.

Good, T. and Brophy, J. (1991) *Looking in Classrooms,* 5th edn. New York: Harper Collins.

Gopnik, A. and Welman, H. (1994) The theory theory. In: L. Hirschfeld and S. Gelman (eds), *Mapping the Mind: Domain Specificity in Cognition and Culture,* chapter 10. Cambridge: Cambridge University Press.

Goswami, U. (1998) *Cognition in Children.* Hove: Psychology Press.

Gottfredson, L. (1988) Reconsidering fairness: a matter of social and ethical priorities. *Journal of Vocational Behaviour,* 29, 379–410.

Graves, D. (1983) *Writing: Teachers and Children at Work.* London: Heinemann Educational Books.

Harlow, H., Harlow, M. and Mayer, D. (1950) Learning motivated by a manipulation drive. *Journal of Experimental Psychology,* 40, 228–34.

Harris, J.R. (1998) *The Nurture Assumption: Why Children Turn Out the Way They Do.* London: Bloomsbury.

Harris, J.R. (1999) How to succeed in childhood. In: S. Ceci and W. Williams (eds), *The Nature–Nurture Debate*, chapter 6. Oxford: Blackwell.

Hausman, P. (1999) *On the Rarity of Mathematically Gifted Females.* Santa Barbara, CA: Fielding Institute.

Hirschfeld, L. and Gelman, S. (eds) (1994) *Mapping the Mind: Domain Specificity in Cognition and Culture.* Cambridge: Cambridge University Press.

Hoban, R. (1975) *Turtle Diary.* London: Jonathan Cape.

Holt, J. (1984) *How Children Fail.* Harmondsworth: Penguin.

Hughes, M. (1986) *Children and Number.* Oxford: Blackwell.

Hull, R. (1985) *The Language Gap.* London: Methuen.

Jackson, P. (1968) *Life in Classrooms.* New York: Holt, Rinehart and Winston.

Jussim, L. and Eccles, J. (1995) Are teacher expectations biased by students' gender, social class or ethnicity? In: Y.T. Lee, L.J. Jussim and C.R. McCauley (eds), *Stereotype Accuracy: Towards Appreciating Group Differences.* Washington, DC: American Psychological Association.

Karmiloff-Smith, A. (1992) *Beyond Modularity: A Developmental Perspective on Cognitive Science.* Cambridge, MA: MIT Press.

Kennewell, S., Parkinson, J. and Tanner, H. (2002) *Learning to Teach ICT in the Secondary School.* London: Routledge Falmer.

Kerry, T. and Sands, M. (1984) Classroom organization and learning. In: E.C. Wragg (ed.), *Classroom Teaching Skills*, pp. 149–79. London: Routledge.

Koestler, A. and Smythies, J. (eds) (1969) *Beyond Reductionism.* London: Hutchinson.

Konner, M. (1982) *The Tangled Wing.* London: Penguin Books.

Kounin, J.S. (1970) *Discipline and Group Management in Classrooms.* New York: Holt, Rinehart and Winston.

Kyriacou, C. (1995) Direct teaching. In: C. Desforges (ed.), *An Introduction to Teaching*, chapter 6. Oxford: Blackwell.

Lee, K. (ed.) (2000) *Childhood Cognitive Development: The Essential Readings.* Oxford: Blackwell.

Lee, K. and Homer, B. (1999) Children as folk psychologists: the development of understanding of the mind. In: A. Slater and D. Muir (eds), *The Blackwell Reader in Developmental Psychology*, pp. 228–52. Oxford: Blackwell.

Lee, R. and De Vore, I. (eds) (1976) *Kalahari Hunter Gatherers.* Cambridge, MA: Harvard University Press.

Lee, Y.T., Jussim, L.J. and McCauley, C.R. (eds) (1995) *Stereotype Accuracy: Towards Appreciating Group Differences.* Washington, DC: American Psychological Association.

Le Fevre, D., Moore, D. and Wilkinson, A. (2003) Tape-assisted reciprocal teaching: cognitive bootstrapping for poor decoders. *British Journal of Educational Psychology*, 73, 37–58.

Leinhardt, G. (2001) Instructional explanations: a commonplace for teaching and location of contrast. In: V. Richardson (ed.), *Handbook of Research on Teaching*, 4th edn, chapter 19. Washington, DC: American Educational Research Association.

Levi, P. (1991) The irritable chess players. In: *Other People's Trades*, p. 133. Translation by Raymond Rosenthal. London: Abacus Books.

Lewis, C. (2002) *Lesson Study: A Handbook of Teacher-led Instructional Change.* Research for Better Schools. Available at www.rbs.org/

Liben, L. (ed.) (1987) *Development and Learning: Conflict or Congruence?* Hillsdale, NJ: Lawrence Erlbaum Associates.

Loehlin, J. (1992) *Genes and Environment in Personality Development*. Newbury Park, CA: Sage.

Ma, L. (1999) *Knowing and Teaching Elementary Mathematics: Teachers' Understanding of Fundamental Mathematics in China and the US*. Hillsdale, NJ: Lawrence Erlbaum Associates.

McCallum, B. (2000) *Formative Assessment: Implications for Classroom Practice*. London: Institute of Education. Available at www.qca.org.uk

Meltzoff, A. (2000) Understanding the intentions of others: re-enactment of intended acts by 18-month-old children. In: K. Lee (ed.), *Childhood Cognitive Development: The Essential Readings*, pp. 151–74. Oxford: Blackwell.

Mercer, N. (1995) *The Guided Construction of Knowledge*. Clevedon: Multilingual Matters.

Munby, H., Russell, T. and Martin, A.K. (2001) Teachers' knowledge and how it develops. In: V. Richardson (ed.), *Handbook of Research on Teaching*, 4th edn, pp. 877–904. Washington, DC: American Educational Research Association.

Nagy, W.E., Herman, P.A. and Anderson, R.C. (1985) Learning words from context. *Reading Research Quarterly*, 20(2), 233–53.

National Literacy Strategy (2000) *Supporting Students Learning English as an Additional Language*, revised edition. London: Department for Education and Employment.

Nias, J. (1989) *Primary Teachers Talking*. London: Routledge.

Nickerson, R., Perkins, D. and Smith, E. (1985) *The Teaching of Thinking*. Hillsdale, NJ: Lawrence Erlbaum.

O'Connor, T. (1983) Classroom humour. Unpublished B.Phil. thesis, University of Newcastle.

Ofsted (1997) *Using Subject Specialists to Promote High Standards of Teaching: An Illustrative Survey*. London: Ofsted Publications Centre. Available at www.ofsted.gov.uk/publications

Ofsted (2001) *Standards and Quality in Education*. London: Ofsted Publications Centre. Available at www.ofsted.gov.uk/publications

Ofsted (2002a) *Achievement of Black Caribbean Pupils: Good Practice in Secondary Schools*. HMI 448. London: Ofsted Publications Centre. Available at www.ofsted.gov.uk/publications

Ofsted (2002b) *Achievement of Black Caribbean Students: Three Successful Primary Schools*. HMI 447. London: Ofsted Publications Centre. Available at www.ofsted.gov.uk/publications

Ofsted (2003a) *Special Educational Needs in the Mainstream*. HMI 511. London: Ofsted Publications Centre. Available at www.ofsted.gov.uk/publications

Ofsted (2003b) *Bullying: Effective Action in Secondary Schools*. HMI 465. London: Ofsted Publications Centre. Available at www.ofsted.gov.uk/publications

Ofsted (2003c) *Good Assessment in Secondary School*. HMI 462. London: Ofsted Publications Centre. Available at www.ofsted.gov.uk/publications

Olsen, D. and Torrance, N. (eds) (1996) *The Handbook of Education and Human Development*. Oxford: Blackwell.

Palincsar, A. and Brown, A. (1984) Reciprocal teaching of comprehension-fostering and comprehension-monitoring activities. *Cognition and Instruction*, 1(2), 117–75.

Perkins, D. (1995) *Outsmarting IQ: The Emerging Science of Learnable Intelligence*. New York: The Free Press.

Peters, R.S. (1966) *Ethics and Education*. London: Allen and Unwin.

Petitto, L. and Marentette, P. (1999) Babbling in the manual mode: evidence for the ontogeny of language. In: A. Slater and D. Muir (eds), *The Blackwell Reader in Developmental Psychology*, pp. 267–75. Oxford: Blackwell.

Piaget, J. (1932, 1965) *The Moral Judgment of the Child*. New York: The Free Press.

Pinker, S. (1997) *How the Mind Works*. London: Penguin.

Pinker, S. (2002) *The Blank Slate*. London: Penguin.

Pollard, A. (1985) *The Social World of the Primary School*, 2nd edn. London: Cassell.

Pollard, A. and Filer, A. (1996) *The Social World of Children's Learning*. London: Cassell.

Resnick, L.B. (1994) Situated rationalism: biological and social preparation for learning. In: L. Hirschfeld and S. Gelman (eds), *Mapping the Mind: Domain Specificity in Cognition and Culture*, chapter 19. Cambridge: Cambridge University Press.

Richardson, V. (ed.) (2001) *Handbook of Research on Teaching*, 4th edn. Washington, DC: American Educational Research Association.

Richardson, V. and Placier, P. (2001) Teacher change. In: V. Richardson (ed.), *Handbook of Research on Teaching*, 4th edn, pp. 905–47. Washington, DC: American Educational Research Association.

Robertson, J. (1981) *Effective Classroom Control*. London: Hodder & Stoughton.

Rogers, B. (1991) *You Know the Fair Rule*. Harlow: Longman.

Rogers, B. (2000) *Cracking the Hard Class*. London: Paul Chapman.

Rogers, C. (2002) Teacher expectations: implications for school improvement. In: C. Desforges and R. Fox (eds), *Teaching and Learning: The Essential Readings*, pp. 152–70. Oxford: Blackwell.

Rowland, S. (1984) *The Enquiring Classroom*. London: Falmer.

Ruddock, J., Chaplain, R. and Wallace, G. (1995) *School Improvement: What Can Students Tell Us?* London: David Fulton.

Rumelhart, D. and Norman, D. (1981) Analogical processes in learning. In: J. Anderson (ed.), *Cognitive Skills and Their Acquisition*, pp. 335–59. Hillsdale, NJ: Lawrence Erlbaum Associates.

Salomon, G. and Perkins, D. (1989) Rocky roads to transfer: rethinking mechanisms of a neglected phenomenon. *Educational Psychologist*, 24, 113–42.

Saxe, G. (2002) Candy selling and maths learning. In: C. Desforges and R. Fox (eds), *Teaching and Learning: The Essential Readings*, chapter 4. Oxford: Blackwell.

Schön, D. (1983) *The Reflective Practitioner*. New York: Basic Books.

Schulman, M. (1991) *The Passionate Mind*. New York: Macmillan.

Searle, J.R. (1992) *The Rediscovery of the Mind*. Cambridge, MA: MIT Press.

Sharp, J., Potter, J., Allen, J. and Loveless, A. (2002) *Primary ICT: Knowledge, Understanding and Practice (Achieving QTS S)*. London: Learning Matters.

Sheppard, L. (2001) The role of classroom assessment in teaching and learning. In: V. Richardson (ed.), *Handbook of Research on Teaching*, 4th edn, p. 1076. Washington, DC: American Educational Research Association.

Sherif, M. (1966) *Group Conflict and Cooperation: Their Social Psychology*. London: Routledge and Kegan Paul.

Shulman, L. (1986) Paradigms and research program in the study of teaching: a contemporary perspective. In: M.C. Wittrock (ed.), *Handbook of Research on Teaching*, 3rd edn, pp. 3–36. New York: Macmillan.

Shulman, L. and Quinlan, K. (1996) The comparative psychology of school subjects. In: D.C. Berliner and R.C. Calfee (eds), *Handbook of Educational Psychology*, pp. 399–422. New York: Macmillan.

Siegler, R. (2002) The rebirth of children's learning. In: C. Desforges and R. Fox (eds), *Teaching and Learning: The Essential Readings*, chapter 3. Oxford: Blackwell.

Slater, A. and Muir, D. (eds) (1999) *The Blackwell Reader in Developmental Psychology*. Oxford: Blackwell.

Slavin, R. (1995) *Cooperative Learning: Theory, Research and Practice*, 2nd edn. New York: Springer-Verlag.

Smith, F. (1992) *To Think: In Language, Learning and Education*. London: Routledge.

Smith, P. (1999) *The Nature of School Bullying: A Cross-national Perspective.* London: Routledge.

Sternberg, R. (ed.) (2000) *Handbook of Intelligence.* Cambridge: Cambridge University Press.

Strachey, L. (1918) *Eminent Victorians.* London: Chatto and Windus.

Task Group on Assessment and Testing (TGAT) (1987) *A Report.* London: Department of Education and Science.

Terman, L. (1925, 1930, 1947, 1959) *Genetic Studies of Genius.* Stanford, CA: Stanford University Press.

Tharp, R. and Gallimore, R. (eds) (1988) *Rousing Minds to Life: Teaching, Learning and Schooling in Social Context.* New York: Cambridge University Press.

Torrance, H. and Pryor, J. (1998) *Investigating Formative Assessment.* Buckingham: Open University Press.

Turnbull, C. (1984) *The Forest People.* London: Triad/Paladin.

Turnbull, C. (1987) *Mountain People.* London: Touchstone Books.

Vosniadou, S. (1994) Universal and culture-specific properties of children's mental models of the earth. In: L. Hirschfeld and S. Gelman (eds), *Mapping the Mind: Domain Specificity in Cognition and Culture*, chapter 16. Cambridge: Cambridge University Press.

Vygotsky, L.S. (1962) *Thought and Language.* Cambridge, MA: MIT Press.

Vygotsky, L.S. (1978) *Mind in Society: The Development of Higher Psychological Processes.* Cambridge, MA: Harvard University Press.

Watkins, C., Carnell, E., Lodge, C., Wagner, P. and Whalley, C. (2002) *Effective Learning.* NSIN Research Matters No. 17. London: Institute of Education.

Weiner, G. (1995) Ethnic and gender differences. In: C. Desforges (ed.), *An Introduction to Teaching*, chapter 13. Oxford: Blackwell.

Wells, G. (1986) *The Meaning Makers.* London: Hodder & Stoughton.

Whiting, B. and Whiting, J. (1975) *Children of Six Cultures.* Cambridge, MA: Harvard University Press.

Wise, S. and Upton, G. (1998) The perceptions of students with emotional and behavioural difficulties of their mainstream schooling. *Emotional and Behavioural Difficulties*, 3(3), 3–12.

Wittrock, M.C. (ed.) (1986) *Handbook of Research on Teaching*, 3rd edn. New York: Macmillan.

Wragg, E.C. (ed.) (1984) *Classroom Teaching Skills.* London: Routledge.

Wragg, E.C. (1993) *Class Management.* London: Routledge.

Wragg, E.C. (2001a) *Class Management in the Primary School.* London: Routledge Falmer.

Wragg, E.C. (2001b) *Class Management in the Secondary School.* London: Routledge Falmer.

Younger, M. and Warrington, M. (1999) 'He's such a nice man, but he's so boring . . .' *Educational Review*, 51(3), 231–41.

Index